LIFE AND LABOUR

OF THE

PEOPLE IN LONDON

LIFE AND LABOUR

OF THE PEOPLE

IN LONDON

EDITED BY

CHARLES BOOTH

VOLUME VI

POPULATION CLASSIFIED BY TRADES

(CONTINUED)

London

MACMILLAN AND CO.

AND NEW YORK

1895

LONDON
G. NORMAN AND SON, PRINTERS, FLORAL STREET
COVENT GARDEN

CONTENTS OF VOL. VI

PART I.—PRECIOUS METALS, WATCHES, AND INSTRUMENTS

PRECIOUS METALS, WATCHES, AND INSTRUMENTS.

PRELIMINARY STATEMENT.

Of workers in the precious metals, watch and clock-makers, and the makers of surgical, scientific, and musical instruments, &c., the census counts 31,589, divided as to age and sex in the following manner:—

Persons represented: (A) Census Enumeration.

ENUMERATED BY AGE AND SEX.

	10—	15—	20—	25—	55—	65.	Total.
Males	591	4498	4486	16,114	2036	1052	28,777
Females	147	892	540	1,000	148	85	2,812
Total........	738	5390	5026	17,114	2184	1137	31,589

Of these, 16,890 are returned as heads of families, and the whole population included in these families adds up to

77,548, the average number in each family, excluding servants, being 4·44, as is shown in the following table:—

Persons represented : (B) Enumeration by Families.

No.	Sections.	Heads.	Total numbers (excluding Servants).	Per family (excluding Servants).	Servants.
18	Gold & Silver Work	4,588	20,622	4·48	1101
19	Watches & Clocks	2,693	11,774	4·37	381
20	Surgical Instruments, &c.	4,150	17,922	4·31	593
21	Musical Instruments & Toys....................	5,459	24,686	4·51	469
	Total................	16,890	75,004	4·44	2544
	Servants		2,544		
	Total population		77,548		

The number of servants kept is large, especially amongst the workers in gold and silver. These 2500 servants attend on 8600 persons, leaving 66,400 who keep no servants. Of the 8600 there are 4800 who have only one servant to four or more of those served, and 2800 who have one servant to less than four persons, or two servants to four persons or over, and another 1000 have two or more servants to each family.

Of the 66,000 without servants, 26,000 occupy more than four rooms per family, or if less than four rooms have less than one person per room; 19,000 live one and up to two persons per room, 13,000 two and up to three per room, 4500 three and up to four, and 2500 live four or more persons to a room.

Crowded : 20·4 %

Not Crowded : 73·6 %

Lower Classes.	4 or more persons to a room 2,595 or 3·3 % } 9·4 %		
	3 and under 4 " " 4,635 " 6·1 %		
	2 and under 3 " " 13,167 " 17·0 %		
	1 and under 2 " " 10,011 " 24·5 %		
Central Classes.	Less than 1 " " 2,902 " 3·9 % } 41·0 %		
	More than 4 rooms... ...23,974 " 30·9 %		
	4 or more persons to a servant ... ... 4,708 " 6·2 %		
Upper Classes.	Less than 4 persons to 1 servant, and 4 or more to 2 servants... ... ... 2,775 " 3·5 %		
	All others with 2 or more servants ... ... 1,087 " 1·4 %		
	Servants ... ... 2,544 3·2 %		
	77,648 100 %		

Social Condition (by Sections).

	3, 4, or more persons to a room.	2 and under 3 persons to a room.	1 and under 2 persons to a room.	Less than 1 to a room, more than 4 rooms, or 4 or more persons to a servant.	Less than 4 persons to a servant.	Servants.	Total.
Gold and Silver Workers, &c..	1723	3160	4874	9020	1845	1101	21,723
Per cent.......	8	14	22	42	9	5	100
Watch and Clock-makers	821	1743	2518	6155	537	381	12,155
Per cent.......	7	14	21	51	4	3	100
Surgical & Scientific Instrument-makers.	1667	3171	5090	7186	808	593	18,515
Per cent.......	9	17	28	39	4	3	100
Musical Instrument-makers, &c..............	3079	5093	6529	9313	672	469	25,155
Per cent.......	12	20	26	37	3	2	100

CHANGES SINCE 1861 IN NUMBERS EMPLOYED.

	1861.	1871.	1881.	1891.
Gold and Silver Workers, &c.	7,400	8,300	8,600	8,600
Watch and Clock-makers ...	5,700	4,900	5,000	4,300
Surgical and Scientific Instrument-makers	2,400	2,800	3,900	8,300
Musical Instrument-makers, &c......................	7,600	8,300	8,600	10,400
Total......................	23,100	24,300	26,100	31,600

Watch and clock manufacture shows a considerable reduction since 1861; but all the other sections have increased, and especially the section which includes scientific instruments. Gold and silver work increased from 1861 to 1881, but in the last decade has stood still.

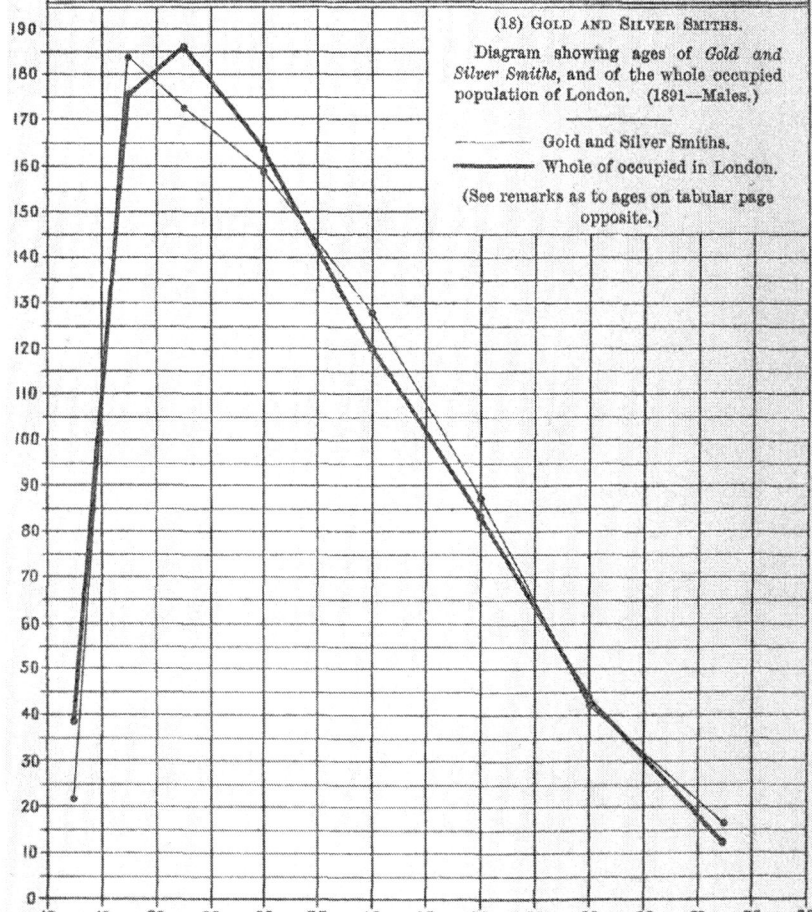

Proportionate Numbers Occupied.

EXPLANATORY NOTE

OF METHOD ADOPTED IN PREPARING THE DIAGRAMS OF NUMBERS OF OCCUPIED MALES AT DIFFERENT AGES.

Of every 10,000 males in London, 6300 are counted as *occupied*. These 6300 males are divided by ages in the following manner :—

Ages.			Proportion per 10,000 of total aged 10-80.	Proportion at each year of age.
10 and under 15			193·5	38·7
15	,,	20	880·0	176·0
20	,,	25	933·0	186·6
25	,,	35	1636·0	163·6
35	,,	45	1201·0	120·1
45	,,	55	830·0	83·0
55	,,	65	434·0	43·4
65	,,	80	192·5	12·8
			6300·0	

The last column, giving the yearly mean, is obtained by dividing the proportionate figures by the number of years which they cover. Thus the proportionate figures for ages 10-15, as representing 5 years, are divided by 5, giving 38·7 as the mean; similarly, for 25-35, covering 10 years, the figures are divided by 10, giving 163·6 as the mean number. The numbers at the different age-periods in each Trade-section or Group are brought to the same scale, and the charts drawn in accordance with the mean figures, as is shown by the indicating points of the curves being placed in the centre of each age-period.

(18) GOLD AND SILVER SMITHS.

Diagram showing ages of *Gold and Silver Smiths*, and of the whole occupied population of London. (1891—Males.)

·········· Gold and Silver Smiths.

———— Whole of occupied in London.

(See remarks as to ages on tabular page opposite.)

Ages. 10 15 20 25 30 35 40 45 50 55 60 65 70 75 80

CHAPTER I.

JEWELLERS, GOLD AND SILVER-SMITHS, &c. *(Section 18.)*

Persons Represented.

Census Enumeration.						Enumerated by Families.					

Census Enumeration.

nsus Divisions, 1891.	Fe-males.	Males.				Total.
	All Ages.	—19	20—54	55—		
Gold and Silver	469	1104	4899	602		7134
Lapidaries, &c.	563	136	655	155		1509
TOTAL....	1032	1240	5554	817		8643

n each of the industries here represented
greater number of the females employed
between 15 and 20 years of age. As to
les, the diagram shows some excess between
and 20, a falling off from 20 to 35, and a rise
ain at the more advanced ages, the latter
ng due principally to the lapidaries.

DISTRIBUTION.

E.	N.	W. & C.	S.	Total.
881	3602	2611	1549	8643

DETAILS OF OCCUPATIONS
(FROM THE CENSUS DICTIONARY).

) Goldsmith, jeweller, engraver, chaser, colourer, stamper; bracelet, brooch, locket, pencil-case, sleeve-link, stud-link maker; silver-smith, mounter, saw-piercer, engraver, chaser.
) Diamond-cutter, lapidary, pebble-cutter, grinder; bullion dealer, gold-cloth maker, gold-leaf wire flatter, burnisher, gold and silver-thread maker, insignia maker, regalia, platinum manufacturer.

Enumerated by Families.

Sex	Males	4487	
	Females	101	

Birthplace	In London	65 %	2975	Heads of Families, 4588.
	Out of London..	35 %	1613	

Industrial Status ..	Employer	18 %	815	
	Employed.......	70 %	3204	
	Neither....	12 %	569	

TOTAL POPULATION CONCERNED.

	Heads of Families.	Others Occupied.	Unoccupied.	Servants.	Total.
Total	4588	4634	11,400	1101	21,723
Average in family..	1	1·01	2·48	·24	4·73

CLASSIFICATION.

Numbers living in Families. %

3 or more to a room	1723	7·9	
2 & under 3 ,,	3160	14·5	
1 & under 2 ,,	4874	22·5	
Less than 1 ,,			
More than 4 rooms 4 or more persons to a servant	9020	41·5	
Less than 4 to 1 servant, and 4 or more to 2 servants	1303	6·0	
All others with 2 or more servants ..	542	2·5	
Servants	1101	5·1	
	21,723	100	

	Inner.	Outer.	Together.
Crowded ..	33 %	16 %	22 %
Not	67 %	84 %	78 %

DISTRIBUTION.

East ..	Inner 1764 Outer 184	1948
North	Inner 1587 Outer 8008	9595
West ..	Inner 458 Outer 1831	2289
Central	Inner 3742	3742
South-East	Inner 101 Outer 1544	1645
South-West	Inner 727 Outer 1777	2504

Inner 8379, or 39 %
Outer 13,344, or 61 %

Status as to Employment (according to Census Enumeration).

Census Divisions (1891).	Employers.		Employed.			Neither Employer nor Employed.		Total.
			Males.		Females of all ages.			
	Males.	Females	Under 20.	Over 20.		Males.	Females	
) Goldsmith, Silver-smith, Jeweller ..	843	36	1104	4073	410	645	23	7134
) (Lapidary	21	4	29	86	116	24	4	284
(Others (gold cloth, wire, &c.)	00	6	107	589	418	30	15	1225
TOTAL..........	924	46	1240	4748	944	699	42	8643
	970		6932			741		

Proportion of Employers to Employed–1 to 7

GOLDSMITHS AND JEWELLERS.

Goldsmiths proper are employed in the manufacture of brooches, bracelets, sleeve-links, lockets, studs, &c., while gold-chain makers and ring-makers and carvers, also workers in gold, form small branches by themselves.

Jewellers, on the other hand, "mount" and "set" those articles only in which precious stones are used.

London is the seat of the English high-class jewellery trade, and Hatton Garden is the centre of the London trade. In Birmingham, the only other place of importance for jewel work, goods are manufactured on well-known patterns in large quantities, but in London, as a rule, very few copies are made of the same design, and it is seldom worth while to make a die. A great many of the men employed on jewellery in London are foreigners, and it is from abroad that the trade is recruited. Neither in power of design nor in technical knowledge can Englishmen compete with foreigners. The French are the best jewellers, and in the workshops their language still prevails, though not so much now as formerly.

Jeweller's work is divided into "mounting," *i.e.* making the mount, and "setting," *i.e.* inserting and making secure the stones. The men who make the mounts, and all goldsmiths, work at tables scooped out in semicircles, and between this hollowed space and the workman's waist a leathern apron is fastened to catch stray particles, called "limels," of the precious metal, or falling stones; and so carefully is any loss guarded against that even the water in which the workmen wash their hands is made to yield up what gold it may contain. Each man as he works has a gas jet at his right hand, for use with the blow-pipe in fashioning the metal. Many have their eyelashes scorched off by the flame.

The mount, having been made according to the order, is sent to the polisher, and then passed on to the setter, who fixes it firmly either in a wooden vice or more commonly in a bed of shellac. The jewels are then placed in the sockets prepared for them in the mount, and the metal is worked up round them until they are securely "set."

A few of the best men work in their own homes, or occasionally are employed on the premises of West End jewellers, but the manufacture is mostly carried on in regular workshops. The wages in good houses range from 9*d* to 1*s* 3*d*, or in very rare cases to 1*s* 6*d* an hour.

Diamond-mounters and setters, with whom are included the mounters and setters of all precious stones, are generally foreigners. Mounters are time workers, and earn about 1*s* 1*d* to 1*s* 6*d* per hour. Setters are generally on piece, earning £3 to £6 when in full work.

Goldsmiths are more often Englishmen, and of these bracelet-makers would make about 45*s* per week, or 11*d* per hour, and so would good ring-makers. Ring-carvers, who cut patterns out of the solid gold, earn rather more, 1*s* to 1*s* 4*d*; but general carvers, who carve gold and silver monograms, and call themselves engravers and piercers, vary more widely, and while a good man will earn 50*s*, a second-class one will not earn more than half this amount. Chain-makers are generally piece workers. They always keep to the same class of work, and 35*s* is stated to be a fair average for a full week, but the year round the men would not make more than 25*s*. Of the polishers, the men, who polish goldsmith's work, get 7*d* to 9*d*, and women, who polish jeweller's work, 5*d* to 9*d* per hour.

Hours of work.—The working week consists of fifty hours, or nine ordinarily and five on Saturday. A few years ago it was fifty-six hours, but was reduced by trades union action, and one of the masters tells us that the amount of work per man remains the same in spite of the shorter hours.

Seasons.—In busy seasons there is a great deal of over-time, and the earnings are large, but this is balanced by short time when work is slack. The three months before

Christmas and the months of the London season are the busiest; August, September, and the three months which follow after Christmas are the slackest of the year. The men stick to one shop, and masters share the work, be it much or little, as far as possible amongst all their regular employees. There are so many so-called secrets and specialities in the way of pattern that the best masters are very chary of taking on new men to meet a temporary demand, and unwilling, also, to part with old hands.

Cheap trade.—What has been said so far applies to the regular factory work, which rests on mutual goodwill between masters and men, safeguarded by trade customs and the action of trades unions. There are, in addition, the small garret masters in and about Hatton Garden and the jobbers in Clerkenwell and round the Tottenham Court Road, who do cheaper work. In Hatton Garden those employed are mostly Jews, and hail from Austrian Poland, while in the neighbourhood of Fitzroy Square the majority are Frenchmen, the trade name for this district being " La petite France." Neither the conditions of employment, nor the work done in the small shops can be called satisfactory. The productions are hawked round among the wholesale houses.

Health and age capacity.—Jewellers sit in a cramped position, and their work is not in any way calculated to develop their muscles; they cannot compare in physique with silver-smiths, but there is nothing in itself unhealthy in the trade. The men do not seem to lose capacity early, and many remain good workmen after sixty years of age.

Each large factory has a shop club of its own, giving 12s to 14s for sickness, and there are also several general benefit societies. Most of the men belong to one or other of these societies, and can claim as much as 20s a week, in addition to their shop allowance, in case of sickness or accident.

Manufacturing Silver-smiths.

There are six divisions of this trade sufficiently distinct to have each its own trades union, none of which, however, date back more than eight years, with the exception of that of the spoon and fork-makers, which is about twenty years old.

(1) Silver plate workers.

(2) Small silver workers (who make fusee cases and small silver models).

(3) General chasers and silver engravers.

(4) Silver-plate polishers.

(5) Spoon and fork-makers.

(6) Spoon and fork-finishers.

There seems to be some jealousy between these different branches as regards their relative importance. The most highly paid are the chasers, and at the other end of the scale are the polishers and burnishers, polishers being men and burnishers, who give the final brilliancy, being generally women.

Wages and Hours.—As with the jewellers, 1s to 1s 3d or even 1s 6d per hour is paid for the very best work, 7d to 1s for ordinary, and 6d to 9d for polishers. There are also special modellers and designers in each large shop at wages from 55s to £7 and £8 per week. The hours worked are fifty to fifty-two, or, in some cases, fifty-six, ending on Saturday at 2 o'clock. Both time and piece are customary, and first-class work is done on both systems, though the very best is generally on time-work.

Process of work.—Silver may be stamped, spun, hammered, or cast into form, but the last named, casting, is not very much used except for the "furniture" (handles, &c.) of a piece of plate. Stamping and spinning are the cheaper methods, and are said to leave the metal soft, while with hammering the pores of the silver are closed and the metal made harder and more durable. Mugs and bowls are often spun, *i.e.* a circular sheet of silver turning on a lathe is gradually pressed against a wooden shape.

Chasing proper is always hand-work, although imitations are largely made with stamps. It can be applied to the finish of shapes, however produced, but hand-work throughout gives most "life" to the lines of the design.

After having been stamped, hammered, or spun, the different parts are put together, and small irregularities removed by the file of the "repairer." The article then passes into the hands of the polisher, who works first with pumice-stone, or, in some cases, with lime and trent sand, and then with rotten-stone, oil, and beer dregs; after this a higher polish is obtained with rouge and swan's down, and finally the "live leather" of the bare hand is reached, and gives that last brilliant burnish for which London silver is renowned.

Health.—There is nothing in the silver trade which can be said to be unhealthy, except the task of polishing; here the fine dust of the substances used has a tendency to get into the eyes, nose, and lungs, producing discomfort and a craving for drink, if nothing more. It is, besides, the less skilled section of the business, and apt, to be relegated to the worst part of the factory.

Seasons in this trade are not so strongly marked as formerly; business is brisker while Parliament is sitting and during the three months preceding Christmas than in the first quarter of the year, but, on the whole, the demand is regular, and depends more upon the general prosperity of the country than upon any particular whim or custom of the buying public.

Irregularity.—There is always employment for good workmen, and probably two-thirds get regular work all the year round, though not always on full time. The best of the piece-hands often do all their work between Tuesday morning and Friday night, making their Sunday last three days. In the four days they will earn 40s or more. These men are said to drink a good deal. It is difficult to say what amount of work there may be for the one-third who are not regularly employed. No doubt it gets gradually less and less in proportion to capacity or character, age or indolence; but there is no large unemployed class, and taken all round it is a prosperous trade for both masters and men.

There is little shifting from one branch to another. Some men may be able to undertake several departments, but it pays them, and also pays their masters best, to devote themselves to one branch only.

Apprenticeship is the only recognized way of learning the different industries mentioned above, but the system is falling into disuse amongst jewellers, goldsmiths, small silver workers, chasers, engravers, and polishers; the silver-plate workers, and spoon and fork-finishers, are practically the only two branches in which the full term of seven years is enforced.

Boys who are regularly indentured to a freeman of the Goldsmiths' Company, can, at the end of their time, themselves become freemen, on payment of a small fee; and, provided they maintain a decent character, be sure of relief whenever they may require it in after life. But more often masters will not be burdened with the training of apprentices, and prefer to take on boys, or to promote sharp errand lads who pick up the trade as best they can.

The employment of boys who are not apprentices is much complained of; only two societies (the Silver Engravers and Spoon and Fork-makers) have obtained a recognition from the masters that not more than one boy should be employed to five men.

GOLD-BEATING.

This is a small and gradually decaying industry in London. Foreign competition has been too severe, and the Germans have successfully attracted most of the English custom. Round about Nürnberg and Schwabach it is a family trade, and leaf can be hammered there much more cheaply than here in England.

In London there are about fifteen masters, employing altogether some ninety men in the busy season, which is spring, when picture-frames are being gilded for the exhibitions, and houses redecorated for the season. In slack times not 30 per cent. of the men can expect work, and must look for casual jobs in other trades as unskilled workers. A few girls (about twenty altogether) are also employed in cutting and light work.

Gold-beating consists in hammering flat pieces of gold into very fine leaf, which can then be applied with the help of gold-size to gildings of every kind. The gold comes in rolls like ribbons from the rolling mills, and is cut off into small squares which are interleaved with sheets of vellum and then hammered. After this, each leaf, which has expanded considerably, is taken out and divided into four, and placed between sheets of the very fine preparation of gut known as gold-beater's skin, and again hammered. This process is again repeated, and finally the leaves are lifted out very gently with a long pair of wooden pincers and smoothed out with the breath, and trimmed and placed in small books of twenty-five leaves ready for the buyer. Out of a golden sovereign *eight hundred leaves of gold* $3\frac{1}{4}$ *inches square can be beaten;* while no less than *two-thirds* of the gold will have had to be trimmed off in the process and returned to the melting pot. This gives some idea of the way in which this metal will spread when beaten.

Some men can get more leaves out of a given piece of gold than others, and some work much more quickly, so that earnings differ. All work is piece-work, and each master settles his own piece prices. In all cases a man is expected to get a minimum amount of leaf from a given quantity of gold, and is paid extra for anything above this amount.

The work is hard, for the hammers weigh from eight to twenty pounds, and in addition great delicacy is needed in handling fine gold-leaf in the later stages. The men hammer standing at a desk made on the top of a block of granite, and the motion up and down starts in the small of the back, and not from the elbow or shoulder.

Wages.—Earnings are very low, and a good man will not average more than 26s to 28s throughout the year. A slow worker is glad to get 21s, and has to be content with six months' work in the twelve. There are no apprentices, and the trade is practically dead, although the best English leaf is said to be better and more durable than any that can be produced on the continent. Dentists, who might be customers, go to Philadelphia, where gold stopping was first invented. There seems to be no reason why they should not buy here, but their habit is otherwise, and they are, perhaps naturally, disinclined to make any change.

GOLD AND SILVER WIRE.

This is used for making gold cloth, damasks, and embroidery for theatrical, military, and court suits.

It is a small industry in London, and not more than three hundred persons are employed even in the busiest season, the majority of these being women. The few men there are only draw the heavy wire, while the women do all the lighter work, and are divided into wire-drawers, flatters, silk-winders and spinners. The "gold" used is made of an alloy of silver and a little copper, into which leaves of pure gold are afterwards rolled. The metal is then gradually drawn by machinery through plates pierced with holes of different sizes, and finally through rubies, sapphires, and diamonds until sufficiently reduced in size. This wire, however, is round, and is not only still too precious, but also too heavy to be worn as embroidery, and must therefore be "flattened" by machines, and afterwards spun round threads of cotton or silk. In this state it is ready as "gold thread" for use by the "lacemen," who make it up and sell to the costumiers and tailors.

The work is fairly skilled, especially when very fine wire is used—1400 yards is the usual length obtained from an ounce of metal, and *twelve times as much* is said to be within the bounds of possibility.

As a rule the girls start as errand girls, and are then put to one of the branches mentioned above. Work is both day-work and piece-work. The business can be learnt in a year or eighteen months, and employment is fairly regular. Christmas is busy for pantomime goods, and the spring for court dresses, while the autumn months are nearly always slack. In slack times it is the custom of the trade to spread the work so far as is possible. Day workers will be given one week in and one week out of work, while those on piece will only be allowed to work half or three-quarter time only, and to make as much as they can in the shortened hours. The women, who are well spoken of as to character, can expect to earn an average of 13s on full time, except the silk-winders, who can make only 6s to 8s for a full week of sixty-five hours.

The women have no trade organization.

LAPIDARIES.

Of these, according to the census, there are 284 in London, who are to be found chiefly in Clerkenwell and Soho. Dealers in precious stones are in Hatton Garden. They are more often than not foreigners, but the majority of the working men are English.

This is quite a minor industry, and is carried on in small shops with never more than six journeymen in one place; many masters only employ a few boys, and others are their own employers, and work by themselves. These masters are very jealous of one another and keen competitors; and it is said that the great number of employers, as compared with those employed, is due to the temptation that there is for a man who has learnt something about stones, and knows how to work them, to add the profits of a dealer to his earnings as a practical workman.

Lapidaries may be divided into two distinct branches: (1) Diamond-cutters; (2) Oriental stone-cutters and General lapidaries.

Diamond-cutters, by right, fashion the rough diamond into the finished article, but there is very little except jobbing work done in London now, for diamonds are great travellers, the larger number of them being found in South Africa, bought and sold in London, cut and polished in Antwerp and Amsterdam, and then finally set in Paris. When Cape diamonds first came over and were worked here, a diamond-cleaver has been known to earn £40 per week, and many could earn £10 or £12. Now there are only irregular repairs to be done, for which a man will get 40s or 50s per week on time-work.

In the _general trade_, in which some are piece workers, some day workers, and some weekly workers, there is greater regularity. The best men are oriental stone or gem-cutters, and confine themselves to rubies, emeralds, sapphires, opals, and the finer stones. The second-class men are known as glass-cutters, and do a cheaper class of work for lockets, &c.

The gem-cutters are busiest during the London season, and more especially before great weddings, and at Christmas time; speaking generally, they are busy in the summer and slack in winter.

In diamond-cutting, the diamond itself is fixed, and the

VOL. VI.   2

wheel is then worked against it. But in gem-cutting the stone is fixed at the end of a stick; this the cutter holds in his hand and presses first against a revolving wheel of lead, over which emery has been sprinkled—and this is the unhealthy part of the work, for some of the lead will fly off and be inhaled and cause lead poisoning—then against a wooden wheel, until finally the last polish is given with putty powder. After this, the gem is ready for the jeweller. The work requires great skill, for the edge of the facet depends entirely upon the steadiness of the man's hand.

A fair gem-cutter can expect to earn between 30s and 40s per week, and a good one between 50s and 60s.

Glass-cutters earn a precarious livelihood, and may make between 20s and 25s, but not more. They are the poorest paid and least skilled of the workmen in the trade.

At the present time (1894) there are a great many young men in the general trade, owing to the practice that has for some time prevailed of taking on boys to do the rougher parts of the work. Apprenticeship is almost dead, and masters instead take on boys with or without premiums, and see what they can make of them. A lad begins at 5s or 6s per week, and a master soon sees whether he is likely to be a success or not. The work requires infinite patience and delicacy; one boy may have it in him to succeed, while another has not; and hence it is that here, as in many other industries, masters refuse to be bound by the strict rules of legal apprenticeship.

In spite of the general improvement in the direction of sobriety there is still some complaint as to the habits of the men; for instance, it was said that often very little work was done on Monday mornings, because no men were there to do it.

TRADES UNIONS.

Trade organization is as follows :—

Numbers in the London Trade (Census 1891).		Name of Trade Society.	Membership in London.		Remarks.
Total.	Of whom are employed males over 20.		In each Society.	In each Division.	
		The London Society of Goldsmiths and Jewellers (1893).	470		Out of work, Strike, and Death Benefits. Incidental fund.
		The London Silver-plate Workers' Society (1885).	90		Out of work, Strike, and Death Benefits, and grant for emigration or travel. Enforce apprenticeship.
		The London Small Silver Workers' Society (1890).	80		Out of work and Death Benefits, and Incidental fund.
7134	4073	The London Amalgamated Society of Chasers and Engravers.	108	854	Used to be separate, amalgamated in 1894. Out of work and Death Benefits, and grant for emigration or travel, and Incidental fund.
		The London Silver-plate Polishers' Society.	40		——
		The London Spoon and Fork-makers' Society.	36		Give out of work pay and other benefits. Very exclusive societies.
		The London Spoon and Fork-finishers' Society.	30		
1509	675	The Gold-beaters' Trade Society (1777).	70	70	Out of work and Death money. Members allowed to work at any shop at the rate of wages existing in that shop.
8643	4748			924	

Thus 924 persons in this section are organized, out of a total number of 4748 males over 20, or 20 per cent.

With subscriptions ranging from 3*d* to 6*d* per week, the benefits given invariably include out of work and death money—namely, 10*s* or 12*s* for eight to thirteen weeks for loss of employment; £3 or £5 at death; and generally half that sum at the death of a member's wife. Many have, too, an incidental fund, made up from voluntary donations, for such purposes as helping members in distress or paying their subscriptions, so that they may still remain in the society.

There are also a great many benefit societies and benevolent institutions connected with the trade, such as :

(1) The Goldsmiths and Jewellers' Benefit Society.

(2) The Globe Benefit Society (Clerkenwell).

(3) The Friendly Society of Goldsmiths and Jewellers (1818).

(4) La Société des Jouailleurs.

(5) The Goldsmiths' Benevolent Institution (for aged and infirm only), founded 1833.

(6) The Goldsmiths' and Jewellers' Annuity and Asylum (1827). (For aged or those totally incapacitated.)

(7) The Silver Trade Pension Society.

(8) The Silver Trade Benefit Society.

So that there is no lack of the means of making suitable provision for old age and infirmity; and it is said that most of the men avail themselves of their opportunities.

There is a good deal of secrecy, both among men and masters in the trade, which is accounted for, probably, by the number of men who are sometimes journeymen and sometimes small masters. In the "silver" trade there are one or two very close societies, which, however, have been persuaded to form part of the "Silver Trade Council," a body representing the six silver societies, whose aim is to concentrate the interest of the trade upon questions affecting the whole or any part of it.

The most remarkable society of all, in point of age, is that of the gold-beaters, which was established so long

ago as 1777, and has still in its possession account books
dating back to 1810. It was never broken up, but at
one period split into two sections, which were rejoined in
1855, and finally reorganized in 1886. The relations of
employers with all the silver trade organizations is of a
rather uncertain character, but in several cases societies
have been applied to by masters in want of men.

Wages Statistics.

In these trades, of the 4748 adult males employed, we
have wages' returns for 412. They work for fifteen firms,
as under—

Jewellers 6	=15 firms usually employing 709 persons, of whom 433 are adult males, but 21 of them belong to other sections, as porters, &c.
Gold and silver-smiths 8	
Gold-wire makers........................ 1	

The earnings of these men in an average week are as
follows :—

Below 20s .... 6, or 1½ per cent.	Under 30s, 16½ per cent.
20s to 25s .... 7 „ 2 „	
25s to 30s .... 54 „ 13 „	
30s to 35s .... 56 „ 13½ „	
35s to 40s .... 71 „ 17 „	30s and over, 83½ per cent.
40s to 45s .... 76 „ 18 „	
45s and upwards... 142 „ 35 „	

412 „ 100 „

Board of Trade returns in 1886 from eighteen firms, employing 228 adult men, compare very closely with the above.

	—20s.	20s—	25s—	30s—	35s—	40s—	45s—
Our returns ...	1½ °/₀	2 °/₀	13 °/₀	13½ °/₀	17 °/₀	18 °/₀	35 °/₀
		16½ °/₀			83½ °/₀		
Board of Trade returns	1 °/₀	2 °/₀	17 °/₀	14 °/₀	14 °/₀	17 °/₀	35 °/₀
		20 °/₀			80 °/₀		

The Board of Trade returns show a reduction, in the slack weeks, of 14 per cent. in numbers and of 25 or 30 per cent. in the amount earned. The busiest weeks were in December, February, and May, and the slackest in January, May, and August, showing no very definite connection with the seasons.

Our returns include information as to 161 women and girls employed, or roughly one-sixth of those returned in the census as engaged in these industries. About half of these earn from 9s to 12s a week, and the greater part of the remainder take more than this, 12 per cent. earning over 20s, as against only 5 per cent. at 5s. Boys' wages are not so good. About 70 per cent. of those returned earn 10s or less, including nearly 20 per cent. whose wages do not exceed 5s. The Board of Trade returns give rather better results, indicating possibly a downward tendency since 1886. Most of the women got 13s or more, and the majority of the lads from 12s upwards.

Social Condition.

Of a total of 4748 adult men employed in these trades, about 3130 come under social classification as heads of families. According to the sample tested there are only 3½ per cent. who earn less than 25s a week, but no less than 28 per cent. live under crowded conditions. Next we have 26½ per cent. who earn from 25s to 30s to compare with 30 per cent. living one to two to a room, and finally actually 70 per cent. who earn over 35s compared to only 42 per cent. of the central class :—

Comparison of Earnings with Style of Life (Gold and Silver-smiths).

Earnings as returned.			Classification of population.		
Below 20s...	6, or	1½ per cent.	3 or more in each room,	1500, or	9 per cent.
20s to 25s...	7 ,,	2 ,,	2 to 3 ,,	3100 ,, 19 ,,	
25s ,, 30s...	54 ,,	13 ,,	1 ,, 2 ,,	4900 ,, 30 ,,	
30s ,, 35s...	56 ,,	13½ ,,	Less than 1 ,,		
35s ,, 40s...	71 ,,	17 ,,	More than 4 rooms	7000 ,, 42 ,,	
40s ,, 45s...	76 ,,	18 ,,	4 or more persons		
45s and upwards	142 ,,	35 ,,	to a servant		
	412 ,,	100 ,,		16,500 ,, 100 ,,	
			Employers' families and servants	5200	
				21,700	

The wide difference between our table of earnings and the condition as to crowding here shown is partly owing to the fact that no returns of wages were obtainable from employers in the poorer portion of these industries. Furthermore, the presence of so many foreigners, who congregate in Central London where rents are high, would also account for a greater degree of crowding than is warranted by the amount of their weekly earnings.

The majority of the English gold and silver-smiths and jewellers live in North London, and come into their work by train or tram. Some bring their dinner with them, and in a few cases masters make provision for the cooking of chops and steaks in the workshop itself: but in many places no meals are allowed on the premises beyond lunch or tea. Both tea and dinner can be heated up over the gas or fire while the cold weather lasts, but the practice is discontinued in summer, when fires and gaslight are reduced to a minimum. In a few shops fifteen minutes is allowed for lunch and tea, but where this is not so refreshments are brought in for the men and taken at the bench during work.

As to dress, ornamental engravers and diamond-mounters wear long blouses, or an old coat, and apron when at work, while smiths work in their shirt-sleeves, and polishers generally cover themselves well up in overalls or old suits of clothes.

In the jeweller's industry nearly every shop has a club of its own, but in the silver trade these clubs are not so numerous, though it is calculated that even here from 1s 3d to 1s 9d of a man's weekly earnings go in subscriptions to different benefit societies.

As a rule, English wives do not work, but many of the French jewellers' wives are skilful polishers, and can make good earnings in this way.

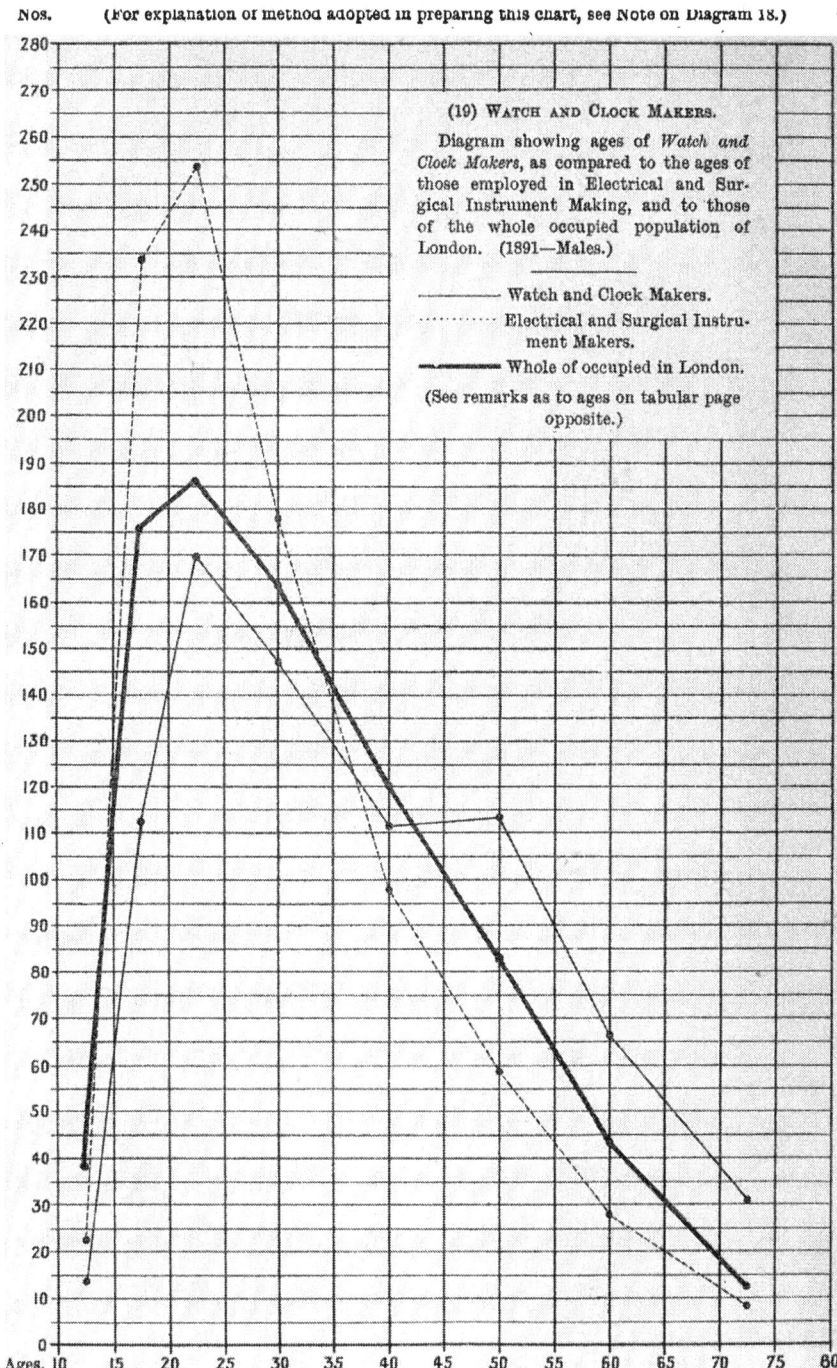

(19) WATCH AND CLOCK MAKERS.

Diagram showing ages of *Watch and Clock Makers*, as compared to the ages of those employed in Electrical and Surgical Instrument Making, and to those of the whole occupied population of London. (1891—Males.)

————— Watch and Clock Makers.

············ Electrical and Surgical Instrument Makers.

▬▬▬▬ Whole of occupied in London.

(See remarks as to ages on tabular page opposite.)

CHAPTER II.

WATCHES AND CLOCKS. *(Section 19.)*

Persons represented.

Census Enumeration.					
Census Division, 1891.	Females. All Ages.	Males.			Total.
		—19	20—54	55—	
Watch and Clock-maker	82	424	3034	741	4281

The number of old men is very noticeable. (See diagram.) There are more between the ages of 45 and 55 than there are between 35 and 45, and probably nearly half the men are over 40 years of age. The explanation is doubtless to be found in the transfer of younger men's work to automatic-machine working.

DISTRIBUTION.

	N.	W. & C.	S.	Total.
	1485	1306	993	4281

DETAILS OF OCCUPATIONS

(FROM THE CENSUS DICTIONARY).

Watch and chronometer-movement making:—Balance, dial, escapement, fusee, hand, jewel hole, pivot, keyless work, &c., &c., makers. Watch and chronometer-case makers, secret-spring makers, &c. Clock-makers. Turret-clock makers, pattern-makers. Founders.

Enumerated by Families.

Sex ...... { Males			2672
Females..............			21
Birthplace { In London	53 %	1416	Heads of Families, 2693.
Out of London..	47 %	1277	
Industrial { Employer	23 %	613	
Status .. { Employed......	49 %	1320	
Neither........	28 %	760	

TOTAL POPULATION CONCERNED.

	Heads of Families.	Others Occupied.	Unoccupied.	Servants.	Total.
Total	2693	2884	6,197	381	12,155
Average in family..	1	1·07	2·30	·14	4·51

CLASSIFICATION.

Numbers living in Families.		%
3 or more to a room	821	6·7
2 & under 3 ,,	1743	14·3
1 & under 2 ,,	2518	20·7
Less than 1 ,,		
More than 4 rooms	6155	50·7
4 or more persons to a servant ..		
Less than 4 to 1 servant, and 4 or more to 2 servants	422	3·5
All others with 2 or more servants ..	115	·9
Servants	381	3·2
	12,155	100

	Inner.	Outer.	Together.
Crowded..	32 %	14 %	21 %
Not ,, ..	68 %	86 %	79 %

DISTRIBUTION.

East ..	{ Inner 1121	Outer 136 }	1257
North	{ Inner 592	Outer 3976 }	4568
West ..	{ Inner 238	Outer 1059 }	1297
Central	Inner 2237		2237
South-East	{ Inner 134	Outer 1152 }	1286
South-West	{ Inner 491	Outer 1019 }	1510
			12,155

Inner 4813, or 40 %
Outer 7342, or 60 %

Status as to Employment (according to Census Enumeration).

Census Division (1891).	Employers.		Employed.			Neither Employer nor Employed.		Total.
			Males.		Females of all ages.			
	Males.	Females	Under 20.	Over 20.		Males.	Females	
Watch and Clock-maker	670	16	424	2143	60	962	6	4281
TOTAL..........	686		2627			968		

Proportion of Employers to Employed—1 to 4

WATCH MAKING.

Changes and fluctuations are common to all trades at all periods, and the present time is full of such movements, but nowhere shall we find a more striking example of the transitional than in watch making, as conducted in London to-day.

Forty or fifty years ago the business had reached a remarkable and balanced perfection. Division of labour and individual skill had each been carried to an extraordinary pitch, and were so applied as to produce either excellent watches at not excessive prices or a really perfect article at a high price. Nothing so good and so durable can be made to-day at any less cost, if indeed it can be made at all; and yet the old system, except in a very few houses, is moribund and will probably pass away.

Its success, until 1870, was such that London watches (or those made under similar conditions, principally at Coventry and Liverpool) commanded the Home, Colonial and American markets. The demand became greater than could be honestly met; the workmen, paid by the piece, were urged to work faster; inferior work was accepted by the masters and passed by the exporters; and, finally, the London watch partly lost its good name. This slip might no-doubt have been recovered but for an obstinate conservative spirit which had been developed in or by the system of manu-facture. The old-fashioned London watch was thick because the "verge" escapement which gave the shape to the ancient "turnip," is vertical; for ladies' use a thinner watch was demanded. The Swiss maker contrived the horizontal escapement, but London makers would not budge; and, later, held out also against the Lancashire lever escapement. Nor would they hear of machine work. A company for the use of machinery was projected; but, opposed by Clerken-well influence, it failed to obtain the charter then necessary, was transferred to the United States, and has been the pioneer of the modern factory system. Thus, the opening being given, other countries and places stepped in, and London lost the lead, never probably to be recovered.

When a machine-made watch, which will last some years and keep very fair time, can be produced for 10*s*, or less, and is sold retail for 15*s* or 20*s*, there is no chance of a large sale for even a decidedly superior hand-made article, which costs five times as much. To this fact London makers must needs adapt themselves, and they tend to do so more and more by using machine-made movements instead of manufacturing the whole watch entirely by hand.

The best work remains. It is as impossible as ever to produce a really fine watch except by hand-work throughout, and in such work no place excels London. But the trade becomes smaller by degrees; the demand tends to dwindle, for perfection in a watch is a rather fanciful requirement; and, further, the men who can do such work die out, being no longer recruited from the pick of a large trade. It is not as if one man could make a whole watch; many men are needed, and, if the result is to be perfect, each in his own line must be a perfect workman. The number of sub-divisions in the trade is inconceivable. We find gold and silver-case makers, pallet-makers, motion-makers, escapement-makers, cap-makers, balance-makers of various kinds, main-spring makers, hair-spring makers, jewellers, fusee cutters, fusee chain-makers, joint finishers, secret springers, engine turners, case engravers and enamellers, dial-makers of gold, of silver, and of enamel, watch-hand makers, and polishers, to say nothing of adjusters and examiners. These men are all necessary to the making of a high-class London watch and are all independent workmen; to each of them the watch goes in the course of manufacture, and between every separate process will be returned to the dealer to be examined and sent out again. Each worker will be found in a separate house, and at Clerkenwell, where they congregate, almost every front-door in certain streets has its brass-plate stating the owner's special occupation. Here he carries on his profession by himself, working in a room with a north light near the top of a house, or, it may be, in a lean-to shed at the back. Every man is apt to consider his own part in the making of a watch the most important, and very few have any knowledge of the business outside of their own particular line. They can scarcely be accounted conscious workers; they are only parts of a wonderfully perfect machine. To this there are a few exceptions. Those who control the working of this machine, *i.e.* the firms whose names are connected with the product, select the most inventive of the men to work on their own premises, and take such special orders as may come in for watches out of the common way. These men must have an all-round knowledge, and so must those who undertake repairs, who if employed on fine work must of course be fine workmen, or they will only spoil what they propose to set right.

While the old-fashioned system changes or dies out, ordinary repairing work is very active. A cheap watch comes oftener for repair than a dear one, and, though the old and very high scale of charges cannot be maintained, the work is still profitable. This has, however, little to do with Clerkenwell, and not much with the men there, who, calling themselves watch-makers, are, as already indicated, in truth only the makers of some particular part of a watch.

Some of them, as their own trade shrinks, may sacrifice their special skill and take to general repairs, but for the most part the all-round watch-jobber is more likely to hail from some provincial town where the whole process of watch making can be learnt.

In the hand-made chronometer every part is constructed specially to suit a given watch, and no part is interchangeable with the same part of any other watch, whereas the idea of a machine-made watch is to have every part interchangeable. A very high finish and polish is given to every part of the hand-made watch, even though the work is useless; and altogether labour is lavished on it at every point. It is costly to make and costly to mend, but then it lasts long, and if carefully handled very seldom requires repairing.

There are now a few factories in London, but so far they compete at some disadvantage with factories elsewhere. A London watch is expected to be a hand-made watch, and for the most part still is so, though, as we have suggested, a hybrid production is perhaps the most likely outcome of the situation.

As to foreign competition, the Americans produce a good-going watch with interchangeable parts; it may be an open question whether our provincial factories are equally successful, but both English and American seems to be outdone at present by the cheap Swiss watch. The demand is so enormous that there may well be room for all. The Swiss also excel and always have excelled in ladies' watches. They make the best watches of small size, paying great attention to outside ornament. They are also very ingenious, and have a reputation for making watches which "do things," *i.e.* repeat, show changes of the moon, &c.

As in all dwindling trades, there are many old men employed. It is, moreover, a healthy trade. Even the eyes, they say, are not materially injured by the constant use of magnifying glasses.

Earnings are less than they used to be. Highly-skilled men receive £2 to £3 for a full week's work where they used to make £3 or £4 for perhaps four days only. Men not absolutely first class have to be content with 25s to 30s per week or less. Their wages have fallen 30 per cent. in the last twenty years, and they have no alternative trade.

CLOCK MAKING.

Strange as it may seem, clock-makers have little in common with watch-makers. Neither would have any idea of the manner in which the work of the other should be done.

The work of making a clock is conducted under one roof, and both by hand and machinery. The men learn to make a clock throughout, and whatever their particular work may be, they do it with conscious reference to its bearing on the action of the whole clock. They are thus necessarily, to some extent, mechanicians, and able at once, without further training, to engage in other branches of work, such as that needed for gas or other metres, automatic penny-in-the-slot machinery, electrical instruments, and even the making of bicycles. This has had an important effect on the trade, which would be larger than it is were it not that the better wages to be had in alternative trades have caused a wholesale desertion of workers in the last two or three years.

The men are aware of the advantages of their position, and are united in resisting such sub-division of work as would remove the possibility of learning how to make a timepiece throughout. On the other hand, the masters declare that their German competitors have an advantage on this score which enables them to beat us in the production of cheap office clocks or dials. We are also beaten, mainly by France, in fancy clocks; in fact, we hardly compete. English makers have never attempted fancy cases. But though the Germans have been able by means of lower wages and more sub-divided work to make dials much more cheaply and sufficiently good as time-keepers to take some of our trade in these, and though we lack the taste to produce fancy clocks in competition with Paris or Vienna, yet no foreigner has been able to touch the English chime clock. For these and turret clocks, as well as dials, London has a speciality, and the whole trade is fairly prosperous.

The danger lies in the future. Youths are now brought up to automatic-machine making only, and though a clock-maker is fully competent to turn his hand to a less complicated mechanism, the man trained to automatic work is by no means able to turn to clock-making. Perhaps technical education may step in to fill this requirement.

Wages are on the level of 8*d* an hour for fifty-four hours. In automatic-machine making a "plus" is given proportionate to the amount of work done, which yields a substantial balance, and comes very near to a piece-work system of payment.

TRADES UNIONS.

The following is the only union in the London trade :—

Numbers in the Trade (Census 1891).		Name of Trade Society.	Membership.		Remarks.
Total.	Of whom are employed males over 20.		In each Section.	In each Division.	
4281	2143	The Union of Clock-makers, Index-makers and Brass workers in General (1892).	94	94	Minimum wage, Strike pay, and Benevolent fund, from which special contributions are made. Is responsible up to 20s for members leaving work unfinished.

Thus, out of a total of 2120 males over 20, only 94 are organized, and these all belong to one comparatively new society, and consist chiefly of index-makers, some of whom have not been brought up as clock-makers at all. In the watch trade there is no organisation; the masters having no association, and the men no union. There are three exclusively benevolent societies which are confined to the trade :—

(1) The Watch and Clock-makers' Benevolent Institution (1815).

(2) The Watch and Clock-makers' Pension Society.

(3) The Watch and Clock-makers' Asylum.

The first of these offers £12. 12*s* per annum as a pension to the "aged necessitous workmen of good character," and £8: 8*s* to their widows.

But all three are failing for want of support, and one is not more prosperous than the other, for the same men belong to all, and there are apparently. no new members forthcoming.

There is also the Horological Institute, where classes are held to teach drawing and the theory of watch and clock-making.

Wages Statistics.

In these trades 2143 adult males are employed, and of these we have wages returns for 147 employed by nine firms as under:—

Watch-makers .... 7 } = 9 firms employing usually 190
Watch and Clock-makers .... 2 } persons, of whom 147 are adult males.

The earnings of these men in an average week are as follows :—

Below 20s .... 12, or 8 per cent. }
20s to 25s .... 18 ,, 12   ,,   } Under 30s, 36 per cent.
25s ,, 30s .... 24 ,, 16   ,,   }
30s ,, 35s .... 23 ,, 16   ,,   }
35s ,, 40s .... 30 ,, 21   ,,   }
40s ,, 45s .... 17 ,, 12   ,,   } 30s and over, 64 per cent.
45s and upwards ... 23 ,, 15   ,,   }

                     147 ,, 100   ,,

With the above returns may be compared those made to the Board of Trade in 1886 by twenty-two firms employing ninety-one adult males, and it will be seen that the proportion at high wages is even larger than we make it.

	—20s.	20s—	25s—	30s—	35s—	40s—	45s—
Our returns ...	8 °/₀	12 °/₀	16 °/₀	16 °/₀	21 °/₀	12 °/₀	15 °/₀
		36 °/₀		64 °/₀			
Board of Trade returns	4 °/₀	7 °/₀	8 °/₀	14 °/₀	13 °/₀	31 °/₀	23 °/₀
		19 °/₀		81 °/₀			

The earnings of the whole trade would undoubtedly be

much lower than the above figures indicate, as the men working on their own account, or employing one assistant, are necessarily not included. These men form a considerable part of the whole trade, and their earnings are in many cases very low.

A few girls are employed at from 8s to 20s, the majority being paid about 10s. Boys at various ages receive from 5s to 20s.

Social Condition.

About 1310 of the 2140 adult men employed in these trades come under social classification as heads of families. According to the sample tested, 20 per cent. of those employed earn less than 25s a week, and may be compared with 28 per cent. who live under crowded conditions. Next we have 32 per cent. who earn 25s to 35s and may be compared with the 29 per cent. who live in small tenements with one to two persons in each room, and, finally, there are 48 per cent. earning 35s and upwards compared to 43 per cent. of the central classes, as follows :—

Comparison of Earnings with Style of Life (Watches and Clocks).

Earnings as returned.			Classification of Population.			
Below 20s...12, or	8 per cent.		3 or more in each room,	800, or	9 per cent.	
20s to 25s...18	,, 12	,,	2 to 3	,, 1700	,, 19	,,
25s ,, 30s...24	,, 16	,,	1 to 2	,, 2500	,, 29	,,
30s ,, 35s...23	,, 16	,,	Less than 1 ,,			
35s ,, 40s...30	,, 21	,,	More than 4 rooms			
40s ,, 45s...17	,, 12	,,	4 or more persons	3800 ,, 43		,,
45s and } 23 upwards }	,, 15	,,	to a servant			
	147 ,, 100	,,		8800 ,, 100		,,
			Employers' families and servant	3300		
				12,100		

The slight discrepancy between the amount of wages earned and the comfort in which the men live is without doubt due to the fact that we have returns for those only who are actually in work. Among watch-makers very many are old men who cannot be certain of regular employment, and depend almost entirely upon the income arising from any savings they may have made in more prosperous times. Those who have not saved, or who have spent all on the better education of their families, earn a precarious livelihood, or, perhaps, rely wholly on such help as can be given by a son or daughter.

Many of the men both live and work in Clerkenwell itself, as stated above, but many, also, are to be found further north in Islington and Highbury. Those who work at home feed at home, while those who work on the premises of their employers generally have their own "cosey corners," whether in a public or eating-house, to which they go for the dinner-hour.

Dress and outfit do not involve much expense. Beyond an apron and the well-known watch-maker's magnifying glass, which he may almost be said to "wear" in his eye when at work, the workman's outfit has no peculiarities.

Nos.   (For explanation of method adopted in preparing this chart, see Note on Diagram 18.)

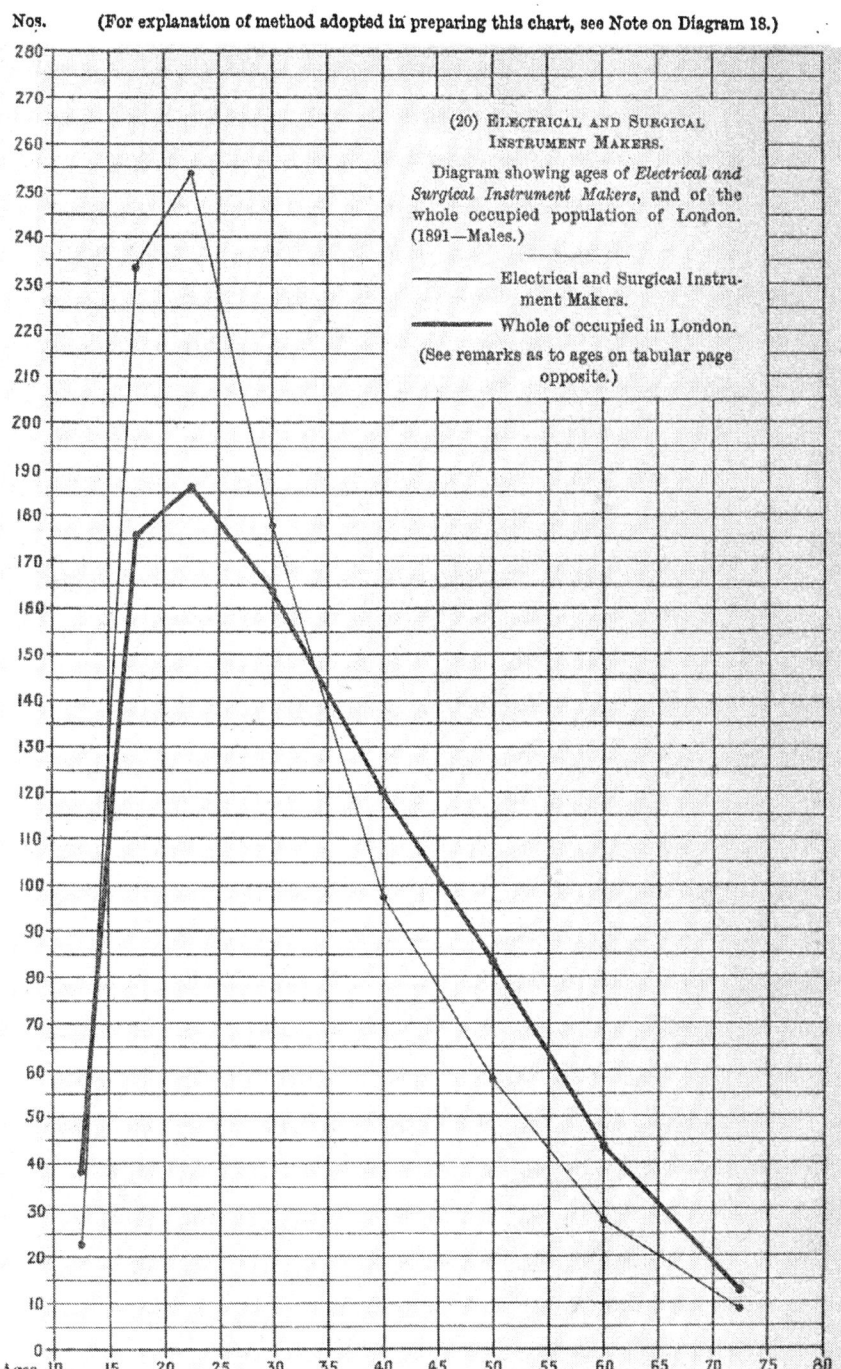

(20) ELECTRICAL AND SURGICAL
INSTRUMENT MAKERS.

Diagram showing ages of *Electrical and Surgical Instrument Makers*, and of the whole occupied population of London. (1891—Males.)

——————— Electrical and Surgical Instrument Makers.

━━━━━━━ Whole of occupied in London.

(See remarks as to ages on tabular page opposite.)

CHAPTER III.

SURGICAL, SCIENTIFIC, AND ELECTRICAL INSTRUMENTS. (*Section* 20.)

Persons represented.

Census Enumeration.						Enumerated by Families.			

Census Enumeration.

nsus Divisions, 1891.	Fe-males. All Ages.	Males.			Total.
		—19	20—54	55—	
Surgical In-truments......	260	117	516	83	976
Philosoph. do.	132	425	1550	245	2352
Electrical do.	129	1028	3598	175	4030
TOTAL....	521	1570	5664	503	8258

Enumerated by Families.

Sex ...... { Males .... 4103 / Females............. 47 }
Birthplace { In London .... 59 % 2440 / Out of London.. 41 % 1710 } Heads of Families, 4150.
Industrial Status .. { Employer ...... 11 % 444 / Employed...... 81 % 3371 / Neither........ 8 % 335 }

t may seem strange that there should be many women in the surgical instrument de. They are employed in making band-s and belts. The electrical trade is full of ung men, 2000 of those employed being ler 25 years of age. The age distribution haracteristic of a new trade. (*See* diagram.)

TOTAL POPULATION CONCERNED.

	Heads of Families.	Others Occupied.	Unoccupied.	Servants.	Total.
Total	4150	3317	10,455	593	18,515
Average in family..	1	·80	2·52	·14	4·46

DISTRIBUTION.

E.	N.	W. & C.	S.	Total.
545	2672	2078	2863	8258

DETAILS OF OCCUPATIONS
(FROM THE CENSUS DICTIONARY).

Artificial limbs, bandages, belts. Blunt and sharp instruments. Deformities' instruments. Probes, respirators, and syringes. Opticians, hour-glass, opera glass, magnetic appliances, meteorological instruments. Photo apparatus, camera, lens-maker. Spirit levels, sun-dials, compasses, spectacles, magic lanterns. Lightning conductors, telegraph tapes, submarine cables. Land cables. Gutta percha wire coverers. Core-maker. Electric light instruments and apparatus maker.

CLASSIFICATION.

Numbers living in Families.		%
3 or more to a room	1667	9·0
2 & under 3 ,,	3171	17·1
1 & under 2 ,,	5090	27·5
Less than 1 ,, / More than 4 rooms / 4 or more persons to a servant ..	7186	38·8
Less than 4 to 1 servant and 4 or more to 2 servants	538	2·9
All others with 2 or more servants ..	270	1·5
Servants	593	3·2
	18,515	100

	Inner.	Outer.	Together.
Crowded..	40 %	20 %	26 %
Not ,, ..	60 %	80 %	74 %

DISTRIBUTION.

East .. { Inner 1189 / Outer 347 }	1536
North { Inner 843 / Outer 5227 }	6070
West .. { Inner 425 / Outer 1793 }	2218
Central Inner 1838	1838
South-East { Inner 212 / Outer 3436 }	3648
South-West { Inner 1221 / Outer 1984 }	3205
	18,515

Inner 5728, or 31 %
Outer 12,787, or 69 %

Status as to Employment (according to Census Enumeration).

Census Divisions (1891).	Employers.		Employed.			Neither Employer nor Employed.		Total.
			Males.		Females of all ages.			
	Males.	Females	Under 20.	Over 20.		Males.	Females	
Surgical instrument maker	111	5	117	420	239	68	16	976
Philosophical instruments, optician..	227	4	425	1377	121	191	7	2352
Electrical instrument maker	189	3	1028	3387	124	197	2	4930
	527	12	1570	5184	484	456	25	8258
TOTAL..........	539		7238			481		8258
	Proportion of Employers to Employed–1 to 13							

SURGICAL INSTRUMENT MAKING.

The demand for surgical and scientific instruments is dependent rather upon the wants of large bodies than upon those of private individuals. Hospitals are the chief customers of surgical instrument makers, while for scientific and electrical instruments the orders mainly come from Home or Foreign Governments, or from telegraph, railway, and mining companies. There is a great and growing demand for photographic cameras, but with this exception the demands of individuals are the demands of specialists. A great surgeon will order a peculiar instrument to suit his particular fancy, or to render an operation possible in some special case; or a leading scientist will need a new instrument, either as a means to or as the result of a new discovery. Those engaged in the trade must, therefore, be prepared to satisfy these various customers. The most accurate individual handiwork is necessary, together with inventive genius of a high order, and must be applied as required to the first construction of the instrument, or, later, to that of the machinery which shall reproduce it by thousands for popular use at the lowest possible price.

A line may, however, be drawn between surgical and scientific or electrical instruments, as the former are never made wholesale by machinery. There is even very little division of labour; a single workman will, out of a strip of best steel, shape and sharpen, or entirely make and put together, an ordinary surgical instrument, needing only the work of other hands in polishing to render it ready for use.*

There are a few large houses engaged in this manu-

---

* To make a surgeon's instrument, a piece of the hardest Sheffield steel is forged roughly into shape and then worked on a lathe, or with a file, until ready for polishing. The polishers sit on low benches with the emery-wheel between their knees.

facture who employ skilled hands ; but the bulk of the work is done by chamber masters, who are often men who have formerly worked in these very houses. A skilled workman of more than usual enterprise, and one who can face the difficulties attendant on keeping accounts, decides that he would rather work for himself. He is not easy to replace, and rather than risk failure with a new hand, his employer agrees to give him work on condition that he shall not manufacture for competitors in the business. The new bond is more elastic than the old, but is very close, and, to some extent, secret. The names of these small makers are not known outside the trade. What they make is stamped with the die of the retail seller, and secrecy is observed on the part of the maker for fear of losing his only customer, and on the part of the retailer because he wishes the world to think he makes all he sells—preferring to claim credit as a manufacturer, rather than only as the possessor of a name which is a guarantee of the goods he offers to the public.

The position of these small men is a strong one. Their shops are the schools of the trade; they attract rising talent, and can produce at once cheaply and well; for under their strict supervision, a boy not only learns the trade, but assists in making his master's business profitable. It is most remarkable that we have here all the peculiarities that mark the sweating system, without any of the evil consequences that usually follow. This, however, applies only to surgical instrument making; with scientific instruments — and especially when, as with magic lanterns, these verge on toy-making — we find amongst chamber masters a much less desirable state of things.

Surgical instrument makers include the makers of artificial limbs and fall under the following heads; the smaller men as a rule confine themselves to one branch only :—

(1) Edge workers.
(2) Blunt workers.
(3) Deformity men.
(4) Artificial limb makers.

Edge workers, making anything which has a cutting edge, earn from 35s to 80s a week, the higher figure being given only to those engaged in making the most delicate instruments, such as are used in eye operations.

Blunt workers are not quite so skilled, and earn from 30s to 50s a week. The wages of *deformity men*, and those who make *artificial limbs*, vary greatly. A man who can make a good spine will earn £3 a week, while one who is proficient at artificial hands may make as much as £7 or £8; but these are special rates. For ordinary work, the wages are 36s to 40s, whether employed on the wood or on the metal portion, and 30s is paid to the finishers who cover the wood with leather and do the padding.

Time-work is the rule in the central shops, where special orders for single articles are taken, or where the first example of a new design is produced; but among chamber masters piece-work prevails, and is possible because the orders are generally for the reproduction of a known pattern in certain quantities. Few industries can boast of such regularity of employment. An average workman can be sure of constant work—overtime is the evil; long hours being the rule rather than the exception. There is very little shifting from branch to branch in the trade itself, or from, or to, other trades, though the men would be capable of turning to bicycle or electrical work.

Surgical instrument makers have no trades union of their own, but are represented by the Scientific Instrument Trade Society. They are too prosperous, it seems, to care to belong, in any great numbers, to this union, or to take any active part in it.

Most of the men have learnt their business under chamber masters. They are not regularly apprenticed, but agree to work three or five years at a very low wage, and expect to learn every branch. If they work, they learn, if they do not, they are soon dismissed. The larger makers are not in favour of apprentices, whether premiumed or not. It pays them better to employ men already trained ; or, if they receive a lad, to train him to one branch only.

With reference to work done in other parts of the world ; Sheffield produces coarser and somewhat cheaper instruments ; the cheapest of all come from Germany, but the hospitals and first-rate operators have a prejudice against them. This is a case in which the very best, and only the very best, possible article can be considered satisfactory, and this superiority London workmanship of Sheffield steel is supposed to give.

PHILOSOPHICAL AND OPTICAL INSTRUMENT MAKERS.

These (including makers of opera glasses, photographic apparatus and magic lanterns) form the second division of this section.

Meteorological and surveying instruments, microscopes, magic lanterns, and photographic apparatus are made largely in London. Opera glasses come almost entirely from Paris and cheap spectacles from Germany, which also competes with our microscopes. Magic-lantern making, except for the very best, is said to be a sweated industry. The very cheapest are imported. The large dealers, who probably call themselves manufacturers, only retail the produce of the garrets, where magic lanterns are turned out so cheaply that, so far, no one has found it worth while to compete with this system by gathering the workers under one roof.

Barometers and thermometers used to be entirely in the hands of Italians working in London. These have now been superseded by English workmen, and traces of the former state of things remain only in the names of two or three old-established and still leading houses.

The usual week varies between fifty-four and sixty hours, and wages are paid at 8d, 10d or even 1s an hour for very highly-skilled men. The lowest union rate is 8d per hour, and where a piece-work price can be set men can earn as much as 1s 2d an hour, and will be found ready to work longer hours than is good for them. Time-pay, with a bonus shared in proportion to work done, is a system frequently adopted, and, in this or other forms, most work is actually paid by the piece. If a man is a good hand at lathe and vice work he is fitted for almost any part in the manufacture of scientific instruments, except glass-grinding for lenses, and with but few exceptions can be sure of regular work throughout the year. A good workman is perhaps at a greater premium in this than in any other trade.

As far as there are seasons at all, autumn and winter are the busiest times : aneroids for autumn touring; thermometers to register the cold in winter, which excites greater interest than the heat in summer; and clinical thermometers for an epidemic like the influenza. For microscopes the chief demand is from chemists, colleges and doctors, and these do not buy them unless their pockets are full—those of colleges from well-paid rents, and those of doctors from an abundance of patients. For retailers of photographic apparatus summer is busy and winter slack, but the men do not feel the seasons to any great extent, as stock does not deteriorate, and can be made up in winter for the summer demand.

With these exceptions the business as a whole depends more upon the general course of trade, and the need of new instruments for new lines of railway, or for the working of new mines, than upon the regular irregularities which in many trades follow the seasons of the year. And while any general depression is at once reflected in the orders for surveying instruments, so, too, is the springing up of enterprise felt before other trades are conscious of it. Such is the case now (1893), and the makers speak with assurance as to a general revival of trade within the next two years.

With scientific and electric instrument making the tendency is to sub-divide the work as much as possible. Few men make the whole of any instrument, and new machinery is introduced every day and helps to make still further sub-divisions possible. Only in this way, say the masters, can the competition of Germany be faced successfully.

ELECTRICAL INSTRUMENTS.

It is especially with regard to electrical work that wholesale production by machinery on a colossal scale follows closely on the heels of scientific investigation and elaborate experimental handiwork. No industry is more modern, nor does any show more vitality and expansive power. It extends in every direction and its enterprise finds work for every kind of labour. The making and laying of deep-sea cables have called for special machinery and special ships; and the preparation of the materials used has created new industries. The perfecting of transmitting instruments and their construction by machinery, which can turn them out by thousands at a moderate price, is an industry in itself, and it, too, calls for the special preparation of necessary and peculiar (non-conducting) materials, of which india rubber is generally the basis. Electric lighting alone includes a hundred trades. The dynamos must be invented, improved and manufactured wholesale. Power must be applied to the creation of electric force in great quantities. Streets must be wired, houses fitted, and lamps supplied. All this has not been done without some wasted effort. There have been costly failures as well as notable successes, but, on the whole, the march of this trade has been a triumph of enterprise out of which labour has greatly profited. And as witnessing the prosperity of the electrical trades, it is remarkable that in a year of exceptional depression (1893) the union secretary stated that he did not know of one *bonâ fide* workman out of employment. The men who were needed have been drawn from many sources—from the watch or clock trade for the making of metres, from wire workers and brass-finishers, from electro-platers and india-rubber workers, and from every branch of engineering. Retired sailors are employed to rig the wires aloft, and navvies and bricklayers to make channels for them underground, and women learn to assist in new processes of manufacture; but, on the whole, as a modern industry it is the trade of young men, and so in many ways abnormal from a social point of view.

. Much of the work is carried on beyond the London boundary. The construction of cables for use by land or sea is confined almost entirely to a few large factories in Silvertown and Woolwich. The employees live on both sides of the Thames, some within, but the larger proportion beyond, the census boundary. Much machinery is used, and a lower rate of pay obtains than in London itself. Cable making is only a semi-skilled industry, and there is much common labour employed. The men earn only $4\frac{1}{2}d$, $5d$ or $6d$ an hour, and the union has as yet obtained no footing among them. In the particulars of wages, which are given later, Silvertown is separately treated.

The manufacture of electricity for lighting is for the most part done within the district to be supplied. Where this is not so, and the generating station is situated at a distance, power is supplied at high pressure and transformed at small stations. The loss on transmission in this manner outweighs, at present, the saving resulting from lower rent and the concentration of the work.

In every central station the work is divided into three departments :—

        (1) Engine-room staff.
        (2) Out-door staff.
        (3) Main staff.

The engine-room is served by day as well as by night—

usually three shifts of eight hours on week-days, and two of twelve hours on Sunday. This gives fifty-six hours work per week on the average, each man having one free Sunday out of three. The best drivers are found in men who, from failing eyesight, have had to abandon railway work. The pay is 35*s* to 45*s* for leading hands, and 25*s* to 30*s* for others. Now that engines are arranged to lubricate themselves, the labour involved is not great, but the drivers must be prompt to detect a fault and able to correct it.

The "out-door staff" make connections with the mains for house work, and are an irregular body. Some companies have their own men for this work, but more usually either engage men as required or apply to the large contractors, who always have gangs of men for the purpose. Good wiremen and jointers get from $7\frac{1}{2}d$ to $9\frac{1}{2}d$ per hour, and are in some measure skilled, but the skill is easily acquired, and the labourers or boys who help them become wiremen themselves in due course. Meter readers also belong to the out-door staff. They begin at 25*s* and rise to 45*s*.

The "main" staff consists of permanent hands whose duty it is to lay and keep in repair the different mains. These are "service-layers," "bricklayers," and labourers, paid 8*d*, $9\frac{1}{2}d$, and 6*d* per hour respectively. They are most busy in the late summer and autumn, when in West London they can work with the least interference to consumers, but there is repair work all the year, except during fogs, when every wire is in full use, and leaks, large or small, must take their chance.

The electric lighting industry has been suffering from a hesitation on the part of consumers, following on the first rush. The light was not uniformly a success. But the trade is settling down, demand and supply are becoming more regular, and it may now be considered as forming a great London industry.

TRADES UNIONS.

Subjoined are particulars of the trade organizations :—

Numbers in the London Trade (Census 1891).		Name of Trade Society.	Membership in London.		Remarks.
Total.	Of whom are employed males over 20.		In each Society.	In each Division.	
3328	1797	Scientific Instrument Makers' Trade Society (1887).	450	516	Has 5 branches in London. Offers out of work pay, and a contingent benefit for Strikes. Relations fair with masters. Minimum wage.
		Barometer, Thermometer and Tube Blowers' Trade and Benefit Society (1890)	66		Offers out of work, Sick, Strike, and Death Money. Strict rules as to apprenticeship. Union and non-union men work together.
4930	3387	The Electrical Trades Union (1889).	285	435	Has 3 branches in London. Offers out of work, Death, and Accident Benefits, and special rates for special cases. Is represented on Arbitration Board of Chamber of Commerce. Minimum wage.
		The Amalgamated Society of Telegraph and Telephone workers (1893).	150		Strike pay and Death levy only. Members are mostly outside telephone men and labourers.
8258	5184			951	

Thus, out of a total of 5184 males over 20, 951 are included in the organizations, or 18 per cent. Taken separately, the proportion is 29 per cent. among surgical and scientific instrument makers, and 13 per cent. amongst electrical instrument makers.

There is no combination among employers.

In considering the question of organization, it is to be remembered that many of those employed may be, and probably are, members of some of the brass-workers' societies, or even of the Amalgamated Engineers, as the

men have been drawn into scientific and electric work
from all sides, and at any rate they are closely in touch
with the trades union movement at many points. For
instance, the Building Trades' Federation refuses to allow
its men to work with any non-union electricians, and
all the branches of the Electrical Trades Union and of the
Scientific Instrument Makers' Society, as well as the
Amalgamated Telegraph and Telephone Workers, are
affiliated to the London Federal Council of Brassworkers.

The Scientific Instrument Makers' Society admits only
those who have worked at the trade five years, and who are
getting not less than 8d an hour. There are no standard
hours and no regular overtime rate, although a good deal
of overtime is worked, especially on Government contracts.

The Barometer, Thermometer, and Tube Blowers' Society
has strict rules with reference to the training of apprentices,
and urges that every effort be used to enforce their order
that "every apprentice should be put under the control and
guidance of one man, to whom alone will be attached the
responsibility of teaching him his business. Such responsibility to be undertaken between the employer and the
workman to whom the apprentice is to be attached, and
that every boy before his articles of apprenticeship be
signed should undergo at least a probationary period of one
month. And, further, that no learners other than apprentices shall be taught in any firm."

The other Society especially involved is the Electrical
Trades Union, established in 1889 and amalgamated in
1890 with the Telegraph and Telephone Construction
Union (a Manchester Society). It has in all 14 branches
with 1700 members, 3 branches with 280 members being
in London; no branch is allowed to have more than 300.
It admits any men who have worked for at least three
years in the trade, and are earning not less than 8d per
hour for winders, 9d for wiremen, and 10d for chargemen.
Overtime one quarter extra for first two hours and time

and a half after. The telephone wiremen—nearly every wireman in London is a society man—used also to belong, but have formed recently (1894) a separate society of their own, in which they include the telegraph workers. One of their objects is to enforce a minimum wage of 26*s* per week for labourers and 30*s* for wiremen.

Wages Statistics.

There are 5184 adult men employed in these trades, and we have wages returns for 1503 in all, but of these 673 are at Silvertown, just beyond the Metropolitan boundary, and are therefore stated separately later on. The remaining 830 are employed by thirty-three London firms, as under :—

Surgical instrument makers	8	= 33 firms employing usually 1445 persons, of whom 1036 are adult males, but 206 of these belong to other sections, as tool - makers, brass - finishers, engineers, engine drivers, stokers, bricklayers, carpenters, French polishers, painters, store-keepers, and porters.
Scientific ,, ,,	5	
Opticians	6	
Electricians	7	
Electric-light supply	6	
Telegraph-cable makers	1	

The wages earned in an ordinary week by these 830 men are as follows :—

Below 20*s*	21,	or 2 per cent.		Under 30*s*, 25 per cent.
20*s* to 25*s*	65	,, 8 ,,		
25*s* ,, 30*s*	121	,, 15 ,,		
30*s* ,, 35*s*	149	,, 18 ,,		
35*s* ,, 40*s*	219	,, 26 ,,		30*s* and over, 75 per cent.
40*s* ,, 45*s*	118	,, 14 ,,		
45*s* and upwards	137	,, 17 ,,		
	830	,,100 ,,		

In this section the Board of Trade returns of wages are not given in sufficient detail to allow of a satisfactory comparison with our own, but by including Silvertown we are

able to make use of both methods of return in showing
the influence of busy and slack seasons on the whole
trade :—

	Busy Week.	Slack Week.	Percentage Reduction.		
			In number.	In earnings per head.	Combined.
Our returns	1389	882	37	4	39
Board of Trade returns	2709	1644	39	10	45

We have here, however, two distinct classes of trade,
and the conditions of each are quite different. There are,
on the one hand, the surgical and scientific instrument
making and electric-lighting firms of the western and more
central parts of London, in which the work is for the most part
highly skilled and employment very constant; and, on the
other hand, there are the large electrical apparatus and
telegraph cable works of the outlying Eastern districts, in
which work is less skilled and a good deal of irregularity
prevails. This will be clearly shown by giving the two
sections separately :—

SURGICAL AND SCIENTIFIC INSTRUMENT, &c., MAKERS.						ELECTRIC APPARATUS AND CABLE WORKS.					
			Percentage Reduction.					Percentage Reduction.			
	Busy Week.	Slack Week.	In number.	In earnings per head.	Combined.	Busy Week.	Slack Week.	In number.	In earnings per head.	Combined.
Our returns	333	336	+1	5	4	920	429	53	4½	55½
Board of Trade returns	159	145	9	22	29	2550	1490	42	9½	46½

It will thus be seen that whilst in surgical and scientific
instruments, &c., the numbers in busy and slack times

differ very slightly (there being in fact in our returns rather more women and boys employed in the slack than in the busy time), there is in the other portion of these trades a reduction of nearly one-half in the numbers employed.

From five firms of the former class statements have been received of the proportion of time and piece-work in busy and slack weeks, and give the following result:—

Men.	Number of Workers.	Busy Week. Average.			Number of Workers.	Slack Week. Average.		
		Wage.	Hours.	Rate.		Wage.	Hours.	Rate.
		s. d.		d.		s. d.		d.
Time-work { Under 5d per hour	5	16 6	57	3½	5	16 0	55	3½
5d to 6d ,,	16	26 6	58½	5¼	15	24 6	53	5¼
6d to 8d ,,	111	34 0	54	7½	107	34 4	55	7½
Over 8d ,,	63	43 0	52	9¾	64	43 4	52	9¾
	195	—	—	—	191	—	—	—
Piece-work { Under 20s per week	1	16 0	—	—	5	14 0	—	—
20s & under 25s ,,	4	21 9	—	—	8	22 6	—	—
25s ,, 30s ,,	5	27 7	—	—	6	27 6	—	—
30s ,, 35s ,,	10	32 10	—	—	13	32 6	—	—
35s ,, 40s ,,	15	37 4	—	—	9	37 9	—	—
40s ,, 45s ,,	14	41 8	—	—	12	42 2	—	—
45s ,, 50s ,,	16	47 4	—	—	8	46 4	—	—
50s and upwards ,,	18	56 8	—	—	11	52 5	—	—
	83	—	—	—	72	—	—	—
Boys—								
Time-workers ,,	71	10 2	57	2¼	74	9 9	52	2¼
Piece- { 10s & under ,,	2	10 0	—	—	9	7 9	—	—
work { Over 10s ,,	14	16 5	—	—	10	15 6	—	—
	87	—	—	—	93	—	—	—

These returns also show the hours worked by piece-hands, and the following restatement of their earnings may be compared with those of men paid by the hour:—

Piece Workers (Men).	Busy Week.				Slack Week.			
	Number of Workers.	Average.			Number of Workers.	Average.		
		Wage.	Hours.	Rate.		Wage.	Hours.	Rate.
		s. d.		d.		s. d.		d.
Under 5*d* per hour	2	20 6	52	4¾	4	16 9	51	3¾
5*d* to 6*d* ,, ...	7	27 5	57	5¾	4	20 6	46	5¼
6*d* to 8*d* ,, ...	13	33 2	52½	7½	16	30 11	49	7½
Over 8*d* ,, ...	61	46 4	54¾	10	48	41 5	50	9¾
	83	—	—	—	72	—	—	—

The remarkable regularity, as well as high average earnings, here shown are further borne out by the following detailed return made by an electric-lighting firm, giving the exact wages and hours worked by six representative men in their employ during one entire year. The men are certainly good examples, and rather above the average:—

	July–Sept.		Oct.–Dec.		Jan.–March.		April–June.		12 months.		Average rate per hour.
	Average hours.	Average earnings.	Average hours.	Average earnings.	Average hours.	Average Earnings.	Average hours.	Average earnings.	Average hours.	Average earnings.	
		£ s. d.		£ s. d.		£ s. d.		£ s. d.		£ s. d.	d.
Fitter	67	2 9 11	69	2 11 6	69½	2 12 4	66	2 9 9	68	2 10 11	9
Engine driver ...	66	2 1 3	85	2 13 8	84½	2 13 3	68½	2 3 4	76	2 7 11	7½
Carpenter	53	1 19 8	53	1 19 6	54	2 0 6	55½	2 1 7	54	2 0 4	9
Wireman	53	1 15 4	52	1 14 6	52	1 14 6	52½	1 14 10	52½	1 14 10	8
Stoker	68	1 16 10	87	2 7 2	88½	2 7 11	76	2 1 1	80	2 3 3	6½
Battery attendant	63	1 11 8	85	2 2 6	84	2 2 1	73	1 18 6	76½	1 18 8	6

The actual hours will not be quite so long, as "added" time is given, *i.e.* on Sundays every hour is reckoned as 1½ hours.

A full week is fifty-four hours, so the rule is to work overtime. As will be seen, the engine driver, stoker and battery attendant have to put up with long hours: in foggy weather their work is very heavy. For this there seems to be no help, unless treble shifts are worked, a plan not always easy to arrange or popular with the men.

As representing the other class of firms, we have the returns from Silvertown as subjoined:—

TELEGRAPH AND ELECTRIC WORKS, SILVERTOWN.

Men.	Number of Workers.	Busy Week. Average.			Number of Workers.	Slack Week. Average.		
		Wage.	Hours.	Rate.		Wage.	Hours.	Rate.
		s. d.		*d.*		*s. d.*		*d.*
Time-work. (Under 5*d* per hour	181	22 8	61½	4½	60	21 0	59	4¼
5*d* to 6*d* ,,	212	30 0	66	5½	105	26 7	60	5¼
6*d* to 8*d* ,,	25	38 9	67	7	24	34 3	57	7¼
Over 8*d* ,,	15	49 7	66½	9	11	45 4	58	9¼
	433	——	——	——	200	——	——	——
Piece-work. (Under 10*s* per week	1	3 0	——	—	2	8 6	——	—
10*s* & under 15*s* ,,	10	11 9	——	—	6	11 2	——	—
15*s* ,, 20*s* ,,	8	18 1	——	—	6	16 6	——	—
20*s* ,, 25*s* ,,	8	22 4	——	—	6	23 4	——	—
25*s* ,, 30*s* ,,	12	28 0	——	—	8	26 10	——	—
30*s* ,, 40*s* ,,	49	34 3	——	—	10	34 3	——	—
40*s* ,, 50*s* ,,	17	45 1	——	—	17	42 4	——	—
Over 50*s* ,,	9	53 11	——	—	——	——	—	—
	114	—	—	——	55	——	——	——
Boys, under 5*d*	133	13 0	58½	2¾	62	11 4	55	2½

It appears that not only is employment much more irregular, but hours are longer and wages lower. As, however, the slack period for different parts of the work does not come at the same time, the irregularity is reduced by the men shifting from one branch to another.

Concerning the earnings of those who are not heads of families, our returns give results for 117 women and girls, and 283 boys and apprentices—a fairly large proportion of the total numbers engaged in the trades. Of the females, half earned 10*s* or less, and the other half more than that, the most usual amounts being 10*s* and 12*s*. The particulars as to boys and lads show almost equal numbers receiving 5*s*, 6*s*, 7*s*, 8*s*, and so at each stage up to 20*s*. At the telegraph works the wages of women are slightly lower, the majority earning from 8*s* to 10*s*. In the Board of Trade returns, which show smaller proportions, earnings of females are stated at 11*s* to 20*s*, and of lads at 9*s* to 20*s*. but few are given at less than 11*s*. There appears to have been of late a considerable increase in the number of women and boys employed in these trades, and this increase is at the lower rates of pay.

Social Condition.

Of the 5180 adult males employed, about 3330 come under social classification as heads of families. According to our wages returns only 10 per cent. of those employed earn less than 25*s* a week, whereas 30 per cent. are living under crowded conditions. Next we find 33 per cent. earning from 25*s* to 35*s* compared to 32 per cent. of those who live in small tenements, but not crowded; and finally 57 per cent. earning 35*s* and upwards, compared to 38 per cent. of the central classes, as follows:—

Comparison of Earnings with Style of Life (Surgical and Scientific Instruments).

Earnings as returned.			Classification of Population.			
Below 20s...	21, or	2 per cent.	3 or more in each room,	1600, or	10 per cent.	
20s to 25s...	65 ,,	8 ,,	2 to 3 ,,	3200 ,,	20 ,,	
25s ,, 30s...	121 ,,	15 ,,	1 ,, 2 ,,	5100 ,,	32 ,,	
30s ,, 35s...	149 ,,	18 ,,	Less than 1 ,,			
35s ,, 40s...	219 ,,	26 ,,	More than 4 rooms			
40s ,, 45s...	118 ,,	14 ,,	4 or more persons to	6000 ,,	38 ,,	
45s and upwards }...	137 ,,	17 ,,	a servant... ... }			
	830 ,,	100 ,,		15,900 ,,	100 ,,	
			Employers' families, servants, &c. ...}	2600		
				18,500		

Of the skilled men in the surgical and scientific instrument trades a large number live in North and South London at some distance from their work, and these either bring their dinner with them and eat it in the shop, or go out to do so.

Telegraph and telephone men, even though they may live near their employers, may have work to do in different parts of London, one day in one place and the next in another, so that they must select the nearest eating-house for their meals.

In Silvertown, on the other hand, both men and women are chosen from the neighbourhood, and in many cases are able to go home for dinner.

There is still some complaint as to drink among scientific and electrical-instrument makers, glass-grinders and blowers. This is partly a survival from old times, when there was more work than workers, and when it was no uncommon thing to send a man round to the public-houses with a bribe to induce someone to come in to finish a job; or, reversing the situation, men used even to "ask for a 'sov.' of the governor to go out for a 'booze'"—and get it. Now employers are much more strict; but whether it is the nature of the work, as in glass-grinding, where the men have a habit of spitting on the lenses for the sake of better lubrication, that makes a man thirsty, or the great demand there is for workmen, and that money easily gained is easily spent, there is undoubtedly still room for further improvement in the matter of sobriety.

The discrepancy in the condition of life and the earnings of the men according to the table given above is partly due to this curse of drink, but, no doubt, it must also be ascribed to the absence of any figures with regard to the less fortunate members employed by small garret masters and magic-lantern makers, from whom we were unable to obtain any information, and among whom lower rates of pay would seem to be usual.

Many of the larger shops have successful sick clubs, to

which the employers also contribute something. For the men 3*d* per week is the usual payment, with benefits of 10*s* or 12*s* for six weeks or so; at the end of the year the money in hand is shared out with the exception generally of a small sum which is left to start the fund well in the beginning of the New Year.

Only in very rare cases do the wives of men employed in the above industries earn money.

CHAPTER IV.

MUSICAL INSTRUMENTS, FISHING-TACKLE AND TOYS. (Section 21.)

Persons Represented.

Census Enumeration.

Census Divisions, 1891.	Fe-males. All Ages.	Males. —19	20—54	55—	Total.
1) Musical Instruments	253	1458	4935	747	7393
2) Fishing-tackle, Toys, Tobacco Pipes	924	397	1413	280	3014
TOTAL....	1177	1855	6348	1027	10,407

The noticeable features here are the number of boys in the musical instrument trade, and of women in toy making. There is an excess of quite young and old people, with a corresponding decline at the intermediate periods; little strength is required. See diagram.)

DISTRIBUTION.

E.	N.	W. & C.	S.	Total.
1236	5591	1601	1979	10,407

DETAILS OF OCCUPATIONS
(FROM THE CENSUS DICTIONARY).

1) Musical-instrument maker, dealer, musical-string maker, brass-instrument maker, organ-builder, piano-maker, action-maker, back-maker, bellyer, case-maker, finisher, fitter-up, polisher, key-maker, tuner, &c.

2) Toy, sports, game-apparatus maker, &c., Tobacco-pipe maker, snuff-box maker, &c.

Enumerated by Families.

Sex	Males		5274	Heads of Families. 5459.
	Females		185	
Birthplace	In London	71 %	3881	
	Out of London..	29 %	1578	
Industrial Status ..	Employer	12 %	658	
	Employed......	76 %	4148	
	Neither	12 %	653	

TOTAL POPULATION CONCERNED.

	Heads of Families.	Others Occupied.	Unoccupied.	Servants.	To
Total	5459	5328	13,899	469	25.
Average in family..	1	·96	2·55	·09	4

CLASSIFICATION.

Numbers living in Families. %

				%
3 or more to a room		3079		12·1
2 & under 3	,,	5093		20·3
1 & under 2	,,	6529		26·0
Less than 1	,,			
More than 4 rooms		9313		37·0
4 or more persons to a servant ..				
Less than 4 to 1 servant, and 4 or more to 2 servants		512		2·0
All others with 2 or more servants ..		160		·7
Servants		469		1·9
		25,155		100

	Inner.	Outer.	Together.
Crowded..	44 %	32 %	32 %
Not ,, ..	56 %	68 %	68 %

DISTRIBUTION.

East ..	Inner 2213	2
	Outer 358	
North	Inner 2275	13,
	Outer 11,367	
West ..	Inner 448	2
	Outer 2053	
Central	Inner 1397	1
South-East	Inner 223	1
	Outer 1623	
South-West	Inner 975	3
	Outer 2223	
		25,

Inner 7531, or 30 %
Outer 17,624, or 70 %

Status as to Employment (according to Census Enumeration).

Census Divisions (1891).	Employers. Males.	Females	Employed. Males. Under 20.	Over 20.	Females of all ages.	Neither Employer nor Employed. Males.	Females	Total.
1) Musical instrument maker	463	26	1458	4741	196	478	31	7393
2) Fishing tackle, toys, games	193	52	314	824	591	234	117	2325
Tobacco pipes, &c.	75	6	83	320	146	47	12	689
TOTAL..........	731	84	1855	5885	933	759	160	10,407
	815		8673			919		

Proportion of Employers to Employed—1 to 11

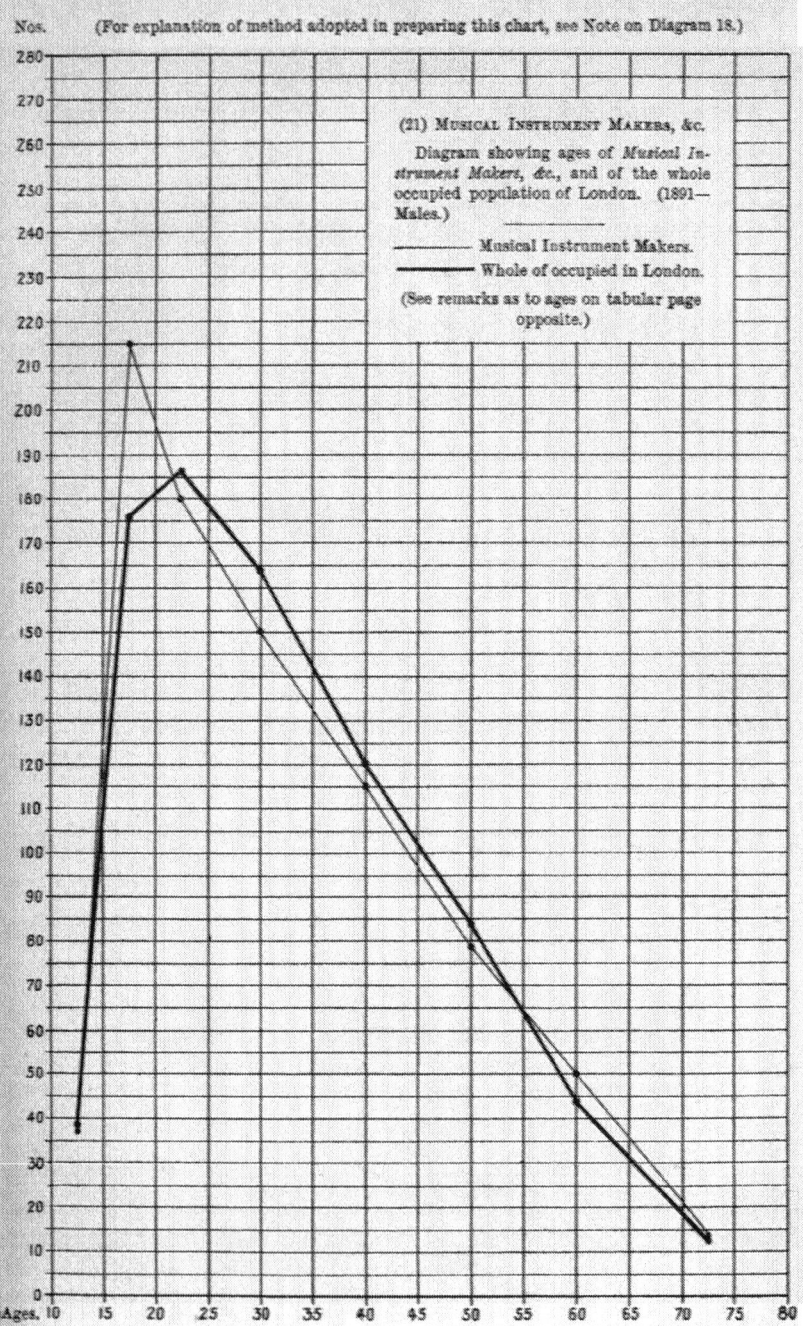

(21) MUSICAL INSTRUMENT MAKERS, &c.

Diagram showing ages of *Musical Instrument Makers, &c.*, and of the whole occupied population of London. (1891—Males.)

——————— Musical Instrument Makers.
——————— Whole of occupied in London.

(See remarks as to ages on tabular page opposite.)

PIANO MANUFACTURE.

Pianofortes, harmoniums and organs are the musical instruments with the manufacture of which this section is chiefly concerned, and of these pianofortes are the most important.

The construction of a piano is a very complicated affair. There is the case with its ornamentation, and within it is the "back," or foundation of the instrument, the "belly," or sounding board, and the strong harp-shaped frame, on which the wires are strung; then there are the "actions" and other internal or external fittings — pedals, key-boards, &c. The manufacture of a piano consists in putting all these parts together, rather than in making them, but all *bonâ fide* manufacturers make "back," "belly," and case. Even the largest firms buy many parts of their instruments ready-made, and most of them import the "actions," or internal machinery, by which the touch of the performer on the key-board is conveyed to the stretched wires. There are some makers of this beautiful mechanism in London, and a few houses make their own, but most are imported from Germany or France; the former country especially excels in this manufacture. London work is said to be less clean, and with our atmosphere this is not surprising.

Piano manufacturers may be divided into three classes:—

(1) The large well-known firms, who have a good name to keep up, and who produce the finest and most expensive instruments.

(2) The smaller, or less renowned firms, whose work is cheaper, though still good and durable.

(3) Small makers working for middlemen, or from hand to mouth, on ill-seasoned material, and shifting out of the class of masters into that of workmen at the bench, or *vice versâ*, as opportunity offers or necessity compels.

The most essential point of all in the manufacture of a

good piano is that the "belly" and "back" should be made of well-chosen and well-seasoned wood; on this more than on any part of the internal mechanism do the tone and permanence of tone depend. Here, then, we find the main difference between first-rate, second-rate, third-rate, or no rate instruments, although at every point the better make is shown in more perfect workmanship.

. The firms of the first class provide more regular employment and more regular hours, and healthy, well-ventilated workshops; but with these advantages discipline is more strict, and in busy times there is less money to be made than in workshops of a lower and even the lowest kind.

. There is a great variety amongst the workshops of the second class, some being admirably appointed and fitted, so as to rank with the first in this respect; others falling off by degrees, until it is difficult to draw a very distinct line between them and the third class, except as to the quality of the materials used—the seasoned character of the wood— which implies at once the intention to produce a genuine instrument, and the possession of sufficient capital to do this, and, if need be, await a buyer.

The last class—the small makers—are, in some ways, the most interesting subject of study, but are the most difficult of access, and in regard to them our information is mostly of a hearsay character. While the business of the large firms proceeds steadily with the regularity of clockwork, the small maker is always at one extreme or the other; working with feverish energy to sell in haste, or entirely out of work. Unseasoned wood bought on a Monday is said to leave the shop with all the outward show of a piano on Saturday! All sorts of expedients are resorted to in order to find a market. The instrument may be hawked about from dealer to dealer, or money may be borrowed on it where it stands. Advertising is greatly resorted to.

The best firms are practically out of reach of the competition of this last class, and are not tried by it; but the makers of good and sound cheap pianos are much affected by such competition, and are loud in their complaints of the third-rate maker and his ways.

Seasons and regularity.—There are very distinctly marked busy and slack seasons in the piano trade, and the smaller the shop the more these variations are felt. The busy months are those of autumn and winter—the months of indoor amusements—while the slack season lasts from April or May to the end of August. In large firms men are not usually discharged unless they are unsteady or troublesome, but shorter hours are worked, and steam may be shut off on Saturday. A footing once obtained in one of these factories is good for a lifetime's employment, and one employee can say that his grandfather, his father, and he have between them worked 150 years for the firm in which he now holds a high position. A preference is given to sons and relations of employees, and it is rather difficult for any outsider to obtain an entrance. In such a firm a good deal is done for the men, and it may be mentioned that in one instance a library of eight thousand volumes is provided for the workpeople, who have also their own volunteer corps.

In the better second-class shops two-thirds of the men can perhaps count on regular employment, but many of these shops, and the majority of the third-class, shut up entirely during three or four months, and some only keep on two or three men. On the other hand, when the busy time comes, work is sometimes kept up till 10, 11 or 12 o'clock at night, with the full concurrence of the men, who, it is believed, would not favour any legal limitation of hours.

Some men who are thrown out of employment in the summer find work as cabinet-makers, this closely allied trade being then most active; in other cases, they may take to regular summer employments, such as professional cricketing, and return to the factory for the winter.

Hours and wages.—The standard hours of work are fifty-four to fifty-six per week, reduced even in the largest firms to forty-eight in summer, and to thirty hours or less in other instances. The general run of wages paid in each department and character of work done is given below, but where there is much loss of time it is difficult to estimate the yearly income.

1. *Back-making.*—The back of a piano is in effect the foundation on which the whole instrument rests. It is made of beech, and upon it the sounding board or " belly " and the iron frame are built up. No more skill is required than for high-class joinery, but the work demands special experience. The wages paid (usually by piece) come to 9*d* or 10*d* per hour, which will mean 40*s* to 45*s* in busy times, dropping to 25*s* to 30*s* in the slack season. The same rates apply to those who make doors and panels, lay on veneer, &c., called " part " makers.

2. *Bellying and marking-off,* *i.e.* making and preparing the sounding-board (of resonant Swiss pine) and fixing it to the back. Wages earned are from 10*d* to 11*d* per hour.

3. *Stringing.*—This is generally done by youths, paid 6*d* an hour.

4. *Fitting-up,* *i.e.* putting the case, &c., together. The earnings vary according to the quickness of the worker, from as little as 8*d* to as much as 1*s* per hour, and may average from 9*d* to 10*d*, with a wide range between busy and slack times in the weekly earnings.

5. *Finishing and regulating;* a branch of work requiring the greatest accuracy and precision, since the finisher has to set up the delicate mechanism of the " actions." A good workman in this branch should earn £2 to £3 per week in one of the large firms, and not less than £2 in second-class establishments. With inferior pianos much less care would be given to this work.

6. Lastly, there are the *polishers,* the only men who are,

as a rule, paid by time, this being the result of a strike against piece-work. These men, who are the roughest and least skilled in the trade, earn usually 8*d* an hour, and make from 24*s* to 30*s* yearly average.

In the making of "actions," machinery is largely used, labour is greatly sub-divided, and wages are lower. A good many boys and women are employed, as much of the work is light. Piano-strings also form a distinct manufacture, which, however, has its home in the Midlands, and not in London.

Sub-contracting.—What is called "contracting" has been very usual in the trade, and, though there is less of it now than formerly, it is still not unusual. Under this system a manufacturer gives out the materials to a skilled artisan, who undertakes to complete the work at a price, and engages and pays those who assist him. The work is done on the manufacturer's premises. A good deal of trouble is saved, as well as some foremen's wages, but the practice has not worked comfortably, and seems to be dying out. The men do not like it because it tends to increase the number of boys employed and to reduce wages, and the masters because they lose control over their factories and over the work done. It is certainly objectionable in a general way, as being liable to bring in the manifold evils of sweating.

Training.—A great many boys and youths are employed in the trade, but very few of them are thoroughly taught; any regular system of apprenticeship has fallen into disuse and is hardly likely to be revived. The "contractors" and small masters employ, perhaps, the largest proportion of young hands, but it must be admitted that they also teach them most. The larger the factory and the more complete the sub-division of the work into departments, the less chance a boy has of acquiring any general knowledge, though in place of this he becomes quite perfect at some one process. For lack of regulation on the question of apprenticeship, the trade is liable to be over-crowded with incompetent men. There are no unions of any power in the trade, or they would probably take up this subject. On the other hand, it must be said that the rates of wages paid do not at present leave much room for complaint.

Health and age capacity.—The trade is, in itself, a healthy one. Where the workshops are roomy, there is nothing to object to on this score. But a dry and rather hot atmosphere is required, and in small shops where the upper part of each room, to within six feet of the floor, is filled with seasoning planks, the conditions are rather stifling. The transition from heat of this kind to the chill of the outer air is very trying, especially at first. Old hands become inured, and the steady warmth while working perhaps suits the old. Men frequently work on till sixty-five or seventy.

Drink.—Pianoforte artisans have had a bad reputation for drink, but a great improvement is remarked as to this. Formerly, it was common enough for a whole shop to join in celebrating successive birthdays by drinking bouts, but this custom no longer obtains. It used to be almost impossible for any young man to hold aloof from these convivialities; now, however, moderate men as well as total abstainers are to be found in almost every shop. It is in the shops where work is most irregular that there is most drinking, and where some of the quickest and smartest workmen are to be found. These men do not want to work every week in the year. Hard work and large earnings, succeeded by idleness and hard drinking, make exactly the life that suits them, and the pinch of want is salt to their existence. The pity of it is as regards their wives and children.

Foreign Competition.—Foreign workmen are not much found in this trade, which, in that respect, differs greatly from cabinet-making. The foreigner's competition is a question of imports. "Actions," as we have said, come largely from abroad, and there is also a considerable, though decreasing, importation of finished pianos. Certain improvements—the introduction of iron frames and a more efficient check action—though invented by Englishmen, were first adopted in Germany. Our manufacturers were more slow to move and consequently lost trade, which, however, they are now recovering.

The trade this summer (1893) is very much depressed. Pianos are a luxury, and the demand for them one of the first to be affected by, and one of the last to recover from, a general contraction of expenditure. On the other hand, there is no luxury which better tests a rising standard of life, and the trade, in its broad lines of expansion, has reflected and still reflects the abounding prosperity of our times.

HARMONIUMS AND ORGANS.

The manufacture of harmoniums or American organs does not greatly differ from that of pianos as regards the condition of the workmen employed. Wages seem to follow the same lines. The work is generally done on piece, and the average earnings are about 36s. The usual hours are fifty-four to fifty-six, and there are the same busy and slack seasons.

Originally harmoniums were all made in France, but since the war of 1870, the English market has been supplied by home factories; and now that American organs have come into fashion, these too have been, to a considerable extent, produced at home, although the woods used in their manufacture all come from America. The difference between the two instruments is interesting. In the harmonium the air is driven through the wind-box, within which are the pipes or reeds. The arrangement of the American organ reverses this. The wind is not driven but sucked through the box, and the reeds are outside, and so more conveniently accessible for tuning or repairs. There is also a difference in the make of the reeds; those of the French harmonium being of cast brass, rough and thick, while those of the American organ, though also of brass, are much more slight and elastic. These instruments have a great vogue amongst our hymn-loving people, and especially in musical Lancashire.

The manufacture of street organs, which is somewhat extensively carried on in London, is entirely in the hands of Italians, masters as well as men.

Organ building, though not a large, is a very peculiar industry. It has no clearly defined busy and slack seasons, but is irregular, because of its dependence on individual orders. There is no working for stock. An organ must be specially designed, and so the trade works from hand to mouth. Each instrument is made and erected in the shop and tested, but is then taken to pieces, in order to be finally put together, and, in effect, re-made, where it is to stand—the church itself becoming the workshop. Hence the men employed are constantly travelling about. For instance, a London firm has at the present time (summer, 1893) one man in their employ at Hong Kong, and another at Dresden, and are about to send off a third to Jamaica. That a number of the men should be scattered in different parts of England is the usual state of things, and whether far or near, they are beyond the supervision of the master's eye. Steadiness of character and sobriety of demeanour and behaviour, good morals and good manners, are thus absolutely essential qualities if those who pay for the organ are to be satisfied. A man setting up an instrument in a church must not forget that there, while he works, others may have come to pray.

Each man must have a thorough knowledge of every branch of the trade, and therefore apprenticeship becomes a reality. Indeed, it is hardly possible that any boy, working at one instrument from start to finish, with the design before him, should not learn the what and why of every part. Another peculiarity of the trade, we are quaintly told, is that of slow pay.

Church effort often goes beyond the funds in hand, and the organ itself must help to fill the offertory plate. On the other hand, times of dull trade and general depression do not seem to affect the demand. Perhaps—who knows ?—they may even act as a stimulus, on the principle of " When the Devil was sick, the Devil a monk would be."

Wages.—The standard rate of wages throughout the trade may be reckoned at 8*d* an hour, or 36*s* for a week of fifty-four hours. The work is principally paid by time, except for " sound-board " makers, who work on piece and earn a little more. The best paid branch of work is that of the " voicers." Voicing is a delicate operation, requiring considerable skill and attention, and is paid at 50*s* or 60*s* a week. All shop workers, except metal-hands—*i.e.* those who do the casting of the pipes—are supposed to get their turn at outside work, taking jobs in regular order.

To men on outside duty, London firms give 21*s* a week extra, and as, in addition, a " tip " may be received if satisfaction has been given, besides the pleasure of change of air and scene, these jobs are jealously sought after, and complaints are heard if all do not have their turn. The workmen in this trade are almost a close corporation. It is described as a regular " father to son " business, and it is not easy for an outsider to get admission. Sometimes, however, the privilege is accorded to a country lad, *protégé* perhaps of the clergyman in whose church an organ has been set up, who, having been employed to help, has shown aptitude.

Provincial competition.—There is no foreign competition, but some provincial factories of recent growth are able to undercut London prices. (They do not, it is said, produce so good an instrument.) To prevent this competition affecting wages, a union has been established with provincial branches, which seems to be increasing its hold on the trade, and to take an enlightened view of its objects. A deputation from this society visited a Birkenhead firm which had brought out an improvement in organ actions, and, in response to some surprise expressed at their taking so much interest in the matter, answered that "they consider a man to be a poor workman whose interest in the trade he follows does not extend beyond the amount of pence per hour he receives for his labour."

GAMES, &c.

Billiard Tables.—The making of billiard tables is the only large industry connected with games, and some difficulty was experienced in obtaining information, for it is a trade full of secrets and jealousy. The regular working hours are said to be from 9 to 8, with 1½ hours for meals and a short Saturday, or 51½ hours in all. The most highly skilled men work by piece, and make 8d to 1s an hour. These are employed on the table itself. Turners and polishers are paid 7½d and 7d an hour by time. The making of a good table demands perfect materials, and also very fine workmanship, especially in fixing, and rubbing to a perfect level the large slabs of slate which form the table; and in building up the cushions, and clothing all with its fine raiment of green. Four men are needed—a turner, a polisher, and two skilled hands. Bagatelle boards involve much less skill.

Winter is the best season, clearly defined from equinox to equinox, but with the best firms employment is regular all the year round, for fashion does not change in these articles, and manufacturers with capital can work for stock. On the whole it is said that 75 per cent. of the men have regular work. Of the rest some perhaps do not want it. They are sure of getting on again when winter comes. At the present moment (summer, 1893) trade is very slack, but the industry on the whole is increasing in harmony with the general demand for amusement and the spread of wealth, and perhaps especially in connection with the working men's club movement.

Only a few of the workmen have gone through a regular apprenticeship; most come from cabinet-making or joinery. The work is in itself healthy, and is usually done in large workshops.

All cues and cue-tips, and most of the appliances for a billiard table, come from France, the French having a monopoly of the secret of properly balancing a cue; otherwise billiard manufacturers do not suffer from foreign competition. There is a colonial and Indian export trade.

Other Games.—Articles used in other games, such as cricket, tennis, and golf, keep a considerable number of skilled men at work in three or four factories, in addition to small workshops and home workers. This, too, is an increasing trade. The wages of skilled artisans so employed would appear to be on a par with the rest in this section, viz. 8d an hour, or 30s to 40s a week. In some cases, however, considerably more will be earned, especially in the very best cricket-bat, tennis, raquet or golf-club work, at which men will make 50s or even 60s a week. The lowest paid branch is that of cricket-ball makers, where the best men engaged do not get over 35s. This is said to be due to the competition of small masters. The wages of less skilled workers range from 20s to 30s, and among these we may place turners and polishers. A considerable number of women and girls are also employed, making from 3s a week at the start to 12s or 14s, and to 17s or 18s for forewomen. Boys, beginning at 5s, rise gradually in five years to two-thirds of man's wages. Piece-work is the rule throughout the trade.

Under the large firms who supply cricketing things, &c., there is great regularity of employment, and 90 per cent. of their employees may count on having work all the year round. There are busy and slack seasons in the departments engaged on outdoor and indoor games, but they dovetail, and men are moved from department to department, or else continue their work, "stocking" for the next busy season. The demand, when it comes, sets in with such a rush that nothing but an adequate stock will meet it. It is here, as elsewhere, the men working for small masters who have to reckon with the possibility of being unemployed for part of the year. Hours are regular in the larger houses—about fifty-six a week. Overtime is not common, and only at exceptionally busy times is any work given out.

In this, as in other skilled trades where labour has been a good deal sub-divided, we meet with the complaint of the difficulty of finding "all round" men on the one hand, and of learning to become all round men on the other. Boys would rather earn than learn, and whether a boy be bound apprentice or not, the master finds that he receives nothing to repay the trouble and expense of teaching. For education, therefore, we perforce turn to small masters, or to the interest that a son will take in his father's work, and the pride his father will take in teaching him.

The manufacture of *fishing-rods and tackle* is not a large London industry. There are a few first-class makers for fly-rods, but even in this branch the names of some provincial makers will occur to fishermen as being in no way inferior to those of London. For cheaper rods and tackle the principal centre of manufacture is Redditch in Worcestershire. A skilled artisan in this branch will earn wages much on a par with the rest of the men in this section, *i.e.* from 30s to 40s. The information received in regard to this branch of industry is, however, only of the scantiest description.

Toys and Small Fancy Goods.

Not much toy making is done in London compared to the importations from Germany, Austria and France. There is here no large toy factory, though there may be two or three employing thirty or forty workers, and the bulk of what is produced is done by small masters working at home with their families, and a few boys or girls. Some articles are made always, and are always the same, such as shell-boxes, common wooden horses, and penny whistles; other things sell solely as novelties. Such are the penny toys hawked about the streets, especially in the City. The maker of these things is probably the inventor also. His lot is not a happy one. He is perpetually racking his brains for some new contrivance. For him Sunday brings no rest, but he must for ever struggle to evolve some novel and fearful implement to delight the young. The happiest idea, the most successful venture, does not run for long, and he must be always ready with something new to follow on. If he hits on something which catches the public fancy, there is indeed some profit while it lasts, but against this has to be set the failures. A few girls and one or two men are all his staff, but after he has paid the former their 6s or 7s, and the latter perhaps 20s each per week, together with the rent of his little workshop and the cost of his moulds and materials, there is in all probability "only just a living in it." Those who tramp the streets to sell the articles must also live, and the maker has to allow them a heavy discount.

TOBACCO PIPES.

In this [section, for lack of a better place, have been included the makers of tobacco pipes. One large firm in London practically monopolizes the business in briar pipes,* but does not manufacture them, only doing the mounting and fitting, for the bowls are all imported. Part of this work is given out to small masters. The men who do mounting earn 8d an hour or about 38s a week. Polishers earn 6d an hour or 25s to 27s a week; and even in so simple an affair there are several other sub-divisions in

* They are made not of "briar," but of the "bruyère" or white Mediterranean heather root.

the work.   The regular hours are 8.30 to 8, with one and
a half hours for meals.   The busiest season is from September
to January, followed by a slight slackness, but not enough
to interfere with practical regularity of employment.
There is no trades union.

The making of white clay pipes is still in London a home
industry.   A man, aided by his wife and perhaps a daughter,
will make the pipes, and himself find a market for them
amongst the publicans; fashion, however, has turned against
the old and hospitable "churchwarden"; while the short
clay is looked down on as rather "low," and almost every
smoker, whether of high or low degree, now carries in his
pocket a " briar " pipe.

TRADES UNIONS.

The extent to which the men are organized is indicated
by the subjoined table:—

Numbers in the London Trade (Census 1891).		Name of Trade Society.	Membership in London.		Remarks.
Total.	Of whom are employed males over 20.		In each Society.	In each Division.	
		Organ Builder's United Trade Society.	100		Out of work, Strike, and Sick Benefits. Insurance of tools up to £5. Has Branches in Liverpool, Manchester and other large towns.
7393	4741	Brass Musical Instruments' Trade Society (1894).	60	360	—
		Piano, Harmonium, andAmerican Organ-makers.	200		—
2325	824	(*Games, &c.*)			
689	320	(*Tobacco Pipes.*)			
10,407	5885			360	

Thus only 360 persons are organized out of a total of

5885 persons over 20 years of age who are employed, or about 6 per cent.

In the pianoforte industry there are no very powerful societies; but among organ builders, the "United Trade Society" is a growing one, and has branches in many parts of England.

The Brass Instruments' Society is composed chiefly of French and German workmen resident in London.

The cricket-bat makers have a club, but otherwise there is no separate society for those connected with the manufacture of the different appliances for games. Some of the turners, however, have joined themselves to the "Amalgamated Cabinet-makers' Alliance."

Tobacco-pipe makers used to have a union of their own, but it failed towards the end of 1893.

Wages Statistics.

In this section 5885 adult males are employed, and as to these we have wages returns for 308, in the service of twelve firms, as under :—

Pianoforte-makers	3	=12 firms employing usually
Organs and harmonium-makers	3	426 persons, of whom 332 are
Billiard-table makers	2	adult males, but of these 24
Games and Toy-makers	2	belong to other sections, as
Tobacco-pipe makers	2	porters, vanmen, &c.

The wages earned in an ordinary week are as follows :—

Below 20s	32,	or 10 per cent.	}	Below 30s, 30 per cent.
20s to 25s	22	„ 7 „		
25s to 30s	40	„ 13 „		
30s to 35s	53	„ 18 „	}	30s and over, 70s per cent.
35s to 40s	50	„ 16 „		
40s to 45s	54	„ 18 „		
45s and upwards	57	„ 18 „		
	308	„ 100 „		

Our returns may be compared with those made to the Board of Trade in 1886 from nine firms, employing 192 adult men, as follows :—

	—20s.	20s—	25s—	30s—	35s—	40s—	45s—
Our returns	10 °/$_c$	7 °/$_o$	13 °/$_o$	18 °/$_o$	16 °/$_o$	18 °/$_o$	18 °/$_o$
Board of Trade returns		30 °/$_o$			70 °/$_o$		
		6½ °/	21 °/$_o$	18 °/$_o$	26 °/$_o$	20 °/$_o$	8½ °/$_o$
		27½ °/$_o$			72½ °/$_o$		

Allowing for the difference between our method and that employed by the Board of Trade these returns confirm each other very closely.

As to regularity of employment it is difficult to speak of the section as a whole because it consists of so many small yet distinct trades. In pianoforte making, which probably employs the largest number of men, detailed returns from two factories show a difference between busy and slack weeks of 8 per cent. in the numbers employed and of 12 per cent. in the earnings. The busy season is in winter, and July and August the time of slackness.

Of lads and boys we have not many returned, but of those given nearly a fourth earn 5s or less, half get from 6s to 10s, and more than a fourth above this. 10s is the amount most commonly paid. The Board of Trade returns of 1886 corroborate this.

The women and girls, of whom there are about 1100 in the trade, earn from 5s to 20s, about half receiving from 8s to 12s.

Social Condition.

Of a total of 5885 adult males employed in these trades, about 4030 come under social classification as heads of families. According to our wages returns 17 per cent. of those employed earn less than 25s a week, and this figure is to be compared with 37 per cent. who live under crowded conditions. We next have 31 per cent. earning from 25s

to 35s compared to 30 per cent. of the next social grade,
and finally 52 per cent. earning over 35s, compared to 33
per cent. of the central classes, as follows:—

Comparison of Earnings with Style of Life
(Musical Instruments, &c.).

Earnings as returned.			Classification of Population.		
Below 20s...32, or 10 per cent.			3 or more in each room, 3100, or 14 per cent.		
20s to 25s...22 ,, 7 ,,			2 to 3 ,, 5100 ,, 23 ,,		
25s ,, 30s...40 ,, 13 ,,			1 ,, 2 ,, 6500 ,, 30 ,,		
30s ,, 35s—53 ,, 18 ,,			Less than 1 ,, ⎫		
35s ,, 40s...50 ,, 16 ,,			More than 4 rooms ⎪		
40s ,, 45s...54 ,, 18 ,,			4 or more persons ⎬ 7200 ,, 33 ,,		
45s and ⎱ 57 ,, 18 ,, upwards ⎰			to a servant ... ⎭		
303 ,, 100 ,,			21,900 ,,100 ,,		
			Employers' families and servants ... 3200		
			25,100		

The considerable discrepancy between the percentage
figures for wages and those for social condition is not
difficult to account for.

The wages returns in this section were supplied to us by
a few of the best firms, and are probably therefore a good
deal above the average, so that the low percentage of those
earning under 30s, and the high percentage of those above
40s, cannot be taken as a general standard for the whole
section. Besides this, account must be taken of a considerable number of persons working in small toy industries, &c.,
in East London, for whom we have absolutely no wages
returns. Could we have obtained particulars of the earnings
of a proportionate number of these, as well as of those
employed in third-class piano factories, and have added
them to our present table, they would doubtless have greatly
altered the respective percentages of wages given, and have
brought them more into line with those of the classification.

The men engaged in pianoforte and organ building, who form the greater number of persons belonging to this section, live for the most part near the factories which lie, generally speaking, in the northern districts of London.

Meals are eaten at home, if the men live near enough to the works, otherwise on the premises, or at some neighbouring cook-shop or coffee-house. There does not appear to be any regular habit throughout the trade in favour of one as against another method.

The working dress consists of a large apron, and men frequently change their coats and trousers, and especially boots, before starting work. Old boots are more comfortable for use while standing about at work, and the trouble of changing is worth taking in wet weather.

A large proportion of the men, if they do not belong to a trade union, are at any rate members of a friendly society. This is probably more frequently the case amongst the workpeople of the large firms who give regular employment, from whom our returns come, than amongst those of the small East End masters, of whom it has already been noticed, that it is most difficult to obtain any information.

Shop sick and provident clubs are also common in the better firms. From 4d to 1s a week would appear to be the average rate of contribution made for the purpose of insuring against sickness, &c. It seems to be rare for wives in this section to add to their husbands income by undertaking any special work on their own account.

PART II.—SUNDRY MANUFACTURES.

SUNDRY MANUFACTURES.

PRELIMINARY STATEMENT.

THE sections which are here treated together (viz. Glass, Chemicals, Soap, Leather, Saddlery, and Brushes), have not much in common. They are, however, especially representative of manufacture in London. They do not any of them involve a large population, yet each is made up of several distinct trades. Nothing in London is more noticeable than the variety of its industries, unless it be the multiplicity of small establishments by which these industries are carried on. The whole number of the occupied divided as to age and sex is as follows :—

Persons represented : (A) Census Enumeration.

	ENUMERATED BY AGE AND SEX.						
	10—	15—	20—	25—	55—	65—	Total.
Males	852	4283	3928	16,678	2116	980	28,837
Females	367	2655	1912	3778	396	214	9,322
Total	1219	6938	5840	20,456	2512	1194	38,159

We have here a large proportion of women and young people. Of those employed, less than half are heads of families, in place of two-thirds or three-fourths, as in the trades previously dealt with. The total population included in these families is 87,652, made up as follows :—

Persons represented : (B) Enumeration by Families.

SUNDRY MANUFACTURES, 1891.

No.	Sections.	Heads.	Total number (excluding Servants).	Per family (excluding Servants).	Servants.
22	Glass and Earthenware	2498	11,486	4·60	179
23	Chemicals, &c.	2285	10,322	4·51	570
24	Soap, Candles and Glue	1056	4,739	4·49	207
25	Leather and Leather Goods..................	8076	37,494	4·64	862
26	Saddlery and Harness	2342	10,450	4·46	128
27	Brushes, Combs, &c. ...	2470	11,085	4·49	130
	Total	18,727	85,576	4·57	2076
	Servants		2,076		
	Total population		87,652		

Of the 18,700 heads of families, nearly 1400 are women, fur pulling (included with leather work) and brush making being the occupations of most of them.

The 2076 servants attend 6752 persons, the remaining 78,824 being without any resident domestic assistance. Of the servant-keeping class, 3700 have only one servant to four or more persons served, 2000 have one servant to less than four in family and two servants to four or more persons, and 1000 live in other families which keep two servants or more.

Turning to the 79,000 (roughly) who have no servant, we find that nearly 25,000 of them live in families which occupy more than four rooms, or have, on the average, more than one room to each person ; 22,000 live with one and under two persons per room, and 21,000 with two to three persons to a room ; over 7000 live three to four to a room, and 4000 individuals form households in which there are four or more persons to each room.

	4 or more persons to 1 room	...	3,025 or 4·4 % } 12·6 %
	3 and under 4 " "	...	7,175 " 8·2 % }
Lower Classes.	2 and under 3 " "	...	20,763 " 23·7 %
	1 and under 2 " "	...	22,068 " 25·1 %
Central Classes.	Less than 1 person to a room	...	2,680 " 3·1 % } 32·6 %
	More than 4 rooms	...	22,213 " 25·3 % }
	4 or more persons to 1 servant	...	3,058 " 4·2 % }
Upper Classes.	Less than 4 persons to 1 servant, and 4 or more to 2 servants	...	2,068 " 2·4 %
	All others with 2 or more servants ...	...	1,020 " 1·2 %
	Servants	...	2,076 " 2·4 %
			87,652 100 %

Crowded 36·3 %

Not Crowded 63·7 %

Social condition (by Sections).

Section.	3, 4, or more persons to a room.	2 and under 3 persons to a room.	1 and under 2 persons to a room.	Less than 1 to a room. More than 4 rooms, or 4 or more persons to 1 servant.	Less than 4 persons to a servant.	Servants.	Total.
Glass and Earthenware	1811	3225	2964	3236	250	179	11,665
Per cent......	15½	27½	25½	28	2	1½	100
Chemicals, &c....	1116	2074	2589	3672	871	570	10,892
Per cent......	10	19	24	34	8	5	100
Soap, Candles,&c.	435	980	1179	1833	312	207	4946
Per cent......	9	20	24	37	6	4	100
Leather	4909	9184	9697	12,419	1285	862	38,356
Per cent......	13	24	25	32½	3½	2	100
Saddlery	1182	2432	2802	3855	179	128	10,578
Per cent......	11	23	26½	36½	2	1	100
Brushes & Combs	1647	2868	2837	3536	197	130	11,215
Per cent......	15	25½	25	31½	2	1	100

CHANGES SINCE 1861 IN NUMBERS EMPLOYED.

	1861.	1871.	1881.	1891.
Earthenware and Glass	3,000	4,000	4,200	5,000
Chemicals......................	2,400	2,900	4,400	5,800
Soap, Candles, Glue, &c.......	3,000	2,500	1,700	2,200
Leather	8,600	9,500	14,200	15,700
Saddlery	3,500	3,900	3,700	3,900
Brushes and Combs............	5,600	5,700	6,400	5,500
Total	26,100	28,500	34,000	38,100

It will be seen that the numbers employed increased on the whole from 26,000 in 1861 to 38,000 in 1891, but the several changes have been irregular. Whilst earthenware, chemicals, and leather show a large and constant increase from one decade to another, saddlery has remained almost stationary, and brush-making has lost in the last ten years all that it had gained in the previous twenty. In the soap and candle trade, there was a steady falling off between 1861 and 1881, but a noticeable revival in the last decade.

Nos. (For explanation of method adopted in preparing this chart, see Note on Diagram 18.)

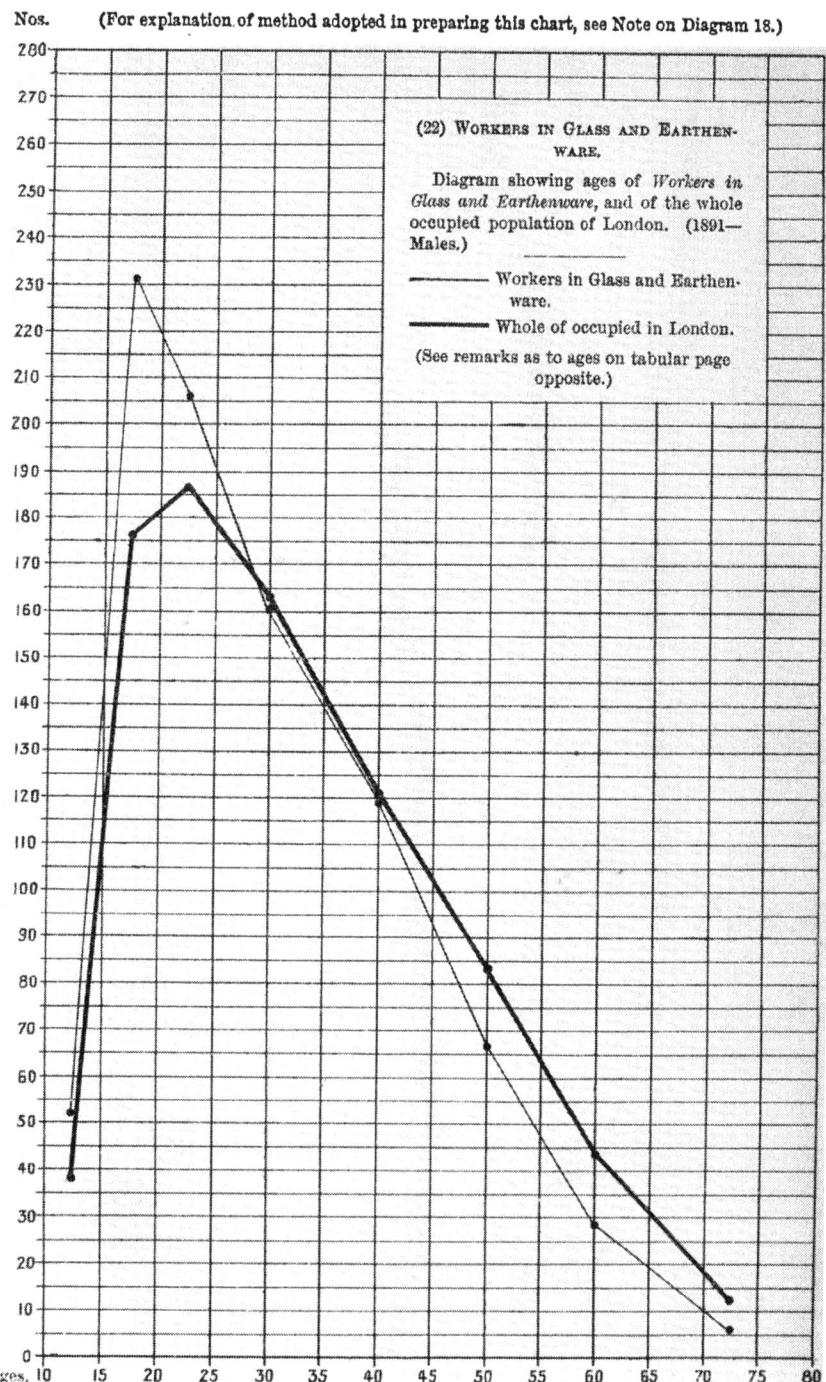

(22) WORKERS IN GLASS AND EARTHEN-
WARE.

Diagram showing ages of *Workers in Glass and Earthenware*, and of the whole occupied population of London. (1891—Males.)

——————— Workers in Glass and Earthenware.

————— Whole of occupied in London.

(See remarks as to ages on tabular page opposite.)

CHAPTER I.

GLASS AND EARTHENWARE. *(Section 22.)*

Persons Represented.

<table>
<tr><th colspan="6">Census Enumeration.</th><th colspan="4">Enumerated by Families.</th></tr>
</table>

Divisions, 91.	Fe-males. All Ages.	\-19	Males. 20—54	55—	Total.
....	175	625	2193	178	3171
...enware	341	377	985	97	1800
...TAL......	516	1002	3178	275	4971

Enumerated by Families.

Sex ...... { Males .... 2444 } Females............. 54 }

Birthplace { In London .... 71 % 1768 } Heads of Families, { Out of London 29 % 730 } 2498

Industrial { Employer ...... 9 % 231 } Status.... { Employed...... 83 % 2076 } { Neither .... 8 % 191 }

TOTAL POPULATION CONCERNED.

	Heads of Families.	Others Occupied.	Unoccupied.	Servants.	Total.
Total	2498	2146	6842	179	11,665
Average in family..	1	·86	2·74	·07	4·67

trades employ a large proportion of ...t show a marked deficiency of men ...onwards, and especially from 50 to 60. ...30 and 40 the line (*see* diagram) ...almost exactly that for the whole ...population of London.

DISTRIBUTION.

N.	W.& C.	S.	Total.
1180	808	2175	4971

DETAILS OF OCCUPATIONS
[FR]OM THE CENSUS DICTIONARY).

...engraver, &c. Stained-glass painter. ...saicist, sanitary pipe, chimney pot, ...e-bottle maker.
...-cotta maker. Enamel maker, cru- ...e maker. Art-ware designer, ...deller, finisher, aquarium maker,

CLASSIFICATION.

Numbers living in Families.		%
3 or more to a room	1811	15·5
2 & under 3 ,,	3225	27·6
1 & under 2 ,,	2964	25·5
Less than 1 ,,		
More than 4 rooms	3236	27·8
4 or more persons to a servant ..		
Less than 4 to 1 servant, and 4 or more to 2 servts.	176	1·5
All others with 2 or more servants ..	74	·6
Servants	179	1·5
	11,665	100

	Inner.	Outer.	Together.
Crowded..	57 %	28 %	47 %
Not ,, ..	43 %	72 %	53 %

DISTRIBUTION.

East	{ Inner	1405 }	1632
	{ Outer	227 }	
North	{ Inner	486 }	2712
	{ Outer	2226 }	
West	{ Inner	88 }	710
	{ Outer	622 }	
Central	Inner	1084	1084
South-	{ Inner	166 }	1098
East	{ Outer	932 }	
South-	{ Inner	2857 }	4429
West	{ Outer	1572 }	
			11,665

Inner 6086, or 52 %
Outer 5579, or 48 %

Status as to Employment (according to Census Enumeration).

Census Divisions (1891).	Employers.		Employed.			Neither Employer nor Employed.		Total.
	Males.	Females	Males. Under 20.	Over 20.	Females of all ages.	Males.	Females	
...s manufacture	216	11	625	1993	153	162	11	3171
...henware, china, &c.	39	—	377	980	329	63	12	1800
	255	11	1002	2973	482	225	23	4971
TOTAL..........	266		4457			248		

Proportion of Employers to Employed–1 to 17

Glass.

Glass manufacture and the inter-connected trades cannot be considered as London industries of the first importance, yet the variety of features they present and the artistic merit of some of the work produced give them an interest greater than may attach to industries in which far more persons find employment.

Of the actual manufacture of glass from the raw material there is but little in London. Old broken glass is mainly used. No plate glass at all is made here. The bulk of London glass-blowing is confined to " small works "—that is, cheap bottles and vials of small size for medicine, essences, or scent. About half a dozen large firms are engaged in this class of work, employing twenty to thirty glass-blowers each, and there are a great number of small shops employing six to ten blowers. Beyond these there are some furnaces at which larger bottles and jars are made, also from refuse glass. Though not a distinct branch of the trade, the blowers of this class hold themselves aloof from the small works blowers and the small works men from them. A man who is a good hand at one sort of blowing seldom can do well at the other, and while small works men are generally London born and bred, the others are mostly north countrymen from Lancashire and Yorkshire. They belong to different trade societies.

The few firms which rise above this common work manufacture their glass from the raw material, and aim at the production of artistic and highly finished ware, for which a large trade has sprung up in the last few years. The demand seems in fact at present to have outstripped the supply. The blowers engaged on this kind of work are called " table-men," and are highly skilled artisans, who usually receive their training on the premises. It is, in fact, most difficult to obtain in any other way men sufficiently skilled to undertake this work ; and while the factories which make common small bottles are overrun by second-rate workmen, turned out wholesale from non-union shops, where the number of boys is not restricted, there is something of a stoppage in the higher branch of the trade for want of really first-class blowers.

A glass furnace at night is one of the most picturesque and weird sights imaginable. As you approach through a dark passage the furnace apertures are seen in the distance glowing like cat's eyes. On reaching the end an extraordinary scene bursts into view. In front of the furnace half a dozen or more dark figures hurry to and fro, now digging long tubes into the red molten glass, which itself provides all the light required ; now drawing them back with a fiery mass at the end, to be first rolled into shape and then waved backwards and forwards in the air, taking a duller and yet duller tint of red as it expands and cools at the end of the blower's tube.

When the glass has been slightly blown it is placed in a mould and blown out further, so as to fit the mould exactly, and then it is allowed to harden. After being extracted from the mould it is knocked off the tube, which then makes another visit to the furnace, while the half-made bottle is taken hold of by the "maker" or "finisher," who picks it up with a four-pronged fork and re-heats the neck in the furnace. The maker is the most skilled workman. He sits generally a few feet from the furnace, and taking the re-heated bottle out of the furnace rolls it rapidly to and fro with his left hand, while with his right he forms the neck, clasping it in an iron mould which, being furnished with a spring, gives under pressure of his hand the required shape.

When finished by the maker the bottles are carried two at a time by a boy, and placed in a " cooling oven," through which they are gradually passed.

The maker or "gaffer," two blowers or " servitors," and a boy, work together, and are termed a " chair." The wages. are paid upon a complicated system, nominally by time, but actually by piece. In " small works" factories, which abide by the union rules, the combined wages of the three men are fixed at 16s per nominal day. The boy is paid separately and generally by the week. Of the 16s, the maker gets 6s, and the blowers 5s each. The making of a certain number of each, kind of bottle constitutes a day's work, and so moderate was the original estimate, or so greatly has the power of production increased, that two days' work, or sometimes even more, may be done in a shift of ten hours. This means 10s and 12s a day (or night) when times are busy. But to make fourteen days in any one week would be rare, and eight nominal days a week are considered a fair average, resulting in 40s to 45s a week wages.

The number of bottles of every sort and size, which shall be counted " a day's work," has been fixed by the union and agreed to between masters and men. These prices only apply to union shops, but the non-union firms, of which there are a considerable number, do not, as a rule, pay lower wages to the men they employ. They economise by largely employing boys and youths, who earn 8s to 20s a week. Production under these conditions is limited to the smallest and most easily manufactured goods.

The work goes on day and night, for the furnace does not sleep. In most of the small glass-bottle factories 7 A.M. and 7 P.M. divide night and day, and in each ten hours are worked, and two set aside for meals, except that Saturday is shortened to six hours. The night hours are from 7 to 11, and 12 to 4, and 5 to 7. The two shifts take night and day service week and week about. Other factories, and those the best, work on a different system, viz. alternate shifts, working six hours off and six hours on, for four days, *i.e.* from 7 A.M. on Monday to 7 A.M. on

Friday; with no work during the rest of the week. This makes forty-eight hours in all. During the three off-days the furnaces are replenished, and prepared for the next week's work.

In the six-hour shift factories it is the custom to pay by nominal hours in place of days, and there are three men and a boy to the "chair." For a first-class chair the gaffer gets $7\frac{1}{2}d$, the two servitors $6d$, and, besides the boy, there is a man called the "foot-maker," who receives $5\frac{1}{2}d$. A chair of the second grade will earn $1d$ or $2d$ less per nominal hour. As with the other factories, the production of a certain number of pieces, varying with the article made, is agreed upon as "an hour's work," and the actual earnings will be about double the nominal rate; or $50s$ to $60s$ for the gaffers, and $40s$ to $45s$ for blowers, as payment for forty-eight hours' work. The foot-maker, who is not found at all in ordinary small works factories, comes rather lower in the scale.

The Trade Societies are strong, and have strict rules as to apprenticeship; and, whether as a consequence or not, there are but few apprentices in the union shops. The members of the union and the trade at large are mainly recruited from boys and youths brought up in non-union establishments, where the proportion of boys to men is in the inverse ratio to that established by the union. This is not the only instance to be met with of the sweating shop figuring as the sole school of industry.

Boys, whether apprenticed or not, make themselves generally useful, and pick up what they can, being occasionally permitted to make an attempt at blowing during off-hours. As they grow older, and have some experience, they may be allowed to fill the place of some absentee, under a special arrangement with the other men working in the chair as to division of wages.

The glass-blowing trade has steadily increased in London

during the last twenty years, but there is keen foreign competition in "small works" which makes it difficult to maintain wages at their present rate. This summer (1893) the trade in small medicine bottles has been rather slack, and the year of the influenza epidemic was spoken of by one master with fond regret as a red-letter time.

The business of those houses which produce the higher class of goods, shows no sign of falling off; on the contrary, as already intimated, more orders come in than there are skilled men to execute.

Stained-glass.—The best English work in making stained windows is done in London. In the past twenty or twenty-five years a great advance has been made in the art, the fruit of much studious inquiry into the old thirteenth, fourteenth, fifteenth, and sixteenth century methods. Interest in the subject seems to have been revived some fifty years ago, and more recently one or two of our best artists have interested themselves in the subject, and have manifestly influenced the development of the craft. The undoubted improvements effected have been the result of outside influence rather than of any growth of artistic feeling among the artisans themselves, and the English glass-painter rarely rises above the position of a mechanical copyist, in spite of the advantages which the character of his work and its surroundings afford.

Considerable skill is required and displayed by both painters and draughtsmen, but they all work under very constant supervision by the heads or managers of the firm. An Italian or French workman might perhaps develop an artistic sense of his own, but this, apparently, an Englishman can rarely do.

The process is as follows:—First, a coloured design is drawn by the artist. This design is then enlarged to full size by a draughtsman, assisted, may be, by the artist, and the lead lines are traced. These lines, called the "cut lines," are then traced on to transparent calico, and on this basis the glass-cutter works. Each section is next numbered with a figure representing its particular colour (*i.e.* the colour basis), and the glass is cut to match and placed in position. The whole is then covered with a brown tint of vitrifying paint and placed in separate portions on easels, so that the light shines through and brings into relief any outlines drawn to assist the glass-painter, who now takes the work in hand, and leaving shadows in the brown tint, clears the lights by the use of a stiff brush. This done, the bits of glass are separated and burned in a kiln, so that the shadow tint becomes fused in the body of the glass. It then only remains to fit the sections together with lead and cement, and the window is complete.

The art is thus rather the combination and shading of bits of coloured glass than anything that can strictly be called painting. Excepting the enamel colours, sometimes used in heraldry, and in windows such as those of the Munich school, there is but one colour actually applied by a painter to the surface of glass, and that is the bright yellow so largely used on white glass. This colour is composed of nitrate of silver. The nitrate is mixed with yellow lake, to make the pigment spread smoothly, and to enable the painter to see what he is doing. It is then burnt into the glass; the greater the heat used the more intense the colour.

Coloured glass must not be free of flaw, nor should it be, on any account, of an even tint. Such imperfections, as they might be deemed, are essential to that beauty of effect which justifies the expression " painted window." More-over, this mysterious beauty, which is born of imperfection, " cometh not by observation." The best and safest plan to follow in forming a mass of colour, is to mix together all the minor shades of the tint required and join the various bits haphazard as they come to hand. If any effort or calculation is applied to their arrangement the orderly human mind inevitably shows itself in some regular alternation of light and dark—some tiresome sequence of effect, or some uncomfortable pattern.

Most coloured glass is tinted throughout, but ruby red* and a dark sapphire blue are in themselves so deep in colour as to appear almost black, and for this reason, and also because of their costliness, are run while in a molten state over a sheet of plain glass in a film— thinner or thicker, according to the depth of colour required.

Coming now to the men employed. Draughtsmen, belonging usually to a well-to-do class, and paying sometimes a high premium for learning the art, receive from £2. 2s to £8. 8s for forty-four to forty-eight hours a week. Painters, who are the majority of those employed, consist of ornamental and figure hands, the former being less skilled and receiving the lower wages. The rate varies from 35s to 60s per week for forty-eight, or it may be fifty-four hours, or from about 9d to 1s 3d or 1s 4d per hour. In this class, apprentices sometimes pay as much as £20 premium.

Glaziers, who cut and fit the glass, &c., earn from 40s to 50s for about fifty-four hours. This is almost entirely highly-skilled work.

Men cannot shift into any other trade if work is slack, and rarely move from one branch to another. But their employment is extremely regular.

In addition to the finer work for church or other stained-glass windows, there is an increasing amount of leaded lighting for ordinary building purposes. This may be done by the same men or by less skilled operators.

The making of vitreous mosaic is a new industry connected with glass. It has only recently sprung up, and we are without any information regarding it.

---

* Made with chloride of gold, copper, or iron.

Glass engraving is another industry falling into this section. It is said there are not above fifty skilled engravers in London now. Owing to the introduction of the cheaper method of producing patterns on glass by sand-blasting, the demand for the better, but far more expensive work engraved at the wheel has declined, and is at present very limited.

The trade, such as it is, is generally passed down from father to son, and few outsiders enter it. Most of the glass engravers work at home for some dealer. A good workman, unless he is working for a special order, when a design is supplied, draws on the glass with his wheel as an artist does on paper with his pencil. The hours worked are very irregular.

Glass bevelling, which would seem to belong here, is accounted a part of cabinet-making, and has been already described in Volume V., under Cabinet-making.

POTTERY.

Pottery in London practically means stone-ware—the making of drain-pipes, chimney-pots, crucibles, chemical jars, or beer, ginger beer and ink bottles. The same factories make also terra-cotta mouldings and ornaments. The only other branch is red-pottery—the making of red chimney-pots, flower-pots and porous pipes—which is carried on in the immediate neighbourhood of London rather than in London itself. No china is made here.

Stone-ware is made of West Country clay, brought to London in hard square blocks. The clay is ground to a fine powder, mixed with water and "rough stuff" compound, and kneaded, and is then ready for the hand of the potter, who, if bottles or jars are to be made, is called a "thrower," and sits before his wheel, on which a lump of the plastic stuff is placed and fashioned as it spins. Any finer touches that may be required are given by "finishers," who smooth the surface and apply any little decorations of line or beading. A finisher's tools are of the simplest; an old tooth-brush handle had served one of them for a number of years. Names or letters are then impressed, and the bottles, having been hardened by drying in the air, are dipped in liquid glaze before being "burned."

The stacking in the kilns is done by men called kiln-setters, and so arranged that the fire passes right through and over, bathing the bottles and jars with flame for a period varying from 65 to 130 hours, according to the class of goods and the intensity of heat used. The principal burners who preside over the firing are among the most important workmen in the factory. Upon their judgment depends the success of each burning, and considerable experience is needed. If the burning goes wrong, goods to the value of £40 or £50, and even £200, may easily be spoilt.*

Plain straight pipes are made by machinery to certain given sizes, and can be turned out in vast quantities without much trouble or skill of handicraft. But if the clay is to be fashioned into pipes of irregular shape, it goes into the hands of the "moulder," who beats and rolls it out flat to the proper thickness, and lays it in, or on, a plaster mould, divided into half sections, so that when the clay is hard, the plaster having absorbed its moisture, the mould can be withdrawn.

Terra-cotta work is made out of Devonshire and Dorset clay, in the mixing of which some skill is needed to produce

---

* In one instance, owing to overfiring, it took a week's hard work, with pickaxe and crowbar, to clear the kiln of the vitreous stoneware, which had all fused together and become solidified.

the right colour. The clay is moulded much as pipes are, but the men employed form a separate branch from the ordinary moulders.

The wages of skilled potters in the two principal branches —throwers and moulders—are estimated as averaging 8*d* or 9*d* an hour, but payment is by piece, and, while some men can make 1*s*, others will not earn more than 7*d* an hour. Average weekly wages, taking busy times with slack, may be put down as 35*s*. A really first-rate thrower, working on large chemical jars, will make as much as £3 a week, but these cases are comparatively few.

The above wages are quoted net. The gross amount earned is greater, but from the throwers there is usually a deduction of about 4*s* 6*d* per week for steam-power. They used formerly to pay boys to turn the wheel, and the boys still assist them, and also the moulders, by preparing the clay and handing them a lump as required. These boys receive 7*s* or 8*s* a week, and are hired and paid by the men.

Terra-cotta moulders are paid by the cubic foot at 6*d* to 10*d* a foot, and when trade is brisk can make good wages, but the work falls very slack in winter. One worker stated his highest week's takings in summer as £2. 19*s* 11*d*, and his lowest in winter as 7*s*, and placed his average at 35*s*.

The head burners get £2 to £3 a week, and have the certainty of regular employment the year round. Their hours are, however, necessarily irregular and often long.

The standard hours in the trade are from fifty-six to sixty a week, but it appears that in many instances skilled piece-workmen are not over regular in their attendance, and stay away from work a day, or even longer, during the week.

The majority of men and boys employed at potteries rank with unskilled labour. To every skilled man there

are usually three to four unskilled men and boys. Besides
the yard labourers, clay-mixers, grinders, &c., who receive
from 20s to 30s, or an average of 23s or 24s for a week of
fifty-nine or sixty hours, being paid mostly by the week,
there are also the kiln-setters, who, like glass-blowers, are
remunerated nominally by time but really by piece, on a
system curious and worthy of notice:

Before the great expansion of the stone-ware trade in
London, kiln-setters were paid at the ordinary rate for
unskilled labour, which was then 4d an hour. When
employers began to extend their business, it became
essential to economise time and space by setting and clearing the existing kilns more quickly. The time usually
occupied over the work was therefore noted, and the
labourers told that they would receive the money to which
those hours entitled them, no matter what time they
took over setting and clearing the kiln. The result has
been that kilns are cleared and reset in half or less than
half the time formerly taken, and in place of 4d the men
earn 9d, or even sometimes 10d an hour, and are registered
in the wages books as having worked one hundred or
one hundred and ten hours in the week, when possibly they
have not actually worked more than fifty. When a new
kiln is erected the amount to be paid for setting and
clearing it is fixed on the basis of the old time-work
system.

The hours worked by the setters are irregular. It is
impossible to tell exactly at what hour a kiln will be cool
enough for clearing, and the men—they work in gangs of
five or six—have often to wait about for an hour or two
before they can start work. For this it is only fair they
should be paid. The work, while they are at it, is decidedly
strenuous—carrying heavy weights down a flight of steps,
perhaps from the potters' shop to the kiln below,—and
it is hot, dusty and stifling when kilns, which are barely
cooled, have to be cleared. The average weekly wages

the year through will be 30*s* to 35*s*, placing them far above
the level of ordinary unskilled labourers.

The irregularity of hours, the periods of idleness, and the
stress and character of the work, as well as the high level
of pay, are enough to account for the bad reputation these
men have for intemperance. They cannot continue at it
later than up to forty-five, or in rare cases, fifty years of age,
and are apt to fall into the ranks of the very irregularly
employed casual labourers and loafers. It is rare that they
save—more commonly they are ready to pay a penny in the
shilling per week to forestall their wages, borrowing from
some petty money-lender of their own rank, till their wages
are mortgaged a week or two in advance, and then every
shilling they receive pays its toll. Betting, even more than
drink, is now the ruling extravagance. As regards intemperance, it is said there is some improvement, but this is more
especially noticeable among the skilled potters.

There is a trades union with two branches—the throwers
and the moulders. They came out together on a question
of boy labour some two years ago. The strike, which lasted
fifteen weeks and was not successful, has left some bitter-
ness between the two branches. Few apprentices are taken
on at the present time, and boys pick up the work how and
when they can by watching the men whom they help.
Where apprentices are taken the term is either seven years
from fourteen, or five years from fifteen or sixteen, and the
latter plan is preferred. Boys are increasingly employed,
especially on small ink-bottles, and where machinery is
used.

The stone-ware trade is healthy, little being heard in
London of the "Potter's rot," and the men continue to
work till fifty-five and sixty, or even later. The glaze used
is harmless. Stone-ware requires a far more intense heat
in the burning than other china or pottery, in order to
produce that fusion of substance or semi-vitrification, which
renders it alike non-porous and almost incorrodible by

acids, and in consequence, whitening, salt, and other non-poisonous materials can be used in place of lead to make the glaze.

There is no foreign competition in the home market (except in electrical ware), but the maintenance of the business on its present scale depends upon export, and on this our hold is necessarily precarious. England has led the way in sanitary engineering, and so in the supply of the material required, for which we have very suitable clay; but it is not to be supposed that England has any monopoly of such clays, and in the United States beds of equal excellence have already been found.

Red pottery, which, as has been said, is a small industry on the confines of London chiefly to the north, is perfectly distinct from the making of stone-ware, and men shift rarely from one branch to the other. To the unpractised eye, however, there does not seem to be much difference between "throwing" a flower-pot or a ginger-beer bottle. Work is paid by the piece, or rather by the "cast"—which is a given number of pots varying according to the size—the price paid ranging from 4d to 5d, and the number of pots from sixty to thirty-two. Standard wages are 32s a week, with average earnings, it may be, of 27s through the year. Lads can earn about 15s at small works. Kiln setters are not paid by the piece, but by the week, and make 24s or 25s. The usual hours are fifty-six. There is said to be keen competition in the trade between large and small makers, to the advantage of the former, who can employ steam power. The clay used is the common London clay, and no great skill is required in mixing. The burning is also easier, requiring much less heat than stone-ware.

TRADES UNIONS.

The extent to which the men in these trades are organized is shown by the following table:—

Numbers in the London Trade (Census 1891).		Name of Trade Society.	Membership in London.		Remarks.
Total.	Of whom are employed males over 20.		In each Society.	In each Division.	
3171	1993	London Glass Blowers' Trade Society.	300	532	Out of work benefit. Pension for disability after ten years. "Oppression money." Price list enforced.
		National Flint Glass Makers' Society of G. B. and Ireland (1849).	91		Offers out of work and "Oppression money." Sick and Death Benefits, and Pension.
		Glass Bottle Makers of Yorkshire United Trade Protection Society.	21		
		Glass Painters' Union (1889).	120		Out of work benefit. Minimum wage 9d per hour; discourages piece - work. Apprenticeship usual. Relations with Employers friendly.
1800	980	Amalgamated Society of Pottery Moulders&Finisherr.	50	79	Give out of work pay only.
		London Affiliated Potters' Trade Society.	29		
4971	2973			611	

Thus in the glass industry 532 males are organized out of a total of 1993 over twenty years of age, or 27 per cent., while among potters only 79 out of 980, or 8 per cent., are members of any organization confined to the members of their own trade.

The trades unions play a very important part in the glass industry, directly consequent on the method of remuneration. When work is paid for by time, or when piece-work is unvarying in character, uniform rates of wages may perhaps be maintained without special organization, by the common rule of one price in one market for any article. But when a price by piece has to be fixed for a great variety of work frequently changing in character, and done at very varying speeds, any approach to uniformity could only be reached by common action well thought-out. The trades union view may be against all piece-work, but in this case piece-work is the main reason for the existence of a union; for while no other system of remuneration would do justice to the employer, some such standard as the union provides is strictly necessary if justice is also to be done to the men.

The London Glass Blowers' Society, as will be seen above, is the most important, and has a very elaborate book of rules. Among other things it declares that "employers should acquaint their men before taking on an apprentice;" and fines any member who applies for "employment to an employer or manager without first obtaining the consent of the men employed in the shop." Any member, too, discharged from a situation for default (as irregularity), falls out of benefit for six weeks or longer, at the pleasure of the committee. The potters, on the other hand, are but poorly represented, and though there have existed societies for all branches, yet they have been ruined by strikes, and their members have left them. In 1889, many of the "red potters" joined the London and Counties Labour League, and obtained a slight increase of wages; but when in June, 1890, a strike was resorted to in order to limit the number of boys employed, the men were beaten, and not a few of them thrown out of work. With financial assistance, a co-operative association was then started; but whether owing to defective management or want of good faith among the workers, it had to be wound up, and is now worked on ordinary capitalist lines under the control of the Labour League.

Wages Statistics.

In the trades included in this section there are 2973 adult men employed. Our wages returns are from fifteen firms, and include 743 adult males, as under :—

Glass manufacturers 1	}	= 15 firms usually employing 966 persons, of whom 805 are adult males, but 62 of these belong to other sections, being bricklayers, carpenters, engineers, stokers, glass-bevellers and silverers, carmen, &c.
Glass-blowers 4		
Glass-benders, bevellers, &c.......... 3		
Glass-painters 3		
Potteries 4		

The earnings of these men in an average week are as follows :—

Below 20s............. 44, or	5½ per cent.	}	Under 30s, 32 per cent.
20s to 25s............. 92 „	12¼ „		
25s „ 30s............. 103 „	14 „		
30s „ 35s............. 113 „	15¼ „	}	30s and over, 68 per cent.
35s „ 40s............. 124 „	16½ „		
40s „ 45s............. 80 „	11 „		
45s and upwards... 187 „	25 „		
743 „ 100 „			

Our figures may be compared with returns made to the Board of Trade in 1886, from four firms of glass-blowers, and three potteries, by omitting from our returns all except potteries and glass-blowers. The result is as follows :—

	—20s.	20s—	25s—	30s—	35s—	40s—	45s—
Our returns.......	7 %	14 %	16 %	16 %	15½ %	9½ %	22 %
		37 %			63 %		
Board of Trade returns	8 %	23½ %	11½ %	13 %	9 %	19 %	16 %
		43 %			57 %		

As to irregularity of employment, five firms made special returns to us which are fairly supported by the returns made to the Board of Trade :—

	Busy Week.	Slack Week.	Percentage Reduction.		
			In numbers.	In earnings per head.	Combined.
Our returns......	449	428	5	23	26
Board of Trade returns	1576	1455	7½	18	24

Our returns place the busiest weeks in May, July, and September, and those of the Board of Trade give August, September and December. The slackest weeks fall in January, July, August and September according to our returns, and in April and June according to those of the Board of Trade. Slackness of work is therefore evidently due to causes other than the seasons, and affects the amount of earnings rather than the numbers employed.

8s to 15s a week is the general range of wages for lads and boys, but at the bottom of the scale about 5 per cent. earn 5s or less, and at the top a similar proportion get 20s or more.

Social Condition.

There are 2970 adult males employed in these trades, and about 2030 are counted as heads of families, and so come under social classification. If we might assume them to be represented by those of whom we have particulars, we should have only 18 per cent. earning less than 25s a week, but compared to this about 48 per cent. are found living in a more or less crowded condition, and all comparison between the scale of earnings and that of social condition appears to break down.

Comparison of Earnings with Style of Life (Glass and Earthenware).

Earnings as returned.				Classification of Population.			
Under 20s...	44	or	5½ per cent.	3 or 4 in each room,	1800,	or 17 per cent.
20s to 25s...	92	,,	12½ ,,	2 to 3 ,,	3200	,, 31 ,,
25s ,, 30s...	103	,,	14 ,,	1 ,, 2 ,,	3000	,, 29 ,,
30s ,, 35s...	113	,,	15½ ,,	Less than 1 ,, ⎫		
35s ,, 40s...	124	,,	16½ ,,	More than 4 rooms ⎪	2400 ,, 23 ,,	
40s ,, 45s...	80	,,	11 ,,	4 or more persons ⎬		
45s and upwards	187	,,	25 ,,	to 1 servant ... ⎭		
	743	,,	100 ,,		10,400 ,, 100 ,,	
				Employers' families ⎫ and servants ...⎭	1265	
					11,665	

The glass factories of London, small and large, are scattered over a wide area, although Bethnal Green may be called the centre of the "small works" industry, and the men do not live as a matter of course near their work. With potters it is otherwise, for although the large potteries of London are situated as a rule at considerable distances from one another, they are to be found in quarters where workmen can obtain dwellings, and are sufficiently important to guarantee regularity of employment to the majority of their employees. We find, therefore, that while men in the glass industry usually get their food from home and eat it either in the factory, or less commonly at a public-house or coffee-house, the potters, living near by, frequently go home to their dinner in the middle of the day.

The friendly societies are well patronized by both glassmen and potters, and the former belong, as we have seen, in considerable numbers to their various trade unions. Factory sick clubs are common, members dividing any surplus funds once or twice a year.

It is possible that in some cases the wives of men in this section add to the week's earnings by some home industry. But, there being scarcely any work in either branch of this section which could well be performed by women, this is not nearly so general as it is in trades in which part of the work is regularly given out to be done by women in their own homes, or even when female labour is employed in the shop.

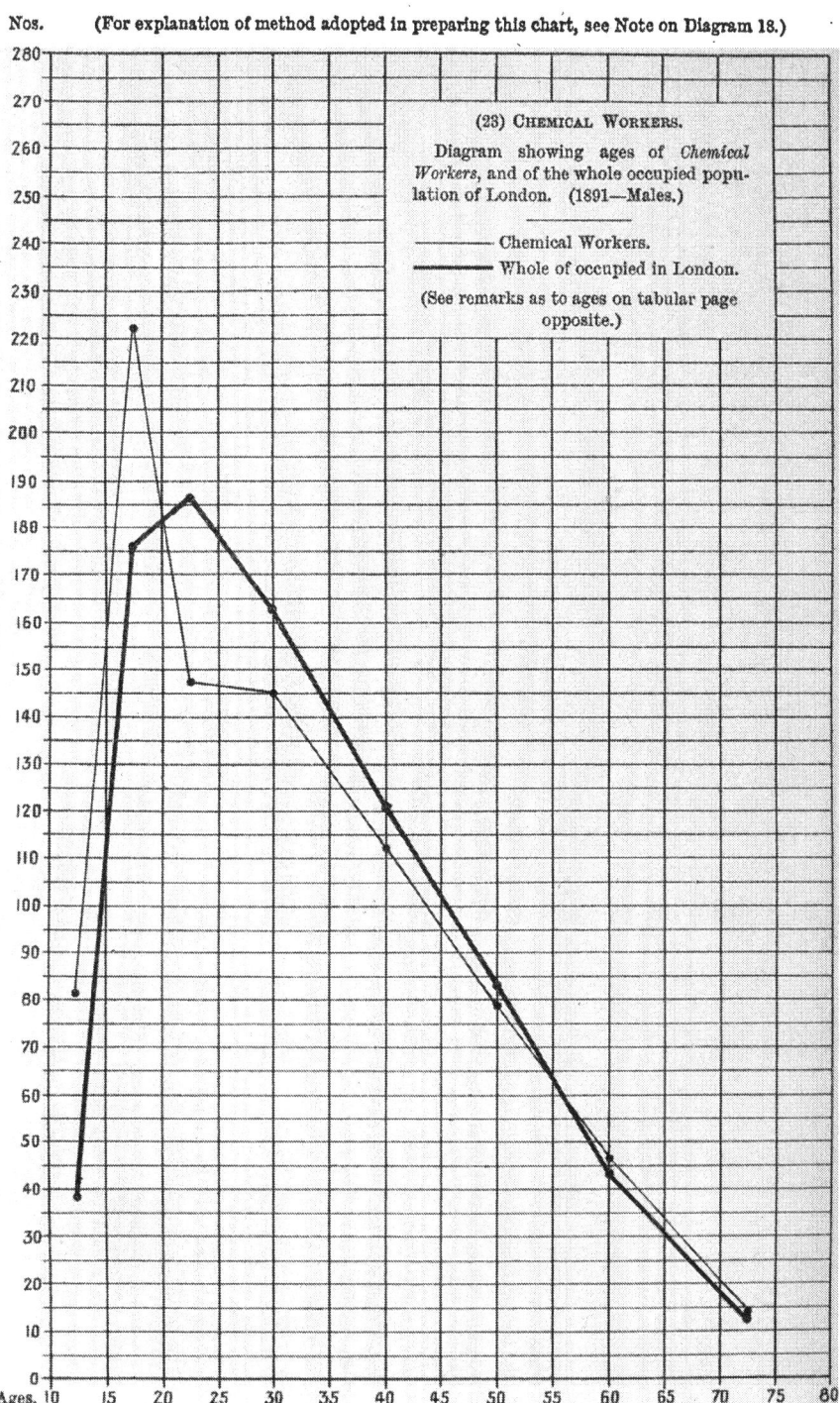

(23) CHEMICAL WORKERS.

Diagram showing ages of *Chemical Workers*, and of the whole occupied population of London. (1891—Males.)

——————— Chemical Workers.
━━━━━━━ Whole of occupied in London.

(See remarks as to ages on tabular page opposite.)

CHAPTER II.

CHEMICALS, &c. (*Section 23.*)

Persons Represented.

Census Enumeration.						Enumerated by Families.			

Census Enumeration.

Divisions, 1891.	Fe-males.	Males.			Total.
	All Ages.	—19	20—54	55—	
nfacturing mist .... paint,	741	207	1158	227	2333
king, &c. powder,	105	218	929	139	1391
hes, &c..	1183	495	393	41	2112
TOTAL....	2029	920	2480	407	5836

rger majority of the females are quite women and girls. As to males the ons of those employed at different somewhat extraordinary, there the diagram shows, a large number followed by a marked deficiency of en, so that it is not till 55 that a proportion is reached.

DISTRIBUTION.

N.	W.& C.	S.	Total.
1434	624	2029	5836

DETAILS OF OCCUPATIONS M THE CENSUS DICTIONARY).

liver oil manufacturer, perfumer, t powder, essential oil distiller, disin- t manufacturer, baking powder, h manufacturer, drysalter. wood worker, aniline dye manufac-, colour grinder, artists' colourman, -lead maker, black-lead grinder, aker. signal, torpedo, rocket-maker, per- n cap maker, pyrotechnist.

Enumerated by Families.

Sex	{ Males	2094
	{ Females	191

Birthplace	{ In London .... 60 %	1379	Heads of Families,
	{ Out of London.. 40 %	906	2285

Industrial Status ..	{ Employer ...... 14 %	328
	{ Employed...... 81 %	1847
	{ Neither .... 5 %	110

TOTAL POPULATION CONCERNED.

	Heads of Families.	Others Occupied.	Unoccupied.	Servants.	Total.
Total	2285	2110	5927	570	10,892
Average in family..	1	·92	2·59	·25	4·76

CLASSIFICATION.

		%
Numbers living in Families,		
3 or more to a room	1116	10·2
2 & under 3 ,,	2074	19·1
1 & under 2 ,,	2589	23·8
Less than 1 ,,		
More than 4 rooms	3672	33·7
4 or more persons to a servant ..		
Less than 4 to 1 ser- vant, and 4 or more to 2 servts.	450	4·1
All others with 2 or more servants ..	421	3·9
Servants	570	5·2
	10,892	100

Inner. Outer. Together.
Crowded..49 % 22 % 29 %
Not ,, ..51 % 78 % 71 %

DISTRIBUTION.

East..	{ Inner 979	2528
	{ Outer 1549	
North	{ Inner 397	3017
	{ Outer 2620	
West	{ Inner 93	466
	{ Outer 373	
Central Inner	573	573
South-	{ Inner 322	2457
East	{ Outer 2135	
South-	{ Inner 657	1851
West	{ Outer 1194	
		10,892

Inner 3021, or 28 %
Outer 7871, or 72 %

Status as to Employment (according to Census Enumeration).

Census Divisions (1891).	Employers.		Employed.			Neither Employer nor Employed.		Total.
			Males.		Females of all ages.			
	Males.	Females	Under 20.	Over 20.		Males.	Females	
uf, Chemist, Alkaline manuf...	226	6	196	987	701	55	7	2178
salter	29	1	11	76	25	12	1	155
paint, ink, blacking makers....	115	1	218	913	97	40	7	1391
powder and cotton manuf. ..	2	—	19	29	26	—	—	76
ees, fireworks, explosives makers	21	3	476	370	1152	12	2	2036
	393	11	920	2375	2001	119	17	5836
TOTAL.........	404		5296			136		5836

Proportion of Employers to Employed—1 to 13

CHEMICAL WORKS, MANUFACTURING DRUGGISTS, &c.

Although the metropolitan area can hardly be considered one of the principal centres of chemical industry in England, the enormous variety of products and processes included makes it impossible to give a separate account of each; books might be filled in describing the products of coal tar alone ; but as regards our immediate object there is no great divergence among the chemical factories of London. Hours and rates of wages of those employed, and methods of learning, are throughout very much alike ; and the proportions as to age and sex are similar.

The ordinary chemical labourer is rather to be called disciplined than skilled. His position is like that of the private soldier in a regiment. The officers are trained chemists—men of scientific education. They are constantly at work in the laboratory, testing the product of the workshops or making fresh experiments. When a new process is to be tried, they themselves superintend its course until the foreman or leading hand in charge has become thoroughly acquainted with it ; and then these men, who answer to the non-commissioned officers, become responsible so long as the process is continued.

Those who act as foremen acquire a rule of thumb knowledge of each process that comes under their care, and beyond this must prove themselves capable of the management of men. But the great body of the labourers need little skill and acquire no special knowledge ; they have only to carry out exactly the orders given. The qualities necessary for a good chemical labourer are, as for a soldier, attention and obedience; and the closeness of the parallel is curiously shown by the preference given in some factories to men who have been in the army.

Besides these trained men, there are the yard labourers, from among the most intelligent and well-behaved of whom the chemical labourers are recruited.

There are thus three classes of workmen with whom we have to deal—

(1) Foremen.

(2) Chemical labourers.

(3) Yard labourers.

The wages of the foremen are from 40s to 50s, paid regularly throughout the year. At the top of the second class stand the leading hands, whose duties are usually confined to looking after one particular branch of the work in one particular room. From among them the foremen will be chosen. They receive 6d or 7d an hour, which would be 27s to 32s for a regular week of fifty-four or fifty-six hours. They perhaps lose a little time if work is slack, and in busy periods may work twenty or even thirty hours a week overtime. Some firms have put a stop to long hours by working two shifts, but this is not at present usual. The long hours are not quite so bad as they may sound, for the work as a rule is light, including much time spent in simply sitting and watching for the moment when the product is matured; or in readiness for action if anything goes wrong. The men, it is true, must not move from the spot, but there is little physical exertion. The rank and file of chemical labourers receive much the same wages as are paid for ordinary unskilled labour in the district. The great majority get 6d an hour, or if paid by the week, 24s to 26s. There are, however, cases in which the rate is lower, varying from $5\frac{1}{2}d$ to $4\frac{3}{4}d$ per hour, or 20s to 22s if paid by the week, and in some districts even 4d per hour is paid to new hands. The men all have the advantage of more regular and lighter work than the yard labourers, and they moreover frequently work overtime. For this they are sometimes paid one-fourth more, and it raises the actual amount earned by the bulk of them to about 30s, one week with another; while the yard labourer, though nominally paid at the same rate, rarely exceeds 24s, and would undoubtedly average much less. Some firms with a river frontage employ their labourers at piece-work to unload barges; and, working in a gang, the men can then earn as much as two or even three pounds each in a week, or perhaps less time. Such chances are balanced by irregularity of work.

The reason why the trained workers do not command a higher price for their labour per hour than the ordinary unskilled labourers lies in the ease with which the necessary knowledge is acquired, and in the fact that this knowledge is of little or no value outside the factory gates. Steadiness of character is in reality the measure of their skill, and steadiness of employment its reward.

In the workshops of the *Manufacturing Druggists* still more care is required of the workman than in the ordinary chemical factory. Any mistake—a bottle wrongly labelled or a medicine wrongly compounded—may lead to serious consequences. To prevent mistakes there is at the head of each room a superintending chemist, responsible for the men working under him, and these men must be steady and intelligent. Untrustworthy characters are weeded out. Not only is drink strictly forbidden on the premises, but the sobriety of the men is said to extend beyond business hours. Nevertheless the wages do not commonly rise above 25s a week. There seems to be fairly regular work throughout the year, but winter, when illness and disease are most rife, is the busiest season. Other chemical products have also their busy and slack seasons, but, as a rule, each firm works at a variety of branches, some of which are slack while others are busy, so that the men can be shifted from one branch to another. Perhaps the only exception is to be found in the coal-tar distilling and pitch industry, the whole of which is busy in winter and slack in summer. The ordinary labourers in this case are said to find employment in the brickfields in summer, and the number of actual chemical labourers at work does not vary so very much, even in this branch.

A large number of young women are employed by Manufacturing Druggists. These girls are quieter and better behaved than those in match factories, or in many other East End industries. Deftness and cleanliness are required from them, and the girls either learn to live up to this standard or the character of the work attracts a better class. Their wages, are, however, no higher—8*s* may be taken as a fair average, beginning at 4*s* 6*d* with new comers, and rising to 10*s* or 10*s* 6*d* for a skilful worker. Forewomen receive 14*s* 6*d* or 15*s*. The hours worked are according to the Factory Acts.

White-lead.

The manufacture of white-lead stands apart from the rest of the chemical industries, not only because of its special unhealthiness (as to which see page 106), but because of other peculiarities. The labour employed is mostly casual; the men are taken on and paid off day by day. Those engaged on the most unhealthy process are paid 7*s* 6*d* per day, but are not allowed to work more than three days in one week. The rest of the men receive 4*s* 6*d* a day, or 19*s* to 22*s* a week for such as have regular work. The hours vary from fifty-six to fifty-nine per week. November and December are the slack months, being those which usher in the winter, when little painting is done. Otherwise the work is fairly regular, though the workers themselves are constantly shifting to and from other forms of casual employment, and are, no doubt, often out of work. The white-lead works are looked upon as the last resource of the starving—of the helpless and lowest class of the unskilled—but there are those who, having once " tasted the lead colic," prefer to apply to the Guardians rather than repeat the experience. Yet, while the more numerous class are those who take short spells at this work from time to time when necessity compels, there are others who, from despair or indifference, acquire a regular habit of working at it, and keep on and on till permanently injured. If they cannot or will not take the first warnings, their last two or three years are spent between the works and the infirmary, the visits to the latter becoming more and more prolonged, till the day comes when they return to their labour no more. Excess in alcohol very generally accompanies lead poisoning. The danger from the lead applies much less to the foremen, for they know better how to take care of themselves and their work involves less risk.

MATCH MAKING.

This industry, which is grouped with chemical works in the present section, also presents some peculiarities partly connected with health. An account of the process of manufacture and the wages paid to the girls, who form three-fourths of those employed, has been given by Miss Collet in a previous volume.* In one respect there is said to be a considerable improvement since the chapter on women's work in East London was written. Miss Collet notices the irregularity of attendance as tending to reduce the earnings of the girls, and so make the wages appear lower than they really are; within the last year, however, there has been more regular attendance than ever before, both in regard to the number of hours worked in the week and the decreased numbers who have left work at the factory to go fruit or hop-picking. The caprice of the moment seems to have less force. Another good sign is that the girls are more cleanly than they used to be, thus greatly diminishing the danger of necrosis—the terrible "phossy jaw." Unfortunately it appears certain that neither cleanliness nor any known preventive is an infallible guarantee against this disease where yellow phosphorus is used, and it is used in all except "safety" matches; that is to say, in all matches not made to ignite solely upon a specially prepared surface. For safety

* See Vol. I. of first edition—Vol. IV. of present edition.

matches, red or amorphous phosphorus is employed, and
this means "safety" not alone to the consumer, but to the
producer. In Switzerland the manufacture of other than
safety matches has on this account been forbidden by
Government action. At present, in this country the
demand for safety matches is decreasing, the old style
being found more convenient, and the additional risk
to the makers is, through ignorance or indifference, dis-
regarded. The buildings and appliances have been
improved, and the home industry, which still exists to
a certain extent on the continent, is fortunately unknown
in England. The modern tendency of some trades to
concentration in the hands of large companies has been
a distinct benefit to the match-makers, by supplying large
and well-ventilated rooms and all the appliances of cleanliness necessary for health.

Girls in match factories work almost invariably by the
piece. The men "dippers," on the other hand, are usually
paid by time, their wages averaging about 24s per week.
There are about four boys employed to each dipper. They
receive 6s to 8s a week. The hours vary between 8 to 7
in winter, and 6.30 to 6 in summer, with one or one and
a half hours for meals.

GENERAL REMARKS ON THE TRADES IN THIS SECTION.

Methods of Training.—There is no regular system of
apprenticeship, and in chemical factories boys are rarely
employed. They are not strong enough for yard labour,
nor sufficiently careful to be trusted to do work requiring
close attention; but young men of nineteen or twenty,
taken on as labourers, may be promoted to more responsible work if they show signs of possessing the requisite
qualities. Among manufacturing druggists, boys, beginning as errand or office boys, are by degrees drafted into
the packing department or into the laboratories. Some of
those employed in the laboratories attend technical educa-

tion classes and try to qualify themselves as certified chemists, in which case they may rise to superior positions in the factory. But more usually the responsible chemists are men of a higher class, who, having passed their examination in pharmacy, and perhaps served some years in a chemist's shop, prefer a regular salary to the chances of business on their own account.

Foreign Competition.—Excepting as regards corrosive acids or dangerous articles, the importation of which is practically prohibited by the freight charge, there is great competition in which this country is too often beaten by Belgium, France, and Germany. Our opponents' success is generally attributed to lower wages, but cannot be explained by this cause only. In the cost of the coarser and commoner articles wages may be the ruling factor, but in the manufacture of more delicate products it is rather to high scientific knowledge and ceaseless experimental industry that success is due. It is said to be in the application of science that English manufacturers are beaten; being, or at least having been, less ready to learn from others and less active in discovering improvements for themselves. Some advance in this respect is noticed, but a first-class chemical education is far cheaper in Germany than in England, and so skilled chemists are more common; and further, it is averred that the professors of chemistry at the foreign universities work hand-in-glove with the manufacturers to an extent unknown in England. Moreover, we have much leeway to make up.

Unhealthiness.—Something has been already said as to the special difficulties of white-lead and match making. Phosphorus and white-lead are, however, not the only poisonous dangers to be encountered. Compounds of arsenic or mercury and many other things are very dangerous to handle. How far to carry State action—where or in what way to regulate, when to forbid, and whether to try for international action, are very difficult questions, and to answer them requires almost exhaustive knowledge. In view of the Government Commission on this subject which has lately reported it is not necessary to make any such attempt here, but a few observations may not be out of place.

It seems, judging by information received from workmen as well as employers, that many of the dangers might be avoided or prevented by proper care, and that care in this instance means cleanliness. It is not enough to provide baths and lavatories; their use needs to be enforced on every individual undertaking dangerous work. The men who run these risks, especially in the white-lead works, are among the least educated and least civilized members of the community; they cannot safely be left to their own devices, and, in fact, we do now at every turn check their natural propensities because we believe it to be for their own benefit or that of others. It is not to be wondered at, that, reckless as they are, they are indifferent to, or sceptical of the dangers that lie in wait about them, and are consequently unwilling to adopt the necessary measures for safety, or to acquire habits of cleanliness to which they are in no way accustomed. As a community, we cannot rightly take advantage either of their ignorance or of the cheap price at which they hold their lives.

TRADE ORGANIZATION.

There are not any unions of the men specially connected with these trades, but many of those employed in one capacity or another—engineers, carpenters, coopers, labourers, &c.—may belong to their own unions, and it is probable that any benefit won by these organizations would be participated in by all hands, more or less.

There is, however, a union among the match girls, which was started by assistance from outside, and

seems to be growing in favour. It appears to have
already taught its members the advantages of organization
and discipline, and it is far from unlikely that the improvement lately noticed as regards both cleanliness and
regularity of attendance is, to a considerable extent, due
to the originators of the movement, who are teaching the
girls that a "feather club" is not all that combination can
do for them.

Wages Statistics.

Of the 5296 persons employed, 2375 are adult men; and
of these we have information as to earnings for 403,
employed by fifteen firms, as under :—

Chemical manufacturers 7	⎫	= 15 firms usually employing
Paint and colour works 2	⎪	836 persons, of whom 663 are
Ink-makers 2	⎪	adult males, but 260 of these
Blacking manufacturers............... 1	⎬	belong to other sections, as en-
Dye-makers 1	⎪	gine-men, blacksmiths, carpen-
Match-makers 2	⎭	ters, coopers, packers, carmen, watchmen, labourers, &c.

The earnings of these men in an average week are as
follows :—

Below 20s............	16, or	4 per cent.	⎫	
20s to 25s............	65 „	16 „	⎬	Below 30s, 37 per cent.
25s „ 30s............	68 „	17 „	⎭	
30s „ 35s............	103 „	26 „	⎫	
35s „ 40s.............	56 „	14 „	⎪	
40s „ 45s............	51 „	13 „	⎬	30s and upwards, 63 per cent.
45s and upwards...	44 „	10 „	⎭	
	403 „	100 „		

Returns made to the Board of Trade in 1886, which
include eight from white-lead and paint works, and two
from varnish and japan works, but none from chemical

manufacturers or dye-makers, and only one from ink-makers, show a considerably lower range of wages, as follows :—

	—20s.	20s—	25s—	30s—	35s—	40s—	45s—
Board of Trade returns (chiefly White-lead or Paint Works)............	4 °/₀	33 °/₀	26 °/₀	26 °/₀	3 °/₀	3 °/₀	5 °/₀
		63 °/₀				37 °/₀	

In chemical manufacture the work is fairly regular, and on the whole there is less loss of time in all these trades than in some others. Overtime when trade is active may make up for wages lost when work is slack.

The remuneration of lads and boys in these trades seems to be good, ranging usually from 9s to 20s a week. Wages of females are lower, the bulk being at 7s to 12s a week, but they are largely either young girls, or married women who do not make full time.

Social Condition.

Of the 2375 adult men employed in these industries, about 1690 are counted in the census as heads of families, and are the men whose earnings and social condition we are attempting to determine.

If we assume that as our returns represent chiefly the chemical workers, while the Board of Trade returns represent chiefly the paint workers, the true average for the whole group is best represented by a combination of the two sets of figures, we find about 26 per cent. who earn in an ordinary week less than 25s, and may compare with them the 32 per cent. who live more or less crowded in their homes. Next we have about 45 per cent. earning from 25s to 35s to compare with 31 per cent. who live one or two to a room, and finally 28 per cent. earning over 35s compared to 37 per cent. of the central classes, as follows :—

Comparison of Earnings with Style of Life (Chemicals, &c.).

Mean of samples tested.	Classification of Population.		
Below 20s......... 4 per cent.	3 or more in each room,	600 or	7 per cent.
20s to 25s......... 22¾ ,,	2 to 3 ,,	2000 ,,	25 ,,
25s ,, 30s......... 20 ,,	1 ,, 2 ,,	2500 ,,	31 ,,
30s ,, 35s......... 25½ ,,	Less than 1 ,,		
35s ,, 40s......... 10 ,,	More than 4 rooms		
40s ,, 45s......... 9 ,,	4 or more persons	3000	37 ,,
45s and upwards 9 ,,	to 1 servant		
100 ,,		8100 ,,100 ,,
	Families with female heads, Employers' families and servants	2800	
		10,900	

In most cases the employees in chemical factories live
near their work, these factories being generally situated
in the poorer districts of London. It results as a natural
consequence that the men frequently go home to meals,
though for those that prefer to eat their food on the
premises, a dining-room, with washing apparatus, is often
provided by the firm. It is usual to wear aprons and
overalls, when engaged upon any dusty employment, while
for those occupied with the manufacture of poisons and
acids special jackets and gloves are sometimes provided.

A majority of the men appear to belong to some friendly
society or shop club, but, as already noted, there is no
regular union among the men of this section.

Nos. (For explanation of method adopted in preparing this chart, see Note on Diagram 18.)

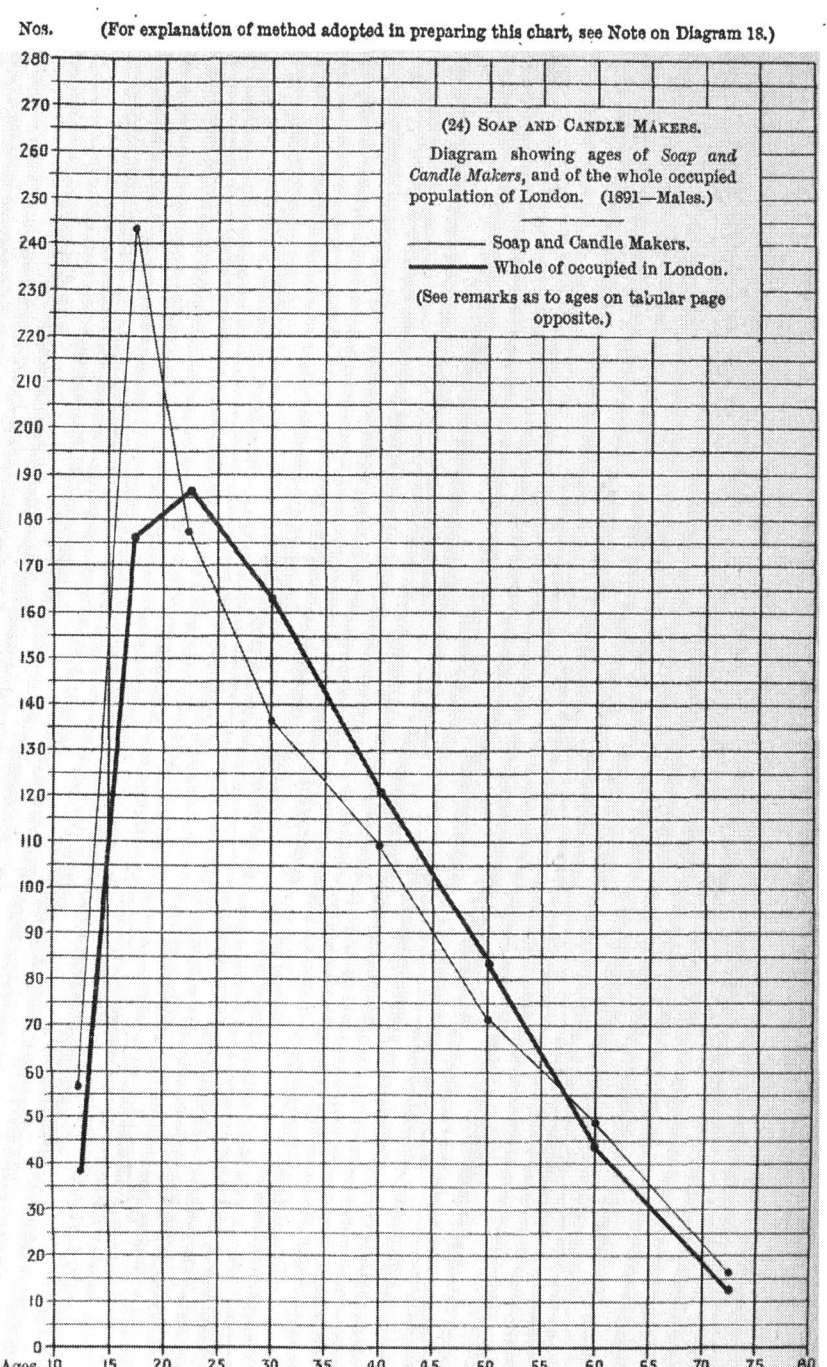

(24) SOAP AND CANDLE MAKERS.

Diagram showing ages of *Soap and Candle Makers*, and of the whole occupied population of London. (1891—Males.)

————— Soap and Candle Makers.
━━━━━ Whole of occupied in London.

(See remarks as to ages on tabular page opposite.)

CHAPTER III.
SOAP, CANDLES, GLUE, &c. (Section 24.)

Persons Represented.

Census Enumeration.					
Divisions, 1891.	Fe-males. All Ages.	Males.			Total.
		—19	20—54	55—	
ow, soap, ... , size, nure, &c...	139	369	849	153	1510
	223	69	392	61	685
TOTAL....	362	438	1181	214	2195

age distribution of the men and boys ed in this trade shows the same rity, of the presence of many boys absence of a reasonable proportion of men, that we have found in the al trade.

Enumerated by Families.

Sex	Males		1003	
	Females...............		53	
Birthplace	In London	63 %	664	Heads of Families, 1056
	Out of London..	37 %	392	
Industrial Status ..	Employer	12 %	129	
	Employed	81 %	856	
	Neither	7 %	71	

TOTAL POPULATION CONCERNED.

	Heads of Families.	Others Occupied.	Unoccupied.	Servants.	Total.
Total	1056	1037	2646	207	4946
Average in family..	1	·98	2·51	·20	4·69

DISTRIBUTION.

N.	W.& C.	S.	Total.
331	216	1195	2195

DETAILS OF OCCUPATIONS
(FROM THE CENSUS DICTIONARY).

ase collector, tallow renderer, stearine ter, glycerine preparer (crude and ned), cart grease, railway grease, t's - foot oil maker, wax taper, at-light maker, dog-cake maker.

tine capsule maker, isinglass roller, e maker, bone boiler, calciner, her, miller, gatherer.

CLASSIFICATION.

Numbers living in Families.		%
3 or more to a room	435	8·8
2 & under 3 ,,	980	19·9
1 & under 2 ,,	1179	23·9
Less than 1 ,,		
More than 4 rooms 4 or more persons to a servant ..	1833	37·0
Less than 4 to 1 servant, and 4 or more to 2 servts.	183	3·7
All others with 2 or more servants ..	129	2·6
Servants	207	4·1
	4946	100

	Inner.	Outer.	Together.
Crowded...	45 %	18 %	29 %
Not ,, ..	55 %	82 %	71 %

DISTRIBUTION.

East..	Inner	775	1184
	Outer	409	
North	Inner	75	705
	Outer	630	
West	Inner	26	292
	Outer	176	
Central Inner		242	242
South- East	Inner	219	1052
	Outer	833	
South- West	Inner	585	1561
	Outer	976	
			4946

Inner 1922, or 39 %
Outer 3024, or 61 %

Status as to Employment (according to Census Enumeration).

Census Divisions (1891).	Employers.		Employed.			Neither Employer nor Employed.		Total.
			Males.		Females of all ages.			
	Males.	Females	Under 20.	Over 20.		Males.	Females	
low chandler,candle,grease maker	38	3	245	598	74	13	5	886
p-boiler, maker	32	2	124	406	54	5	1	624
e, size, gelatine, isinglass maker	22	—	21	61	53	5	1	163
nure maker, bone boiler	13	1	6	53	—	6	—	79
ers	57	4	42	121	158	55	6	443
	162	10	438	1149	339	84	13	2195
TOTAL.........	172		1926			97		2195

Proportion of Employers to Employed–1 to 11

SOAP.

The trades dealt with in this section lie in two groups—the one dealing with animal grease, or animal and vegetable wax, and with their oils; the other with gelatinous animal matter, bones and blood. These trades are really quite distinct, but it has been numerically convenient to bring them together in this section, and they have something in common in that they together deal with the refuse parts of animals.

Soap is a combination of fat or fatty oils with some alkaline body.* The fats used are of the most disagreeable nature, being largely obtained by boiling down refuse obtained from slaughter-houses, and from restaurants or private houses. This latter, known as " town stuff," is particularly unsavoury. Such is the low origin of even the most dainty toilet soap.

The material is collected by agents or by the carts of the manufacturers themselves. Each load is deposited in the mixing room, where it is melted in huge copper pans, care being taken to combine different fats in due proportion. This first boiling, or " rendering," as it is called, frees the grease from impurities. It is boiled a second time, and while hot is treated with alkali to produce saponification. The soapy liquid must be kept boiling, but must not boil over. The men have to stir it as a cook would stir a sauce, only on a very large scale, and moreover they have to keep down ebullition by cooling the surface, tossing small quantities into the air with long scoops or ladles. After several days boiling the liquid is allowed to stand, when all remaining impurities either rise to the top as scum or sink to the bottom as dregs. Before the mass is cool, the central clarified portion of the liquid is drawn off into upright iron cases or frames, with movable sides, there to solidify. When the stuff is cold

* This refers to hard soap. Soft soap is made with potash.

the sides of the frame are taken down, leaving a solid block of soap. This is then wire-cut into slabs, and these again are divided into the familiar bars of household soap, ready for sale to the retailers.

If fine toilet soap is to be made, the first product is either remelted and further refined, or it is "milled" by being cut into thin strips and exposed to the air, and then crushed together into one mass without actual melting or any more boiling; and finally it is given its distinctive character, colour and scent. Some firms do not make the soap from the start, but buy ordinary yellow soap as the raw material of their manufacture, and limit themselves to the finishing processes.

CANDLES.

Up to the fifteenth century all candles were produced by "dipping," "rolling," or "pouring," and the old methods still apply to the original materials — tallow and real beeswax; otherwise the method now adopted is that of "moulding."

The materials used for mould or "composite" candles are the stearine derived from tallow, and the solid portion of animal, vegetable, or mineral oils—mainly sperm, palm and paraffin. Metal moulds are used, up the centre of which runs the plaited thread which forms the wick. The moulds, set together by hundreds in a frame, are "jacketed," so that they can be surrounded with cold water, or with hot steam, at pleasure; they are kept hot while being filled, and then cooled off. The wicks having been severed, the candles, which are made in a reversed position, are pushed out of the moulds by the tip piece, which, being smaller than the bore of the mould, is driven up through it. By the same action fresh wicks are stretched and the process is repeated. A more elaborate mould is required to produce "self-fitting ends."

Real wax adheres too tightly to the mould to be successfully manipulated in this manner. At one time wax candles were rolled out of softened wax, but "pouring" followed by rolling is the method now usually employed. The process of "pouring" is exactly the reverse of "dipping"—both form the candle by successive layers of the hot liquid, which is made to cling first to the bare wick and then to the growing candle, and allowed to harden layer by layer. When half made the candles are larger at the upper end, and must be inverted if uniformity in size is desired. The tallest church candles are left of "taper" shape; they might not otherwise carry their great weight safely. When the pouring is finished, but before the wax is hard, the candles are rolled by hand on a wet marble slab, and when round and smooth are cut into the required lengths and their tips trimmed.

Tallow dips, which may still be seen in some shops, hanging like bunches of carrots, are made of tallow which has simply been "rendered"—that is, boiled with a weak acid to clear it from fleshy and other impurities. The process of alternate dipping and cooling till the desired thickness is attained may be easily imagined. The plan of dipping is also used for the so-called "snuffless dip," a cheap candle made of very soft stearine. For this a plaited wick is used, whereas the wick of the regular tallow dip is unplaited.

The "snuffless dip," which is a step towards the more perfect mould, finds its place as a cheap "go-to-bed" candle. A very small piece of a very thin candle suffices for this purpose among the mass of the people, and this kind of candle yields a pleasant little light, easy to blow out, and free from the expiring smell of old-fashioned tallow. The genuine article, however, still finds its place in trade; cheap, unbreakable, and not easily extinguished, it is unequalled for some purposes as a workman's candle.

As a cheap illuminant, the candle has no chance against petroleum and gas; and, except in Roman Catholic churches and some old-fashioned houses of the rich, the beautiful soft light of burning wax is now replaced by electricity. Nevertheless, such is the convenience and the excellence of the candles now made, that more are used than ever. Our standard rises in this matter. The desire for brilliant lighting is insatiable. Gas is proposed to supersede candles, but both are used and both are improved. Old lamps are exchanged for new in an endless series of improved construction. Petroleum competes with gas, and electricity with both; but there is room for all three, as also, it would seem, for every invention that increases our control of light.

GENERAL REMARKS.

A larger quantity of soap is used in summer than winter, as more washing is done in hot than cold weather, but the difference is not great, and as fashion in soap does not change quickly, the manufacturers can work for stock when the immediate demand is not brisk. The result is fairly even employment throughout the year.

Not so with candles, which are only needed in the dark, so that in winter there is a much greater demand. Moreover, hot weather is against the setting of the wax or composition, so that there is a disadvantage in making goods in summer for the winter trade. The men are, however, mostly kept on, though a few may be dismissed and all may make short time.

Both for soap and candles trade was good in 1891, and the business done has not decreased since. But there is a general complaint of provincial competition, which has made the London trade less profitable.

The factories lie for the most part along the banks of the Thames, and may be smelt from afar. There are a few small makers of common soap, but candle making is now mostly confined to large factories. The plant required is expensive and occupies much space.

The making of soap and candles, like the manufacture of chemicals, lies on the border-land between skilled and unskilled labour. All that can be taught can be acquired in a few weeks by men, or in a few months by boys; yet the work is not ordinary labourer's work, and no master would willingly replace his old hands by untrained men.

As among the dockers and chemical workers, the greater number of the men employed are London born.

Our returns show that there is as much piece-work as day-work, and the tendency is said to be in favour of the piece-work system. The material is given out for the making of so many candles or so much soap, to be finished by certain men at a given price. The earnings are generally shared equally.

Where time-work is the rule, the foreman sees that a certain amount of work is got through in a given time, but even so, more work naturally is done and more money made in an hour on piece than on time. The wages of time workers usually rise with length of service, because steadiness and regularity are the qualities in request, and custom sustains this advantage of the old hand over the new-comer, even when capacity begins to fail. The work is healthy, and men soon become accustomed even to the smell of the mixing-room.

Women and girls are employed to make boxes and to wrap up fancy soaps. They all work on piece, and earn from 7s 6d to 15s a week, according to the speed at which they work.

GLUE, SIZE, &C.

Glue and Size Making is not a large trade in London, and has always been in the hands of the Irish since, and even before, the days of the famine. The work is ill-paid as well as unattractive and rheumatic. The same material is used to make both glue and size, viz. scraps and parings of hides and skins, cut off in the course of preparation for tanning. Size is simply half-boiled glue, not dried.

The process of manufacture consists first in washing the pieces in acid and water, to get rid of the lime with which the hides have been impregnated by the tanner. The parings being then clean and fresh, the gelatine in them is liberated from the animal fibre by boiling with water to make size, or with "mother liquor" to make glue. Mother liquor is the liquid that is obtained after boiling the parings three times for size. The hot liquid size clarifies as it cools into a jelly, and is sold in that state. The glue is boiled until sufficiently strong—usually eight hours—and is then run all hot into troughs, where it is allowed to cool for three days, turning into a very stiff jelly. It is then cut into slices, which are laid upon nets and exposed to the air—the drying by a strong east wind being best. The pattern seen on glue is an impression of the meshes of the net.

Size is used by painters to give body to whitewash and to prepare surfaces for other work, and has besides a thousand uses in manufacture, more often perhaps on the side of immediate appearance than of lasting wear.

Amongst many other trades glue is, of course, used in cabinet-making and enters largely into the making of matches, the heads of which are dipped in a solution of glue to prepare them for the phosphorus.

Gelatine is a highly refined form of glue, and can be made from pieces of any skin selected and treated with care. It is used to stiffen jelly, and brightly coloured thin sheets of it serve to decorate Christmas crackers. This sheet gelatine is made by pouring the liquid smoothly on to glass, when it hardens in a thin film.

Isinglass, the most approved form of gelatine for cooking purposes, especially for invalid diet, is made from fish bladders, the best being those of the Caspian sturgeon. No preparation is needed beyond washing and cutting into strips. The rougher pieces are used to clarify beer. They are reduced by acid to a thick liquid, known as "finings," a certain quantity of which is commonly put into every barrel of beer, where, in the course of settling down, it takes all impurities with it. Some brewers make their own.

There is not much skill needed by the operatives in glue or size making. Wages are from 20s to 25s. In all branches the amount of skill requisite is soon acquired. As for seasons, summer is busy and winter slack; in one factory in 1892, glue was boiled on 239 and size on 187 days, out of a possible 304 days. In this factory, the men work from 6 to 6, with one and a half hours for meals. On Saturday work ceases at 4. The hours of the women are rather shorter.

Blood Refining is an even more disagreeable trade than glue making, and allied to it are bone and manure works. These trades lie midway between chemicals and glue in style of work and remuneration.

Sausage-skin Dressing is remarkable for the perfection and purity of the finished article, starting as it does from so foul an offal. In character and in remuneration the work is very similar to leather dressing, described later. Not much of it is done in London. The men employed are all Germans, and live near the slaughter-houses.

Paste Making, also included in this section, is something like size making, but the gluten is mostly vegetable.

Dog Biscuits.

Of the making of dog biscuits, which the census places in the same category with soap, as using animal refuse from which soap grease has been extracted, it is unnecessary to say much. It is doubtful whether the men would so return themselves as to be included in the section. They are more likely to appear as biscuit bakers.

The meat fibrine, which gives this food its distinctive

character, does not form any large proportion in the mixture of which the dough is made, and the general process is the same as that employed in making ship's bread. The paste, cut into cakes and stamped, is baked by being slowly passed through large ovens on travelling plates. The oven work is very trying, and men cannot keep at it for long without an interval in the fresh air.

Organization.—In this group of trades there seem to be from first to last no trades unions.

Wages Statistics.

The census returns 1149 adult men as employed in these trades, but our information shows a larger number than this, returns having come in to us from 14 firms, employing 1276* male adults as follows :—

Soap-makers........................... 4	}	= 14 firms usually employing 2702 persons, of whom 1585 are adult males, but of these 309 belong to other sections, as seed-crushers, oil-millers, case-makers, coopers, carpenters, engineers, carmen, and warehousemen.
Soap and candle-makers 3		
Glue and size-makers.................. 2		
Gelatine-makers 2		
Tallow melters and bone crushers.. 2		
Dog-cake maker 1		

The earnings of these men in an average week are as follows :

Below 20s 121,	or 10 per cent.	}	Under 30s, 57½ per cent.		
20s to 25s 292	„ 23 „				
25s „ 30s 312	„ 24½ „				
30s „ 35s 207	„ 16 „	}	30s and over, 42½ per cent.		
35s „ 40s 166	„ 13 „				
40s „ 45s 82	„ 6½ „				
45s and upwards... 96	„ 7 „				
1276	„ 100 „				

---

* This probably includes a number of men who live outside the metropolitan boundary.

Our figures may be compared with returns made to the Board of Trade in 1886, from firms employing 900 persons, of whom 366 adult males come under this section :—

	—20s.	20s—	25s—	30s—	35s—	40s—	45s—
Our returns	10 %	23 %	24½ %	16 %	13 %	6½ %	7 %
		57½			42½		
Board of Trade returns	3 %	33 %	50 %	4½ %	7 %	1 %	1½ %
		86			14		

The difference between the two returns is very marked, but may be explained. The 10 per cent. under 20s of our return falls to 3 per cent., because the Board of Trade figures are based on the nominal full week's earnings, whereas ours give the actual sums earned. Of those who nominally earn 20s to 25s, some actually receive less than 20s; thus our 23 per cent. compares with 33 per cent. on the Board of Trade list. But above this level, owing to payment of overtime, which is prevalent, the actual wages exceed the nominal. There are few— only 14 per cent.—whose rate of wages is over 30s, but, if our information is correct, no less than 42 per cent. do make more than 30s in an average week.

As to regularity of employment, seven firms made special returns, and the results are closely borne out by the Board of Trade figures for 1886. Our returns showing 9½ per cent. reduction in numbers, with 9 per cent. reduction in average earnings, and the Board of Trade 10 per cent. and 9 per cent. The busy weeks are found in January, February, March, April, May, June, July and December, and the slack weeks in January, April, June, August, October, November and December. August to November is undoubtedly the slackest time on the whole, but with candle-making it begins and ends sooner.

Five firms gave detailed returns of busy and slack weeks,

and one sent particulars of an average week only. By combining these statements we are able to make the following comparison between time-work and piece-work:—

Men.	Busy Week (5 firms).				Slack Week (5 firms).				Total Average (6 firms).			
	Men.	Wages.	Hours.	Rate.	Men.	Wages.	Hours.	Rate.	Men.	Wages.	Hours.	Rate.
Time-work.		*s. d.*		*d.*		*s. d*		*d.*		*s. d.*		*d.*
Under 5*d* per hour	141	22 5	63½	4¾	110	20 8	59½	4	150	21 8	61½	4¼
5*d* to 6*d* „	145	31 2	69¾	5¼	133	27 5	60¾	5¼	180	28 10	65	5¼
Over 6*d* and under 8*d* per hour......	43	34 2	61½	6½	33	35 1	65¼	6¼	43	34 8	63¼	6½
Over 8*d* per hour...	16	58 7	68½	10¼	16	48 6	56¾	9¾	16	53 0	63	10
	345	—	—	—	292	—	—	—	389	—	—	—
Piece-work.												
Under 15*s*	20	10 6	—	—	41	11 4	—	—	31	11 0	—	—
„ 20*s*	33	17 3	—	—	30	17 0	—	—	34	17 1	—	—
„ 25*s*	33	23 2	—	—	54	23 5	—	—	47	23 4	—	—
„ 30*s*	30	27 5	—	—	104	26 11	—	—	70	27 0	—	—
„ 40*s*	127	35 2	—	—	60	34 0	—	—	110	34 10	—	—
40*s* and upwards ...	106	45 4	—	—	20	50 3	—	—	68	46 0	—	—
	349	—	—	—	309	—	—	—	360	—	—	—

It will be seen that the difference shown in the numbers employed between busy and slack weeks is here 13 per cent. Time workers and piece workers are nearly equal in numbers. The effect of slackness is, as might perhaps be expected, greatest on the *numbers* of time workers, and on the *money earned* as regards the piece workers. In the busy weeks two-thirds of the piece workers received over 30*s*, and one-fourth over 40*s*, while in the slack weeks the proportion was reversed, two-thirds receiving less than 30*s*, and one-fourth less than 20*s*. We may perhaps assume that it is those who earn *least* in busy times who earn *nothing* when work is slack. Amongst the time workers this is evident; of those earning less than 5*d* an hour one-fifth drop out altogether, and of those from 5*d* to 6*d* only one-tenth. Of those earning over 8*d* an hour none are discharged. The exceptional reduction in the numbers of those making 7d per hour may perhaps be partly due to some of them being put to other work, for it is remarkable that those who still work at this figure actually worked more hours—65¼ in the slack as compared to 61½ in the busy weeks; whereas the rest worked much shorter time in the slack weeks, those paid over 8d twelve hours less, those paid 5d to 6d nine hours less, and those paid under 5d four hours less. Even in a slack week a little overtime is worked in these trades.

The hours of piece workers may to some extent be gauged by some of the returns, which gave the time worked also :—

Piece workers, earning—

Under 15s for	....	57 hours, or	2¼d per hour.
15s and under 20s for	56	,,	3¾d	,,
20s	,,	25s ,,	57	,,	5d	,,
25s	,,	30s ,,	55	,,	5¾d	,,
30s	,,	40s ,,	62	,,	7d	,,
40s and upwards... ,,	65	,,	9d	,,

On piece, in busy times, men work long hours and fast, so earning the maximum rate per hour. In slack times they spin the work out—the time put in is rather less and the money earned per hour very much so.

It is difficult to assign a different rate of pay or distinctive earnings in different departments. The men may be classed in each department as :—

Time-work.

(1.) Unskilled men earning 20s to 25s.

(2.) First-class labourers, *i.e.* those whose work, while requiring no actual skill, yet necessitates a certain use of intelligence and judgment, 25s to 30s.

(3.) Skilled, *i.e.* the foreman and leading hands in each department, earning over 30s.

Piece-work.

(1.) Slow workers, 20s to 30s.

(2.) Medium ,, 30s ,, 40s.

(3.) Quick ,, 40s, upwards.

The women and boys included in this section are occupied in wrapping and packing, and in making night-lights and tapers. For boys there is an almost even number at each rate from 6s to 15s, with a smaller number earning up to or over 20s. From 9s to 15s is the usual range for females, but 16 per cent. earn more and 18 per cent. less than this amount. The children and female relations of the men are quite as likely to be engaged in box-making, &c., and so included in other sections of the census, as to be counted here.

Social Condition.

Of the 1150 adult men employed in these trades, about 810 come under social classification as heads of families. According to our wage returns, 33 per cent. of those employed may be supposed to earn less than 25s a week, a figure which compares closely to the 31 per cent. who live under crowded conditions. Further, 40½ per cent. appear as earning from 25s to 35s, as compared to 30 per cent. of those living in small tenements, but less than two persons to a room; while the 26½ per cent. who appear as earning over 35s compare with 39 per cent. of the central classes, as follows :—

Comparison of Earnings with Style of Life (Soap, Candles, &c.).

Earnings as returned.			Classification of Population.		
Under 20s...121	or 10	per cent.	3 or more in each room,	300,	or 7 per cent.
20s to 25s...292	„ 23	„	2 to 3	950	„ 24 „
25s „ 30s...312	„ 24½	„	1 „ 2	1150	„ 30 „
30s „ 35s...207	„ 16	„	Less than 1 „ ⎫		
35s „ 40s...166	„ 13	„	More than 4 rooms ⎪	1500	„ 39 „
40s „ 45s... 82	„ 6½	„	4 or more persons ⎬		
45s and over 96	„ 7	„	to 1 servant ... ⎭		
	1276 „ 100	„		3900 „ 100	„
			Families with female ⎫ heads, employers' ⎪ families, servants, ⎬ &c. ... ... ⎭	1000	
				4900	

As is shown above, the men, as a whole, live in rather less crowded conditions than their earnings would appear to warrant. This may be accounted for by the fact that soap and candle-making is for the most part carried on in the outskirts of London, where the comparative cheapness of rent enables the men to live near the factories, thus saving them any expense in respect of daily tram or train fares in getting to or from their work.

Some go home for meals, others bring their dinners with them, and in several of the larger factories there is a special place or dining-hall provided for those employed. The presence of so many large factories, and the greater centralization of effort thereby rendered possible, will account also for the different shop-clubs, both athletic and friendly, which are the rule rather than the exception in the firms connected with the soap and candle industry. From three pence to one shilling per week will be spent in this way, and membership of the shop sick club is sometimes compulsory for those who do not already belong to a friendly society paying substantial sick benefits.

As to dress, nearly all the men change a part of their clothes and put on aprons and blouses, as the work is dirty. Glue and size-makers wear aprons and leggings made of coarse sacking.

It seems to be unusual for the wives of men employed to earn money, though, no doubt, there are some who do so. With glue-makers, however, nearly all the women are married, and wives of the employees.

Nos.   (For explanation of method adopted in preparing this chart, see Note on Diagram 18.)

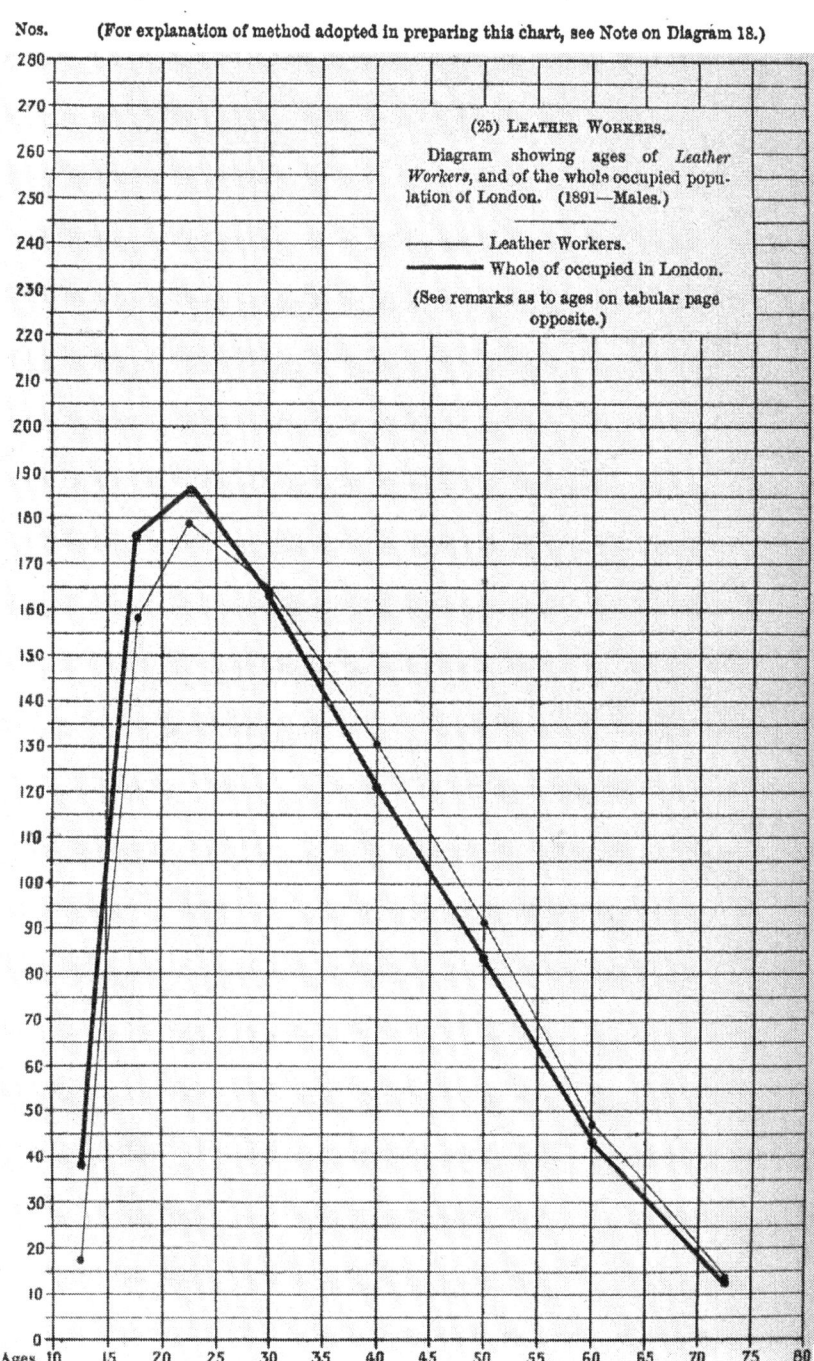

(25) LEATHER WORKERS.

Diagram showing ages of *Leather Workers*, and of the whole occupied population of London. (1891—Males.)

————— Leather Workers.
━━━━━ Whole of occupied in London.

(See remarks as to ages on tabular page opposite.)

CHAPTER IV.

LEATHER DRESSING, TANNING, &c. (*Section 25.*)

Persons Represented.

Census Enumeration.						
Divisions, 91.	Fe-males.	Males.				Total
	All Ages.	—19	20—54	55—		
er and er ...... rier, er Goods, ment,&c.	3059 1156	531 1088	3376 5328	410 791		7376 8363
TOTAL....	4215	1619	8704	1201		15,739

Enumerated by Families.		
Sex ..... { Males .... Females	7309 707	
Birthplace { In London.... 62 % Out of London 38 %	5007 3069	Heads of Families, 8076
Industrial Status.. { Employer .... 13 % Employed .. . 81 % Neither ...... 6 %	1007 6579 490	

TOTAL POPULATION CONCERNED.

	Heads of Families.	Others Occupied.	Unoccupied	Servants.	Total.
Total	8076	8230	21,188	862	38,356
Average in family ..	1	1·02	2·62	·11	4·75

omen are employed as fur-pullers and er-case making. Many of the fur-are married, and from 25 to 35 is the est age. More girls are employed in making, the leading ages being 15 Age distribution of males is practi-nal. (*See diagram.*)

DISTRIBUTION.

N.	W. & C.	S.	Total.
2855	1803	7947	15,739

DETAILS OF OCCUPATIONS (IN THE CENSUS DICTIONARY).

ner, fur-dresser, dyer, seal skin sser, cap and mantle-maker, wool-ler, dyer and rug-maker. Fell-nger.

er, leather-goods maker, dealer, rocco, patent leather, japanner, h and harness currier. Chamois ver, manufacturer, hide splitter, sian leather dresser, portmanteau, sing-case, bag frame, mill-bands, y leather goods, parchment, vellum er, dealer.

CLASSIFICATION.

Numbers living in Families.		%
3 or more to a room	4909	12·8
2 & under 3 ,,	9184	23·9
1 & under 2 ,,	9697	25·3
Less than 1 ,, More than 4 rooms 4 or more persons to a servant ..	} 12,419	32·4
Less than 4 to 1 ser-vant, and 4 or more to 2 servts.	948	2·5
All others with 2 or more servants ..	337	·9
Servants	862	2·2
	38,356	100

	Inner.	Outer.	Together.
Crowded..	46 %	22 %	29 %
Not ,, ..	54 %	78 %	71 %

DISTRIBUTION.

East.. { Inner Outer	5771 594 }	6365	
North { Inner Outer	711 5695 }	6406	
West { Inner Outer	371 991 }	1362	
Central Inner	2561	2561	
South- { Inner East { Outer	11,182 5233 }	16,415	
South- { Inner West { Outer	3447 1800 }	5247	
		38,356	

Inner 24,043, or 63 % Outer 14,313, or 37 %

Status as to Employment (according to Census Enumeration).

Census Divisions (1891).	Employers.		Employed.			Neither Employer nor Employed.		Total.
			Males.		Females of all Ages.			
	Males.	Females	Under 20.	Over 20.		Males.	Females	
rier, Skinner, &c.	379	44	410	2213	2940	162	64	6212
ner, Fellmonger	33	—	121	990	10	9	1	1164
rier, Leather Goods, &c.	679	39	1083	5027	1066	354	40	8288
hment and Vellum	2	1	5	51	9	6	1	75
	1093	84	1619	8281	4025	531	106	15,739
TOTAL..........	1177		13,925			637		

There are on the average 8 men and 4 women employed to each Employer.

TANNING.

Bermondsey is the centre of the London leather trade. Here is the leather market, and here round the market are the tan-yards in which the raw hides are treated until they become leather. Men in the streets tramp about in heavy clogs; some have high boots, while others have their legs tightly bound in matting to protect them from the damp and dirt in which they work. The whole atmosphere of the place is redolent of tan and of the more unpleasant smell of market hides.

The London manufacturing business used to be far larger than it is at present; but rents have risen and tan-yards have given way to warehouses or dwellings; thus provincial tanneries have taken the lead, and whether for heavy, medium, or light leather, Bermondsey has lost her supremacy. In London, however, a little of everything is done, and it is enough, taking all together, to give the tone to the markets of the world. Moreover, London is still the central exchange for East Indian and Australian tannages, and buyers from all parts compete at the periodic sales held in Mincing Lane, where in the course of the year millions of skins are put up at auction.

Heavy leather.—The manufacture of heavy or medium leather, as carried on in Bermondsey, may be divided into two stages—tanning and currying. The manufacture of the lighter kinds is called leather dressing.

By tanning the raw hide is turned into leather; and by currying, this leather, being treated with fatty matter, is rendered soft and waterproof. The tanner receives the hides fresh from the London slaughter-houses, or salted or sun-dried from the importers' wharves. These hides are unhaired, and washed and scraped until they are pure fibre and gelatine, when they are placed in pits containing tannic extract, and the result is leather.

In every tan-yard there are three distinct divisions—the beam-house, the pits, and the shed. The pits are of two kinds: first, for liming; second, for tanning. In the beam-house, the raw hide is treated after liming and before tanning, and the men employed are known as unhairers and fleshers. The men who "work in the limes" are called jobbers, and it is their duty to soak and handle the hides in pits containing a solution of lime till the skin swells, the pores open, and the hair is loosened ready for the operations of the unhairer. After the hair has been rubbed or scraped off, the hides go back into lime and are again soaked and "handled," that is, pulled out and left to drain and then put back into the pit, which has meanwhile been well "plunged," or stirred with a sort of wooden rake. Finally, when they are sufficiently swollen with lime they are ready for fleshing, or the removal, with a special two-handled knife, of the fleshy membrane that adheres to the flayed pelt. These men and the unhairers are called beam-men, and the place in which they work the beam-house, because they work the hides on rounded beams placed in an inclined position rising from the ground to the man's stomach. The beam for unhairing is made of wood, and that for fleshing of iron. The workman leans over and pushes the knife downwards from him, driving the hair or flesh before it. The unhairer works with a blunt knife, while that of the flesher is sharp. There is another process, which consists of shaving, done in the same manner with a very sharp knife. This is called "frizing," and applies to light skins only; it has been partly superseded by splitting and by machine shaving.

Unhairing can be quickly learnt, but fleshing requires considerable practice and frizing great skill. Men generally begin as unhairers and work up to the position of fleshers. The conditions of work in these departments are not very pleasant; the men must always stand in the damp. Lime jobbers wear booted clogs and leggings, while the beam-men besides these use a stout leather apron, a very useful and necessary precaution, as, in reaching over, their body is pressed against the upper portion of the wet limey hide as it lies upon the beam.

Lime jobbers, at $4\frac{1}{2}d$ or $5d$ per hour, earn from 25s to 30s a week throughout the year, often working over-time. Beam-men all work on piece, and earn from 20s in slack to 50s in busy times. This may possibly yield 30s a week on the average—rather more for the fleshers, whose wages will hardly fall so low as 20s, and rather less for the unhairers, who at best will scarcely make as much as 50s.

There are no particular seasons. One yard is often busy while another is slack. Frost will at times stop work.

The larger hides are not dealt with in one piece, but are cut up in various ways before the process we have been describing has begun. This is partly for convenience in handling, but also because different portions—the butt, the belly, &c.—make altogether different leather, and must undergo distinct methods of treatment. So far as our description has yet gone, there is little if any difference, but after the beam-men have done their work, the hides, or portions of hides, are sorted into various classes. Butts for heavy leather go straight to the tanning pits, but other sorts, needing to be completely freed from lime, go through a process usually called bating, but sometimes also known by other names. It consists of soaking the hides in an unsavoury bath, in which the fibre softens and is purged of lime and any grease or filth which remains in the pores of the skin. To complete this process the hide or skin is scudded or scraped over with a sort of knife, the blade or edge of which is of smooth slate or stone, and some-times of glass.

The hides being now placed in the tan-pits are there impregnated with a gradually strengthened tan, by being moved from pit to pit; and at each change of pit, if not oftener, they are laid in heaps to drain. Much physical strength is needed for this "drawing" of the pits, and with it a particular knack or jerk in hooking, lifting, and throwing the hides. The period during which the hides remain in tan varies from three to twelve or fifteen months. Science continually tries to shorten the process and succeeds in doing so, but hitherto it has always been at the cost of durability in the leather.

The men in this department earn 23s or 24s for sixty hours' work. With overtime, which will commonly be five hours extra per week, they will earn rather more, and if on piece may make as much as 32s.

Some hides when half tanned are put through a machine, which cuts or splits them into two halves of such substances as may be required, or the thickness of the hide afford. Split hides are used wherever lightness and cheapness are required, and Bermondsey is famous for their production. There are four men to each splitting machine, of whom the senior and responsible man receives 2d a hide, and earns from 45s to 50s ; the second man has about 28s, and the others, whose business it is to pull the hides through from the reverse side of the machine, will earn 24s to 26s for a full week, varying according to the amount of work done.

The unsplit hides when fully tanned pass into the hands of the shed-men, who, with the aid of rather modern machinery, or in old-fashioned ways by hand, clean, strike out, and, by rolling, rapping, or rubbing, give a smooth and polished surface to the leather, which is then ready for the currier. Split hides, and those which, originally thin, have been shaved to a light substance, are not finished for the currier, but are merely smoothed out ; for this men are paid 4½d and 5d an hour, and earn throughout the year 26s or 28s a week. Their hours are long because they often must work on Sundays. The regular shed-men, engaged in finishing heavy leather,

commonly earn from 30s to 35s, but the wages paid vary a
good deal, and are affected by overtime, which in some
factories is systematic, and by piece-work payment.

The men learn their business as they can. They begin
as labourers in each department, and take such opportunities as offer of learning the more skilled work. In the
beam-house the lime jobber helps the shavers and unhairers
when they are busy, or even pays them to teach him their
craft. In the yard among the pits, as we have said, no
skill is needed, beyond a knack in tossing the skins into
. packs to drain. The work is heavy, and the fine physique
of the men at once attracts attention.

Light Leather.—In light, as opposed to heavy leather,
labour is the principal item in the cost of the finished
article. Light leather goods, sometimes split and sometimes not, are either tanned much in the same way as heavy
leather, or dressed in sumac, or with oil (as wash-leather),
or cured in alum and salt. Such leather is used for black
and yellow boots, chair coverings, bookbindings, gloves,
hat leather, and bag linings, pocket-books, and a thousand
minor purposes, and the object aimed at is to finish skins
in such a way that they shall be pleasant both to look at
and to handle, and even to smell. For glove leather the
skins are stuffed with yolk of egg, and many strange
substances are used in the effort to produce soft leather.
They are then dyed, and finally shaved or ground down
to the desired thickness. Glove leather, which is very fine,
will not stand shaving, and is, therefore, "grounded," or
scraped with a knife and rubbed with an emery block.
For many purposes splitting is resorted to; of the two
halves, the outer or grain side is used to make imitation
morocco, and the inner or flesh side to make wash or
so-called "chamois" leather.

It is very difficult to arrive at any exact estimate of the
men's earnings, for there is a system of piece-mastership
prevailing in Bermondsey which is entirely confined to

light leather factories; in heavy leather tanneries it has apparently no counterpart.

A master will go to some responsible man and give him a certain number of skins, the work to be done at an agreed price and by a certain time, and to be of a given quality; and in some cases, as we have heard, a commission will be paid on every shilling saved off the sum at which a master is willing to give the goods out. This man is then at liberty to employ whom he likes, on the master's premises, either on day or piece, and at the lowest rates for which he can get the work done. This system is open to some abuse, and leads to very great sub-division of work. 24s to 26s seems to be the general wage paid by the sub-contractor to the men whom he employs. A time worker under this arrangement leaves the moment his work is done. " Brass me up first, and then I'll go," is the phrase for asking for payment before leaving.

Glazers, *i.e.* those who put the gloss on to the leather, get 32s or 33s for a week, varying between fifty-seven and sixty hours. Shavers are more highly paid, as their work is very responsible. They have a strong trade society, and a monopoly of the better men, so that they can command their prices. Payment is by piece, and they would seem to make an average of 40s throughout the year. However, as there are, roughly, three times as many shavers as there are members of the Society, there may be many who earn considerably less.

In Persian leather dressing, which consists in preparing hard, tanned skins, used for cheap boot and shoe linings, glacé kid, &c., more machinery is employed than in the other light leather departments. There is also a somewhat unhealthy process for finishing the leather known as "fluffing," the object of which is to make the leather softer, and to partly shave it anew and smooth the surface, back or front, by pressing it on the flesh side against a rapidly revolving emery wheel. The leather flies off in fluff and is inhaled. Dust extractors are usually arranged to minimise this risk. The work requires no particular skill, and ordinary wages are paid for it.

Some yards in the light leather trade open at 6, others at 7 or 8. There is no rule, and piece-workers may come in to work when they please. In a large factory each department has a different season, according to the purpose for which the leather is produced: for boots and shoes the spring and summer, for furniture and bookbinding the autumn and winter, for hat linings the spring, and so on. Yet there is little shifting from one department to another; a skilled man in his own department would be unskilled in any other. All through the trade overtime is frequent, either because of seasonal press of work, or because the piece master has undertaken more than can otherwise be accomplished by the men he has, or prefers to employ, in the time agreed.

CURRYING.

Heavy leather which must be made soft and pliable is sent from the tanner to the currier. As a rule it is not rolled, and leaves the tanner in the form known as " dressing leather." Some master curriers make a speciality of coach and harness work, and others of currying boot leather, or mill-band, leather hose, and valve making. Formerly it was the duty of a journeyman currier to receive a dressing hide, and then to attend to every process of currying himself. Now there is greater sub-division, owing to the introduction of machinery, especially among mill-band makers.

Of all the departments coach work is the most regular and the best paid, and the best work is said to be done in London.

The journeyman currier is a highly skilled workman. His business is to reduce a hide to the required thickness all over by shaving it with a sharp two-handled knife. He works much in the same way as a flesher, but he shaves a hide after instead of before tanning, his knife is straight instead of curved, and has the edge turned, and he stands over his hide at a beam which is square-faced and nearly upright, instead of being slanting and round.

The majority of these men are piece workers, and earnings in a busy season vary from 45s for a good man to 36s for one who is less proficient. Shoe work is rather less well paid, but is not a large London industry, since only about fifty or sixty men are employed in this branch. Piece prices are partially regulated by an elaborate price-list of the Curriers' Trades Union, which sets a minimum wage for time-work at 45s for men on coach work, and 40s for those on boot work. These prices seem to be rather more than the men actually get, but in any case a man in regular work can make good wages, and 35s to 40s was given by a master as a fair weekly average for a steady man doing a full week's work, varying from forty-eight to fifty-four hours.

A master currier also employs table-men and machine-men.

The machine-men, generally day workers, earn 35s, and have to attend to the machines for scouring the hides. Table-men take the hides that have been shaved, and press them out over large mahogany or marble tables, in order to make the surface quite smooth. It is hard work and requires much practice to do well. They earn from 26s to 30s—more often it is 30s—as a full week's wage.

After being treated in these various ways, the hides are "stuffed" or covered over with grease and hung up until they have absorbed a sufficient amount, when they are ready for the buyer.

Mill-band makers employ their own curriers, and also men as sewers to join the different lengths which go to make mill-bands. These sewers are generally piece workers, and are those who are most uncertain of regular employment. The amount of work available varies very much. A machine-sewer earning on piece 50s to 60s in a

busy week, will get but 26s to 30s when slack, and there is
the same variation among hand-sewers.

Patent Leather.—Those hides which must be japanned for
carriage splash-boards and all the various uses of patent
leather, are simply scoured, shaved, and dried, and stuffed
with cod-oil by the currier. They are then sent to the
japanner.

Of journeymen japanners and enamellers there are
probably less than one hundred in London, nearly all of
whom belong to their trade society. They take the leather
from the currier and nail it on boards, which are then put
into an oven. When the leather is thoroughly dry, the
enamel is spread by means of a certain tool called a sleaker,
which ensures a regular thickness. With every man there
is a boy, who works behind him, and has to smooth the
surface with his hand and make it even. The leather,
which has been hardened by the heat of the ovens, is then
hung over pits of damp tan where it absorbs the moisture,
and when sufficiently "nourished" is returned to the
currier.

All work is piece-work and the men count on making an
average of 40s per week throughout the year.

Seasons.

Curriers are busy in the coach department, where
leather is prepared for the hoods of Victorias and large
open carriages, from January until June, in anticipation of
the demand during the London season; and for saddlery
in June and August; while for harness leather there is
a pretty regular demand throughout the year since the
custom of donning new harness on May Day has died out.
Japanners are busiest in spring and summer and often
slack in winter. The men, however, do not turn to anything else; they are given 12s per week by their Society
when out of work, and prefer to wait until trade is
brisk again.

Habits.

The general charge against men employed in tanneries, that they drink to excess, would seem to be borne out by the appearance of the neighbourhood. In every street and at every corner there is fresh temptation to " turn in and take a glass," and the work is trying—damp and cold out of doors, while indoors there may be rapid alternation between steam-heating and an icy wind blowing through the open lattices of the drying sheds. Piece workers are generally free to slip out when they please, and the wants of others are catered for by the visits of a man with a can of beer at stated times.

Trade has been much depressed this year (1893) by financial troubles in America and Australia. But hides and skins have been so cheap that employers have not been afraid to increase their stocks, and the men have not suffered much.

FELLMONGERING.

This work consists of getting the wool off the sheep-skin, so as to leave the pelt. The skins are soaked and washed and covered on the flesh side with slacked lime, and folded or piled till the pores enlarge and loosen the wool. The men are paid for this work 22s to 26s. The method of pulling the wool depends on its length. If long, it is plucked off by hand and roughly sorted at the same time— different classes being thrown into different boxes. If short, it is rubbed off upon a beam with the same kind of knife used in unhairing hides, and is then not sorted. The pulled wool is carried to the stoves—heated rooms, with perforated floors—or spread to dry in a current of cold air. All this is piece-work, and the men employed earn from 24s to 40s, averaging fully 30s. The pelts go to the leather-dresser.

FUR-SKIN DRESSERS AND FURRIERS.

London is the central mart in Europe for seal-skins, and vies with any as a depôt for all other furs. Buyers of all nations attend the sales, and from our metropolis the skins are distributed to all parts. Hence London starts with a slight initial advantage.

The furriers buy the skins at the sales, and send them to be dressed and dyed according to order by the fur dressers, who make these operations their special business.

The preparation of seal-skins is very elaborate. They are blubbered, or rubbed over with a blunt knife, and washed to free them of their natural grease, and allowed to dry; then soaked and laid on a hot floor, so that the fur only is dried, preparatory to getting rid of the long hairs, which are individually removed. After this they are fully dried, and then softened and dressed by the working in of other grease. Small skins of all kinds are "tubbed," that is, when they have been greased they are thrown into large tubs in which a man treads on them with bare feet until they are completely cured. It is a curious sight, on entering a room, to see a row of these tubs each with its Jack-in-the box bobbing up and down. Every man is naked except for a vest, and a rough cloth which is tied round his waist and attached to the rim of his barrel. With hands resting on either ledge up and down he treads, and earns 20s to 25s piece-work. Skins cured by this process are said to be softer and silkier. It is disagreeable work and undertaken mostly by foreigners.

The pelt side of all fur skins is smoothed by shaving; the hair side of the seal-skin is dyed; and so finally the skins are ready for the furrier.

Unhairers or blubberers work from 8 to 7, with intervals for meals. The shavers' hours often fall later, as they follow up the other men, and they may keep on till 10 or 11 o'clock in order to complete the day's work. The dyers obtain the most regular work, and the secrets of the trade are confined to this department. Employers do not like men who have learnt anything of these secrets to go elsewhere, and so employment is constant. They are day workers, and while the head men will receive as much as £5 per week, those under them, who have merely to obey their orders, can be sure of 24s to 28s. A few were seen who had only made 18s per week, but this was considered to be exceptionally low. For the other men all the work is on piece, and during the busy season a good deal of money can be made, 50s being a fair average week's wages. But the busy season only lasts four or five months, and during the rest of the year, or a large part of it, the men are "out of work"—that is, they support themselves as best they may. Their slack time falls in spring and summer, and they may perhaps get work as builders' or painters' labourers, or take a turn with a coster's barrow. In their own trade the skill required is not very great, and the trade is overcrowded, high wages even for so short a time being attractive. The union does what it can to limit apprentices, but its main task has been to fix the prices for dressing, and every process for every kind of skin, from a giraffe to a mouse, has its price.

There are only four or five large factories in the trade. The rest of the work is done by small men—German Jews for the most part—who bring over "greeners" for the busy season, paying them 8s or 10s a week, and providing food and beds, which are often the tables and forms in the workshop where they work all day. These men are, of course, outside the union rules.

As soon as the work of the fur-dresser is completed, the furriers receive back their furs, and themselves employ cutters and nailers, who are men; and sewers, machinists, liners and finishers, who are women.*

Cutters of the first class earn £5 or even £7 a week, and

* See chapter on Women's Work by Miss Collet. Vol. IV.

have constant work.　The second class, £3 to £5; the third class, £1 to £3.　They are almost invariably Germans, and are the best paid of any employed in this industry.　But they suffer in health from the fur, which gets into their eyes and lungs, so that they are not long-lived, and generally past work at fifty.　These men become chamber-masters, and their former employers are glad to give them work. They employ their own families to do the sewing and finishing.　In this way it becomes a family industry, in which a man and his wife and his daughters—or his sisters and his cousins and his aunts—all find a place.　Sewers, if quick workers, can in busy times make 15s, or even more, when using a machine.　Piece-work is the rule in the East End; and earnings vary with capacity.　One worker we have seen could barely make 8s, working very long hours, but admitted that she was slow, and that a nimble-fingered woman at her side drew 15s in a busy week.　The work is hard, and to some extent unhealthy.

Owing to Behring Sea difficulties there has been less employment to be had this year (1893) than previously, and machinery is gradually ousting the hand-sewers.

HATTERS' FURS.

A hatter's furrier buys hare and rabbit skins from collectors all over the country, or bids in the Mincing Lane auctions for those imported from Australia or elsewhere. The skins have to be opened and stretched, and the strong hairs pulled out, so as to leave only the fine fur—finer than silk, and known in the trade as wool—which, shorn from the pelt and assorted according to quality, is sold to hat manufacturers, and used by them in the making of felt.

The work is mostly done in Southwark, in the neighbourhood of the Marshalsea Road, and the bulk of those employed are women.　There are about eight firms engaged in the trade, giving work to from eight hundred to twelve hundred persons, according as business may be brisk or slack. Of these only about one hundred are men.

All the men have regular work throughout the year, and are mostly on day-work, earning 24s to 28s a week. They attend, amongst other things, to a necessary chemical process called carrotting, which makes the fur "felt" more easily.

The women are by no means so regularly employed, partly from the nature of the work, and partly from the character of those who take it up. Fur-pullers form the majority, and many of them are married women with husbands in casual employ, and, both as to hours and days, they come and go as they will.

The factories open at 8.30, but the work is given out over night, and the masters do not mind at what hour the women arrive. They are, of course, paid by piece. This suits a married woman, who can then see her husband out of the house, if not to work, and the children safe in the street, if not to school, before she turns the key in the door and repairs to the factory. Amongst women of this class manners are rough and tongues coarse, and girls who are content, or allowed, to work alongside of them are of the lowest class—not necessarily bad, by any means, but rather free in behaviour and language.

In the factories they sit in long double rows with a pile of skins before them. They bend over their task, taking the skin in the left hand and holding it fast between their knees, while with the right hand they grasp the long hairs between the edge of a blunt knife and their thumb, protected by a rubber finger-stall, and then with a slight wrench extract the hairs one by one. The pulled hairs fly about, and the air is filled with floating particles of fluff, which cover and coat the hair and face and clothes of the women in a way that is very picturesque. It is, however, horrid stuff to breathe, and, being altogether an unhealthy industry, a natural disinclination to pursue it excepting when money is absolutely necessary for food or rent is not surprising. It is said that respirators, if the women could be persuaded to use them, would become clogged with the particles which would "felt" under the influence of the breath.

The wages do not differ from those which women and girls seem almost invariably to receive. A fairly quick worker will make 10s for a whole week, a fast worker something more; but to earn 6s or even 4s is far more usual, by reason of slowness, dawdling, or lost time.

Those who work the machines for clipping the fur from the pelt are rather a better class, have more regular employment, and are better paid. They are day wage earners, but have to perform a certain task. They earn 12s to 15s per week. Sorters also are day workers of a superior class.

Winter is busier than summer. This is due rather to the supply of labour than to the demand for goods. The work, disagreeable at best, is unendurable in hot weather, and when hop or fruit-picking in the country offers as an alternative, it is gladly accepted.

There was once (1891) a union of fur-pullers, but the untutored habits of its members (there are many in the trade who can neither read nor write) were such that it could not be kept together, and so it failed. There are a few women who do pulling in their own homes; nothing can be said in favour of this practice, and only pity felt for those who find themselves compelled by necessity to adopt this means of keeping body and soul together.

PORTMANTEAUX AND TRUNKS.

This work is carried on in the City and West End. In the West End it is all done by hand and by men, except the silk and stuff linings for bags, and one man will take a portmanteau or bag and finish it throughout; whereas, in the City, women and boys help in the lighter parts of the work, and machines are used to do straight sewing.

Retailers are hardly ever themselves manufacturers, they only undertake repairs on their own premises.

The best journeymen work for the wholesale makers only, and the names which appear stamped on the bags and portmanteaux are, in most cases, not those of the makers, but of the retailers.

Fitted and leather-lined case makers are the most skilful among the workmen, and are known in the trade as the "lords." Work is both on time and piece, but more often the latter. On time a good man will earn 38s to 45s for a week of fifty-four hours, while on piece, working the same number of hours, he will make from 45s to 50s. In this branch the men must be able to suit their work to a buyer's fancy. They also make the best solid leather portmanteaux.

Dress-basket makers, and those who make the ordinary black portmanteaux of covered mill-board, go by the name of "the commons." Among them good men earn 35s to 38s, and second-rate hands 25s, generally on piece. In the busy summer months, when people travel or prepare to travel, earnings are rather higher, and some overtime is worked; on an average men would add about one day a week to their usual time for about two months—but, *en revanche,* there is often short time from October to March, except for those engaged on fitted cases, for which Christmas presents make a winter demand. This is a trade which was once noted for its hard drinkers, but of late years there has been some improvement.

FANCY-LEATHER WORKERS AND POCKET-BOOK MAKERS.

Under this heading are included dressing, Gladstone, and all kinds of leather-bag makers besides the pocket-book makers who make purses, bag-fittings, despatch boxes, blotters, note books, card cases, &c. The manufacture of these articles forms a large and increasing industry in London, which is the chief centre of the trade, and gives employment not only to a great number of males, estimated at about seven hundred, but also to nearly as many women and boys, for deftness of finger and neatness is required more than physical strength, especially in small work.

Dressing-bag makers are the most skilled men, and earn the highest wages. They are nearly always on time, and fair workmen need seldom be out of employment. They shift so little that the majority of the men are said to be brought up and to remain in one shop all their lives. Two or three men generally work together on one bag, earning 26s to 42s each for the full week of fifty-four hours.

In Gladstone-bag making the work is sub-divided among men, women, and boys as follows :—(1) The cutter who cuts the leather to shape; (2) the machinist who joins the pieces together, and (3) the framer who fixes them roughly on the frame and then hands them to the stitchers and liners, who are women, while a boy is generally given the handle to make. They are all time workers. Cutters earning 30s; framers, 28s to 34s; good machinists, 16s to 25s; good stitchers, 12s to 14s; and liners about 15s, though the very best will make as much as 18s or £1. Making handles, a youth can earn 16s, while in some shops there is enough work to employ one skilled man at 30s on this job alone.

The Fancy Leather Workers' Union, which admits men only, have put forward a minimum scale of wages which the members try to enforce, and with fair success, except in the lower skilled branches of the trade. Their rate for best bag hands is 34s; for cutters, 30s; for rivetters, framers, stiffeners, and preparers, 28s; for pocket-book makers, 33s; and case makers, 30s. Second-rate men earn anything from 20s to 30s, and the work is so much sub-divided, and so many boys are employed, that it is difficult to establish any standard rate for men.

From a return which the Society was good enough to send us, in May, 1894, for sixteen firms in London, employing 336 males and 177 females, it is to be remarked that 194 were society men, who were presumably earning at least the

minimum rates given above; while 142 males and the 177
females already mentioned were outside the Society, and
were distributed as follows :—

Men ...	52	Bag-makers.
	6	Case-makers.
	37	Pocket-book makers.
Improvers or Apprentices...	33	Bag-makers.
	2	Case-makers.
	12	Pocket-book makers.
	142	**Males.**
Female machinists...	46	Bag.
	5	Pocket-book.
Female stitchers and liners	91	Bag.
	2	Case.
	33	Pocket-book.
	177	**Females.**

No return was made as to wages, and it seems probable
that the rates given above are higher than those usually
earned. Some work is taken home, and the family
helps. A few retailers are also manufacturers, but the
majority are not, and many of the wholesale makers are
foreigners. Gladstone, or "empty," bag work has the
same busy season as portmanteaux, but for pocket-book
makers June to Christmas is the busy season, and November
the busiest month in the year, when overtime is very
common, and though not now so frequently worked as
formerly, as much as ten hours extra (in the week) is not
unusual. On the other hand, after Christmas things are
very slack, and men, women, and boys often get no work
at all, and are glad enough to work short time.

In the cheaper class of goods there is great competition
from abroad, but good work holds its own, and has not yet
been touched by foreign makers, although the men fear
that owing to the decay of the apprenticeship system and
the great sub-division which obtains at present, it will not
for long be possible to produce the very best, and the
reputation of English goods will suffer.

TRADES UNIONS.

The men in these industries are organized as follows:—

Numbers in the London Trade (Census 1891).		Name of Trade Society.	Membership in London.		Remarks.
Total.	Of whom are employed males over 20.		In each Society.	In each Division.	
8288	5027	London United Patent Leather Dressers' Society (1866).	72		Out of work, Sick, Death Benefits. Equal number of masters and men settle disputes. Apprentices limited. Union do not work with non-union men.
		The Mutual Society of Curriers (1891).	17		Out of work pay only.
		United Society of Journeymen Curriers of Great Britain and Ireland (over 100 years).	242		The usual Benefits and Old Age Pension, and help in need. Relations good. Union and non-union men do not work together. 1080 members in Great Britain.
		Spanish and Morocco Leather Finishers' Society (No. 1).	120		These are all small and exclusive societies, allowing only the most skilled to belong. Their members make good money, and are willing to work long hours when occasion offers. The Light Leather Shavers enforce apprenticeship, five to seven years.
		London New Friendly Society of Spanish and Morocco Leather Finishers (No. 2) (1868).	101	1372	
		Light Leather Shavers' Trade Society (1800).	80		
		London Society of Grounders (1861).	133		
		London Portmanteau and Trunk Makers' Society (1866).	140		The usual Benefits given and help when in special need. Relations fair. Union and non-union men work together.
		Pocket-book and Fancy-leather Case Makers' Society (1834).	79		
		Amalgamated Trade Society of Fancy Leather Workers.	268		
		Persian Leather Dressers' Society (1888).	120		
8288	5027	(Carried forward)		1372	

Numbers in the London Trade (Census 1891).		Name of Trade Society.	Membership in London.		Remarks.
Total.	Of whom are employed males over 20.		In each Society.	In each Division.	
8288	5027	(Brought forward)		1372	There are very few of them now (1894). Only one firm makes parchment in London. Society has removed to Mitcham.
75	51	The United Vellum and Parchment Makers of Great Britain.	79	79	
6212	2213	The London Society of Skinners (1854).	145	665	Out of work and Strike Benefits.
		Journeymen Furriers' London Trade Union (1889).	150		Out of work and Strike Benefits. Relations with masters friendly. Rules in German and English.
		The Fur Skin Dressers' Union (1889).	370		Death levy only; hardly recognized by the masters.
1164	990	The United Tanners' Society (1863).	40	40	Out of work Benefit only. Union work with non-union men. 72 in Society altogether.
15,739	8281			2156	

Thus (excluding the parchment makers) out of a total of 8230 employed males over twenty, 2077 are organized, or 25 per cent.

There are, in addition, two societies which are exclusively for benefit purposes.

(1) The Spanish Leather Dressers' Benefit Society (f. 1801), with 120 members drawn from every section of the trade.

(2) The Pocket-book and Leather-case Makers' Pension Societies.

The subscriptions to the trade societies range from 3d to 1s 6d per week, and benefits vary with the amount of subscription. Some societies are too poor to offer anything except moral support, while others give 12s or even 16s per week out of work pay for periods varying between ten and twenty-six weeks. One (the Curriers) offers pay for as

long a time as a year, but this is exceptional. Sick benefit
is generally at the same rate as out of work pay. Strike
pay is rather more, while for death money anything
between £3 and £10 is given (generally helped by a special
levy), and half the sum on the death of a member's wife.
A few offer something extra, e.g. the Curriers give a
limited number of pensions to those over sixty, and help
members to emigrate; they also lend money for boots, and
give tramp allowance; while the Patent Leather Dressers
make up the money of those in partial work to 14s if still
entitled to full benefit, and the Leather-case Makers give
something for loss of tools by fire.

Although the industries considered in this section do
not give a large percentage of members of trade societies,
since only 25 per cent. are organized; still, portions of
the trade form marked exceptions, e.g. the Patent Leather
Dressers and Spanish and Morocco Leather Dressers claim
very nearly all those working in these two branches as
actual members.

In the heavy leather industry there have been attempts
at organization, but without success, and there appears to
be a great want of cohesion among those employed in this
branch. In 1890 a society called the "Amalgamated
Leather Trades Union" was started, but in spite of a
membership of 2400 it failed in 1892, owing to internal
dissensions. In the light leather portion, on the other
hand, there are plenty of trade societies, but they are
small and so exclusive that their influence outside their
own particular clique is insignificant. Even when the
men meet on common ground to pay in their subscriptions
to the Spanish Leather Dressers' Benefit Society, they are
said always to separate and form small groups of those
employed in their own particular branches. Thus finishers
congregate and drink a friendly glass with finishers, and
shavers with shavers, &c., and it is rare to see any
intermingling of the two.

Wages Statistics.

Of the 8281 adult workmen we have wages returns for 665, employed by twenty-one firms, as under :—

Leather manufacturers	8 ⎫	= 21 firms, usually employing
Curriers and finishers	3 ⎪	945 persons, of whom 762 are
Fellmonger	1 ⎪	adult males, but of these 97
Mill-band and hose makers.........	2 ⎪	belong to other sections, as
Parchment and vellum	1 ⎬	felt - makers, hair workers,
· Furriers	2 ⎪	locksmiths, carpenters, brass
Portmanteau and trunk makers...	2 ⎪	finishers, engineers, stokers,
Bag-frame makers ·....................	2 ⎭	carmen, and watchmen.

The earnings of these men in an average week are as follows :—

Below 20s ....79, or 12 per cent.	⎫		
20s to 25s............101 „ 15 „	⎬	under 30s, 44 per cent.	
25s „ 30s............115 „ 17 „	⎭		
30s „ 35s............111 „ 17 „	⎫		
35s „ 40s............ 73 „ 11 „	⎬	30s and over, 56 per cent.	
40s „ 45s............101 „ 15 „	⎪		
45s and upwards... 85 „ 13 „	⎭		

665 „ 100 „

Our figures may be compared with returns made to the Board of Trade in 1886 by twenty-five firms employing 1073 persons, of whom 437 were male adults belonging to this section.

	−20s.	20s—	25s—	30s—	35s—	40s—	45s—
Our returns	12 %	15 %	17 %	17 %	11 %	15 %	13 %
		44 %			56 %		
Board of Trade returns	1 %	23 %	8 %	13 %	13 %	27 %	15 %
		32 %			68 %		

The difference between the two returns is mainly accounted for by the difference in method. The 12 per cent. in our return who took less than 20s did not, we may suppose, work the whole week, and must be added to those taking 20s to 25s to compare with the Board of Trade returns. Otherwise the proportion at each rate compares as closely as could be expected for small samples from such various trades.

The difference in numbers employed in busy and slack weeks is less than 10 per cent. amongst leather workers, but cannot be stated exactly, as part of the work is given out in block to one man who shares it with others, of whose number there is no exact record. Of these men no notice is taken in our returns. We, however, know that the total amount paid in this way by one firm was £321 in a busy week, as compared to £196 in a slack week. The amount earned falls much more than the numbers employed. In the Board of Trade returns the average earnings are as 33s to 22s, while the numbers employed are as 100 to 86.

In portmanteau and trunk making it is as 42s to 28s, while the numbers vary only from 100 to 94—showing an extreme degree of irregularity in the amounts earned, with comparative steadiness in the numbers employed.

From seven firms we have more elaborate particulars, as follows :—

Leather Trades—Earnings and Hours Worked—Adult Males.

		Busy Week.				Slack Week.			
Rate fo Pay.		Number of Men.	Average.			Number of Men.	Average.		
			Wages	Hours.	Rates.		Wages	Hours.	Rates.
			s. d.		d.		s. d.		d.
Time-work.	Under 5d per hour	105	21 2	60	4¼	89	16 8	44¼	4¼
	5d to 6d ,,	59	27 4	58½	5¾	58	24 6	51¼	5¾
	6d to 8d ,,	20	37 7	64	7	23	29 3	52½	6¾
	Over 8d ,,	4	47 6	57	10	4	43 0	51½	10
	Total Time-work	188	—	—	—	174	—	—	—
Piece-work.	Under 15s per week	2	14 0	—	—	6	12 4	—	—
	,, 20s ,,	4	17 0	—	—	15	17 3	—	—
	,, 25s ,,	9	21 8	—	—	15	21 8	—	—
	,. 30s ,,	10	27 1	—	—	25	27 2	—	—
	,, 40s ,,	47	3311	—	—	35	33 9	—	—
	40s and upwards	61	49 9	—	—	24	44 9	—	—
	Total Piece-work	133	—	—	—	120	—	—	—

This return does not give a complete account of piece-work, as it omits the cases already alluded to in which one man receives the whole pay for work shared by him with several. So far as the figures go they show that such piece workers as have work at all, earn nearly as much money in slack as in busy times, and that time workers fall off more in the amount earned than in numbers, there being a great reduction in the hours worked.

In each branch of these industries a proportion of those employed earn labourer's wages, and may average less than 25s a week. Amongst tanners there are unhairers and yardmen; amongst fellmongers there are those who soak and pile the skins; amongst fur-skin dressers there are tubbers and pelt-side men and the undermen dyers; and amongst portmanteau makers and fancy-leather workers there are second-rate hands employed on black leather.

Our returns include only fifty women and girls; of these few make less than 10s, and an unusually large proportion make over 20s a week. The Board of Trade returns confirm these good rates of pay for a limited number of women, employed in the manufacture of leather and leather goods, to which our returns mostly apply. But in this section it is as furriers and hatter's furriers that most of the females work; of these the Board of Trade returns include no less than one thousand, of whom the largest proportion are reported as earning 8s or 9s a week.

The earnings of 140 lads and boys in our returns are evenly distributed from 5s to 20s a week. The Board of Trade returns range from 8s to 15s, the largest number receiving 13s to 15s.

Social Condition.

In these trades, 8281 adult men are employed, and about 6000 come under social classification as heads of families.

According to the small sample provided by our wages returns, 27 per cent. of those employed earn less than 25*s* a week; whereas 39 per cent. live under crowded conditions. Next, 34 per cent. earn from 25*s* to 35*s*, as compared to 32 per cent. who live in small tenements, but less than two persons to each room; and finally, 39 per cent. earn over 35*s* and compare with 29 per cent. of the central class. It is to be remembered that these trades are carried on in parts of London where crowding is not a certain test of want of means.

Comparison of Earnings with Style of Life (Leather, &c.).

Earnings as returned.	Classification of Population.
Under 20s... 79, or 12 per cent.	3 or more in each room, 3000, or 10 per cent.
20s to 25s...101 ,, 15 ,,	2 to 3 ,, 9000 ,, 29 ,,
25s ,, 30s...115 ,, 17 ,,	1 ,, 2 ,, 9500 ,, 32 ,,
30s ,, 35s...111 ,, 17 ,,	Less than 1 ,,
35s ,, 40s... 73 ,, 11 ,,	More than 4 rooms
40s ,, 45s...101 ,, 15 ,,	4 or more persons to 9000 ,, 29 ,,
45s and over 85 ,, 13 ,,	1 servant
665 ,, 100 ,,	30,500 ,, 100 ,,
	Families of women and of Employers and servants ... 7800
	38,300

Tanners, fellmongers, and leather-dressers mostly live in the immediate neighbourhood of their work in Bermondsey, where rents are high. A few have moved outwards in the direction of Rotherhithe, Camberwell, and the parish of St. George the Martyr in Southwark, but not beyond walking distance of the factory in which they work, and the majority go home both to breakfast and to dinner. Tea is more often brought in or obtained at the nearest coffee-house, and is sometimes dispensed with altogether in favour of beer. Furriers and portmanteau and case-makers, on the other hand, live in all parts of London, while fur-skin dressers are found mainly in the Whitechapel district. The majority of these live some way from their work, and therefore either bring their meals with them and eat them in the shop (when allowed), or go to a coffee tavern, where a better dinner and better accommodation is to be had than in a "public," so much so, that it will generally be preferred even by those who are fondest of their glass. Fur-pullers both live and work in Southwark.

Reference has already been made to the prevalence and causes of insobriety in tan-yards, and to this we must also add that complaints are made with respect to fur-skin dressers, who suffer much from the extreme heat of the drying rooms; to fur cutters, who are affected by the throat irritation caused by the dust and fluff which rises from the fur, and to portmanteau makers. There seems to be no special reason why these last should drink to excess, but, in spite of some improvement, the custom still prevails.

As to dress, those who have to move amongst or handle wet hides and skins wear leggings of leather, or a sack tied tightly round each leg, and clogs, and, instead of a coat, put on a "slop" or blouse made of tanned calico. A few also wear gloves, and beam-men, in addition to leggings, are cased in overalls. Furriers put on aprons and sometimes blouses, while portmanteau makers have aprons and a special pair of boots, since their habit of supporting and moving the portmanteaux with their feet is very detrimental to the toes and uppers of ordinary boots.

On the whole, there is a marked absence of prospering friendly organizations either within or without the work-shop. In large factories there is generally a sick club of some kind, but even then very few men belong to it. Those who provide for sickness prefer to join societies like the Odd Fellows or Foresters, not especially connected with the trade.

The wives of the less-regularly employed men all through these industries earn money, and one calculation given for the wives of those employed in tanneries put the proportion of those who help the family income by working in jam factories, charing, &c., as high as 50 per cent. In the same way, wives of men in the fur trade nearly always have to earn money to tide over the long periods of slackness, during which their husbands are out of work.

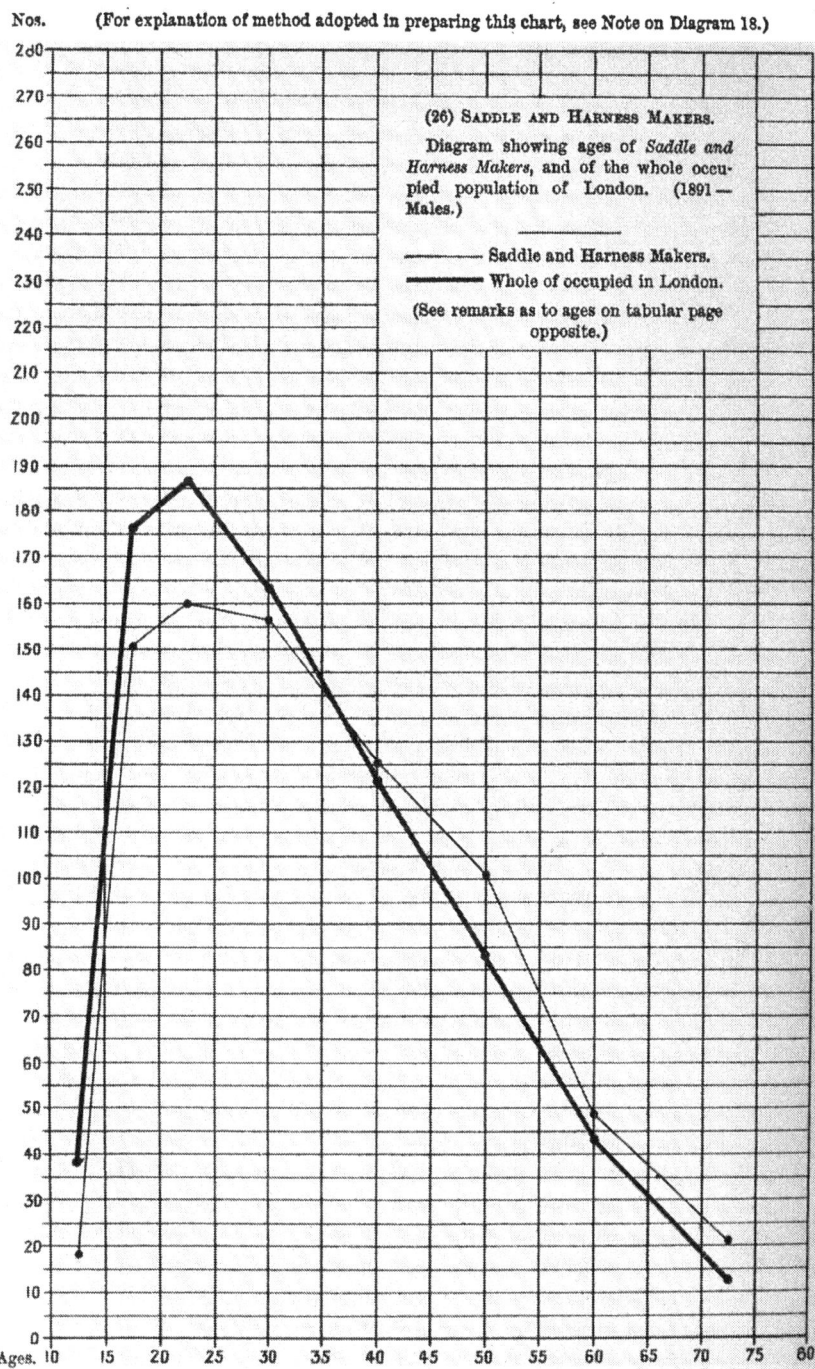

(26) SADDLE AND HARNESS MAKERS.

Diagram showing ages of *Saddle and Harness Makers*, and of the whole occupied population of London. (1891 — Males.)

——————— Saddle and Harness Makers.
━━━━━━━ Whole of occupied in London.

(See remarks as to ages on tabular page opposite.)

CHAPTER V.

SADDLERY, HARNESS, &c. (*Section* 26.)

Persons Represented.

Census Enumeration.

us Division, 1891.	Fe-males.	Males.				Total.
	All Ages.	—19	20—54	55—	
...ery........	182	494	2724	477	3877

greatest number of women employed ...tween 15 and 20. For women over 20 ... is a sudden drop until the ages 35-45 are ...d, when the number rises, showing that ...d women take to the work they have ...in their youth, which they are able to ...home. The diagram for males shows ...comparatively few boys are employed, ...at at fifty, and again in extreme old age, ...trades find work for considerably more ...he normal proportions.

Enumerated by Families.

| Sex ...... | Males .... | 2303 |
| | Females............. | 39 |

Birthplace { In London .... 42 % 993 / Out of London.. 58 % 1349 } Heads of Families, 2342.

Industrial Status .. { Employer...... 16 % 375 / Employed...... 71 % 1672 / Neither........ 13 % 295 }

TOTAL POPULATION CONCERNED.

	Heads of Families.	Others Occupied.	Unoccupied.	Servants.	Total.
Total	2342	2281	5827	128	10,378
Average in family...	1	·97	2·49	·05	4·31

DISTRIBUTION.

	N.	W. C.	S.	Total.
...	866	1138	1211	3877

DETAILS OF OCCUPATIONS

(FROM THE CENSUS DICTIONARY).

...r, harness, and whip-maker, including ...rse clothing, bit and bridle, cantle, ...lar, and chain-maker; embroiderer, ...rse milliner, lace-maker, pannel, pad, ...ns and rosette makers; chaise, hunting, ...d military saddles; saddle-trees, spring ...rs, spurs, stirrups, and military harness ...kers.

CLASSIFICATION.

Numbers living in Families.		%
3 or more to a room	1182	11·2
2 & under 3 ,,	2432	23·0
1 & under 2 ,,	2802	26·5
Less than 1 ,,		
More than 4 rooms }		
4 or more persons }	3855	36·4
to a servant ... }		
Less than 4 to 1 ser-		
vant, and 4 or		
more to 2 servts.	150	1·3
All others with 2 or		
more servants ..	29	·2
Servants	128	1·2
	10,578	100

	Inner.	Outer.	Together.
Crowded..	45 %	25 %	34 %
Not	55 %	75 %	66 %

DISTRIBUTION.

East ..	{ Inner 1528 / Outer 162 }	1690
North	{ Inner 796 / Outer 1589 }	2385
West..	{ Inner 376 / Outer 1591 }	1967
Central	Inner 978	978
South-	{ Inner 290 / East Outer 1516 }	1806
South-	{ Inner 727 / West Outer 1025 }	1752
		10,578

Inner 4695, or 44 %
Outer 5883, or 56 %

Status as to Employment (*according to Census Enumeration*).

Census Division (1891).	Employers.		Employed.			Neither Employer nor Employed.		Total.
			Males.		Females of all ages.			
	Males.	Females	Under 20.	Over 20.		Males.	Females	
...ry, Harness, and Whip-maker	411	13	494	2440	166	350	3	3877
TOTAL..........	424		3100			353		

Proportion of Employers to Employed–1 to 7.

SADDLE, HARNESS, AND WHIP-MAKERS.

The makers of gear for horses are essentially English workmen. There is absolutely no foreign competition, and much of the best work is done in London. The men employed are known as—

    (1) Brown saddlers.
    (2) Black saddlers.
    (3) Harness-makers.
    (4) Horse-clothing makers.
    (5) Saddle-tree makers.
    (6) Collar-makers.
    (7) Whip-makers.

The handiwork of all these men (assisted by a few women) can be bought at a saddler's.

The retail saddler is almost always himself a practical man. He works in his own shop, and his men work alongside of him. He is one of the few surviving illustrations of the mediæval workshop. His tools are simple and the work is good; there is none of the hurry, noise and bewilderment of machinery; and there is no mystery in production; for every passer by may look in through door or window and watch the men at work.

The West End manufacturer is generally an employer of brown saddlers and harness-makers only, and these work upon his premises. In the East End, which here means the neighbourhood of Finsbury, there are also women machinists who make horse clothing.

Saddle-trees, black saddles, horse collars, and whips are very seldom made upon saddlers' premises. They form separate industries, and are not carried on under the same roof.

The making of saddlery and harness is mostly paid by piece, and elaborate attempts have been made to classify and price every possible variety of work. Prices are fixed by the union for nearly one thousand different operations, varying in price from 50*s* to 1*d*. No list could be exhaustive, and where this list fails it is suggested that 9*d* per hour should be taken as the basis of price. As to bridle cutting, the framers of the list sorrowfully admit 'that no two shops could be found in London which practised the same mode of doing work, and that differences in style or stitching make it impossible to tabulate one scale to meet all requirements. No doubt, however, the list acts as a guide and regulator, and assists in the maintenance of a standard scale of pay throughout the trade, whether piece or time or task be adopted as the measure of wage. For members of the union a minimum wage of 30*s* for a standard week of fifty-six and a half hours is enforced if the work be on time.

Brown Saddlers are the best paid men in the trade. They make riding-saddles only, and earn from 40*s* to 60*s* for a full week's work, according to their ability, but out of this a sum varying from 5*s* to 10*s* is paid to the woman or boy who stitches the flaps, &c. One woman may sometimes stitch for two men, if they work slow and she fast. Except in the best West End shops, it is unusual for a brown saddler to do this work himself, but by a custom of the trade he employs his own stitcher, and what he pays for this is a discount on his wages. In any case he calculates to earn 9*d* to 1*s* an hour for himself and very likely his wife or son or daughter does the stitching. The industry is recruited mainly from the country, where most of the men now working in London have served some sort of apprenticeship. London makers want finished workmen, and will not be burdened with boys, whose room is more valuable than their work.

In making a saddle the wooden frame supplied by the saddle-tree maker is first taken, and across it canvas bands are stretched, forming a springy bed, which is then covered by a special quality of serge; in this material a slit is made and the stuffing is introduced, and then worked into place through the meshes of the cloth until the saddle is padded as required, or, as the men say, until the "seat is set." The leather (pigskin) is then damped and blocked on, and nailed down, so that it may take the shape of the seat, but as soon as dry is taken off again, and prepared for the "skirts," which are seamed on. Then the seat is replaced or "drawn on" to the saddle-tree, and is ready for the flaps and panels. In the West End trade all is man's work, including flaps and panels, but in less good work women do the seaming and stitching, and also the sewing for the flaps after they have been cut out and prepared by the men.

Black Saddlers are those who make harness saddles, and are also known as chaise saddlers. Some are journeymen and some are small masters or work alone at home on their own account. The difference in social position is very slight. In this branch also the men do the heavier part and the women and boys sew the flaps and skirts. In the best houses one man, with the woman or boy he employs, will finish a saddle throughout. With small masters there is greater division of labour, showing a drift towards the ordinary conditions of sweating. Black saddlers earn from 25s in a slack week to 40s or 50s in a busy one, after paying their assistants.

Harness-makers may be taken generally to describe those who make all portions of harness except the collars and chaise saddles. There are also a few bridle cutters in London who, besides their own immediate trade, cut out and sew leather post-bags and small solid leather cases, but bridles chiefly come from Walsall, and those produced in London are made more often by harness-makers, who can earn 35s to 40s, if on good work, but if on lower-grade work only make from 25s to 35s. Almost all large carriage and coach-building firms employ, by force of old custom, a few harness-makers. The trades used formerly to be far more wedded than at present.

Horse clothing is made entirely by the wholesale firms. The women who work the sewing machines earn from 10*s* to 15*s*.

Saddle-trees.—The making of saddle frames or "trees" is a different industry altogether. They are made out of split beech-wood, rivetted together with iron supports. The saw is not used, but each piece is hewn with the hatchet and pared into exact shape with a very sharp two-handled knife. The worker has a breastplate of wood, fastened with straps across his shoulders, and cuts towards himself, as some mothers do when cutting bread and butter from a large loaf.

The introduction of machinery has been successfully resisted in London. That it would rob the men of their work is the first reason given; but it is also said that wood thus split, following the grain, like a split oak fence, is far more durable than if sawn into shape. All work is on piece, and there is always, it is said, work for those who will, as when home orders fail the masters are able to make stock for export, in which London does a large trade, and the supply of workers is limited by the action of a very strong union, which forbids apprenticeship, except to the sons of journeymen already in the trade. Those who are good workmen and steady can count on earning 40*s* a week throughout the year. All do not stick to their work; it is, indeed, admitted alike by masters and men, that it is not a very uncommon thing for men in this line to remain "on the booze" for weeks together. There seems even to be a tradition in favour of the practice, so strong that education has not been able to break it down entirely.

The following are detailed accounts of the earnings of two men, the statement of A being for two years and of B

for three-quarters of a year. The former is a good and
steady workman; the latter is also a fair workman but not
so steady :—

	1891.	1892.	1893.
A. 1st qr. (13 weeks)	£25 2 7...	1st qr. £28 14 6...	1st qr. £24 1 9
2nd ,, ,,	29 13 2...	2nd ,, 22 8 5	
3rd ,, ,,	26 18 9...	3rd ,, 20 6 4	
4th ,, ,,	28 4 9...	4th ,, 28 6 5	
	109 19 3	99 15 8	
Weekly average...	2 2 3	1 18 4	

In 1891, A took a short holiday at Easter, making only
9s 10d in Easter week, but he made up for it by earning
60s 11d in the next week. He then worked on till
Christmas, putting on another spurt in the week ending
December 20th, when he again made 60s. He then
knocked off for a fortnight, and during the fortnight drew
20s on account, working himself out of debt in the week
ending January 10th. In the beginning of April he lost
a week, and again in the middle of that month, the former
being Easter week. In the latter he drew 40s on account,
and worked it off in the week ending April 25th, when he
made 76s 11d. Again he took a week at the August Bank
Holiday, drew 35s on account, and worked double tides the
following week, making 75s 6d. In September, 1892, he
lost three weeks—I do not know the reason, but he may
have been ill. This it was that mainly made the difference
between the two years. He worked hard the last quarter,
and took no holiday at Christmas. It is this man's custom
frequently to draw small sums during the week, amounting
sometimes to 2s, sometimes to 4s or 5s, while at other
times for weeks together nothing is drawn. These drawings
I take to be for pocket-money.

The record of B is less satisfactory : 1st quarter,
£21. 4s 8d; 2nd quarter, £9. 14s 5d; 3rd quarter,
£11. 4s 1d; eight weeks, £9. 16s 11d. Total, £52. 0s 1d
for forty-seven weeks, or 22s 2d per week.

B does not usually earn as much as A in the week when he does work, but in his largest week he made more than A ever did, earning no less than £4. 6s 8d; he often makes over £2, and on one occasion £2. 16s. It would, therefore, seem that the *powers* of earning of the two men are not dissimilar. B was off work the first week in December, drawing 30s on account, and earned 56s the following week to make up. He also took a week at Christmas, and was again off work the second week of the New Year, and on every pay day he had had money on account, making it necessary, as they say, to start work the next week "on a dead horse." In February he went off for a month, and after working one week, lost four weeks more. Again, in June and July he only worked one week out of nine, and undoubtedly the cause of his idleness was drink. For both men equal opportunities offered. The moral of this comparison needs no pointing.

Those who do the metal work on the saddle-trees are called rivetters, and they, too, earn about 40s a week. When rivetted together, the trees are covered with thin canvas, laid on smoothly with brown size. A woman usually does this, and will make about 12s a week.

Horse-collar Makers comprise fore-whale fitters, bodyers, and finishers. The fore-whale is the hard rim which runs round the front part of the collar. The after-whale is the broader and softer part which fits to the horse's shoulder. Both are made of straw covered with leather; but in the case of the fore-whale a leather tube is stuffed with straw, rammed in very hard with a steel rod, whereas the after-whale is moulded in straw and afterwards covered with leather and padded with serge, the stitching of the cover being women's work.

The men employed earn about 30s a week throughout the year after paying for female assistance. Their wives often do the work.

Whip-makers employ stick dressers, stick finishers, riding-whip makers, thong-makers and braiders; these last being women machinists who braid hunting crops. Holly sticks are used for driving whips, and come from the Southern counties, or sometimes from France, but the French stick is not so strong. The sticks are bought by the whip-maker and kept two years to season, and are then sent to the whip-stick dresser, who works at home. The business is confined to a few families, and the art handed down from father to son. The dresser pairs off the bark and chips the knots, and, where required, adds an artificial knot. The skill needed and the price paid vary with the class of stick—anything from three halfpence to 5s a stick may be charged. To some men no one would entrust the best class of work, while others would take nothing else. In busy times 35s to 45s will be made, but the yearly average would be a good deal less, perhaps 25s to 30s for capable men. The finishers, working on the master's premises, are those who "quill up," attaching the quill to the top of the stick and the thong with it. They also fix on the handle, and sometimes the metal mounting. They earn 30s to 35s in busy times, but not more than 25s throughout the year. Hunting crops require skilled work. The best are made of whalebone and cane combined, and then braided with gut.

Thong-makers' wives often plait the thongs, but the women "braiders" are not usually the wives of whip-makers.

There are still a few small men who make whips at home and hawk them round the cab stands, but they are dying out.

Military Work.—The making of military harness is accounted a separate industry. Those engaged on it shift from employer to employer, according as one house or another is successful in obtaining Government contracts. Their work is heavier and coarser than that required for the civil trade, and their earnings not so high. They make on an average $6\frac{1}{2}d$ an hour on piece-work, and seem to be in a much better position now than they were prior to the inquiry of the Sweating Commission.

Considering the section as a whole, neither men nor masters have much cause for complaint. There are seasons, but even in ladies' side-saddles there is little change of fashion, and a master can safely make for stock. The work is healthy as well as regular, and not over-laborious. Men may still do good work well on in life.

TRADE UNIONS.

The extent to which the trade is organized may be gathered from the following particulars :—

Numbers in the London Trade (Census 1891).		Name of Trade Society.	Membership in London.		Remarks.
Total.	Of whom are employed males over 20.		In each Society.	In each Division.	
3877	2440	The London Saddle and Harness Makers' Trade Protection Society (1872).	658	825	Out of work, Strike and Death allowance. Enforces minimum wage. Relations with masters good.
		The London Chaise Saddlers' Trade Protection Society (1890).	47		Usual Benefits. Union and non-union men do not work together.
		The London Saddle-tree Makers' Trade Society (1890).	40		Will only teach sons of journeymen. Enforces price list.
		The London Horse Collar Makers' Trade Society (1872).	80		Out of work, Sick and Death Benefits.

Thus, 825 males are organized out of a total of 2440 over twenty years of age, or 34 per cent.

There is also an " Amicable Benefit Society of Saddlers and Harness Makers, Bridle Cutters and Collar Makers," which was founded so long ago as 1779. To this many employers subscribe annually, and any man working in the trade may also become a member, whether he belongs to one of the societies given above or not. Sick benefits, varying from 16*s* to 5*s* per week, are offered, and £14 at member's death, with half that sum at the death of his wife. And in addition to this there is a flourishing " Pension Fund Association," with 142 subscribers (1893), which offers a pension of £20 per annum obtained by ballot, for those who are aged and infirm and have subscribed at least five years to the funds.

Wages Statistics.

There are, as already stated, 2440 adult men employed in these trades. As to these we have wages returns for 207 men working for fifteen firms, as under :—

Saddlery and Harness-makers 11	= 15 firms usually employing
Whip manufacturers 2	257 persons, of whom 207 are
Saddle-tree maker 1	adult males, all belonging to
Collar-maker ....:................... 1	this section.

The earnings of these men in an average week are as follows :—

Below 20*s* .... 8, or 4 per cent.		
20*s* to 25*s* ....10 ,, 5 ,,	Under 30*s*, 32½ per cent.	
25*s* ,, 30*s* ....48 ,, 23½ ,,		
30*s* ,, 35*s* ....50 ,, 24 ,,		
35*s* ,, 40*s* ....19 ,, 9 ,,	30*s* and over, 67½ per cent.	
40*s* ,, 45*s* ....23 ,, 11 ,,		
45*s* and upwards ...49 ,, 23½ ,,		

207 ,, 100 ,,

Our figures may be compared with returns made to the

Board of Trade in 1886 by eight firms employing 128 persons, of whom 99 were adult males.

	−20s.	20—	25s—	30s—	35s—	40s—	45s—
Our returns	4 %.	5 %.	23½ %.	24 %.	9 %.	11 %.	23½ %.
Board of Trade returns	32½ %.			67½ %.			
	1 %.	14 %.	5 %.	42 %.	18 %.	2 %.	18 %.
	20 %.			80 %.			

It is probable that ordinary full week's wages, as returned to the Board of Trade, are somewhat more for the day-wage men at the bottom of the scale, and somewhat less for the piece workers at the top of the scale, than the actual earnings. The returns agree in putting the largest section of the men at 25s to 35s a week, with a considerable section at 45s and over.

Busy and slack weeks, according to the Board of Trade returns, fall irregularly. The busy ones were in November, January, May, and two in July, the slack ones were two in December, and one each in May, September, and November. The numbers employed varied about 20 per cent., and the average wages about 20 per cent. also.

As to the earnings of those who are not heads of families, we find a number of girls and women usually earning from 10s to 15s a week. The boys commence at 5s, the usual earnings being 8s to 12s.

Social Condition.

Of the 2440 adult men employed, about 1640 come under social classification as heads of families. According to the small sample provided by our wages returns, only 9 per cent. earn less than 25s a week, whereas no less than 42 per cent. live under crowded conditions. Next, 47½ per cent. earn from 25s to 35s as compared to 32 per cent. who live in small tenements, but less than two persons in each room; and finally, 43½ per cent. appear as earning over 35s, whereas only 26 per cent. belong to the central classes, as follows:—

Comparison of Earnings with Style of Life (Saddlers, &c.).

Earnings as returned.			Classification of Population.		
Under 20s... 8, or	4	per cent.	3 or more in each room,	1000, or	12 per cent.
20s to 25s...10 ,,	5	,,	2 to 3 ,,	2500 ,,	30 ,,
25s ,, 30s...48 ,,	23¼	,,	1 ,, 2 ,,	2800 ,,	32 ,,
30s ,, 35s...50 ,,	24	,,	Less than 1 ,,		
35s ,, 40s...19 ,,	9	,,	More than 4 rooms		
40s ,, 45s...23 ,,	11	,,	4 or more persons to	2200 ,,	26 ,,
45s & over .49 ,,	23½	,,	1 servant ...		
207 ,,	100	,,		8500 ,,	100 ,,
			Families of Employers and servants ...	2000	
				10,500	

Our sample is evidently much too favourable, and it seems plain that those working on their own account without assistance are not so well off as the men working in the larger shops. Several causes may lead to this apparent contrast between earnings and social condition. Saddlers, especially when busy, pay a woman or a lad 5s to 10s a week for stitching, which amount would come out of their earnings; while one of the most poorly paid branches of the trade—the manufacture of military accoutrements was removed from London soon after the 1891 census was taken, and does not appear in our statistics of wages.

As a rule, the men live at some distance from their work, West End workers coming from the West and South West districts, and East End men from the East and North East, so that only in very rare instances are they able to go home to dinner. The numbers of those who bring their food with them and eat it in the shop, and of those who both buy and eat it in a coffee tavern are about equal. Dinner in the shop does not occupy the full hour, and after it a stroll with a friend and a pipe is usual. Public-houses here, as elsewhere, do not often attract men for the midday meal.

All men wear aprons, and generally work in their shirt sleeves; there is no dress peculiar to the trade. The majority are members of a friendly society, if not of a trade union also, and, in addition, there are a few shop clubs for sickness or for making small loans, whose surplus funds are usually shared out either at Christmas time or immediately before the annual beanfeast.

On the whole, it is not usual for the wives (except of thong-makers) to earn wages. Such women's work as there is has already been mentioned above, where reference has also been made to the prevalence of drink in certain sub-sections of the trade.

CHAPTER VI.

BRUSH-MAKING. *(Section 27.)*

Persons Represented.

| Census Enumeration. | | | | | | Enumerated by Families. | | | | |

<table>
<tr><td colspan="6">Census Enumeration.</td></tr>
<tr>
<td rowspan="2">Census Division, 1891.</td>
<td>Fe-males.</td>
<td colspan="3">Males.</td>
<td rowspan="2">Total.</td>
</tr>
<tr>
<td>All Ages.</td><td>—19</td><td>20—54</td><td>55—</td>
</tr>
<tr>
<td>Brush-makers,&c.</td><td>2018</td><td>662</td><td>2339</td><td>522</td><td>5541</td>
</tr>
</table>

Enumerated by Families.

Sex ...... { Males 2142
{ Females 328

Birthplace { In London .... 76 % 1876
{ Out of London .. 24 % 504 } Heads of Families, 2470.

Industrial { Employer ...... 12 % 288
Status .. { Employed ...... 77 % 1904
{ Neither .... 11 % 278

Females are most numerous between the ages of 15 and 20. There is then a sudden fall from 440 for that quinquennium to 312 for 20 to 25, but a good many seem to work on, as there are still 417 for the decade 25 to 35. After 35 the decrease is rapid and regular, being about 30 per cent. for every 10 years.

The age line for Males (*see* diagram) shows the usual features of a trade in which machinery and factory work is superseding older methods of manufacture. Quite young people enter and the old linger, but of men in the prime of life there is (for the time) a great deficiency.

TOTAL POPULATION CONCERNED.

	Heads of Families.	Others Occupied.	Unoccupied.	Servants.	Total.
Total	2470	2798	5817	130	11,215
Average in family..	1	1·13	2·36	·05	4·54

DISTRIBUTION.

E.	N.	W. & C.	S.	Total.
1919	1464	518	1640	5541

DETAILS OF OCCUPATIONS (FROM THE CENSUS DICTIONARY).

Hair, bristle worker, brush and broom manufacturer ; hair, bass, bristle dresser, &c. Brush drawer, borer, polisher, finisher. Pan hand. Tooth-brush maker, drawer, fashioner. Bone, ivory cutter, turner. Tortoise-shell, india-rubber, horn, &c. Comb-maker, polisher, &c.

CLASSIFICATION.

Numbers living in Families.		%
3 or more to a room	1647	14·7
2 & under 3 ,,	2868	25·6
1 & under 2 ,,	2837	25·4
Less than 1 ,,		
More than 4 rooms } 4 or more persons } to a servant .. }	3536	31·5
Less than 4 to 1 servant & 4 or more to 2 servants ..	161	1·4
All others with 2 or more servants..	36	·3
Servants	130	1·1
	11,215	100

	Inner.	Outer.	Together.
Crowded..	48 %	30 %	40 %
Not	52 %	70 %	60 %

DISTRIBUTION.

East ..	{ Inner 2822 } { Outer 574 }	3396
North	{ Inner 266 } { Outer 2695 }	2961
West..	{ Inner 61 } { Outer 266 }	327
Central	Inner 748	748
South- East	{ Inner 567 } { Outer 880 }	1447
South- West	{ Inner 1891 } { Outer 445 }	2336
		11,215

Inner 6355, or 57 %
Outer 4860, or 43 %

Status as to Employment (according to Census Enumeration).

<table>
<tr>
<td rowspan="3">Census Divisions (1891).</td>
<td colspan="2" rowspan="2">Employers.</td>
<td colspan="3">Employed.</td>
<td colspan="2" rowspan="2">Neither Employer nor Employed.</td>
<td rowspan="3">Total.</td>
</tr>
<tr>
<td colspan="2">Males.</td>
<td rowspan="2">Females of all ages.</td>
</tr>
<tr>
<td>Males.</td><td>Females</td>
<td>Under 20.</td><td>Over 20.</td>
<td>Males.</td><td>Females</td>
</tr>
<tr>
<td>Brush and broom-makers, hair workers..</td>
<td>276</td><td>36</td><td>563</td><td>1869</td><td>1836</td><td>214</td><td>60</td><td>4854</td>
</tr>
<tr>
<td>Bone, horn, ivory, tortoise-shell workers.</td>
<td>42</td><td>2</td><td>99</td><td>360</td><td>79</td><td>100</td><td>5</td><td>687</td>
</tr>
<tr>
<td></td><td>318</td><td>38</td><td>662</td><td>2229</td><td>1915</td><td>314</td><td>65</td><td>5541</td>
</tr>
<tr>
<td>TOTAL........</td><td colspan="2">356</td><td colspan="3">4806</td><td colspan="2">379</td><td></td>
</tr>
</table>

Showing on the average 8 male and 5 female employees to each employer.

Nos. (For explanation of method adopted in preparing this chart, see Note on Diagram 18.)

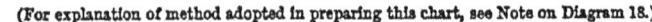

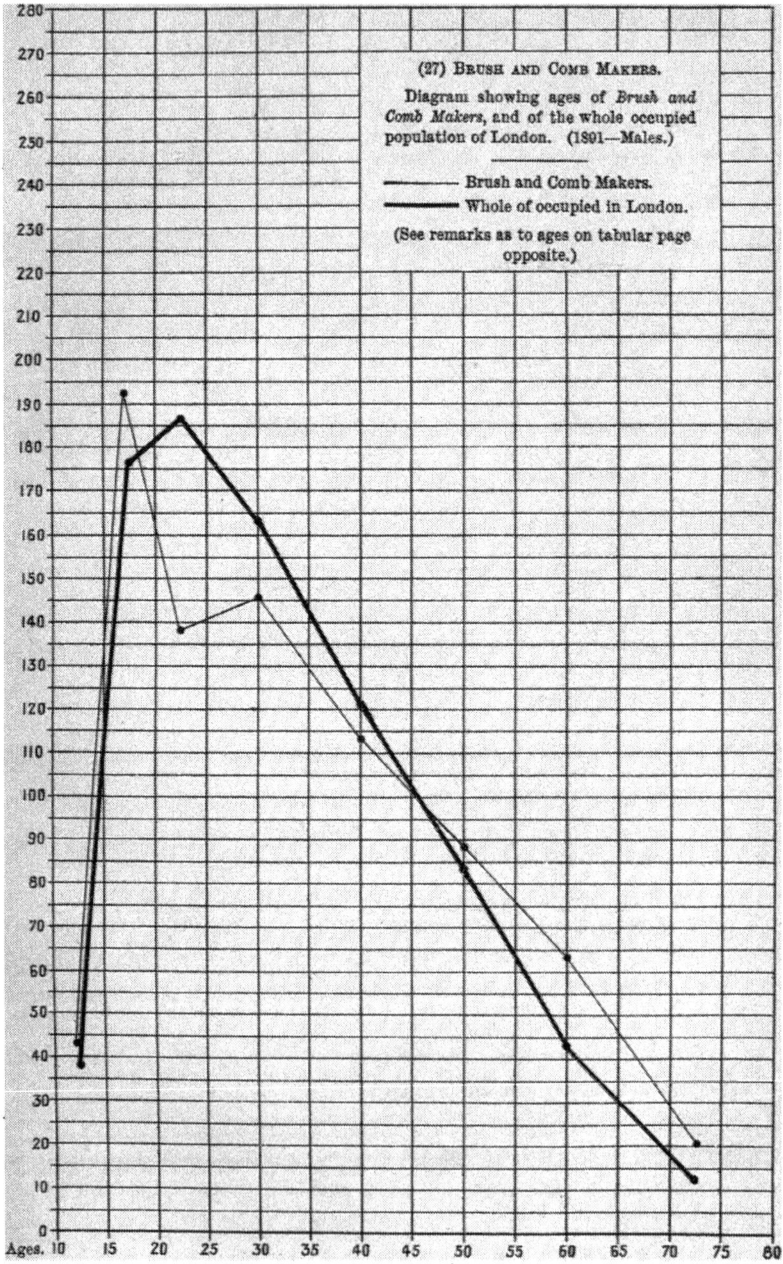

(27) Brush and Comb Makers.
Diagram showing ages of *Brush and Comb Makers*, and of the whole occupied population of London. (1891—Males.)
Brush and Comb Makers.
Whole of occupied in London.
(See remarks as to ages on tabular page opposite.)
280 270 260 250 240 230 220 210 200 190 180 170 160 150 140 130 120 110 100 90 80 70 60 50 40 30 20 10 0
Ages. 10 15 20 25 30 35 40 45 50 55 60 65 70 75 80

Household and Fancy Brushes.

There are four main branches of Brush manufacture:—

(1) Household (brooms, scrubbing brushes, &c.).

(2) Fancy (hair brushes, tooth brushes, &c.).

(3) Painters (house painting and artist's brushes).

(4) Mechanical (brushes for tube and bottle cleaning).

The first two have many points in common, and may be considered together. It would indeed not always be easy to draw a very distinct line between "*Household*" and "*Fancy*" brushes. The principal divisions of the work are as follows:—

(1) Borers or drillers—men.

(2) Hair hands or bristle dressers—men.

(3) Drawers—women.

(4) Panners—men (household brushes and brooms only).

(5) Trimmers—women.

(6) Finishers—men.

(7) Polishers—women.

(1) *Drillers.*—The men who drill the holes in the face of the brush, through which wires are drawn to make fast the bristles, are paid by the piece, as is the case in brush-making generally, excepting where machinery has superseded hand work. A borer who works quickly, on straightforward work, can bore as many as three thousand holes in an hour, but he could not maintain such a speed for long. The work is hard, and a man who is growing old or weakly will not bore half the number. The operator stands at a table or bench, the weight of his body supported on his left leg, while his right turns the wheel. On the flat of the table he firmly rests his elbows, and leans his chest against a raised portion of it. In this position he is able to manipulate to a nicety the backboard of the brush, which he holds in both hands pressing it against the revolving bit or drill at the exact spot and at the requisite angle, and withdrawing it as each hole is made.

Almost every kind of brush—and their name is legion—
requires holes drilled at special intervals, and it may be
at different angles. A man must have a steady hand and
eye, together with great practice, to do the work both
quickly and well. "Scales" or "patterns"—metal or
wooden plates already pierced in the required fashion—
are frequently used by beginners to prevent mistakes.

In the best shops drillers can earn 30s to 34s a week if
ordinarily quick and regular at their work. But many
of those employed by small masters have, besides possibly
a lower scale of pay, intermittent employment, even though
hey may combine the duties of boring and finishing;
and of those who might have constant work some are
irregular in attendance, and may earn only 25s one week
and 35s the next. As they work independently and are
paid by the piece, the men can please themselves as to times
and hours.

The larger firms now do a good deal of this work with
machinery, handled by women who are paid by time;
and it is probable that the use of machinery will extend
in brush-making.

(2) *Bristle Dressers.*—The preparation of bristles consists in sorting them according to thickness and length,
thickness being tested by a metal comb with teeth at
graduated distances. They are usually subjected to two
sortings, the best being first picked out to be used in the
manufacture of brushes of a superior kind. The rest are
then sorted a second time by the small makers of cheap
brushes, who may still find a quantity suitable for their
purpose. The bristles finally rejected for brush purposes,
are used in the stuffing of furniture. Good bristles are
dear.*

The men engaged in this work earn 30s to 50s a week,
partly according to quickness in working (for it is by

---

* Bristles come principally from Russia—the best from Siberia. The
rise in price is bringing them from other places, as China, India, &c.

piece), and partly according to the character of the bristle
—finer bristles needing finer work. Again, we speak of
the best houses when we quote these figures, and of
steady men.

(3) Brushes are either "drawn" or "pitched in," the
latter process being confined almost entirely to household
brooms and brushes. The *drawers* are women, except in
the case of "bass"* or palm fibre drawing, which is
generally considered as man's work. These women work
with astonishing rapidity. The wire loop is pushed through
each hole in the brush board in turn, the correct number
of bristles inserted, and the loop is then drawn quickly
back, so that the doubled bristles stand out straight from
the face of the board. All this is done with such speed that
the eye can scarcely follow the process. Workers are paid
according to the number of holes drawn.

Those who are employed in factories or workshops for
eight or nine hours a day, on household brushes make
10*s* to 12*s*, or even 15*s* a week, but on fancy brushes not
so much. The fancy work is rather lighter but is paid
less, mainly because it can be done equally well in the
homes, and mostly is so done. Home workers rarely give
their full time, having usually other claims on it. They
seem to earn from 3*s* 6*d* to 8*s* a week.

(4) Those who do the "pitching in" are called *Panners*,
because they sit by threes and fours round a pan filled with
hot pitch. Each man has beside him the stocks of brooms,
ready bored, together with a bundle of the fibre of which
the brush is to be made, from which he picks out as much
as will be required to fill one hole. He dips one end of the
fibres in the pan, and then binds the tarred end with thread

---

* Bass dressing in London is a small dependent industry, not usually
carried on within the brush factory. Those engaged in the trade have been
returned in the census with the mat-makers, and some account of their
work will be found in Chapter III. of Part IV.

or hemp and inserts it in its hole, giving the stock a slight twist as he does so, and the cooling of the pitch fixes the fibre firmly. It is a simple process, but considerable practice is needed to become expert enough to earn "good money" at it. The same men both drill and pan, and are paid according to the number of holes made and filled. For ordinary sizes the trade price is fifteen knots a penny, and a good workman may make as much as 10d an hour, but the amount of work done by different men varies greatly. By "trade price" is meant that recognized by the Union, and at a good factory where these rates are paid panners earn up to 40s or even 45s in a busy week; but work in this branch falls off in summer, so that an average of 30s to 35s throughout the year is declared to be a fair statement of the earnings made under the most favourable circumstances. Those who work for small masters will average a good deal less, 20s or 25s perhaps.

(5) *Trimmers* are women whose duty is to trim with scissors the irregularities in the length of the bristles. They are paid by time, and are said to earn 8s to 10s a week.

(6) *Finishers.*—This work, which is necessary in the case of drawn brushes, is done by men. It consists in cutting the brush board to its proper shape after the bristles are attached, and in putting on the back, which serves to cover the reverse of the holes, and is as much needed for cleanliness as for appearance.

Finishers in a good factory, where full wages are paid, and regular work can be had, average 30s to 35s a week, the takings ranging from 25s working single-handed, up to 50s if working with a boy, who will receive 6s, 8s, or 10s, according to age and skill. The small masters pay less, and their work is also more irregular.

Some finishing is done by machinery; the men who work the machines are paid by time, the leading man receiving as much as 40s to 50s, and the rest about 25s. Where machinery is used, a considerable number of boys are also employed.

(7) *Polishing* is done mostly by women, who earn pretty good wages, 15s or 16s being not uncommon; but, as with most piece-work, the amount earned varies very much, and the average is lowered by those who, being less regular or less quick, earn only 6s to 10s. One woman working at home in this branch stated she had made as much as 20s, and, as far as she is personally concerned, considered 15s a fair average.

With home workers and in small shops these branches are not always distinct—the same man may bore and finish, the same woman draw and trim.

Work in bone and ivory is a special branch of the fancy trade, which should be mentioned before we pass on to mechanical or paint brushes.

Ivory is little worked now. Its uses are almost entirely confined to knife handles, piano keys, billiard balls, umbrella handles, and little fancy articles. The best brushes now have silver backs, and such as one sees with ivory backs are mostly made in France. Tooth or nail-brushes of bone employ, however, some 150 skilled men in London, besides a number of women. The handles are made from the shin bones of cattle, boiled, cleaned, and cut into four strips, and trimmed roughly to the required shape with a circular saw. The men who do this earn about 35s a week. It is a disagreeable, dusty job, but to mitigate its discomfort a wet saw is sometimes used. From the cutters the pieces pass to the fashioners, who with plane and file give each handle its proper shape. These men make 23s to 28s. It is hard work, and men cannot continue at it to so great an age as they can at other portions of the brush trade.

The handles, when shaped, are placed in a revolving cylinder with whitening and water, and after twelve hours of tumbling come out smooth and polished. They then pass to the drillers, who are mostly women, working with the aid of machinery, and earning 8s to 10s a week. The holes are not pushed completely through, but are afterwards met by channels cut in the back, which, when the bristles have been drawn in and made fast, are filled up with cement. The "graver" who cuts the channels earns about 30s. The women who draw the bristle earn wages similar to those paid for other fancy brush-work. Nearly all are home workers. Women also fill up the grooves, and stamp the handles with the names they are to bear, and do the packing, earning 8s or 9s on the average.

PAINT-BRUSH MAKING.

This is a totally distinct class of manufacture. It includes all kinds of brushes used for anything in the nature of painting, from large slap-dash whitewash work to the most delicate "camel's" hair brush (so-called); and the men employed are, on the whole, more highly paid than either "household" or "fancy" workers.

After the bristles have been sorted or dressed, they have to be affixed to their handles with resin or cement, and then tightly bound round, either by hand or machinery, with wire or glued string. Paint-brush makers frequently earn over 40s, and in some cases up to 60s. The average, taking good weeks and bad, is said to be not much under 40s. There seem to be three reasons for the high level of pay.

(1) That the materials (bristles) used are very expensive, and saving in cost of labour is, therefore, not so important as the best possible work.

(2) That there is no division of labour—the same man makes the brush throughout, being given only the handle and the prepared bristles.

(3) That the men are a compact body, united in a strong union.

These three reasons are evidently inter-dependent.

MECHANICAL BRUSHES.

These are made with wire, into which bristles or bass is twisted. They are usually of cylindrical shape for cleaning tubes, large or small, from those of a marine boiler to that of a pipe stem. They include chimney-sweep's brushes. None of these are made to any great extent in London. The larger kinds come from the north. The trade here, so far as it goes, is for small sized brushes and is in the hands of small men, working often with the help of their families only. As such, they are prosperous, not having up to the present been hit by any severe competition, whether home or foreign.

GENERAL PARTICULARS OF THE TRADE.

Methods of Training.—The teaching of the trade follows naturally where boys are employed to help the men. Many employers decline to take regularly-bound apprentices, and it would seem that in this, as in other trades, the old system is making way for one which allows greater freedom to both parties. The trade unions have strict rules, however, on this subject, by which, or by some tacit understanding with their men, the best firms are guided; so that, excepting as regards some of the "sweating shops," no complaints are heard as to boy labour.

Sweating.—Some shops of doubtful reputation in this respect are in a fairly large way of business, but for the most part the "sweaters" are small masters. In these cases the scale of wages is lower, employment more irregular, and the class of work inferior; but how much so, it is not easy to say exactly, or to what extent the inferiority of work applies to every one employed.

Foreign Competition is mainly felt in the lower branches of the brush trade, that is, as regards brushes in which labour forms a heavy item in the total cost. The same rule applies to the competition of machine-made brushes, whether made at home or abroad. In one way or another the old South London industry in common household brushes is being undermined. But men employed on better work are in a stronger position. It does not pay to make by machinery brushes into which expensive materials enter—change of shape and fashion is too frequent, and perfection of finish too important—and against importations best London-made brushes can hold their own.

Effects of the Strike—Inferior Work.—The strike of 1891, after which the rates of wages were to a great extent settled by the joint consent of masters and men, and embodied in a recognized price list, seems to have benefited those who work for the higher-class firms. These firms have been able to adhere to the "fair" rates without being greatly hampered with foreign or machine competition. But in regard to the common and cheaper work the strike gave foreign and machine-employing manufacturers their opportunity, and the position of those working by hand on this class of work has become worse and worse, until it appears not unlikely that they and their employers may disappear together under the apparently inexorable law of the survival of the cheapest.

Those engaged in this cheap work are mostly home workers or the smallest of domestic employers. Tabard Street is the centre of their trade, and has been so since the days when it was the Kent Road, and the materials for their brooms could be cut in the surrounding marshes. There, three or four persons often work in a room not more than 10 feet square, which serves at once for parlour, kitchen and workshop. In bad seasons such as the present (1893) they are frequently obliged to hawk their wares in the streets. Their working hours are very irregular; at times they know no rest, sitting far into the night, and at others must remain idle or risk making for stock goods that will perhaps not easily find a buyer.

It is impossible to say what their average week's earnings are, but it seems that 20s to 22s is looked upon as a satisfactory recompense for a week's work of a man, woman and child, with material thrown in.

Effect on health.—The work is by no means unhealthy, except possibly bristle-dressing, which involves the breathing of a disagreeable dust. The fumes of the pitch in panning are antiseptic, and are said (as among barge-builders) to have kept influenza at bay. Nor does the work entail any severe physical strain, except for those engaged in boring and bone-fashioning. In these branches men begin to lose capacity after forty-five years of age; otherwise men of regular habits engaged in brush-making frequently keep at the bench, and even earn good wages, up to sixty, sixty-five, or, in exceptional cases, seventy.

Horse-hair Workers.

Though not entirely connected with brush-making, horse-hair workers are included in this section. The work consists of sorting according to colour and then again according to thickness and length. The men who do this are known as sorters and drawers; the latter pass the hair through a graduated comb, as is done with bristles. Sorting is shared by women, who, when employed, seem to receive the same rate of pay as the men, earning 25s to 30s for a standard week of fifty-six hours. The longest hairs, those over 18 inches in length, are used for making cloth, and called weaver's hair, the shorter lengths are termed brush hair, while the finest are curled and used for stuffing furniture. Curling, which is done by very tight plaiting or twisting into ropes, is entirely in the hands of men known as "curlers," and, requiring strength as well as skill, in the best-paid branch. Like all the rest, it is piece-work, and as much as 40s may be made in a good week. Besides these men, there are also carders, who, regarded as unskilled, are not admitted to the union. They receive 6d an hour.

There are no particular seasons for this work, which varies in amount according to the market, and in slack times is shared amongst the employees. The men are nearly all members of the Horse-hair and Fibre Workers' Union. The trade is a very close one. The number of boys employed is strictly limited by the union, and most of them are sons of men engaged in the trade. There is no regular apprenticeship.

COMB-MAKING, &c.

Comb-making is not a large industry in London, but the best work, whether in tortoise-shell, ivory or india rubber, is said to be still produced in London by men who work with their wives and families, taking orders from the West End shops. As a skilled trade carried on by journeymen under an employer it is said to be dying out. Cheap machine-made combs come from the North—those made of horn from Aberdeen, and those of vulcanite from Edinburgh. The work when done by hand consists first in shaping with a small saw and then in "grailing" the teeth—that is, iu tapering them and fining off their edges with a file. This is highly skilled work. Journeymen employed at cutting and grailing earn from 30s to 32s on piece.

Ivory-cutting also appears to be dying out in London except as regards the turning of billiard balls, though London is still the principal market for ivory. Turners and cutters make about 32s a week. This is partly a home industry.

TRADES UNIONS.

Particulars of the trade societies are subjoined :—

Numbers in the London Trade (Census, 1891).		Name of Trade Society.	Membership in London.		Remarks.
Total.	Of whom are employed males over 20.		In each Society.	In each Division.	
		The United Society of Brush-makers (1786).	346		Offers the usual Benefits and Travelling and Emigration money. Is responsible to masters for work left unfinished up to 40s.
		The Amalgamated Society of Brush-makers (1889).	70		Out of work and Strike pay only. Admits women at half contributions for half Benefits.
4854	1869	Ivory and Bone Brush-makers' Trade and Protection Society (1890).	120	922	Relations with masters good. Out of work pay.
		Painting Brush-makers' Provident Society.	198		Has a Price List approved by Master Brush-makers' Association.
		Horse-hair and Fibre Workers' Union.	188		Gives Strike pay. Limits the number of boys in the trade.
687	360	(*Bone, Ivory, &c.*)	—		—
5541	2229				

There is also a Master Brush-makers' Association.

Thus out of a total of 1869 males over twenty years of age employed in the brush and bristle industries, 922 or 50 per cent. are organized. The subscriptions to, and benefits offered by, the above societies vary very widely. The United Society of Brush-makers demands as much as 1s 9d per week, but in return pays out of work benefit for a year, gives £5 to emigrate to America and £10 to those on their way to Australia, and a pension of 4s to 6s to those incapable of work, as well as ordinary benefits. The subscriptions to the other societies vary between 6*d* and 2*d* per week, and their members have to be content with benefits in proportion.

The "United" is one of the oldest societies in the kingdom and has a trade-plate dated 1786, which came into its possession when the King's Lynn branch was dissolved. There is also a price list extant dated 1805 (Webb, p. 66). Being old, it has a most elaborate rule book, and strict regulations as to apprentices, to the effect that boys may not be bound before thirteen nor after sixteen years of age; the number that any master may have is fixed with reference to the total number of men in his employ; and, further, no apprentice is allowed to leave his master before the full term of seven years has expired. There are, besides, some minor regulations of interest, which give an insight into a few of the difficulties with which the ruling powers in trade societies have to contend. For instance, it is enacted that no opposition be made by any of the divisions to the introduction of steam power; that no money be allowed for beer on club nights; and that "we pay a rental for our accommodation at our club houses,"— for club houses are generally public-houses, and the host is content to levy rent indirectly. And again, women's work is discouraged by the expulsion of any members who may bore "pan or machine work" for them. Members are also asked to help the funds, when they can, with loans to bear interest at 5 per cent.

There is some friction between the "Amalgamated" and the "United." The former is comparatively a new society and purely a trade organization, and is apparently stronger in the provinces than in London, having, it is said, lost a large number of London members after the strike which occurred in 1891.

As a whole the trade is well organized, and in most cases union will not work with non-union men, so that the various shops contain either one or the other, and not, as in so many other industries, a mixture of the two. The relations between the societies and the employers are very friendly.

Wages Statistics.

2229 adult men find employment in this group of trades. As to these we have wages returns for 367, employed by twelve firms, as under :—

Brush-makers 6	
Paint-brush makers 2	=12 firms usually employing
Tooth-brush maker 1	763 persons, of whom 367 are
Bristle works 1	adult males, all of them
Comb-makers............................. 2	belonging to this section.

These returns no doubt represent the best houses, rather than the whole trade. The earnings in an average week are as follows :—

Below 20s............	20, or	6 per cent.			
20s to 25s............	31 ,,	8	,,	Under 30s, 32 per cent.	
25s ,, 30s............	66 . ,,	18	,,		
30s ,, 35s............	89 ,,	24½	,,		
35s ,, 40s............	71 ,,	19	,,	30s and over, 68 per cent.	
40s ,, 45s............	58 ,,	16	,,		
45s and upwards...	32 ,,	8½	,,		
	367 ,,	100	,,		

Three brush-making firms, employing 140 men, gave details, from which we find that nineteen-twentieths of the work is paid by piece, and the exact average earned was 31s 5d, but some made as much as 55s or 60s, and others as little as 12s 6d. One of the comb-making firms, employing thirty-three men, also return nearly all as piece workers. Their earnings varied from 54s 11d to 15s 10d—the average being 32s 3d.

The only return that we have giving busy and slack weeks separately, shows 50 per cent. reduction in numbers, as well as fully 30 per cent. reduction in amount

earned. This return being from one of the best firms
in the trade, it is evident that employment in it, on the
whole, must be very irregular and uncertain. The following
figures, extracted from the wages books of two journeymen
finishers, both of them sober hard-working men, will go
far to support this statement, and also tend to show that
trade has been worse recently than it was three or four
years ago.

The first, A, in forty-two consecutive weeks, ending
January, 1889, earned £46. 13s, or an average of 22s 2d
per week. The highest week gave 30s 6d, the lowest 13s.

The second, B, in a period of thirty-one weeks, ending
in the summer of this present year (1893), earned £22. 5s,
or an average of 14s 4d; the highest week being 25s 6d,
and the lowest 7s 4d. A worked successively for two firms
—one in East and one in South London, and B for several
small firms on the south side. Both men evidently live
from hand to mouth, drawing money on account, sometimes
day by day. One is married and one not. To the married
man (B) there were at times only a few pence due on
Saturday night owing to drawings made in the course of
the week.

There are 1483 women and 535 girls returned as employed in brush-making, &c., of whom 328 are heads of
families. There are, also, 662 males under twenty years of
age. We have particulars for 320 females, and the
most common rates of wages are 11s and 12s; about
one-fourth get above that amount, rising in some cases to
over 20s, and another fourth earn below 9s. The wages
of 76 lads and boys are given, and of these half get 10s
or less, and half from 11s to 20s or more, the general range
being 9s to 15s.

Social Condition.

Of the 2200 adult men employed, about 1650 count as

heads of families, and so come under social classification.
Of the sample tested only 14 per cent. appear as earning
less than 25*s* in an average week, whereas 39 per cent. live
under crowded conditions.   On the other hand, there are
in the sample 42½ per cent. who earn from 25*s* to 35*s*,
against 31 per cent. who live one to two in a room, and
43½ per cent. who earn over 35*s* to compare with 30
per cent. of the central classes, as follows :—

Comparison of Earnings with Style of Life (Brushes, &c.).

Earnings as returned.			Classification of Population.		
Under 20s...	20, or	6 per cent.	3 or more in each room, 1000, or 11 per cent.		
20s to 25s...	31 ,,	8 ,,	2 to 3 ,,	2500 ,,	28 ,,
25s ,, 30s...	66 ,,	18 ,,	1 ,, 2 ,,	2800 ,,	31 ,,
30s ,, 35s...	89 ,,	24½ ,,	Less than 1 ,,		
35s ,, 40s...	71 ,,	19 ,,	More than 4 rooms		
40s ,, 45s...	58 ,,	16 ,,	4 or more persons to	2700 ,,	30 ,,
45s and } upwards }	32 ,,	8½ ,,	a servant		
	367 ,,	100 ,,		9000 ,, 100 ,,	
			Families with female heads 1000		
			Employers' families and servants 1200		
			11,200		

Members of this section live, as a rule, in Bermondsey,
Hackney, and Bethnal Green, in the neighbourhood of the
majority of brush manufactories of London; and they do
not, therefore, have to traverse such long distances to go
to their work as men working in a trade more scattered
over the town, or peculiar to the WestEnd.   Their going
home to meals depends naturally upon the distance between
their homes and the works, and it appears that the majority
either eat their meals in the shop, bringing food with them,
or make an arrangement with a neighbouring coffee or

public-house; some bringing food with them but eating it in a tavern or coffee-shop.

The dress worn by brush-makers consists of a calico apron, with the occasional addition of a blouse. Not unfrequently an entire working suit is donned as soon as the shop is entered, so as to prevent the dust and smell of materials used adhering to clothes in ordinary wear.

A great number of employees in this section, probably nearly all those in regular employment, belong to a trade or friendly society, and the amounts subscribed vary from 6d to 3s a week—a sum which, in the latter case, may possibly approach one-twelfth of the weekly income. The larger shops often have sick funds of their own, to which the employers contribute.

In the majority of cases wives, working either in the shop or at home, earn money as well as their husbands; in fact, a good many marriages, if made in heaven, originate ostensibly in acquaintance begun in the shop, and the wife does not cease to work.

PART III.—PRINTING AND PAPER TRADES.

PRINTING AND PAPER TRADES.

PRELIMINARY STATEMENT.

THE total number of persons employed in these trades, divided by age and sex, is as follows :—

Persons represented : (*A*) *Census Enumeration.*

	ENUMERATED BY AGE AND SEX.						
	10—	15—	20—	25—	55—	65—	Total.
Males	3154	12,466	10,322	30,459	3120	1408	60,929
Females	1630	8976	6058	8620	755	315	26,354
Total	4784	21,442	16,380	39,079	3875	1723	87,283

It will be seen that the number of males under twenty, and of females at all ages, is very considerable. The women and girls outnumber men and boys in paper manufacture (which includes, and in London mainly consists of, the making of envelopes, carton boxes and paper bags) and in bookbinding. Altogether there are only 33,154 heads of families. The total population included in these families is 148,856, made up as follows :—

Persons represented : (B) Enumeration by Families.

No.	Sections.	Heads.	Total number (excluding Servants).	Per family (excluding Servants).	Servants.
28	Printing	18,048	81,365	4·42	854
29	Bookbinding	4289	18,117	4·22	124
30	Paper	3008	12,307	4·08	251
31	Stationery	3423	14,899	4·35	857
32	Booksellers, &c.	4386	18,646	4·25	1436
	Total	33,154	145,334	4·38	3522
	Servants		3522		
	Total population		148,856		

Of these heads of families, 2574 are women.

The 3522 servants attend on 11,871 persons, the remaining 133,463 being without resident service. Of the servant-keeping class, 7000 have only one servant to four or more persons served; 3300 have one servant to less than four, or two servants to four or more, in family, and 1600 live in other families keeping two or more servants.

Turning to the 133,000 who have no servant, we find that 47,000 live in families which occupy more than four rooms, or have on the average more than one room to each person; 39,000 live with one and under two persons per room; 29,000 with two to three persons to a room; 11,700 live three to four to a room, and 6800 individuals form households in which there are four or more persons to each room.

Lower Classes.	4 or more persons to a room	6,878 or 4·6%	12·5%
	3 and under 4 ,, ,,	11,707 ,, 7·9%	
	2 and under 3 ,, ,,	29,094 ,,	19·5%
	1 and under 2 ,, ,,	38,610 ,,	25·9%
Central Classes.	Less than 1 person to a room	5,445 ,, 3·7%	36·3%
	More than 4 rooms ...	41,729 ,, 28·0%	
	4 or more persons to a servant	6,913 ,, 4·6%	
Upper Classes.	Less than 4 persons to 1 servant, and 4 or more persons to 2 servants ...	3,350 ,,	2·3%
	All others with 2 or more servants	1,608 ,,	1·1%
	Servants	3,522 ,,	2·4%
		148,856	100%

Crowded: 32·0%

Not Crowded: 68·0%

Social Condition (by Sections).

Section.	3, 4, or more persons to a room.	2 and under 3 persons to a room.	1 and under 2 persons to a room.	Less than 1 to a room. More than 4 rooms, or 4 or more persons to 1 servant.	Less than 4 persons to a servant.	Servants.	Total.
Printing.........	10,961	17,338	23,155	28,837	1074	854	82,219
Per cent......	13	21	28	35	1½	1½	100
Bookbinding......	2947	4580	5431	5014	145	124	18,241
Per cent......	16	25	30	27½	1	½	100
Paper Manuf'ture	2777	3372	3023	2758	377	251	12,558
Per cent......	22	27	24	22	3	2	100
Stationery.........	985	1746	3163	7673	1332	857	15,756
Per cent......	6	11	20	49	8½	5½	100
Bookselling	915	2058	3838	9805	2030	1436	20,082
Per cent......	5	10	19	49	10	7	100

CHANGES SINCE 1861 IN NUMBERS EMPLOYED.

	1861.	1871.	1881.	1891.
Printing	17,800	23,400	30,000	40,000
Bookbinding	7,800	9,900	12,900	15,900
Paper Manufacture	4,200	5,500	9,900	14,700
Stationery	4,500	6,000	7,100	8,900
Bookselling	4,700	5,400	5,900	7,800
Total	39,000	50,200	65,800	87,300

All these Sections without exception show very large increases in numbers.

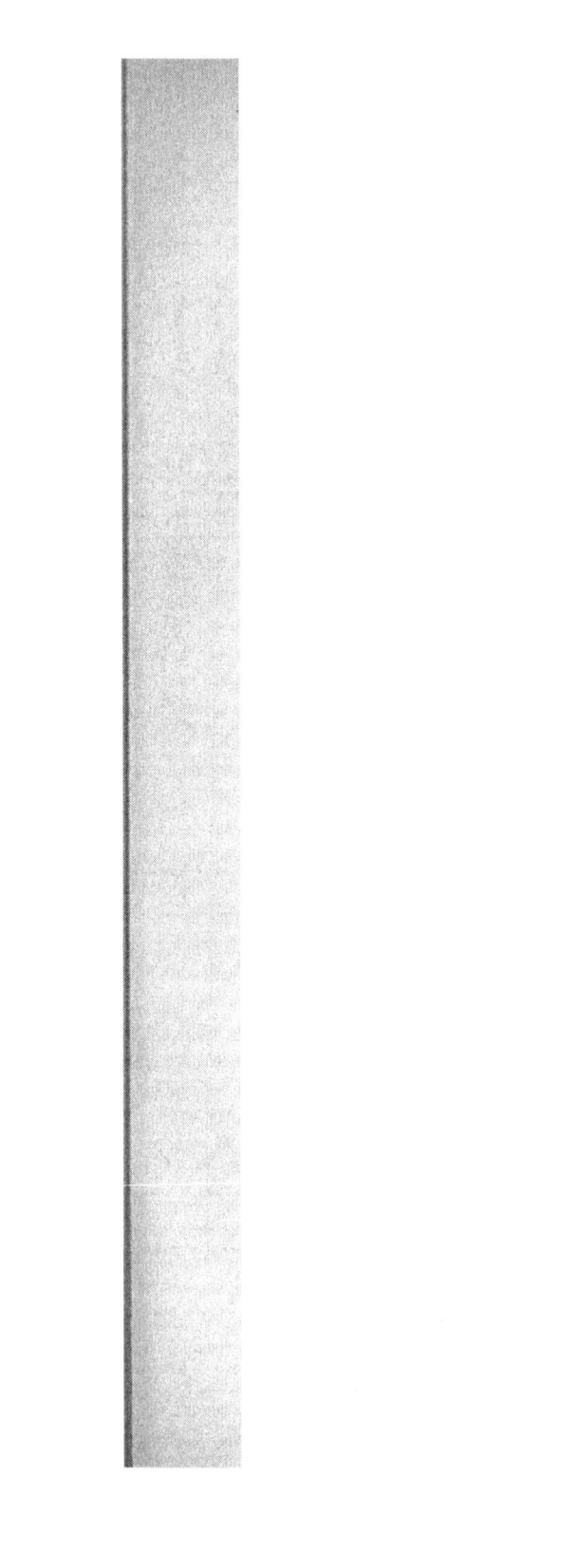

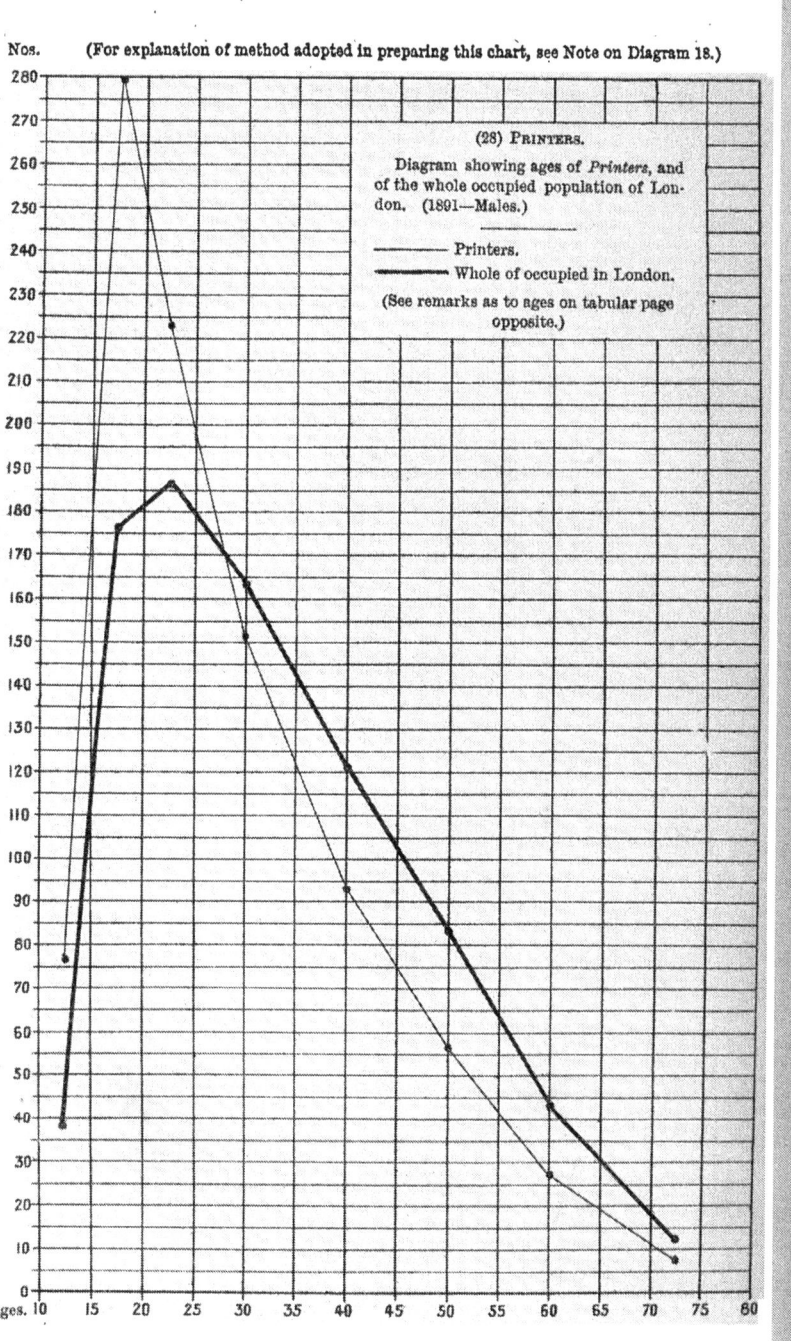

(28) PRINTERS.

Diagram showing ages of *Printers*, and of the whole occupied population of London. (1891—Males.)

——————— Printers.

━━━━━━━ Whole of occupied in London.

(See remarks as to ages on tabular page opposite.)

CHAPTER I.
PRINTERS. *(Section 28.)*

Persons represented.

Census Enumeration.

Divisions, 1.	Fe-males. All Ages.	Males. −19	Males. 20−54	Males. 55−	Total.
...er .... graph-	1316	9988	21,784	1921	35,009
......	809	737	3637	437	5040
...AL....	2125	10,745	24,821	2358	40,049

...ade more than any other absorbs our ...e small proportion of men at all ages ...n the diagram) is merely the counter- ...r feature of the curve. There is no ...o suppose that either the growth of ...e, or any changes in method have ...these proportions, and if so it is ...at a large number of printer's boys ...her work when they reach manhood.*

DISTRIBUTION.

N.	W. & C.	S.	Total.
9835	7577	16753	40049

DETAILS OF OCCUPATIONS (FROM THE CENSUS DICTIONARY).

...t-press printer, music printer, ...rical printer, overseer, clicker, ...sitor, turnover, typesetter, reader, ...r, pressman, layer-on, taker-off, ...ne minder, cropper hand, ware-...man, cutter, machine ruler, ruler's ...ed, stereotyper.

...h printer, chromolithographer, litho. ...er stippler, stone grainer, prover, ...pressman, litho. machine minder, ...on, taker-off, music lithographer, ...lithographer, transfer - engraver, ...graphic printer, copper-plate ...r, steel-plate printer, map and ...colourer and seller, map engraver, ...d and label writer, caligraphist, ...ar addresser.

Enumerated by Families.

Sex	Males	17,846	
	Females	202	
Birthplace	In London .... 66 %	11,942	
	Out of London 34 %	6106	Heads of Families, 18,048.
Industrial Status	Employer .... 5 %	983	
	Employed .... 92 %	16,595	
	Neither ...... 3 %	470	

TOTAL POPULATION CONCERNED.

	Heads of Families.	Others Occupied.	Unoccupied.	Servants.	Total.
Total	18,048	16,060	47,257	854	82,219
Average in family..	1	·89	2·62	·05	4·56

CLASSIFICATION.

Numbers living in Families.		%
3 or more to a room	10,961	13·2
2 & under 3 ,,	17,338	21·1
1 & under 2 ,,	23,155	28·0
Less than 1 ,,		
More than 4 rooms	28,837	34·9
4 or more persons to a servant ...}		
Less than 4 to 1 servant and 4 or more to 2 servants	853	1·3
All others with 2 or more servants ..	221	0·2
Servants	854	1·3
	82219	100

	Inner.	Outer.	Together.
Crowded..	50 %	20 %	34 %
Not ,, ..	50 %	80 %	66 %

DISTRIBUTION.

East	Inner 9269	10,802
	Outer 1533	
North	Inner 3254	21,289
	Outer 18,035	
West	Inner 1066	3924
	Outer 2858	
Central Inner 10,767		10,767
South-East	Inner 2598	14,315
	Outer 11,717	
South-West	Inner 12,811	21,122
	Outer 8311	
		82,219

Inner 39,765, or 48 %
Outer 42,454, or 52 %

Status as to Employment *(according to Census Enumeration)*.

Census Divisions (1891).	Employers. Males.	Employers. Females	Employed. Males. Under 20.	Employed. Males. Over 20.	Employed. Females of all ages.	Neither Employer nor Employed. Males.	Neither Employer nor Employed. Females	Total.
P...er	827	39	9988	22,365	1266	313	11	35,009
Lith., copper and steel-plate printer	177	2	506	2571	88	153	6	3503
Map and print colourer and seller ..	17	—	49	175	72	62	12	387
Ticket and label writers	36	3	202	169	619	114	7	1150
	1057	44	10,745	25,480	2045	642	36	40,049
TOTAL.........	1101		38,270			678		40,049

Proportion of Employers to Employed-1 to 35

* ...om two firms we have particulars of 18 boys who entered the trade. Of these, 3 ...w...s emigrated, 2 became soldiers, 1 a milkman, 1 a ship's steward, 1 a school-board visitor, ...i...rance agent, 1 a photographer, 2 reporters, 1 a reader, and 5 remained printers. In only ...of...e 18 cases was the boy's father in the trade.

The London Printing Trade.

In 1871 no less than 46 per cent. of the printers enumerated in the census for England and Wales belonged to London; in 1881 the proportion was 43 per cent.; and in 1891, 40 per cent. These figures show a continuously reducing proportion, although in the same period the proportion which the population of London bore to that of the whole country rose slightly (from 14·3 per cent. to 14·5 per cent.). The growth of the trade has, however, been enormous everywhere. In London, the numbers employed in it have risen in the twenty years from 23,000 to 40,000, and it is certain that in addition to the 40,000 enumerated in 1891 there are some who, though employed in London, live beyond the Registrar General's boundary, *e.g.* at Walthamstow, &c. Whether we take 46 per cent. of the trade as it was in 1871 or 40 per cent. as it is now, the proportion is extraordinarily large. Except bookbinding no other important trade is so distinctly metropolitan in its character, and this peculiarity is still more clearly marked if we consider the printing of newspapers and periodicals apart from that of books, for as to the printing of books London is at some disadvantage in cost compared to the provinces.

Since Caxton's time, printing has developed in many directions, involving new methods and new materials. Consequently, with printing proper, or typography, there are included in this Section lithography and various forms of printing from engraved blocks or plates, and even from gelatine films. Typography uses lead and lithography limestone, while engraving is usually done on wood, steel, or copper; and in the modern developments of printing in connection with photography many substances have been utilized. A more scientific division than that afforded by the substance used is to be found in the mode in which the impression is obtained, thus :—

(1) In letter-press printing, the prominent surface of the type used receives the ink and imparts it, under pressure, to the paper.

(2) In lithographic printing, a perfectly smooth surface of stone is so affected by application of grease, and so protected where not greased by being wet, that marks made upon it with grease retain ink for transmission to the paper, while the rest of the stone remains clear.

(3) In steel or copper-plate printing the lines to be reproduced on the paper are incised. Ink is applied to the whole surface of the plate, and is then wiped off, leaving only the incised portions charged.

I. LETTER-PRESS PRINTING.

. This trade is by far the most important of those with which we have to deal, and the men engaged in it are quite distinct from those employed in the other branches. They include compositors or typesetters, readers, pressmen, machine managers or minders, stereotypers, and with these may be included the printer's labourers, warehouse-men, cutters and others, of whom the greater number find their employment in letter-press printing.

The compositors outnumber all the rest. They are generally accommodated at the top of the building in which they work, a good light being essential.

The desks or frames at which the men stand, are furnished with two shallow wooden trays, one of which, set a little higher than the other, is also tilted upward and forward at a greater angle. These trays or " cases," as they are called, are divided into compartments or " boxes " to hold the different types. The upper case holds the capitals and the lower one the small letters. The compositor stands facing these boxes, holding his " composing stick " or receptacle for the type in his left hand, while with the right he picks up the letters, &c., for the reproduction of the manuscript, which is placed before him. When a few lines are complete they are transferred from the "stick," on which they have been arranged, to a long tray, the width of which is adjusted to that of the column of print. This tray is called a galley, and the proof drawn from this first arrangement of the matter is the "galley proof." The reader compares this proof with the "copy" (as the original is called, with a lack of logic peculiar to the English race), and returns it for any necessary corrections before a "clean" proof is "pulled" for the author.

Besides setting the type, it is the compositor's duty to arrange the matter in pages, in such manner that when the printed sheet is folded the order shall be correct, and finally he has to "lock" these pages tightly in an iron frame or "chase," after which the "forme," as it is now called, is ready to go to the machine-room for the printing.

In connection with their trade union the compositors in each printing establishment are organized as a "chapel,"* and one of the members, chosen amongst themselves as "father of the chapel," becomes the medium between the union, the individual men, and the employers. In very large establishments there may be two or three "companion-ships"† each of which forms a chapel, and in such cases one of the "fathers" would be known as the "imperial father" and would represent the whole body with the employers and with the Society. Each chapel has a fund—subscribed by the men—from which cases of distress are relieved.

The "reader," or "corrector of the press," as he prefers to be termed, has not only to note mistakes in printing, but to attend to the sense of the printed matter and throw back a query to the author when needful. If not himself a

---

* The peculiar use by printers of the words "chapel," "father," and some others, is very old, and said to date from the setting up of Caxton's press at Westminster Abbey.

† An abbreviation of this word causes a compositor to talk of his "ship" in place of "shop" or "works."

practical _compositor he must in any case be familiar with
the work and technique of printing, and should also have a
considerable fund of general knowledge and quick per-
ception. With his attendant boy, he may be found in a little
den partitioned off from the bustle of the composing-room;
a link between the compositor and the writer. In small
offices a compositor may check his own work with a boy to
read, but in houses where books and newspapers are
printed, men with special qualifications are engaged, some
being paid a high salary. Many managers and editors
graduate at the reader's desk.

In old times, when the compositor had completed the
"forme," it was sent to the pressman to work off, and indeed
still is so sent, except that the introduction of machinery has
changed the name of the workman employed from pressman
to machine minder or manager.* Hand presses are,
however, still used for proofs, or when the number of copies
required is small, or for fine work which needs constant
personal care.

Pressmen remain a distinct body of men, numbering
perhaps five hundred in London, and find fairly regular
employment, because although the use of the hand machine
has decreased, the supply of labour has been even more
restricted. Young men prefer the less laborious work on
the machines, and are, moreover, naturally drawn towards
an increasing trade.

The machines in any printing establishment, are usually
placed, on account of their great weight, in the basement
adjoining the driving engine.

Machine managers are responsible for the printing.
They receive the formes from the composing-room and
fasten them on the machines. Their duties include many

* In England the term "press" is restricted to hand-printing machines,
excepting that the machine perfected by the proprietors of the *Times* is
called the "Walter Press." Otherwise the term "machine" is always used
for printing presses driven by mechanical power.

points small in themselves yet constituting the difference between good and bad printing. Care must be taken that there is no dust or dirt on the forme, and that the type is perfectly level. Any unevenness, either in the forme or in the machines, must be neutralized. This is termed "making ready." If there are any illustrations or diagrams, the lights and shadows must be adjusted to a nicety by "over-lays" or "under-lays," which increase the pressure where required. The printer needs to understand different qualities of ink, and must see that the ink is evenly distributed by the rollers; and correct "lay," that is the accurate adjustment of the forme to the machine so as to maintain uniform margins, must be obtained. If after the machine starts the impression be in any way defective he should be able to find out the reason and provide a remedy. It is also his duty to see that he has the necessary rollers, ink, paper, &c. He must keep count of the number of sheets printed, and learn how to handle white paper without leaving on it traces of his almost necessarily dirty fingers. All this is work requiring no little skill.

A considerable number of men, who come under the general designation of printer's labourers, are employed in the machine department in addition to those who actually manage or mind the machines. The nature of their work is indicated by the special names borne: thus we have "paper wetters," "layers on," and "strokers in," referring to the paper; "cropper" or "platen" hands for the small machines;* and "brakesmen," "oilers," "reel," and "fly" hands for those with rapid rotary action. These, who may be either men or boys, are all semi-skilled workers, though the amount of skill needed varies from the mechanical operation of "stroking" sheets of paper along the feeding board of a printing machine (with a piece of

---

* In these machines, used for hand-bills, cards and small work, the pressure is obtained by means of a plate and not by a roller. The original maker was named Cropper—hence Cropper or "platen" hands.

wood tied to the wrist), to the complete knowledge of "making ready" and of inks, which a good platen or cropper hand requires. There is no special apprenticeship for any part of this work. The lads enter the office as "feeding" boys, and pick up one branch or another as inclination or opportunity may direct.

Until recent times the work of "laying on" and "taking off" was mainly done by boys; but a good deal of overtime is usually worked during the busy season, and since overtime has been forbidden by law for lads under sixteen, men have been employed instead, especially for newspaper printing where the size and weight of the paper renders the change from boys to men doubly expedient.

When a book may run to several editions it is usual to work from a stereo reproduction instead of from the original type. The men who make these stereo-plates are called stereotypers. This process is also adopted when a large number of copies are needed quickly, the plan being to make and work from several stereos; and for the rapid rotary machines stereo-plates are necessary. It is the business of the stereotyper to make the mould and produce the stereo-plate, and one or two of these men are found in all large offices. On daily papers several are employed. There are numerous processes, but all are somewhat similar. That which is most usual is called the "paper" process, and is as follows:—When the stereotyper receives the forme from the composing room he first ascertains (as the press-man or machine minder would) that it is properly fastened up and perfectly level. The face of the type is then oiled, and a thick sheet of a moist pulp, composed of brown paper and blotting paper pasted together, and called a "flong," is placed upon it and beaten down with a brush so as to sink into the interstices between the letters and take an impress of their shapes. It is then dried, hardening as it dries, and, placed in a suitable receptacle, forms the mould into which the molten metal, a mixture of lead and antimony, is poured. For rotary machines the stereo is made in a semi-circular, or rather semi-cylindrical shape.

The tale of those employed is completed by the warehouse-men and cutters, who take charge of and prepare the paper for the printer's use, and also pack the finished printing for dispatch to the customer.

Letter-press printing has four main sub-divisions, in each of which the work has its peculiar characteristics. These are: book printing, newspapers, parliamentary work and commercial or jobbing work. There are also some minor divisions, such as music printing.

Book-work proper, as distinguished from periodicals, is leaving London. With few exceptions the London firms engaged in this trade have provincial houses, and thus themselves organize the competition between London and Provincial, and, it may be, also between union and non-union, labour. London wages (as we shall presently see) are maintained at a high level, partly by trades union action, and the advantage in cost of printing in the provinces is considerable. Compared with 36s or 38s weekly wages in London, the rate at Edinburgh and Bristol is 30s, at Perth 27s, at Aylesbury and Ipswich 26s and 25s, and in some Irish towns falls as low as 20s. It is not to be supposed that as good work, or as much, is done at the low rate, but that provincial work is cheaper is proved by the fact that the share of London in this work grows less. Foreign printers—Dutch or French—also compete, and, it is said, can afford to take still lower prices.

With *Magazines* it is different. Their position approaches that of newspapers, which must be printed where they are published. Some of the magazines are printed outside London, but probably not many outside of the influence of London rates of wages.

Weekly and Monthly Journals fall into the same category as magazines and other periodicals, but the *Daily Papers* form a distinct group. In this group, itself divisible into morning and evening journals, large staffs of compositors, stereotypers and machine men are employed. The work done for morning and evening journals is in some respects similar; for both, rapidity of production is the most important point. Seldom publishing more than one edition, the demand for which extends over several hours, the morning papers can readily attain the requisite speed of production by multiplying the number of machines. The evening journals hold their own by the issue of successive editions, for each of which some of the pages are altered and fresh stereo-plates needed. Keen rivalry also exists betwixt these journals as to which shall first announce such news as the result of an election or an important race. Many ingenious devices are resorted to in order to save time, and papers containing the result of an event are often on sale within ten minutes of the decision being given. For this purpose rapid distribution is as essential as fast machinery, and each of the evening papers has a service of light carts to deliver the editions to the newsvendors immediately on publication.

A great difference in the character of employment springs from the time of day at which a journal is produced. Those engaged on a morning paper necessarily come at night, the bulk of their work falling between 6 P.M. and the small hours of the morning; while the business hours for an evening paper lie between 7 A.M. and 7 P.M. Otherwise the work required is very similar in character. At first little to do, and then a rush, reaching its climax when the time for going to press approaches. As " copy " comes from the editors it is received by the " overseer " of compositors and cut into small sections, called " takes," which are numbered consecutively and given out to the men. When the compositor has set his few lines he will put them in their proper place on a galley, which will also receive the preceding and succeeding " takes," each being numbered to maintain the proper order. In some offices a man is set apart to arrange the takes in galleys. Proofs are pulled, if the article is long, without waiting for its completion, and sent one to the editor and one to the reader, to be returned to the composing-room for correction. Each compositor takes his turn at correcting. The type, set up, is then arranged in pages, and when a page is complete it is stereotyped in the manner already described, and the stereo-plates sent to the machine department, while the original type stands ready for the preparation of a new edition, or, in the case of permanent advertisements, for the next day's issue.

The cylinders of the best existing rotary machines accommodate two sets of plates of a daily paper, and thus produces two copies of the paper at every revolution. The paper passes into the machine from a large reel. As the sheet passes through it is divided down the middle, cut, folded, counted and delivered on to a tray in quires of twenty-six. In addition, supplementary sheets can be introduced and the inner pages fastened in their place with paste. All this work proceeds automatically, and at such a speed that it is more than one man's work to pick up the quires and place them on an adjoining bench, where they are tied into bundles for the publishing office. The latest improved rotary machines can work up to 13,000 revolutions per hour, and in actual practice does maintain a speed of 11,000 revolutions, which, working with two sets of plates, is equivalent to 22,000 copies per hour.

The work on daily papers is practically uniform from year's end to year's end, the busy season only involving a larger proportion of small type, and so slightly increasing the compositor's earnings. For weekly or monthly papers the stress of work, instead of coming at a particular hour of the day or night, comes on a particular day of the week or month. For a journal published on Saturday morning there would be little for compositors to do on Saturday itself or on Monday, beyond distributing the type of the previous issue. But, after Monday, each succeeding day would be busier till Thursday or Friday, when a number of extra men will generally be called in. Some of these outsiders—" grass hands," as they are termed—may also work at other offices, but in many cases these two days will represent their entire week's work. In the machine-room this irregularity is even more marked than with the compositors, but a smaller number of men are involved. With machine managers, too, a number of jobbing hands, both minders and labourers, will be called in.

There is a wholesome and natural tendency to reduce this irregularity by concentrating in one office the printing of various journals published on different days, and from this tendency some improvement may be hoped.

It used to be not uncommon for the proprietor or manager of a newspaper to agree to pay the overseer a certain sum for the production of the paper, leaving him to make his own arrangements with the men. The men and their unions object to this system of " farming " as tending to " sweating," and it is dying out.

Parliamentary Printing consists of the official reports of debates, minutes of evidence given before parliamentary committees, and general work done for the Houses of Parliament. For committees dealing with private bills only the necessary official part of the work is done by the Queen's printers, the promoters of opposed bills print and pay for the reports. Thus, private bill work is divided amongst a number of firms. While Parliament is sitting official work is fairly regular, but at other times there is a considerable decrease in the numbers employed. With private bills not only is the busy period shorter, but, as different printers are employed, the fluctuations in particular offices are great even during the season. This, however, is partly met by the men's practice of shifting from office to office. The work is done under great pressure as to time and always in the night. About 5 or 6 P.M. the printer will be informed that the day's evidence and speeches of Parliamentary counsel will extend to so many folios, and will calculate the number of men needed to set the matter during the night so that some twenty copies may be delivered by 9.30 A.M. He has a few trusted men who remain always on hand, and he fills up the number required from a body of compositors who subsist by this work and who are always on the look out for it. These men are of two classes : (1) fast " whip " hands, who prefer the large, irregular earnings attached to this work, and who, being well known as quick and reliable workmen, seldom lose a night if there is any work going and they wish to have it ; and (2) other men whose irregular mode of life will not allow them to retain a permanent situation, and who come to depend for their living upon a night's work here and there and now and then.

The earnings of these men are greater for the time they work than those of any others in the trade. It is all piece-work, and a guinea a night is attained by some. In one firm the average earnings of the men for ninety nights was 17s 4d per night per man, varying from £3. 17s to £5. 5s a week for those who worked five nights in a week.

Jobbing, or general printing, includes many kinds of work : posters, hand-bills, cards, programmes, and commercial printing of all kinds. Within recent years there has been marked improvement in the character of this work, and printing which was thought good enough, and even excellent, a short time ago, would not pass muster now. The move-ment was initiated by the introduction from America of new styles of type, which gave a clear, sharp impression. Now all the type founders vie with each other in producing new founts. Jobbing work employs a large section of the trade ; nearly all the smaller offices in the suburbs depend on it, and competition is keen. The suburban firms have not only to compete with great city houses, provided with all the advantages of a large and varied stock of type, but, also, on altogether different ground, with operative printers who invest their savings in a small printing plant and use it and their spare time to supplement their wages, by doing work for small tradesmen, local societies, or churches. Jobbing work offers opportunity for the display of skill and taste, and men who have these qualities readily obtain wages above the minimum rates of 36s or 38s. Men must be specially trained for it. Those who have been accustomed to newspaper or book printing are very little good at jobbing work. Payment is usually by time.

Seasons.—In letter-press printing the busiest part of the year is from October to Christmas; demand then continues brisk till Easter, when there is a lull followed by a slight recovery, and after this there is a gradual decline until August and September, which are the dead months in the trade. The few letter-press printers who are busy in these two months are those who print the parochial lists of voters, &c., this being the only special work at that time.

During the slack time the "grass" and jobbing men fare very badly; some of the regular men may be discharged, and those who are retained work short time. The distribution of work depends on the employer, who will manage to keep on those men whom it is his interest not to discharge.

There is very little shifting from shop to shop among the regular hands, and men who are out of work do not seek outside employment even in another branch of their own trade. The lines of demarcation are very clear—a compositor never works at the machine, or *vice versâ*. Within the branch there is some shifting, as from book-work to general printing, but this applies only to a small proportion of the men and these the highly skilled. As a rule, if a man goes at all to other work he leaves the trade altogether.

Training.—A seven years' apprenticeship is the ordinary

method of learning letter-press printing. Beginning by
learning the type and the boxes and making himself
generally useful, in two or three years the apprentice should
become an efficient typesetter. Whether his knowledge
goes much further would depend partly on himself, but
more on the character of the shop. A medium-sized office,
doing general work, is the best school for a lad who
desires to obtain a thorough knowledge of the trade. In
very large offices he is apt to be kept to one department,
and to be paid a piece-rate wage which encourages him to
do, and do only, the one thing he can do best. In very
small shops the plant is so small and the range of work so
limited that complete training becomes impossible. The
incomplete training given to apprentices in the larger firms
is a matter of complaint with the men. In some houses
lads are fined if found in any department other than their
own. The employers reply, and no doubt truly, that the
boys themselves prefer earning to learning. The best
interests, however, of the boys and of the trade demand that
they should be properly taught their business, and the
better class of masters recognize this by passing the lads
through each branch, and by allowing them to leave early to
attend technical classes, and even by paying a portion of the
fees for them. Owing to the defective character of London
training many employers, when they need men, advertise
in the provincial papers in preference to applying to the
London societies. The men who come up from the country,
even though they themselves join the Society, absorb the
chances of employment otherwise open to young Londoners.
Many compositors are unemployed because they have only
learnt one part of their business—type setting—and that
part being increasingly done by machinery it is the more
necessary that lads should learn those branches of the trade
which, requiring taste and judgment, the machine cannot
perform.

The proportion of apprentices to journeymen affects the

condition of employment considerably. The compositors' union endeavours to restrict the numbers, but is only -partially successful, as there are several large firms in which the Society has no influence, as.well as small shops, which make great use of apprentice labour and "flood the trade" with it. Probably the small shops are the worst offenders. Thus, in one suburban office two men are employed with no less than seven lads, who earn from 7s to 17s a week. This is an extreme case, but does not stand alone. The rule advocated by the men allows only one apprentice to three journeymen.

In the machine department the conditions are better. The men are more completely organized and can more generally enforce the rule (which, with them, allows two apprentices to four journeymen, with an additional apprentice for every three additional journeymen). In some houses the lad is taught to use the hand-press before going to the machine. Among the pressmen the old custom still obtains of placing the apprentice in charge of a man who is responsible for teaching him and also for the work that he does, the pressman being paid a certain sum for his trouble.

Improved Machinery.—Improvements in letter-press printing machinery have followed rapidly upon one another; and fast machines, such as have been referred to, are all of very recent construction. The history of the *Times* is a record of the successive introduction of improved machines to be superseded in a few years by others of a newer and faster type. The work on all these machines follows after that of the compositors, the connecting link being that of the stereotyper. A further step is taken by the application of machinery to composing. These machines, after a long and not always successful effort, are now forcing their way into use. There are several of them, but only two are used to any extent in London, of which one sets actual type by means of a key-board, while the other arranges the matrices which line by line receive the molten metal—thus dispensing altogether with loose type. Each of these machines has its advantages and disadvantages. Neither, it must be said, is very well adapted for any except rather simple and straightforward work, but on such work one man will do as much as four or five men setting type in the ordinary way. Amongst the benefits due to these machines is economy of space, and it may be confidently expected that these or other like inventions will gradually supersede hand type-setting for a large part of the compositor's work, especially for newspapers, cheap reprints of books, and for small type.

To a certain extent the adoption of composing machines will benefit London printers, enabling them to compete for book-work, the difference between the cost of labour on the machines in London and the country being much less than in hand composition, and perhaps disappearing altogether if allowance for carriage has to be made.

II. LITHOGRAPHIC PRINTING.

This process was invented in 1796 by a Bohemian, named Alois Senefelder, and has become an important branch of the printing trade. It was introduced into England early in this century, and in 1839 applied to printing in colour, or chromo-lithography as it was called by M. Engelman the first patentee.

The stone used is a close-grained limestone, cut into slabs three or four inches thick—the best stones come from Bavaria. The slabs are very heavy, the largest size (60 by 40 inches) weighing fully 8 cwt., while 4 or 5 cwt. is a common weight.

As a substitute for stone, zinc plates are now coming into use. They are backed with wood and much lighter to handle, but do not take the grease so well as the stones, and need more care in the printing.

The men employed in lithography are (1) stone

preparers, (2) artists or draftsmen, and (3) printers. The stone preparers smooth and polish the surface, or "grain" it for chalk drawings, and are known as grainers and polishers. They usually work in the basement, where the stones are kept because of their weight. The first process of preparation, which is done with water and another stone, removes all trace of any previous drawing and makes or keeps the stone perfectly smooth. It is then polished with pumice or snake stone so as to remove scratches, and the surface is ready for the artist. For graining, after the stone is rubbed level, it is ground with sand of the requisite character. The proportion of large stones used has increased owing to the practice of printing several drawings or several copies of the same design on one stone to economise labour, and the men who handle such stones must be strong. Boys assist in this work, but the men object to the practice as dangerous.

The artists or draftsmen are the most important section of those employed. They prepare the designs, draw them on the stones, arrange the combination of colours for chromolithography and the order and manner in which they shall be used—subject always to the supervision of the employer and the satisfaction of the customer. Three grades are recognized : (a) trade masters, who have their own shops and work for the large firms; (b) piece workers; and (c) journeymen or weekly wage earners. The two last work on their employer's premises. [For wages paid, see under organization.]

Lithographic printers form two distinct groups, viz. provers or pressmen, who use the hand presses, and machine minders; the latter differ little from those engaged in letterpress printing; the former make transfers on the stones, pull proofs, make corrections and touch up the work.

Boys and girls are employed to lay on and take off the sheets of paper. The former being the more difficult operation, lads of about eighteen are usually engaged for.

it. The lay is arranged by the machine minder, and the paper is fed carefully to "grippers" which seize and carry it into the machine. Sometimes to obtain exactness in chromolithography two needle points are projected upwards through a brass plate in the "feeding table" and make minute perforations in the sheets of paper as they pass into the machine. The person feeding the machine in the second and subsequent printings has to place the sheets of paper so that the sheet is seized by the grippers as in the first instance, or so that the needles as they rise go through the original holes. On this the exact adjustment of the colours depends.

In the slack time men are discharged. Provers, if good men, may be retained, but the machine minders seldom. Men do not shift from one branch to another. Artists, printers and polishers are quite distinct, and even machine minders will not work as provers or *vice versâ*. As a rule, they could not if they wished. A prover may learn to use the machine, but the passage in the other direction is much more difficult. Seasonal variation depends mainly on the chromo work, as about three-fourths of the men are engaged on that branch. From Easter to Whitsuntide there is a gradual increase of work, and the busier time is sustained till Christmas, being at its height from August to October. But for the past three years it is complained there has been no season to speak of.

Foreign competition in lithography is confined to the best class of coloured work. Many if not most Christmas cards and booklets are to be seen marked "Printed in Germany," although not infrequently they bear also the certificate "designed in England." Even in design the Germans try to meet our national prejudices by the adoption of English landscapes and English faces in their own designs. France also competes for this work, and possesses some secrets which we seem unable to penetrate. Some say foreigners are better and more intelligent workmen, others blame the trades unions or point to the lower wages on the continent. Others, again, accuse modern mercantile England of lack of business enterprise or of scientific insight compared to that of their foreign rivals. Perhaps all these causes have their effect. For posters and work of the large coarse kind England holds her own, but as between London and the provinces there is competition, and in this rivalry the country has an advantage in wages and rent.*

Like other branches of the printing trade, lithography is developing in many directions, mostly connected at present with the use of photography; and expedients for economising labour are being continually introduced.

For music printing both letter-press and lithographic methods are used. The trade is in few hands.

III. Copper-plate Printing.

Lithography, photogravure, and other processes have largely taken the place of steel and copper-plate printing for book illustrations; and but little remains of a once important trade. Copper-plate printing used to be entirely hand work, but machines have now been adapted for this class of printing. Bank-notes, scrip, and shares of all kinds are produced in this way. Even the printing of visiting cards, which formed a large but poorly paid section of the trade, is failing the copper-plate printer, some of the " card" houses introducing boys for this work, while if more than a few hundred cards or headings are wanted, the impression is transferred to and printed from the stone. Not only is engraving the plates costly, but the printing process is much slower than either letter-press or lithographic printing.

* It is noteworthy that the great posters which served to advertise Kiralfy's exhibition of " Constantinople in London" were printed in the United States.

IV. Minor Connected Trades.

Chromo-block Printing is mainly used for book illustrations, children's toy books, and similar work. A block is
prepared for each colour. There are only a few London
houses engaged in the trade and foreign competition is keen.
If work must be done quickly the London firms obtain the
order, but if time can be given the foreigner has the
preference. Men need a special training, and employers do
not discharge a man if they can avoid it.

Photogravure and other Processes.—A number of new
processes have been introduced under various names,
most of which are connected with the development of
photography, and are coming into use for book and other
illustrations. They depend mainly upon the preparation of
the plate or block. The actual printing follows one of the
three methods already described, but as the elevations and
depressions of the surface are usually very slight, great
care is necessary to obtain good results. In *photogravure*
the photograph is transferred to a copper-plate, and etched
in with an acid solution, the printing being done in much
the same manner as copper-plate etchings or mezzotint
engravings. In *collotype printing* the picture is reproduced on a film of collodion, and printed on a litho or
special press. None of these processes are of much importance in London, being only employed by a few firms. The
production of the half-tone and other photographic blocks,
now largely used for illustrating letter-press work, is more
important, several firms being engaged in the business.
It is, however, more properly a development of engraving
than printing.

Machine Ruling.—A number of other trades have grown
up with the development of printing, some for the supply of
printers' materials, others to undertake some portion of
the work; of these, machine ruling is one of the most
important. Most of the large printing firms employ some

machine rulers in connection with account-book making, but the smaller men take their ruling to one or other of about fifty houses that make a speciality of the work, and are known as machine rulers to the trade. About five hundred men are employed, and working with each man is a boy or girl, called a "putter in," to pass the paper into the machine, and with some machines there is another boy or girl to receive the sheets as they are ruled and place them on racks to dry. The essential feature of the machine is an arrangement by which a number of pens can be fixed at any distance from each other, and the paper be passed beneath them. The operator keeps the pens charged by means of a piece of flannel soaked with ink. Aniline or other inks are used, diluted to the required shade, and as many different colours as there are pens can be used at the same time. The newest machines rule both sides of the paper at once, and some are capable of an automatic lifting of the pens, or any of them, so that lines of varying length may be ruled. The lines drawn are, of course, parallel one with another, and to produce vertical as well as horizontal lines the paper must pass twice through the machine. Double lines are drawn by pens with double nibs.

Other subsidiary trades included in this section are those of ticket writers, stencillers, and map mounters, but the number of persons engaged in these occupations is small, especially when compared with the printers. It is, however, noticeable that they include nearly one-third of the limited number of women connected with printing.

Wood-type Cutters are included with type founders in the census, but may be mentioned here together with *Printers' Joiners,* who are counted with carpenters and joiners, but whose special business is to make type-frames, cases, galleys, composing sticks, &c. Both are distinct trades, whose work is connected entirely with printing offices. The wood-type cutters are mostly paid by the day, but have a set task to do. Wages are usually 7*d* or 8*d,* but may be as low as 6½*d* per hour. The smaller wooden type is cut by machinery, the larger by hand. Apprentices are taken in the proportion usually of one lad to two men. Printers' joinery is done by small masters specializing on some articles and disposing of their work to printers' brokers. A few firms do all parts of the work. Piece-work is general, earnings ranging from about 30*s* to 36*s*. Employment in both branches is fairly constant and men do not change employers much.

HEALTH.

Chest diseases are the great scourge of the printer. Dr. Arlidge published in 1892 an analysis of the causes of death of 799 members of the London Society of Compositors, who died in the ten years 1880-9. Of these, no less than 448 were due to pulmonary complaints, of which phthisis, bronchitis, and pneumonia were the most fatal—and the proportion of those dying of these diseases between twenty and forty years of age was still greater, being 184 out of 290. Nor is it only the compositors who suffer; amongst lithographers, out of 27 recorded deaths 14 were attributed to the same causes. Some part of the excessive mortality from these and other diseases may, it is suggested, be due to a tendency to select weakly children for this trade in preference to an out-door trade, but undoubtedly the explanation is mainly to be found in the heated and vitiated atmosphere in which the men often work, and this is especially the case with compositors. The fingers must be warm and supple to set type quickly, and consequently a high temperature is preferred. Fearing draughts, the compositors will stop every cranny by which fresh air can enter, and at night, especially, when gas lights are freely used, the work is done in an atmosphere that is overpowering to an outsider. These conditions are being improved by the rebuilding of old offices with properly arranged ventilation, and by the use of electric lighting.

The working years in these trades vary considerably. A compositor, if he escape the lung complaints that hurry many to an early grave, may live to a good old age, and retain his "case." There are many competent workers over sixty. Machine work is harder, and only a few exceptional men could continue at it after reaching fifty-five years of age. Beyond this age, also, few lithographic artists and printers remain. Failing sight drives them out of the field. Stone polishers, who have to move the heavy lithographic stones, cannot reckon upon work after reaching fifty, although if a man be a good grainer he will probably obtain work until he reaches sixty.

ORGANIZATION AND WAGES.

In all these trades wages and hours are, to a great extent, controlled by combination among the men. Every branch has its union, and the majority of those employed are members—excepting only in the case of lithographic printers, where the proportion of unionists is small. On the whole, the societies concerned count over seventeen thousand members,* while the total number of males over twenty years of age returned in the London census as employed in these trades is 25,480.

In what follows, the organization, wages, &c., of each branch will be considered separately. Federation has been attempted unsuccessfully on a national scale, and a similar attempt to combine the London societies has only been partially successful, the older unions standing aloof owing to sectional jealousies, especially as regards voting power. Among the individual unions there is a certain amount of over-lapping of sphere, particularly in reference to the semi-skilled workers; but for the most part the various

* Some of the members of these societies live beyond the London boundaries, but not in sufficient number to affect materially the figures given above.

branches of work are quite separate trades, for each of which
special apprenticeship or distinct training is required, and in
which there is little or no shifting of men from one to the
other.

Letter-press printing—Compositors.—The London Society
of Compositors is by far the largest organization connected
with the London printing trade. In its present form it
started in 1848 with eleven hundred members, replacing
the old Society of Compositors which carried its records
back to the beginning of the century, the recognized
objects being to procure employment for its members and
afford them temporary relief when out of work. The new
society progressed with few fluctuations, and within the last
decade its growth has been rapid, the membership rising
to over ten thousand in 1893, or double what it was in
1882. Its accumulated fund increased in the same period
from £12,000 to £23,700.*

The society is divided into two sections: the book and
news departments; the former including all except those
who work on the *daily* newspapers. There is an entrance
fee of 5s, and a weekly subscription of 10d to 1s. The
rate was only 8d in 1891, but was raised (by ballot of the
members) to 9d in 1892, to 10d in 1893, and to 1s in 1894,
in order to check the depletion of the funds consequent on
payments of out of work benefit, and to augment the reserve.
The numbers of unemployed increased from 1545 in 1890
to 2031 in 1891, and to 2256 in 1892, and the amount paid
in a still more serious ratio from £5500 in 1890 to £10,600
in 1891, and £11,900 in 1892, or about 5½d per week per
member. In 1893, the number of unemployed claimants
rose to 2447, or about one in four of the membership, but
there was a slight decrease (£40) in the amount of relief
given. Probably this is due to the fact that less additional

---

* In 1890 the fund reached £29,000, but the numbers of unemployed in
1891-3 reduced the balance by £6000.

out of work pay was voted than in the two preceding years, the limit per member being £15. 12s, as compared with £19. 16s in 1892 and £20. 8s in 1891.

The men attribute this lack of employment to the unsettled state of trade following the revision of the scale of wages (in 1891), complicated by the Baring financial troubles, the Hansard failure and the American Copyright Act. The employers point out that the increased rate of pay attracted a large number of men to London, while at the same time it necessitated on their part greater economy in the use of labour; and we have seen that the use of mechanical systems of typesetting has been pushed forward.

Until 1861, out of work allowance depended upon an optional provident fund, but in that year this benefit was made the first object of the society. Unemployed members may draw 12s per week for sixteen weeks in any year,* or £9. 12s in all, but not more than seven weeks' pay can be drawn from January to July. Men partially employed and not earning more than 16s in any week have their money made up to that sum, or to 19s if engaged on night work. Members of over twenty years standing, if unable to earn 15s a week, may apply for superannuation, and receive 4s to 6s a week. The death benefit for members varies (according to length of membership) from £4 to £15, and for members' wives one-third of these sums may be drawn. Assistance is also given to replace tools or clothes destroyed by fire, and to assist members to emigrate.

The society has its own freehold premises, with library and reading-rooms. Its income amounted to £20,900 in 1893.

The recognized hours of work are from 8 A.M. to 7 or

---

* The number of weeks during which the provident benefit may be drawn has been frequently increased. Since 1884, the only year in which extensions were not granted was 1887.

7.30 P.M., with one and a half hours allowed for dinner and tea. On Saturday work ends from 12 to 2 o'clock, and in some offices the men leave earlier on certain days of the week, working an extra hour on others. The result, on the whole, is fifty-four hours' work for day workers. Night work is either on piece or specially remunerated.

For fifty-four hours' work the union rate of wages is 38*s*, and below this rate the members may not work. This amount may be taken as the earnings of the ordinary time worker in full employment, except in some non-union houses, where 36*s*, the standard wage previous to 1891, still obtains. Many men, however, earn considerably more, 40*s* or 42*s* being paid for the more capable men on time. Piece-work, of which there is a good deal, brings higher but less regular earnings. In most offices both time and piece workers are employed, the proportion varying according to the kind of work done. For newspaper and parliamentary printing, payment by piece is the usual system. The piece rate is reckoned by the 1000 "ens" ("n" being accepted as the standard size of a single letter), and varies according to the size of the type from $11\frac{1}{2}d$ per 1000 for "diamond," a very small type, to $7\frac{1}{2}d$ for "brevier" and larger sizes. The character of the work also makes some difference. For reprints the rates are about $\frac{3}{4}d$ per 1000 less, and for morning newspaper work about $1\frac{1}{2}d$ per 1000 more.

The time workers are usually regular employees, and are known as "'stab" hands (meaning on the "establishment"); they are recruited from the ranks of the piece workers, and do the more responsible work or any copy which does not readily come under the piece scale. When work slackens the piece hands are the first to drop out of work.

The earlier editions of "The London Scale of Prices for Compositors' work," a booklet of over fifty pages, issued by the society, gave a fairly complete history of wages since 1810, when a scale was arranged by masters and men in conference. Since that time it has been revised six times, the last occasion being in 1891, when the scale was re-modelled by a similar conference, the earlier agreements being embodied in the new scale. The "'stab" wage was at that time raised from 36s to 38s per week, and a half-penny per 1000 ens added to the piece rates, with some minor changes chiefly affecting overtime.

From the union point of view, the employers are considered "fair" if they pay their compositors on the London scale of wages, and otherwise their works are "closed" to members of the society, who are not allowed to work with non-unionists; but some of the closed houses are unionist in other departments, while some on the "fair" list in the Compositors' Guide are "rat" shops with other societies. This causes confusion under the recent regulations, which confine public contracts to "fair" houses.

The *"Correctors of the Press"* have, strictly speaking, no trade union, but they are represented by an association with a benevolent fund. Each member, of whom there are 333, is pledged to inform the secretary of any vacancy so soon as he is aware of it, and the secretary must send the information immediately to the first two on the unemployed book. Most of the members belong to the Society of Compositors. There is no fixed rate of pay for this work, but it ranks with or above that of compositors.

Stereotypers have a minimum rate of 36s a week, but very few earn less than 40s, and the average wage is about 42s a week. Men who can do stereotyping, electrotyping, and finishing, get 45s, whilst finishers earn 42s a week. The men employed on daily newspapers obtain still higher rates. For weekly papers the work is sometimes done by contract.

Of *"Pressmen"*—those, as we have seen, who work on the old hand-machines—there are said to be five hundred in London, of whom 360 are members of the Amalgamated Society of Pressmen, an organization which dates from 1834, and into which have been absorbed an older society and a number of small societies called "gifts," which assisted men to obtain work and provided funeral benefit. The Amalgamated Society provides out of work benefit to the amount of 10*s* per week for ten weeks in the year, gives £8 at death, and dispute pay up to 30*s* per week "if requisite." In common with the other printing unions, this society's resources were strained, and its reserve reduced during 1892-3. Among pressmen time workers receive 38*s* for the week of fifty-four hours, while piece workers vary from about 26*s* to 40*s*, according to the speed of their work. The price is fixed by complicated scales which differ in different houses, but usually recognize three kinds of work—ordinary, fine, and difficult, the rate being reckoned per "token" or 250 sheets. For ordinary work, the token is considered an hour's work, so that a job may be termed indifferently so many tokens, or so many hours ; in some classes of work a token occupies much more than an hour.

Machine Managers for letter-press work are also paid a minimum of 38*s* for a week of fifty-four hours; but the standing wages of most of the men who have regular employment are 40*s* or 42*s* without overtime, and with overtime may average 45*s* per week. There is no piece-work. The normal hours are from 8 A.M. to 7 P.M., and till 2 o'clock on Saturday, but there is much night work; and overtime, although discountenanced by the men's society, is unavoidable, especially during the busy season from October to December. It is paid for at from 1*s* to 1*s* 3*d* per hour, and if extending after midnight an extra 1*d* per hour is charged. The varying demand for commercial printing—usually wanted as quickly as possible—accounts for part of the pressure, but the chief cause of the irregularity lies in the production of weekly and monthly periodicals. The pressure recurs with a certain regularity, and there are a number of jobbing hands who depend on work of this kind. Some may get a full week's work by

combining employment at different establishments, one or
two days or nights at each; while others only obtain, or
can only reckon on obtaining, one or two nights a week
(usually Thursday and Friday) during the slack season, and
must make shift to live on that. In the busy season these men
may earn as much as, and often more than, the regular
hands. A night's work consists of twelve hours, from 7 P.M.
to 7 A.M., with one and a half hours allowed for refreshments—the pay for it according to union rules for overtime
would be 13s 6d or 14s.

The trade union connected with these men, and called
the Printing Machine Managers' Society, probably contains
a larger proportion of the men belonging to its own
section than any other society in the trade. It has over
1600 members (1894), and it is said that only about
150 eligible men remain outside. It is strict as to
membership; applicants must have served an apprenticeship and have been in charge of a full-sized printing
machine for three years. Entrance fee is 5s; subscription
3s 6d per month. It gives unemployed benefit, 10s for
thirteen weeks, but reduces this to 9s and 8s for those who
join the society after thirty-five or forty. £20 for funeral,
or £10 in case of death of wife, for members of four years'
standing. Superannuation allowances, 5s per week after
fifty-five, may be voted to members of fifteen years' standing
Assistance also is given to members emigrating. The
society is governed by a council of twenty-one elected by
ballot. As with the compositors, the members in each
society house form a "chapel" with its "father," who is
elected every three months, each member being compelled
to take his turn. This society is one of the few in the
printing trade that has been able to live within its income
during the recent hard times.

Printers' Labourers.—Platen-machine minders have a
small union of their own, and the rest of the assistants
and semi-skilled men are represented by the " Printer's

Labourers' Union," a society founded in 1890, to which it is said three-fourths of those who are eligible belong, or about 1500 out of 2000. Lads working at the trade can join when eighteen years of age. The entrance fee is 5s, and subscription 4d per week. Relief to the unemployed is given at the discretion of the committee by vote from the general fund; the only fixed benefit is that at death, being £10 for a member and £5 for the wife.

Minimum wages for a week of fifty-four hours are fixed by the society at 30s for brake hands, oilers, wetters and general hands, with 9d per hour overtime; or at 36s for forty-eight hours if night work, with 10d per hour overtime. For wetters' assistants and reel and fly hands, 26s with 7d for overtime; or 30s and 8d for night work. For men working on "flat" machines, 20s with 6d overtime. For jobbing the rate is 6d per hour. This society added £200 to its reserve fund in the six months ending July, 1893.

The separate society called the Platen Printing Machine Minders' Society, already referred to, was established in 1890. It numbers 150 members. The entrance is 2s and subscription 6d per week. It promises unemployed benefit, 10s per week for four weeks in each half year, and strike benefit at the discretion of the committee. It aims to "raise the standard of wages and minimize piece-work." The recognized hours are fifty-four, and the union rate of wages varies from 25s to 30s according to the size of the machine, with 8d to 10d for overtime. There is some feeling between the members of this society and the "Machine Managers," who, regarding platen minders as labourers, object to their "making ready" the machines. The platen minders, however, regard themselves as skilled men, and their ambition is to obtain charge of a cylinder machine and become themselves machine managers—when, no doubt, they would think as machine managers do of the pretensions of other platen men to follow in their footsteps. That

they do obtain promotion seems probable from the fact
that there are no men in the society over thirty-five.

Warehousemen and Cutters are admitted to the Printer's
Labourers' Union, but these men have two unions of their
own, viz. "The Amalgamated Society of Printers' Warehousemen" and "The Printers' and Stationers' Warehousemen, Cutters' and Assistants' Union." The former
was formed in 1893 by the combination of two older
societies—the "London" and the "Caxton." It has
now five hundred members, paying 4d or 5d per week
according to age at time of entrance. Its objects are "to
obtain a minimum wage of 30s for warehousemen and
cutters and 24s for assistants, to provide out of work
benefit, and to regulate the relations of workmen and
employers." To be eligible, men must be at least
twenty-one years of age and have been four years at the
trade. The benefits are £5 at death or £2. 10s at death of
wife, and 10s per week for ten weeks if out of work.
There is also a benevolent fund. The other union mentioned has rather a wider scope. It is a general society,
but the London section, with nearly five hundred members, is
by far the largest branch. The subscription is 6d per
week, and for this the union provides £10 at death, £5
at member's wife's death, and 12s when out of work for six
weeks and 6s for six weeks more. This society includes
among its objects the reduction of hours of labour and
restriction of overtime, as to which it has very precise rules;
one forbids members to work more than one night a week
for their employer, or, if in regular employ, to work at
night at all for any employer but their own. It is estimated
that there are two thousand to three thousand men engaged
as warehousemen and cutters, so that not more than 50
per cent. of the men are unionists.

Lithographic Printers have four societies :—

(1) The Lithographic Stone and Zinc Preparers' Society,
established in 1889, with 180 members; subscription 4d

per week and levy of 6*d* in favour of the relatives of any member who dies. This society gives sick benefit and out of work benefit, in each case 8*s* per week for six weeks in the year. Otherwise its objects are the regulation of trade customs and the maintenance of a scale of wages adopted in 1891; viz. leading hands, 30*s*; grainers, 28*s*; polishers and shifters, 25*s* per week. The 30*s* seems to be very rarely paid, otherwise these rates agree with our returns. Overtime is paid at 8½*d* per hour.

(2) The London Circuit of the National Society of Lithographic Artists, with over three hundred members. This society has three different scales of subscriptions and benefits. The lowest of these, which most of the members adopt, is 6*d* per week, with 4*s* entrance, entitling the members to 12*s* a week for five weeks, and 10*s* for four more weeks in case of sickness; and the same amounts for eight, instead of nine weeks, if unemployed, and at death £5 for members of six years' standing. The society also keeps a register of the work done by members, so that employers can have some guarantee of its quality. A studio has also been opened at the society's rooms, where "life" and other art classes are held for the members. The wages earned vary greatly. As to those of the "trade masters" we have no evidence; those of the other men may be from 35*s* to £8 or more per week, depending on ability. The larger part receive from 42*s* to 50*s* per week, and few earn less than 40*s*, although the union minimum is 35*s*, but this minimum is intended for engravers, of whom a few belong to the same organization. Overtime is worked in the busy season, and some men are employed by more than one firm, doing extra work elsewhere after finishing at their regular place. The hours are fifty-three or fifty-four, but the rule is not rigorous—many of the men think forty-four hours enough for an occupation which requires so much care. Young men are preferred; they bring new ideas to the work. Older men fall into grooves.

(3) The London Society of Lithographic Printers (established 1833). This society has now seven hundred members. It provides out of work, sick and death benefits, and legal aid when needed. Since 1889 its expenditure has exceeded its income, mainly through a large increase in the number of the unemployed, and it has had to revise its scale of benefits.

· (4) The Amalgamated Society of Lithographic Printers, a national society, established 1880. This society has forty branches, and over 2500 members in all. The London branch has 350 members. Its resources, like those of the preceding society, have been strained by the expenses of recent years, and in 1893 it was obliged to levy on the members to maintain its reserve fund. Both these societies (3 and 4) endeavour to limit the number of apprentices, but without success in London, owing to the large non-union element.

The minimum wages for a pressman are 36s a week, and for a machine minder 40s. Most of the pressmen get more than their minimum, 40s and 42s being ordinary rates, and good workers in colour make 50s and 55s. Some are paid by piece, especially on black work, such as bill-heads. Parliamentary and legal work is also paid by piece, and, like Parliamentary letter-press, is night work. Of the machine minders there are many working at 36s and 38s, and others at 40s and 42s. Some employers give a "bonus" according to amount of work done, but the unions oppose this practice. There is no regular piece system with the machines, but the employers expect a certain quantity of work per day, the amount depending on the class of work. Overtime is paid "time and a quarter," or by some chromo printers, $13\frac{1}{2}d$ per hour. There is not much overtime, however, except in the small houses, where employment is irregular at all times.

The lads engaged in "putting on" earn 12s to 15s a week, with, in some cases, a bonus on the number of reams

printed.   The "taking off" boys are younger and are paid
7s or 8s a week.   Girls or young women when employed on
this work earn about the same wages as boys or lads,
continuing at it till a greater age.   They are said to be
quicker, cleaner, and more careful than boys, and are
preferred by some of the men because they do not
grow up into competitors as machine minders, like the
boys.

Copper-plate Printers have two societies, the "Philanthropic" and the "Friendly."   Both are small, and the
majority of the men are not unionists.   Wages for time
workers are 36s to 42s; but piece-work is the rule.   The
work is varied in character and there is no recognized scale
of prices except for ladies' and gentlemen's visiting
cards.   Each man has to make his own bargain with the
employer.   Earnings on piece ordinarily vary from 25s to
35s, but exceptional men may get as much as 50s.   In the
slack season few of the men would receive 30s, and some
not exceed 17s or 18s per week.   The busiest time is
from October to Christmas and the slackest about
August.

The *Machine Rulers* have their society (London Society of
Machine Rulers), started in 1873.   It has now 170 members,
and provides out of work and strike pay, death benefit and
superannuation.

TRADES UNIONS.

The following is a complete list of the Trades Unions belonging to this Section :—

Numbers in the London Trade (Census 1891).		Name of Trade Society.	Membership in London.		Remarks.
Total.	Of whom are employed males over 20.		In each Society.	In each Division.	
		London Society of Compositors (1848).	10,268		Centralised Society. Committee elected yearly. Gives Unemployed, Dispute, Superannuation, Death, and Emigration Benefits.
		London Printing Machine Managers' Trade Society (1839).	1650		Gives Unemployed, Strike, Death, Superannuation Benefits, and assists members to emigrate or leave the trade.
		Amalgamated Society of Pressmen (1834).	360		Benefits: Unemployed, Strike, and Death allowances.
		Platen Machine Minders' Trade Society (1890).	150		Gives Unemployed Benefit. Strike pay at discretion of Committee.
35,009	22,565	Printer's Labourers' Union (1889).	1561	15451	Gives Death Benefit. No regular Unemployed pay, but relieves members in distress.
		Printers and Stationer's Warehousemen, Cutters and Assistants' Union (1889).	472		Out of work Benefit only. Strongly opposed to overtime. Union and non-union men work together.
		Amalgamated Society of Printers' Warehousemen (1893).	510		Offers out of work and Death Benefits. Formed by the amalgamation of the Caxton and Old London Societies.
		Federated Society of Stereotypers and Electrotypers (London Branch) (1893).	310		Offers out of work and Dispute pay.
		London Society of Machine Rulers (1873).	170		Offers out of work, Dispute, and Death Benefits; Superannuation to twenty years' members.
35,009	22,565	(*Carried forward*)		15,451	

Numbers in the London Trade (Census 1891).		Name of Trade Society.	Membership in London.		Remarks.
Total.	Of whom are employed males over 20.		In each Society.	In each Division.	
35,009	22,565	(Brought forward) National Society of LithographicArtists, Designers and Writers, and Copperplate and Wood Engravers (London Circuit), (1886).	302	15,451	Offers out of work, Sickness, and Death Benefits. Three scales of subscription with benefitscorresponding in amount. Few wood engravers; these men have their own Society now.
		London Society of Lithographic Printers (1833).	621		Offers out of work, Dispute, and Sick Benefits. Superannuation after fifty-five years of age. Insurance of members' clothes and tools against fire.
3503	2571	Amalgamated Society of Lithographic Printers (London Branch), (1880).	350	1636	Gives out of work. Sick and Death Benefits. Superannuation for members of twenty years' standing.
		Lithographic Stone and Zinc Preparers' Society (1889).	180		Offers out of work and Sick Benefits. Levies members at death.
		London Society of Litho MusicPrinters (1890).	43		Out of work Benefit, varying with length of membership.
		Friendly Society of Copper-plate Printers (1837).	70		—
		Philanthropic Society of Copper-plate Printers (1841).	70		—
387	175	(Map and Print Colourers and Sellers.)	—	—	—
1150	169	(Ticket and Label Writers.)	—	—	—
40,049	25,480			17,087	

The printers seem to have a special aptitude for organization. There are several trade benevolent societies, the most important being the Printers' Pension, Almshouses and Orphan Asylum Corporation, which has almshouses at Wood Green, collects in the workshops, and distributes annually old age pensions amounting to between £2000 and £3000. Of social societies the number is legion, some coincident in extent with the chapel, others of wider range. In some cases the association with the house where a man learnt his trade is maintained, much as "Old Boys" cherish the memory of their school.

The employers are well organized. The Printing and Allied Trades' Association, founded in 1890, includes all the principal firms. On joining it, an employer agrees not to conclude any modification of the terms of labour with the men without first submitting the matter to the committee, and if the workpeople propose a change the same course is to be followed. Most of the proprietors of the daily papers belong to the Newspaper Society, which was started in 1836 to protect the interests of provincial newspapers, but has since widened its basis and now includes most of the London newspapers. In addition, the Printing section of the London Chamber of Commerce may be said to represent the whole trade.

Wages Statistics.

In these trades 25,480 adult men are employed, and of these we have wages returns for 2164, in the service of fifty-five firms, as under:—

General printers .... 24 ⎫
Printers and lithographers 18 ⎪ = 55 firms employing usually 4563 per-
Parliamentary printer ... 1 ⎪ sons of whom 2449 are adult males, but
Music printer .... 1 ⎪ of these 285 belong to other sections, as
Printers and stationers ... 6 ⎬ engravers, die-sinkers, stamp-cutters,
Printer and binder .... 3 ⎪ rubber-stamp makers, stationers, car-
Machine ruler .... 1 ⎪ penters, engineers, engine drivers,
Lithographic artists ...... 1 ⎭ stokers, clerks, travellers.

The wages of these men in an ordinary week are as follows:—

```
Under 20s............ 89, or  4 per cent.  ⎫
20s to 25s...........222  „  10½  „        ⎬  Below 30s, 25½ per cent.
25s „ 30s............243  „  11   „        ⎭
30s „ 35s............214  „  10   „   ·    ⎫
35s „ 40s............587  „  27   „        ⎬  30s and over, 74½ per cent.
40s „ 45s............415  „  19   „        ⎭
45s and upwards...394  „  18½  „
                    ─────
                    2164  „ 100   „   ·
```

A comparison may be made between our figures, and those obtained in 1886 by the Board of Trade from twenty-five firms, employing 3983 persons, of whom 1670 were adult men belonging to this section.

	—20s.	20s—	25s—	30s—	35s—	40s—	45s—
Our returns ...	4 °/₀	10½ °/₀	11 °/₀	10 °/₀	27 °/₀	19 °/₀	18½ °/₀
Board of Trade returns	25½ °/₀			74½ °/₀			
	1½ °/₀	6 °/₀	9 °/₀	9 °/₀	48 °/₀	15 °/₀	11½ °/₀
	16½ °/₀			83½ °/₀			

Wages are now 2s a week higher than in 1886, but this gain, which should make our return show the higher figures, is more than counterbalanced by the substitution of actual earnings, in our return, for nominal full weeks' wages in those of the Board of Trade. It will be noticed, however, that here, as in some other trades, the proportion of those earning quite high wages is greatest when the actual money received is taken as the basis. This may be explained, probably, by the effect of night work or overtime.

As to regularity of work, we have particulars of numbers employed in busy and slack weeks from twelve firms, to combine with the Board of Trade figures as below.

	Busy Week.	Slack Week.	Percentage Reduction.		
			In numbers.	In earnings per head.	Combined.
Our returns	1625	1481	9	19½	26½
Board of Trade returns	4295	3722	13	19½	30

Busy and slack weeks fall in almost every month—it would seem that one shop is busy when another is slack, and if it were not that the trade is, on the whole, over supplied with workers, it might be supposed that men could secure pretty regular work by shifting from shop to shop. As it is, however, the men stay by their shop and earnings are shared. The piece-work system lends itself to this, and an analysis of the returns shows that compositors who are piece workers suffer more from insufficient work than machine minders. But these, on the other hand, have in slack times a larger proportion entirely out of work.

From detailed returns given by ten employers, the following comparisons are made as to the numbers employed at different rates in busy and slack weeks, with average earnings and hours:—

Men.		Busy Week.			Slack Week.		
		Men.	Wages.	Hours.	Men.	Wages.	Hours.
	Per Hour.		*s. d.*			*s. d.*	
	Under 5*d*	46	21 2	62	64	20 8	59
Time-work	5*d* and 6*d*	74	27 4	60½	36	25 9	56
	Over 6*d* to 8*d*	53	32 2	56	53	30 10	53
	„ 8*d* to 10*d*......	221	45 0	58	213	40 4	54
	„ 10*d*	65	59 11	63½	36	53 3	56½
		459			402		
	Under 15*s*	4	8 0		18	11 3	
	„ 20*s*	2	19 0		13	16 3	
	„ 25*s*	7	22 10		25	23 1	
Piece-work	„ 30*s*	11	26 4	} 81°/₀	17	26 8	} 30°/₀
	„ 35*s*	10	32 0		14	31 9	
	„ 40*s*	18	37 5		10	37 3	
	„ 45*s*	18	42 8		5	42 10	
	45*s* and over	60	60 5		2	57 6	
		130			104		

The piece workers—mostly compositors—are here shown to suffer the greatest reduction of wages, only 30 per cent.

of those employed earning more than 30s a week in slack time, compared with 81 per cent. in the busy week.

According to the census, 2045 women and girls are employed in these trades, and we have particulars of wages earned by 647, as follows :—

5s and under	 84	or 13 per cent.	⎫
6s ,, 7s	 55	,, 8¼ ,,	⎪ Below 12s, 49½ per cent.
8s ,, 9s	 88	,, 13½ ,,	⎬
10s ,, 11s	 93	,, 14½ ,,	⎭
12s ,, 13s	109	,, 17 ,,	⎫
14s ,, 15s	 72	,, 11 ,,	⎪
16s ,, under 20s	...107	,, 16¼ ,,	⎬ 12s and over, 50½ per cent.
20s ,, over	 39	,, 6 ,,	⎭

647 ,, 100 ,,

As to boys and lads under twenty, there are 10,745 employed, and we have particulars for 1305, as follows :—

5s and under	 96	or 7¼ per cent.	⎫
6s ,, 7s	327	,, 25 ,,	⎪ Below 12s, 68½ per cent.
8s ,, 9s	271	,, 21 ,,	⎬
10s ,, 11s	195	,, 15 ,,	⎭
12s ,, 13s	135	,, 10 ,,	⎫
14s ,, 15s	 97	,, 7½ ,,	⎪
16s ,, under 20s	...131	,, 10 ,,	⎬ 12s and over, 31½ per cent.
20s ,, over	 53	,, 4 ,,	⎭

1305 ,, 100 ,,

Social Condition.

Of the 25,480 adult men employed, about 16,420 come under social classification as heads of families. Tested by our wages returns, only about 15 per cent. earn less than 25s, whereas 37 per cent. live under crowded conditions. Next we find 21 per cent. earning from 25s to 35s, compared to 30 per cent. who live in one, or up to two, in each room, leaving no less than 65 per cent. earning over 35s, as compared to 33 per cent. of the central classes.

Comparison of Earnings with Style of Life (Printing Trades).

Earnings as tested.	Classification of Population.
Under 20s... 89 or 4 per cent.	3 or more in each room, 11,000 or 14½ per c'nt.
20s to 25s...222 ,, 10¼ ,,	2 to 3 ,, 17,300 ,, 22¼ ,,
25s ,, 30s...243 ,, 11 ,,	1 ,, 2 ,, 23,200 ,, 30 ,,
30s ,, 35s...214 ,, 10 ,,	Less than 1 ,,
35s ,, 40s...587 ,, 27 ,,	More than 4 rooms
40s ,, 45s...415 ,, 19 ,,	4 or more persons } 25,500 ,, 33
45s and } upwards } 394 ,, 18¼ ,,	to a servant
—— ,, —— 2164 ,, 100 ,,	77,000 ,, 100 ,,
	Employers' families and servants 5219
	82,219

Printing and its allied trades being largely concentrated in the East Central and West Central districts, but few of the men live near their work. They are spread over all the outer ring, South-East London being the most favoured district. The only noticeable concentrations are in Walworth, south of the Thames, and in the neighbourhood of the Caledonian Road on the north, a regular colony of printers existing in each place. The men who live in these districts generally walk to their work, convenience of situation, with this aim in view, being a principal factor in the choice of residence. In the remoter districts, excepting the neighbourhoods served by the Great Eastern suburban trains, personal matters, such as proximity of relatives, govern the choice rather than economic reasons. The cheap service of workmen's trains has no doubt attracted many of the men, and accounts for the number of printers living at or near

Walthamstow, Edmonton, Tottenham, and other suburban stations on this line.*

Those who live so far from their work cannot go home to their meals. Tea is usually taken in the shop; it may be made on the premises or obtained from a neighbouring coffee-house, the former being the common practice. As regards the mid-day meal, a much greater diversity is found, in a measure reflecting the social differences that must exist in a body of men representing so many different, although allied, trades. Even amongst the compositors, while no distinction is recognized by their society, the morning newspaper hand is socially as much above the City jobbing compositor as the latter is above the book " comp," the difference in earnings and regularity of employment accounting for this. As a rule, compositors go to a coffee or public-house. Where the latter has a dining-room, the dinner is better and the charges slightly higher than at the coffee-house, and attract the " comfortable " section of the men. Some also, who cannot afford sevenpence or ninepence for the coffee-house dinner, go to the public-house taproom or bar, bringing with them some of their food, and buying their ale, cheese, or pickles of the publican. Stereotypers, warehousemen, and labourers usually have their dinner at the works; the former are shut off from the rest of the workmen, and can easily cook a chop or steak at their furnace. Economical motives induce the warehousemen and labourers to bring their food from home, perhaps making tea or coffee, their facilities for this being better than in other departments where the number of men is greater.

Aprons are generally worn in all branches; some compositors keep an old coat also, and machine men often wear blouses. Overalls are worn by lithographic stone-

_____

* The cost of the journey from Walthamstow to Liverpool Street and back by workman's train is twopence a day; to Penge, about the same distance south, it is fourpence.

preparers, and sometimes by warehousemen when wetting paper for printing.

Most of the men belong to a trade union, and the greater number to a friendly society or sick club also. Perhaps the proportion of men in friendly societies is greater here than in most trades, as, with few exceptions, the men's unions do not give sick pay, and the men, the prudent section of them at least, have an extra inducement to make special provision for this contingency. There are two strong societies connected with the trade, the Compositors' Permanent Sick Fund and the Sick Fund Union. In the large offices there is usually a sick club; in smaller establishments the "chapel" fund is the only resource. The cost of maintaining these associations varies from 10d to 2s 6d a week per man and the proportion of income spent in this way ranges from about 2½ per cent. to 5 per cent. of a man's earnings. As a rule, the compositors' provident expenditure is greater than that of other printers.

In the more highly paid branches of the trade the wife seldom works unless the husband is unemployed, or other misfortune has befallen the family. The leaders of the men see that the standard of life is not higher in trades where husband and wife work than in those where only the man works, and they consequently oppose it "as not worth while." Amongst compositors there is a tendency to start a small business that the wife can look after. Warehousemen frequently find their wives amongst the folders employed in the office, and such women will often continue their work, or resume it as necessity arises.

CHAPTER II.

BOOKBINDERS. (*Section 29.*)

Persons Represented.

	Census Enumeration.					Enumerated by Families.			

Census Enumeration.

Census Division, 1891.	Fe-males.		Males.			Total.
	—19	20—	—19	20—54	55—	
Bookbinders ..	4014	5429	1388	4520	501	15,852

This is largely a trade of women, but the proportion stated above is probably too great, being exaggerated by the inclusion of women engaged as folders in printing offices. The age line for males follows much the same course as that for printers; many boys are employed who must seek other work when they come to be men. (*See* diagram.)

DISTRIBUTION.

E.	N.	W. & C.	S.	Total.
3084	3156	3832	5780	15,852

DETAILS OF OCCUPATIONS
(FROM THE CENSUS DICTIONARY).

Leather binder, forwarder, finisher, cloth binder, backer, rounder, case-maker, blocker, book-edge gilder, marbler, folder, collator, sewer, head bander, vellum or account-book binder, portfolio maker, leather case book maker, straw board liner, bookbinders' material dealer, book mounter, clasper.

Enumerated by Families.

Sex	{ Males	3473 }	
	{ Females	816 }	
Birthplace	{ In London .... 81 %	3461 }	Heads of Families
	{ Out of London.. 19 %	828 }	4289
Industrial Status ..	{ Employer ...... 6 %	272 }	
	{ Employed...... 91 %	3886 }	
	{ Neither .... 3 %	131 }	

TOTAL POPULATION CONCERNED.

	Heads of Families.	Others Occupied.	Unoccupied.	Servants.	Total
Total	4289	4301	9527	124	18,2..
Average in family..	1	1·03	2·28	·03	4·3..

CLASSIFICATION.

Numbers living in Families.		%
3 or more to a room	2947	16·2
2 & under 3 ,,	4580	25·1
1 & under 2 ,,	5431	29·8
Less than 1 ,,		
More than 4 rooms }	5014	27·5
4 or more persons }		
to a servant .. }		
Less than 4 to 1 servant, and 4 or more to 2 servts.	101	·6
All others with 2 or more servants ..	44	·3
Servants	124	·5
	18,241	100

	Inner.	Outer.	Together.
Crowded ..	52 %	26 %	41 %
Not ,, ..	48 %	74 %	59 %

DISTRIBUTION.

East..	{ Inner	2991 }	3..
	{ Outer	331 }	
North	{ Inner	646 }	.46..
	{ Outer	4030 }	
West	{ Inner	190 }	..7..
	{ Outer	389 }	
Central	Inner	3550	3..
South-East	{ Inner	529 }	25..
	{ Outer	2005 }	
South West	{ Inner	2660 }	35..
	{ Outer	920 }	
			18,2..

Inner 10,566, or 58%
Outer 7675, or 42%

* In North London the majority of those employed are men; in the other districts there is a large excess of women. The total population concerned, as compared to the number employed, is consequently greater in the North than elsewhere.

Status as to Employment (according to Census Enumeration).

Census Division (1891).	Employers.		Employed.			Neither Employer nor Employed.		Total.
			Males.		Females. of all ages.			
	Males.	Females.	Under 20.	Over 20.		Males	Females	
Bookbinder	259	42	1388	4621	9344	141	57	15,85.
TOTAL..........	301		15,353			198		
	Proportion of Employers to Employed—1 to 51.							

Note.—The proportion of Employed to Employers is probably too large. Master vellum binders would frequently be returned as printers or stationers.

Nos.   (For explanation of method adopted in preparing this chart, see Note on Diagram 18.)

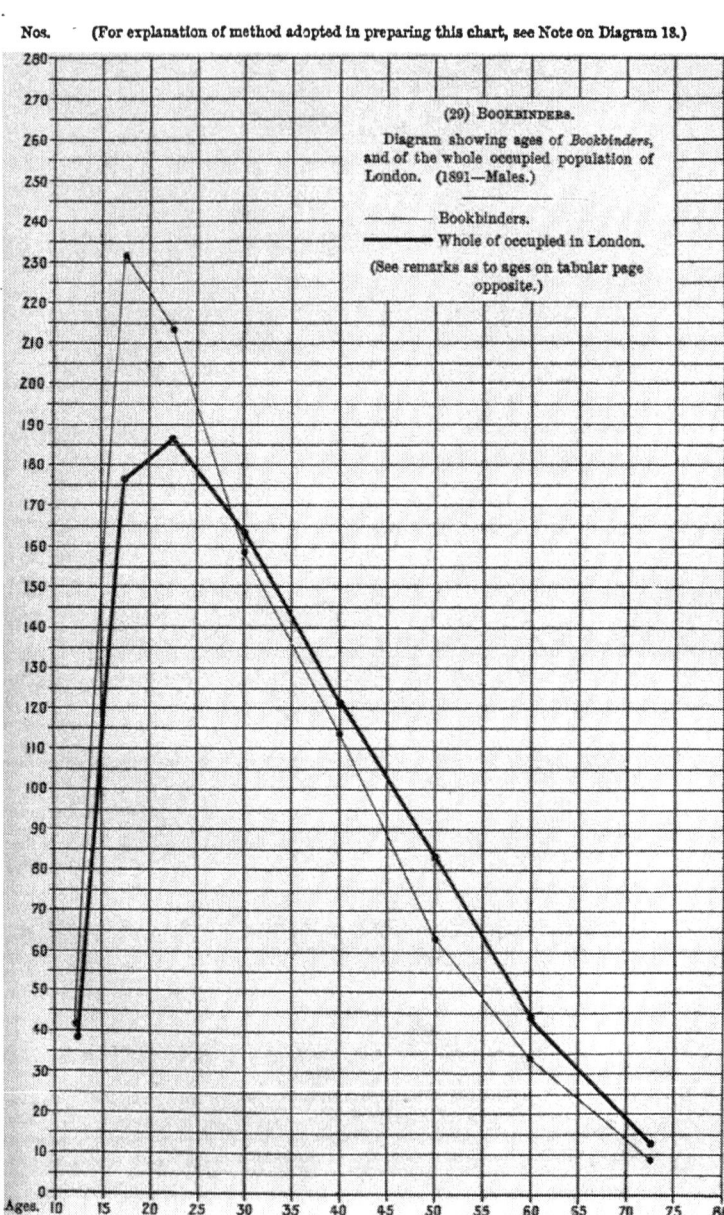

(29) BOOKBINDERS.

Diagram showing ages of *Bookbinders*, and of the whole occupied population of London. (1891—Males.)

——— Bookbinders.
——— Whole of occupied in London.

(See remarks as to ages on tabular page opposite.)

Introductory.

The art of bookbinding has a longer history than that of printing. The common expression "bound in boards" carries our thoughts back to the days before paper or print, when the monks, after working for weeks and months, or perhaps years, with pen and pencil on sheets of parchment, enshrined the product of their toil between oaken boards, lavishing time and ingenuity on the ornamentation of the case that it might be a worthy receptacle for the written thoughts they had lovingly transcribed. Since those days the change is great indeed; but the best binding follows the same methods, and the old words are used, even if in a somewhat new sense.

The bookbinding trade of England is concentrated in the metropolis to an extent even greater than we have seen to be the case with printing. In 1891, out of a total of 25,736 employed in England and Wales, no less than 15,852 lived in London. Previously the proportion of Londoners had been still greater, indicating a tendency, at any rate since 1881, towards dispersion, similar to and closely connected with that observable in the printing trade. In London itself we find most of the large binderies in the same district, and that a very central one; there are few that are not within half a mile of Holborn Viaduct. But again, as with printing, there may be traced some signs of decentralization—a movement, in this case, towards the suburbs, in search of lower rents, more space, and cleaner air.

The trade consists of two main divisions :—

    I. Letter-press binding.

    II. "Vellum," or account-book binding.

These divisions answer to the two meanings given in Dr. Johnson's dictionary to the word "book" as a "volume in which we read," or "a register in which a trader keeps an account of his transactions"; but the second class includes now the whole series of modern blank books, from the banker's heavy ledger to the smallest pocket diary or cash account.*

In most large towns the distinction extends to the employees, a binder qualified in both branches being very exceptional. In London the trade customs differ in these two branches, and, since 1892, the hours of work differ also. In the smaller provincial towns an apprentice will learn both classes of work, but if he comes to London he must choose which part of the trade he will follow, and, if a unionist, will then join the corresponding society.

I. LETTER-PRESS BINDING.

Letter-press binding may be sub-divided into three sections :—

  (1) Cloth work—comprising nearly all the new books or ordinary reprints issued by London publishers.
  (2) Bible work—including prayer and hymn books, covered in leather, and classics or poets for school prizes or presents.
  (3) Modern or extra binding and miscellaneous work.

The business of the first two (cloth-work and bible-work) is to produce thousands of similar covers for books of which the sheets have never before been folded or bound, but come to the binder direct from the publisher's warehouse or the printer's shop. The last of the three divisions concerns the binding or re-binding, for public or private libraries, of books found worthy of this dignity, or this amount of care for their preservation, and is thus essentially

---

* The name "bookbinder" is ordinarily confined to letter-press work, as the more important and legitimate branch of the trade, and "vellum-binder" is used for the others.

a retail trade, a handicraft and an art; whereas the others are wholesale manufactures, relying upon machinery at every point in attaining the form of perfection at which they aim. But all methods of binding adopt the same general principles in folding, fastening, and covering the sheets of paper of which each book is made.

When the printed sheets reach the binder they are folded and then gathered together in order for binding. For this purpose they are distinguished by a progressive number or letter to be found at the bottom of the first page of each sheet, as can be seen by reference to the present or any other book. Folding is women's work. Until quite recently the folding machine was only used for newspapers and pamphlets, but it is now increasingly employed for ordinary book work. The women fold "to print"—that is, they bring the top of each printed page exactly level with the opposite page; the machine can only fold "to paper"— that is, bring the edges of the paper level, and consequently, unless the printing is quite accurate, the printed pages will not face each other exactly.

The folded sheets, now forming a complete volume, are beaten with a heavy hammer or rolled into compact shape, and are then collated to be sure that no sheet is missing or misplaced, and that any illustrations are properly inserted. All this (except the beating or rolling) is women's work. The loose volume is then pressed a little before the sewing. Books when bound for a second time require, of course, no folding—the cut pages are merely put together for re-sewing.

In preparation for the sewing, the backs are usually notched or "sawn in" to admit the cords to which the sheets are to be fastened. Notching is a new fangled idea. The old plan was to bind with a flexible back, and the cords, passing round the back, were merely covered with the leather. The effect of this is preserved in the bands by which the detached backs now in vogue are still divided.

The sewer (who again is a woman) uses a sewing press, in the structure of which lies the whole secret of binding. It consists of a flat bed from which rise two upright pillars supporting a cross bar. To this bar are attached the "lay" cords—usually five in number—which pass through the bed of the press, and are drawn tight and made fast on the under side. To these cords each folded sheet is attached in turn. The woman sits with her left arm round the vertical bar, and the sheet to be sewn is laid flat on the bed of the press (or on the top of the sheet last sewn) with its back edge against the cords. It is then opened and the needle is passed backwards and forwards through the folds of the paper, the thread at each stitch being looped round one of the lay cords. Sheet after sheet is sewn in this way till the book is complete, and when detached from the press (which in truth is not a press but a frame), a short length of each cord is left at the sides. When the sewing is complete the first and last sheets are pasted down, the end papers and waste leaves (which serve to protect the rest) are attached, and the book is ready for the process called "forwarding."

It is the business of the "forwarder" to "glue up." The glue is applied very hot, being rubbed well into the back, and any surplus removed while it is yet liquid. The back is then allowed to become partially dry, but before the glue has lost its flexibility the book is "rounded." Rounding consists in knocking or pulling over the outer sheets, and all more or less, from the centre outwards, so that the back takes a convex and the front a concave shape. Unbound books, that is, books which are issued in limp paper covers, are not rounded, but with stiff sides rounding is necessary if the book is to open freely.

The book is then screwed tightly in a press between boards arranged so as to expose the back, which is hammered till the sheets are beaten over the edges of the boards, and in this way prepared to receive the sides. The sides, of mill board or straw board, having been cut to the exact size and covered with paper, are attached to the book by the ends of the cords (those to which the sheets have been sewn), being laced through holes in the boards and pasted down.

The book now returns to the press, and to all intents is bound. Extra strength, if needed, may be added in various ways, but the addition of the loose back, with its pretentious bands, is not one of them, as the only purpose it serves is to hide the true back of the book. But the loose back is an ingenious structure. A piece of paper folded in three or four thicknesses is glued to the true back of the book in such a way that two adjacent folds of the paper are not fastened together, and the parting between these surfaces forms the hollow shown when the book is opened and the true and false backs separate. The imitative raised bands are then glued on and the book is ready for dressing in its cloth or leather covering.

Before the back is affixed, while the book is still, so to speak, in its shirt sleeves, if the leaves are to be cut, the cutting is done with a "plough," and when cut are probably marbled or gilt, as will be described later, the work being seldom done on the binder's premises.

It is in the covering and finishing that there is most difference between cloth work, bible work, and extra or miscellaneous binding. Most of the shops doing extra or miscellaneous work are small, and the employer is often himself a skilled workman—probably a finisher. He may employ two or three men and a woman or two, and will work by their side. Some are family shops, where the workers are all relatives of the employer.

For extra work, the leather for the cover, or whatever material is used, is stretched and pasted over the back and sides. Finishing is the ornamentation of this cover, and usually takes the form of patterns impressed on the leather by hand tooling. This work affords room for much taste as well as skill, and the result may be either utterly commonplace or exquisitely artistic. The finisher's kit consists of a number of wooden-handled metal tools with various devices—pallets, fillets, rolls, &c., which combine with lines to form the designs on the back and sides of the cover. The tools are heated for use. Similar tools, engraved with letters, are used for lettering, and there are polishing irons for smoothing the surface of the leather. As the tool in what is called blind work, that is when the design is not gilt, has to be passed over the patterns several times to produce a polished surface, great care and steadiness of hand and eye are needed to keep it exactly in the same path. To affix gold leaf the patterns are touched with a preparation of white of egg, called " glaire," to which the leaf adheres. The tools are then again used at a very exact temperature; if they are too hot the gold will be dull, if not hot enough it will not adhere to the leather, and for different leathers a different degree of heat is requisite.

For bible work the cover or case, as it is called, is made in one piece, back and sides together. Into this the book is glued. But while the case is still detached, designs are stamped upon it in a press. This is the work of the blocker. The same system applies to cloth work. In gold blocking a considerable number of women and boys are employed, the usual plan being for the women to lay on and the boys to clean off the gold, while the blockers simply tend the presses. Varnishing when needed is done by women.

Underlying all similarity in the general principles adopted, we have, as the main difference between the three divisions of the trade, the extent to which machinery is used. For cloth work the folding machine is introduced wherever possible, and the gathering facilitated by the use of a revolving table. In the next process the sewing machine has superseded the hand worker. Besides machines using thread there are others for wire, but this plan of fastening is only used for very temporary work, as the wire rusts and the sheets then break away. Rounding is also done by machinery. The result is that in a cloth "forwarding shop" each man is attending to a single operation. One is working a rounding machine, another a backing machine, others are "glueing up" or putting the books in their cases. The rooms are furnished with hydraulic presses. Everything is arranged with a view to wholesale production. For the qualities of the artist there is no demand. Quickness and cleanliness are the attributes most needed.

In these shops piece-work is common. In some cases men work together, at a piece price shared amongst a group of men.

As to busy and slack seasons, cloth work shows the greatest variations, the weekly wages paid by some employers in the autumn being double the amount paid when slack. Work is brisk for about seven months, the activity culminating at Christmas, slackening in March and April, and being at lowest ebb in July. Bible work is much more regular, but is subject to special fluctuations. It has suffered severely this year (1894) by the stoppage of the American demand in 1893, due to tariff legislation and commercial collapse. Extra leather work is usually busiest in the winter months, but 1893-4 was a bad season, affected also by cessation of American orders and bad trade generally. May and June are said to be usually the worst months. In some shops in the slack season the men are put on short time all round and the work is shared among them, but the more general custom is to have a regular staff retained at all times and to take on such extra hands as are wanted during the busy season. This is shown by the out of work benefits granted by the unions; the same men receiving relief year after year until they are fortunate enough to obtain a permanent place.

There is little shifting from one branch of the trade to another. "Forwarders" and "finishers" cannot interchange. A leather binder may take up cloth work, or may go from best to common work, or, as it is said, from "inboard" to "out-board" (the edges in the case of best work being cut after the boards are attached), but a cloth hand can seldom work in a leather shop. Nor is there much shifting from shop to shop except amongst quite casual workers. If a man obtains a foothold in a shop he rarely shifts.

Scrap-album Making is a minor branch of cloth binding. It is confined to a few shops and gives employment to about 150 men. These men—forwarders, case-makers, and blockers—belong to the trade, but are not regarded as the equals of the other men, as their earnings are usually less.

Book-edge Gilding and Marbling are distinct though small trades, the work being usually given out to a number of small employers, known as gilders or marblers to the trade. Most of the gilders shops are in Clerkenwell, and the staff of the largest employer does not exceed forty men and boys even in the busy season. There are probably not more than six who employ as many as ten men, and most are quite in a small way. The process is as follows :—The uncovered books, with the edge turned upwards, are screwed tightly in a press between loose boards. The number placed in the press at one time varies with the thickness of the book, but must not be so great that the edges will not remain rigid under the pressure of the tools. The book edge is then scraped with a sharp piece of steel which removes thin shavings and leaves the edges perfectly even and smooth. The surface is then polished with black-lead and covered with "glaire," and the gold leaf laid on. When dry it is burnished with smooth flint or snakestone. Bending over the press and leaning his weight upon the tool, the workman moves it across the edges without scratching or leaving any mark, and a last polish is given with the "live leather" of the palm of his hand. Sometimes the edges are coloured and then gilt. "Gilt on red" edges are now largely used in bible work.

In this, as in other branches, there has been since 1891 less work to be done, and this has stimulated competition amongst the masters, particularly in some of the non-union shops where a system of "swim" work is adopted, the plan being for a number of men, each doing a portion of the work, to follow each other up from press to press, each completing his part of the work and then passing on to the next.

The marbling of book edges is combined with the staining of marbled paper, and, like the gilding, is a special trade; but at large printing offices a marbler is often employed to do the edges of ledgers and cash books. Marbling is a very persistent freak of taste in imitative decoration. The patterns, which certainly have a beauty of their own and are not particularly like marble, are produced, as regards lined patterns, by the running in and combing out of colours placed upon the surface of a solution of gum in the marbler's trough; and as to spotted patterns, by dropping on gall from which the colour flies. The colour thus twisted and arranged, rests on the gum and is picked up by the paper or book edge on these being brought in contact with it.

II. Vellum Binding.

A vellum or account-book binder's shop is seldom more than a department of some large printing or stationery firm, and the hours and working conditions are apt to be governed by those of the trade with which it is associated.

Binding in boards is the skilled part of the trade. Large ledgers must be very well and strongly bound, for they are heavy and have to stand long, and often hard, usage. They are designed to contain the permanent record of transactions extending over, and liable to be referred to during, many years, and it is essential that the pages should hold together. Perfection in this respect is required irrespective of cost, but the demand for a book that shall be both strong and cheap is increasing. All binding in boards is, however, not of this character, and some work which still goes under this name approaches very closely to the manufacture of note or exercise books known as "flush-work," and so-called because the edges are cut flush with the cover.

When the paper, which is nearly always ruled, is received from the "machine-ruler," it is folded and sewn by girls. In the large shops a girl will keep to folding or sewing, but in smaller establishments will do both. About half the folders and sewers are time workers; piece-work is only found in some of the larger workshops. The system of sewing is quite distinct from that followed in letter-press binding. No sewing-press is used, and tapes or strips of vellum replace the "lay cords" as the bases to which the sheets are attached. Some skill is required to sew the sheets accurately. The sewing-machine is not used for good work, but is being introduced for the production of cheap work in large quantities. After sewing, the back is glued and boys paste on the outside sheets, and the book then goes to the cutter, who cuts the edges, and to the "marbler," after which it passes to the "binder" or "forwarder," who puts on the sides and back, and to the finisher for whatever finish may be needed, much as already described for extra letter-press binding.

In "flush-work" of the commoner kind, boys are largely employed. Division of labour is introduced wherever possible, the more difficult parts being given to the men. On the whole very little skill is required, and, doing one kind of work constantly, the lads are soon able to get through as much of what they are set to do as a man could. The books are covered with American cloth or marbled paper on thin paste board; or, in some cases, stiff boards are used. The covers are simply glued to the tapes to which the sheets have been sewn and pasted down on the first and last pages.

The busy season in this trade lasts from October to February, and is caused by the special demand for new account-books and diaries at the beginning of each year. The slackest time is during the summer holiday months.

CONDITION AND PROSPECTS OF THE TRADE.

The great reductions in the price of paper and other materials used in the production of books, and the numerous inventions that have facilitated this production, have greatly increased the output and brought books within the reach of all classes just when, by the spread of education, there has begun to be a general demand for them. This movement towards cheapness has compelled the binder to seek by all means to reduce the cost of binding also, and in this he has succeeded, for a book that would have cost 2s to cover ten years ago can now be done for 9d, but the work is not so good, and the increase of such work is turning the mechanic more and more into a *machine-minder*.

Competition is not nearly so keen as in the printing trade. There is practically none from abroad, and, with the exception of Edinburgh and one or two provincial towns, the trade is not highly developed outside of London. Books printed in provincial places are still brought to London to be bound; but there are signs of a change, which, as we have seen, is reflected in the census returns. In a few of the Midland towns, well-equipped establishments are springing up, and if the movement continues they may affect the London trade. Otherwise the existing competition is between the London houses. Some connect the development of provincial competition with the eight hours movement and the agitation in 1892, by which the concession in hours was won, and claim also that irrespective of the shortening of the hours, the London trade was much disturbed by the struggle and has scarcely regained its equilibrium. These causes, aggravated by general depression of trade, are certainly sufficient to account for the lack of employment complained of. It may, however, safely be said that 1893 was a better year than 1892, and it may be hoped that with reviving trade a normal condition of things will before long be re-established.

TRADE ORGANIZATION, WAGES, &c.

These trades are well organized, and the present condition of the trade cannot be understood without a knowledge of the work done and influence exercised by the unions, especially in connection with the partly successful attempt to establish an eight-hour day.

The societies concerned are as follows :—

		No. of Members.	
(1) London Consolidated Society of Book-binders	Founded 1784.	1270	2285
(2) Society of Day Working Bookbinders ...	,, 1850.	414	
(3) London Branch of the Bookbinders' and Machine Rulers' Consolidated Union	,, 1858.	601	
(4) Vellum (Account Book) Binders' Society	,, 1823.	391	
(5) Book Edge Gilders' Trade Society	,, 1890.	111	
(6) Society of Women Employed in Book-binding	,, 1874.	200	

The Day Workers' Society was formed by a secession from the older union of a number of men opposed to piece-work; but it is difficult to avoid piece-work in some branches of the trade, and there is now a feeling in favour of the re-union of the two bodies.

The London Branch of the National Union was formed for the convenience of members who came from the Provinces to London, and admits vellum-binders and book edge gilders as well as bookbinders proper, but the bulk of the London members are letter-press binders.

The three societies work harmoniously together, and

since 1889 have had a joint trade committee which conducts negotiations with the employers, and in 1893 concluded an agreement with the Bookbinders' Section of the Chamber of Commerce, as representing the employers, which defined the parts of bookbinding to be regarded as unskilled labour or as work for women. This committee has also made statistical inquiries as to the condition of the principal shops from a unionist point of view.

The return for 1891 includes 151 of the largest shops, employing about 3500 men and boys, but in 1892 the number falls to 127 and 3000 respectively, the decline being due to the exclusion in the latter year of the vellum-binders' shops :—

	Shops.	Men.	Apprentices.	Boys.	Unionist Men.	Non-Unionists.	Per cent of Unionists.
1891.	151	2666	563	283	2261	405	85
1892.	127	2193	526	219	1927	266	88

This table, it will be seen, shows that from 85 per cent. to 90 per cent. of the men are unionists. This proportion would be reduced if all the smaller shops were included, but would still remain high. It is estimated that there are about 340 bookbinding firms in London, of which 150 are large, providing work for about 3000 men and 5000 or 6000 women or girls and boys; another 100 are smaller shops, which may provide work for about 400 men, and the remaining 90 would be working binders who employ occasionally, and of whom half may be counted as working on their own account.

A "shop council," consisting of delegates from various shops, has been formed to give expression to the men's opinions upon the organization of shops; the observance of trade customs; the maintenance of trades union principles, to combat the "laxity and indifference of many in our trade," and to enable the delegates to compare notes, and so promote an active interest in trade matters.

The result of the strike for an eight-hour day was a heavy blow to the vellum-binders' union. When established in 1823 it had 62 members, and by steady growth their numbers had reached 424 in 1889. In the next two years the membership was doubled, reaching the highest point in 1891, with 843 members and £2500 cash in hand. Then came the contest, and at the end of 1893 we find the union slowly retrieving its position, but still £500 in debt to the other unions for assistance received during the strike, and with only 400 members; and although the ill-feeling developed is passing away, it is still so strong that in some of the shops men dare not avow themselves unionists.

The book edge gilders, on the other hand, were early successful in obtaining an eight-hour day—they struck, but the strike lasted only a few hours—and also in restricting the number of apprentices to one for every five journeymen, and in August, 1893, the union went so far as to refuse, for the time being, to permit any new apprentices to be taken on—a regulation it has been able, so far, to enforce in the union shops. In this trade two conditions are present which are very rarely combined, viz. a compact body of workmen and comparatively numerous small employers; with the result that union organization practically controls the trade.

The organized movement to obtain the eight-hour day or, to speak more precisely, the week of forty-eight hours work, dates from October, 1890, when a mass meeting of the men called by the three societies passed a resolution to call a conference of representative employers and workmen to consider the question. The demand was for forty-eight in place of fifty-four hours without reduction of wages, over-time to be paid as time and a half. It was not till February that any action was taken, by which time the vellum binders had joined with the others. The employers were invited to meet the men on March 23rd, but declined to do so, stating that they considered the proposal uncalled for, as the work was easy and necessarily subject to seasonal fluctuations. Nevertheless, the men held the conference, and a few employers attended. In June their perseverance was rewarded. Nine representatives from each side met, and the employers offered terms which led, in September, to a provisional agreement which (a) conceded the forty-eight hour week, from January 1892, without reduction of time wages; (b) added 10 per cent. to piece-work rates; (c) fixed overtime rate at time and a quarter after forty-eight hours, and time and a half after fifty-seven hours; and (d) increased the proportion of apprentices, as asked by the employers, from one for four, to one for each three journeymen employed.

But difficulty arose with the printing houses having binding departments, who refused to alter the hours for what was only one branch of their business. The men employed in these shops are mostly vellum binders, and as the dispute proceeded the cleavage between the two branches of the trade affected the results. First, however, both sides held together. The printer-binders withdrew from the agreement that had been provisionally made, and a strike begun by the vellum binders of one firm in November (1891), extended to a few other houses. Some printing firms offered to increase the rate of wages from 32s to 34s a week in lieu of shorter hours, but that was declined, and the strike dragged on, but became gradually limited to the vellum binders, for the book-binders and their employers came to terms on the basis of the September agreement. At length, after a struggle of twenty weeks, in which feeling ran very high, the vellum binders were obliged to accept the offered 2s, and in some cases to go in without any advance. The union lost half its members, and from some shops unionists were and are excluded altogether.

Moreover, the collapse of the strike reacted on the book-binders. In April, 1892, the men were informed that as the agreement had not been enforced throughout the trade, the employers regarded it as null and void, and, as a practical result, the overtime rate between forty-eight and fifty-four hours has been repudiated. The men retain a normal forty-eight hour week and are paid overtime for all hours beyond, but only at ordinary time rate till fifty-four hours are reached, and then time and a quarter.

With the alteration of hours more stringent regulations were introduced as to time. Five minutes " grace " in the morning is no longer given; men must be at the bench, ready to start work, at the hour, and must not drop their tools till the bell rings ; whereas in the old days they cleaned up and washed their hands in their employers' time. The day has been shortened at its beginning (many of the shops start now at 9) and so omit the hour in which supervision was most lax before the men all settled down to work. Now the whole staff begin work at once. The result is that the reduction in amount of work done is not nearly so great as the reduction in the number of hours.

Overtime, being much discouraged by the unions, has been greatly reduced since 1892. Before that time, long hours were systematically worked in many shops. Except during the busiest season, or in shops where space is much limited, there is very little overtime now. Men used to be able to make up in this way for time lost in the slack months, but it is doubtful if this can be done now in any branch of the trade—certainly it cannot in either bible or extra work. The trade as a whole may be better off, or on the road to be better off, but at present there are more unemployed than formerly, and even those who have the most regular work earn less; one employer tells us that with him they average 2s a week less.

Wages.—The union minimum rates are for forwarders, 32s;

and for finishers, 36s, for forty-eight hours. The rates actually paid vary in the three branches. In extra leather work more is usually given; some finishers have as much as 46s, and the average would be about 40s; but in certain shops assistant finishers are employed, who earn only 32s. In bible work forwarders earn 32s to 42s, or an average of about 36s, and blockers 34s to 38s. Time wages in cloth work tend to the minimum, but still vary upwards from 32s to 35s for forwarders and rather more for blockers. On piece-work the earnings rise to 40s. Case making is paid much the same, in fact it may be said that wages all round are 32s to 40s, extra skill or extra effort being paid at the higher rate. With scrap album binders the average is near the lower limit.

Semi-skilled men are employed in the larger shops to do various operations connected with cutting, rolling and pressing, and in carrying the paper or books from room to room. Porters receive usually 20s to 24s, though some earn as little as 16s. The others vary from 24s to 30s.

Previous to their one day strike, the book edge gilders worked fifty-four hours for a minimum of 32s. They now work forty-eight hours with a minimum wage of 34s. The actual average rate of wages is about 36s. With them there is no piece-work, but a man is expected to do a certain fixed quantity of work. In the slack season short time is general, and the volume of work having contracted considerably since the eight-hour day was adopted, few men average full time. Overtime, when it occurs, is paid as time and a quarter after forty-eight hours. Marblers work forty-eight to fifty-four hours and earn about 36s.

Women folders and sewers, excepting those on extra or miscellaneous work, are paid by piece. Girls begin at 2s a week, are paid half the piece rates in six months, and after a year are given the full rates. The amount of work done by each individual, as usual, varies much. Folding one thousand sheets, crown octavo, would be paid 9d or 10d, and take from two and a half to four hours, or from 2¼d to 4d an hour. When busy a quick folder would earn over 12s a week, and sewers a little more, but the average is much lower as time is lost "waiting," especially in slack times. One woman (a medium folder and sewer) averaged 8s 9d for seventy-two weeks of work, and there were six weeks interspersed when no work at all could be had, making the true average more nearly 8s. On time, 3d an hour is paid, or 10s to 12s a week. Collators may be by time or piece, and are more highly paid, rising to 14s or 15s. Machine sewers, usually time workers, earn as much as 15s or 16s.

Mode of Learning, and Period of Working Life.—There are two recognized ways of entering the trade: by apprenticeship, or as a binder's son. A bookbinder has the privilege of having one son taught the trade without being apprenticed. Men who learn in this way have to prove their ability before they are admitted to the society. This custom, however, is falling into disuse, and most of the lads are apprenticed. It is thought better for lads to learn where they cannot appeal at any moment to their father.

Lads enter the shop at about thirteen on trial, and at fourteen are apprenticed for seven years. A shop doing a variety of work would be preferred. If put to leather binding a lad would become a forwarder or finisher; in a cloth shop or on bible work he would learn what they have to teach. Apprentices start at 4s or 5s a week, and may make 15s to 21s at the end of their time, the usual step being 2s per week each year. Some employers give a little extra pocket money as "coaxers" to lads who work well. In cloth shops, where piece-work prevails, apprentices are sometimes paid two-thirds of the ordinary piece rates, a plan which increases their earnings several shillings a week.

The objection that a lad may become expert at a small section of the trade, but cannot become a craftsman, applies as strongly here as in the printing trade, the only exception being some of the West End leather shops and certain bible houses where pains are taken to pass the boys through every department in turn.

In vellum binding, flush work is usually picked up. In the best work an agreement may be signed for a number of years, but a young man can hardly obtain a knowledge of his trade without moving from shop to shop, and in London there are comparatively few apprentices in this branch. On the whole, however, it cannot be said that in bookbinding apprenticeship is dying out, and this forms a marked contrast to most other London trades.

It is difficult to define the age at which capacity is lost in this occupation. Binding is not heavy work, and as far as "extra" binding is concerned a man can continue to work longer than in many trades, and there is always something to be learnt, but this does not apply to cloth shops, as an old man could not keep up the required pace. Even in these shops a man who has lived a regular and healthy life could and probably would work till sixty-five, or even later if in a permanent situation, but after fifty or fifty-five the chance of obtaining fresh employment would be small. Blockers require keen vision and some have to retire because of failing sight.

Like printers, bookbinders are especially subject to chest diseases. Bending over press or bench, being constantly in the shop, and often taking their meals in the close atmosphere in which they work, conduces to this result. The mortality from this cause is not so great as with compositors, but is considerably above the average. The workshops on the whole compare favourably with those in other trades. There is not in them the hot vitiated air often found in large printing offices; but the shops vary greatly amongst themselves in discipline generally as well as in hygienic conditions. In some the rules are' so numerous and minute that they are known in the trade as "nurseries"; in others there is only one rule—an inexorable one—that the quantity of work must be done.

TRADES UNIONS.

The trade organizations connected with bookbinding are as follows :—

Numbers in the London Trade (Census 1891).		Name of Trade Society.	Membership in London.		Remarks.
Total.	Of whom are employed males over 20.		In each Society.	In each Division.	
15,852	4621	London Consolidated Society of Journeymen Bookbinders (1784).	1270		Gives out of work and Superannuation Benefits. Relieves sick members and widows of members by a "petition."
		Society of Dayworking Bookbinders (1850).	414		Gives out of work, Dispute, and Superannuation Benefits. Allows petitions in sickness or at death.
		Bookbinders' and Machine Rulers' Consolidated Union (London Branch), (1836).	601	2987	Has fifty-two branches and about three thousand members. Provides out of work, Death, and Superannuation Benefits.
		Vellum (Account Book) Binders' Trade Society (1823).	391		Provides out of work, Death, and Superannuation benefits. Relieves sick members from Benevolent Fund.
		Book Edge Gilders' Trade Society (1890).	111		Only benefit is out of work pay.
		Society of Women engaged in Bookbinding (1874).	200		Gives Death and Sick Benefits. Membership changes quickly, owing to the women leaving the trade, removing or marrying.
15,852	4621			2987	

Thus, out of a total of 4621 adult men employed, 2787 are organized, or over 60 per cent.

The employers have two organizations: the Bookbinding Section of the London Chamber of Commerce and the Printing and Allied Trades' Association. To the latter most of the vellum or account bookbinders belong, whilst the bookbinders proper belong to the former. Many of the large firms are connected with both organizations.

All the workers' societies provide an allowance for unemployed members, the men's unions giving 10s or 12s a week for ten or twelve weeks in the year, and the women's 5s for eight weeks. The cost of superannuation is restricted by limiting the number of recipients to some proportion of the total membership—in the Dayworkers' Society it is one annuitant to eighty members. With one exception they also provide, in some form, for death or distress; the two oldest societies doing this by means of a "petition." These petitions are a survival of the early days of trade unionism, the relief being given in this way in order to evade a regulation of some of the early friendly societies forbidding membership with more than one such society. Although members cannot claim this relief as a right, when afflicted in any way they can petition the society, and the committee may grant a weekly allowance or a definite sum provided the total does not exceed £15 on each petition.

Whilst no direct provision for sickness is made by the men's trades unions, many of the shops have a sick fund, and there is a strong society called "The Bookbinders' Pension and Asylum Society," well supported by both employers and workmen. The latter subscribe 5s or more a year, and they or their widows become eligible for the benefits in old age. The asylum provides a home for twenty-four inmates, and there are in all thirty-eight pensioners receiving allowances varying from 6s to 11s a week. The annual income is £1200, of which about one-third is collected in the workshops.

Wages Statistics.

In this trade 15,353 persons are employed, of whom 4621 are adult males. As to these we have wages returns for 370, employed by thirty firms as under :—

Bookbinders...................	20	⎫ = 30 firms employing 1102 persons, to
Book finishers	1	⎪ whom have been added 297 persons
Account bookbinders	3	⎪ engaged in bookbinding whose employers
Gold blockers	2	⎰ are printers, and 411 men from other
Book and card edge gilders	3	⎱ returns obtained through the trades
Bookbinders' engineers ...	1	⎪ unions, making 1810 persons in all. Of
		⎪ these, 799 are adult males, but 18 belong
		⎭ to other sections, as carmen, porters, &c.

The wages of these men in an ordinary week are as follows :—

Under 20s............	39, or	5 per cent.	⎫	
20s to 25s............	89 ,,	11½ ,,	⎬ Below 30s, 28 per cent.
25s ,, 30s............	90 ,,	11½ ,,	⎭	
30s ,, 35s............	323 ,,	41½ ,,	⎫	
35s ,, 40s............	128 ,,	16 ,,	⎬ 30s and over, 72 per cent.
40s ,, 45s............	51 ,,	6½ ,,	⎪	
45s and upwards...	61 ,,	8 ,,	⎭	

781 ,, 100

Our returns may be compared with those furnished to the Board of Trade in 1886 by ten firms, employing 1101 persons, of whom 258 were adult males belonging to this section.

	—20s.	20s—	25s—	30s—	35s—	40s—	45s—
Our returns ...	5 %	11½ %	11½ %	41½ %	16 %	6½ %	8 %
		28 %		72 %			
Board of Trade returns	—	8 %	8 %	57 %	17 %	5 %	5 %
		16 %		84 %			

The effect of piece-work and irregularity of employment upon wages is well shown by a comparison of the two tables. The Board of Trade returns being based on *rates* of wages, none are returned under 20s, and the number in the group including the minimum standard rate (30s to 35s) is very large. Our returns being based on actual earnings, show that although there is a distinct tendency towards keeping the majority near the normal wage, these other influences diminish or increase earnings according as trade is slack or busy, or the workman's opportunities are restricted or increased by individual capacity or good fortune. As the Board of Trade figures refer to a period before the rise of wages, the real difference is probably more marked than the figures indicate.

The influence of season affects these trades strongly, as the following comparison between the number employed and earnings in busy and slack weeks will show :—

	Busy Week.	Slack Week.	Percentage Reductions.		
			In numbers.	In earnings per head.	Combined.
Our returns	509	419	17¼	21¼	35
Board of Trade returns	1266	1051	17	37	47½

The busiest months appear to be October, November,. December, and January, and the slackest months, May, June, July, and August. February and March are also slack sometimes.

For all workpeople in the trade, the slack summer months involve a reduction of wages, but entire loss of work is felt most by the men, as is shown by an analysis of our returns.

	Busy Week.	Slack Week.	Percentage Reductions.		
			In numbers.	In earnings per head.	Combined.
Men	206	145	29½	14½	39½
Boys	34	34	.....	18½	18½
Women	269	240	11	19¼	28

Most of the men are time workers, and when the pressure of work diminishes some are discharged. The women, being piece workers, hang on and divide whatever work offers amongst them, working slowly, or beguiling idle moments by sewing, knitting, or reading, consequently only those who can employ their time profitably at home or elsewhere absent themselves. The boys, being on trial or apprenticed, are not discharged, but take less money.

It seems probable that increased irregularity of work and more stringent conditions have neutralized much of the advantage gained in rise of wages in recent years.

The women and girls outnumber the men and boys in this trade, and from 1881 to 1891 increased more rapidly than the male employees, but since 1891 the women's province has been more clearly defined and, to some extent, restricted, so the rate of increase may not be maintained. The number of employed females given in the 1891 census is 9344, and of these we have particulars as to earnings for 756 :—

5s and under ......119 or 15½ per cent.			
6s ,, 7s............ 63 ,, 8½ ,,			Below 12s, 42½ per cent.
8s ,, 9s............. 79 ,, 10¼ ,,			
10s ,, 11s............ 58 ,, 8 ,,			
12s ,, 13s............166 ,, 22 ,,			
14s ,, 15s............131 ,, 17 ,,			12s and over, 57½ per cent.
16s ,, under 20s...107 ,, 14 ,,			
20s ,, over .... 33 ,, 4¼ ,,			

756 ,, 100 ,,

With the exception of the learners, nearly all are piece workers, and even the learners after a short probation are given some portion of their earnings in this way. The large number at the lower rate of pay is not compensated for, from the worker's point of view, by the proportion, also no doubt large, who on this system can earn over 16s a week.

Of boys and apprentices 1388 are counted. Our returns give the earnings of 135 of these as follows :—

5s and under	17 or 13	per cent.
6s „ 7s............	34 „ 24½	„
8s „ 9s............	27 „ 20	„
10s „ 11s............	13 „ 9½	„
12s „ 13s............	12 „ 9	„
14s „ 15s............	13 „ 9¼	„
16s „ under 20s...	12 „ 9	„
20s „ over	7 „ 5½	„
	135 „ 100	„

Below 12s, 67 per cent.

12s and over, 33 per cent.

Most of these lads are either apprentices or boys on trial—engaged with an understanding that if they display aptitude they will be apprenticed.

Social condition.

Of the 4621 adult men employed, about 3150 come under social classification as heads of families. Tested by our wages returns only about 17 per cent. earn less than 25s a week, whereas 44 per cent. are living under crowded conditions. Next we find 53 per cent. earning from 25s to 35s, as compared to 32 per cent. living one and up to two in each room; and, finally, we have 30½ per cent. whose earnings are 35s or over, compared to 24 per cent. of the central classes as follows :—

Comparison of Earnings with Style of Life (Bookbinders).

Earnings as tested.			Classification of Population.			
Under 20s...	39, or	5 per cent.	3 or more in each room,	2950, or 17 per cent.		
20s to 25s...	89 „	11½ „	2 to 3 „	4600 „ 27 „		
25s „ 30s...	90 „	11½ „	1 to 2 „	5400 „ 32 „		
30s „ 35s...323 „		41½ „	Less than 1 „			
35s „ 40s...128 „		16 „	More than 4 rooms			
40s „ 45s... 51 „		6½ „	4 or more persons	4050 „ 24 „		
45s and upwards	61 „	8 „	to a servant			
	781 „	100 „		17,000 „ 100 „		
			Employers' families and servants	1241		
				18,241		

As a rule bookbinders do not live near their work, but the proportion resident within walking distance is considerable, districts north or south of the centre being more favoured than those east or west. Clerkenwell, Islington, Holloway, Kingsland, Vauxhall and Kennington, all contain large numbers of binders. A certain number live in the outskirts and use the workmen's trains, but the proportion is not so great as amongst printers, for bookbinders usually start work later, especially since the adoption of the eight-hour day. The latest workmen's trains at cheap fares reach the London termini about 7 A.M., rendering the loss of an hour or an hour and a half inevitable before commencing work for men coming by them. One of the results of this may possibly be the high percentage of persons living under crowded conditions, which is much larger amongst bookbinders than the proportion earning low rates of pay appear to render necessary.

Few go home to meals. Where the men are allowed to have their meals in the shop, a considerable number avail themselves of the privilege, and the more so, as in such shops facilities for boiling water or cooking are often available. Many firms, however, do not permit the men to eat their food in the workshop, so that the bulk of the men use some coffee-house or tavern. In nearly all cases the women (folders and sewers) have their dinner on the premises, special provision being made for them even in houses which deny this privilege to the men.

Some firms do not stop work for tea, but where work is continued late enough to make tea necessary, it is had on the premises. As to dress, both binders and book-edge gilders work in their shirt sleeves, wearing an apron over the waistcoat. Many also keep a pair of old slippers for shop wear.

Excepting some vellum binders, nearly all the men belong to one of the bookbinders' trade societies. A non-unionist would be most unlikely to obtain and certainly could not retain work in an ordinary binder's shop. About half the men belong to friendly societies ; many subscribe to the Binders' Pension Fund, and those engaged in a large shop will probably belong to the " sick fund " which is found in most of these houses, though not in smaller establishments. The maintenance of all these organizations cost the men from 1s 6d to 2s a week.

It is exceptional for wives to contribute to the family income. There is, however, a distinct tendency for book-binders to marry book-folders or sewers, and in that case the women will often continue at or come back to their work during the earlier years of married life.

CHAPTER III

PAPER MANUFACTURES. (*Section* 30.)

Persons Represented.

Census Enumeration.

Census Divisions, 1891.	Fe-males.		Males.			Total.
	—19	20—	—19	20—54	55—	
(1)Paper manuf.	242	325	184	505	77	1333
(2) Card, enve-lope maker	973	1307	222	510	38	3050
(3) Paper-box & bag maker	3071	4435	307	615	90	8518
(4)Paper stainer	36	112	269	516	80	1013
(5)Other w'rk'rs in paper ..	62	84	82	482	95	805
TOTAL	4384	6263	1064	2628	380	14719

This, like book-binding, is an employment of women. The age line for males follows a course similar to that of book-binding and printing, with the same consequence as to a large proportion of boys employed. (*See* diagram.)

Enumerated by Families.

Sex ...... { Males 2143, Females 865 }

Birthplace { In London 78 % 2357, Out of London.. 22 % 651 } Heads of Fami 3008.

Industrial Status .. { Employer 10 % 288, Employed 83 % 2489, Neither 7 % 231 }

TOTAL POPULATION CONCERNED.

	Heads of Families.	Others Occupied.	Unoccupied.	Servants.	T
Total.	3008	3058	6241	251	12
Average in family ..	1	1·02	2·08	·08	

DISTRIBUTION.

E.	N.	W. & C.	S.	Total.
5809	2529	2680	3701	14,719

DETAILS OF OCCUPATIONS (FROM THE CENSUS DICTIONARY).

(1) Rag sorter, grass boiler, beaterman, machine-man, finisher.
(2) Envelope cutter, stamper, cementer, black borderer. Card, pattern-card maker, stamper, Christmas-card maker.
(3) Paper and card-box maker, cutter, coverer, scorer, paper-bag maker.
(4) Paper stainer, paper hangings manufacturer, dealer, colourer, grainer, flocker, machine hand.
(5) Alphabet cutter, bill-poster, distributor, board man, lamp-shade maker, paper collar and cuff maker, stove-ornament maker.

CLASSIFICATION.

Numbers living in Families.		%
3 or more to a room	2777	22·1
2 & under 3 ,,	3372	26·9
1 & under 2 ,,	3023	24·1
Less than 1 ,,		
More than 4 rooms 4 or more persons to a servant ..	2758	22·0
Less than 4 to 1 servant,& 4 or more to 2 servants ..	221	1·7
All others with 2 or more servants .	156	1·2
Servants	251	2·0
	12,558	100

	Inner.	Outer.	Together.
Crowded ..	61 %	30 %	49 %
Not	39 %	70 %	51 %

DISTRIBUTION.

East .. { Inner 3717, Outer 451 }
North . { Inner 326, Outer 2460 }
West .. { Inner 68, Outer 567 }
Central Inner 1813
South-East.. { Inner 380, Outer 697 }
South-West. { Inner 1288, Outer 791 }

Inner 7592, or 60 %
Outer 4966, or 40 %

Status as to Employment (according to Census Enumeration).

Census Divisions (1891).	Employers.		Employed.			Neither Employer nor Employed.		Total
			Males.		Females of all ages.			
	Males.	Females.	Under 20.	Over 20.		Males	Females	
(1) Paper manufacturer	65	4	184	466	547	51	16	1333
(2) { Envelope maker	5	2	62	137	1792	4	4	1916
{ Card, pattern-card maker	38	5	160	341	561	23	6	1114
(3) Paper-box, paper-bag maker	103	46	307	518	7311	84	149	8518
(4) Paper stainer.....................	45	4	269	520	143	31	1	1013
(5) Others	42	2	82	477	136	58	8	805
	298	63	1064	2459	10,400	251	184	14,719
TOTAL..........	361		13,923			435		

Proportion of Employers to Employed–1 to 38 (Males 9, Females 20).

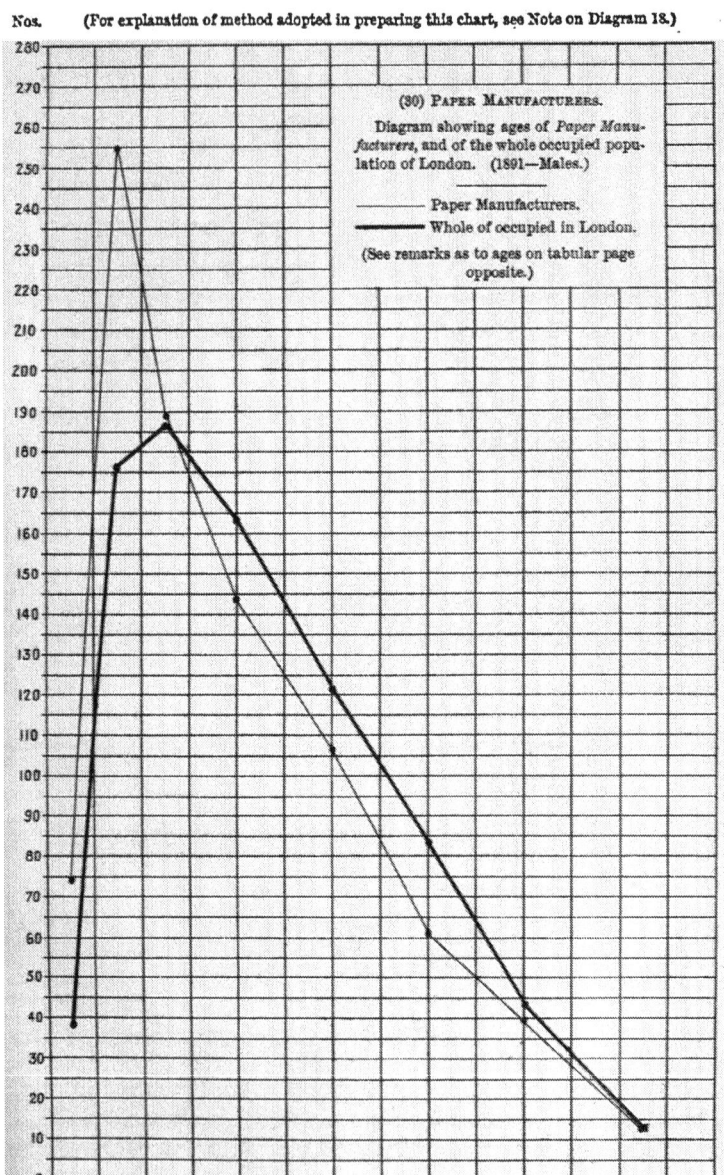

(30) PAPER MANUFACTURERS.

Diagram showing ages of *Paper Manufacturers*, and of the whole occupied population of London. (1891—Males.)

————— Paper Manufacturers.
————— Whole of occupied in London.

(See remarks as to ages on tabular page
opposite.)

Ages.

PAPER MAKING.

Of the actual manufacture of paper little is now done in London, only one paper-mill being situated within the metropolitan area. The industries included in this chapter are concerned rather with the preparation and packing of paper goods, and so, to some extent, overlap with the trade of wholesale stationers.

In the paper-mill the esparto grass is prepared by machinery, under the tendence of women, who earn about 10s for a week of sixty hours, working from 6 to 6, with intervals for breakfast and dinner. Men are employed to boil and break and beat the fibre and mix it with the wood pulp and other materials. Others attend the beautiful machines through which the pulp passes in its transformation from pulp to paper, and yet others reel and cut and pack the product. Beatermen and machine men are the skilled paper makers. They earn 32s a week. The others receive 26s, and there are labourers employed to assist at 18s or 20s a week.

The machines work continuously from Monday morning to Saturday afternoon, and the men form two shifts of twelve hours each, taking day and night service in alternate weeks. For breakfast and dinner one and a half hours are allowed, and there are similar intervals in the night; but the men in charge of the machines cannot leave their post, and must take their meals where they stand. The work is not laborious, and is very regular. The long hours in the mill form the main drawback from the workman's point of view.

ENVELOPE MAKING.

In former years envelope making was concentrated in the neighbourhood of Cannon Street, and millions of envelopes were distributed annually from the large paper warehouses there. High rents and the difficulty of obtaining additional accommodation has slowly altered this, and the City establishments are now mainly warehouses, envelope making and its connected industries having migrated to other districts where rents are cheaper, and room for expansion can be obtained. Most of the newer factories are situated in Southwark, and nearly half the workers are resident in South London.

Envelope making is largely a machine industry, hand-work being confined to the manufacture of peculiar sizes, and to some minor parts of the trade, such as black bordering. Men are employed to cut the paper, and the rest of the work is done by women and girls, of whom there are eight or nine to each man.

The sheets of paper from which the envelopes are made are placed on the bed of a machine, and cutters (shaped like the opened envelope) are placed upon them, edge downward. The bed of the machine then rises, and an upper plate descends, forcing the cutters through the paper, and cutting about a hundred sheets in one operation. The men who work these machines earn 28s to 30s a week.

The shaped paper then goes to the flap-gumming machines, which gum the upper flap, and are tended by girls. After this gum has dried the paper is passed to the girls who mind the folding machines. These machines gum the lower flap, fold the two side flaps upon it, and deliver the envelopes into a tray by the side of the girl who is tending the machine. She counts them into packets of twenty-five, and fixes a band around each packet.

Machines work fast, but neither is there anything leisurely about the work-rooms in which hand-made envelopes are manufactured. The workers are packed much closer together than in the other rooms, where each machine demands space; and although the rattle of machinery is absent, there is in place of it a constant rustle as the paper is rapidly folded and turned. The girls work at low benches, surrounded by the materials and their finished work. The operations are very varied. Some are making the envelopes, others marking black borders, while some are engaged on embossing crests or monograms, others in printing advertisements on tradesmen's envelopes.

Piece-work prevails, though learners begin at weekly wages. The earnings of the average worker range from 10s to 13s. Women who are exceptionally quick may take as much as 18s. Learners will receive from 4s to 7s a week. The hours of work vary. One large house commences at 8.30 and works until 6 o'clock, except on Thursday and Friday, when work is continued till 7 P.M., and the closing time on Saturday is 1 o'clock. Many firms, however, work regularly to 7 or 8 P.M. Ten minutes are allowed for lunch at about 11 o'clock, an hour for dinner, and (in firms working late) half an hour for tea. The busy time is usually from October to Christmas.

CARD AND PATTERN-CARD MAKING.

The industries included under this heading are usually found connected with other trades, of which they form a subordinate part. Card-cutters mostly work at wholesale stationers, and pattern-card making is frequently combined with the manufacture of fancy boxes. It is regarded as one of the best paid branches of this work, the women earning from 15s to 18s a week. The manufacture of Christmas cards is associated with the large lithographic printing firms, but is not an extensive industry in London. There are a few houses which confine themselves to the preparation of fancy cards, and returns received from such firms show that the men earn from 27s to 35s a week; the girls from 6s to 10s.

PAPER AND CARDBOARD-BOX MAKING.

This is the most important trade in this group, and, with paper-bag making, provides employment for 8500 out of the 14,700 persons included in the section. So far as it affects the women—who greatly outnumber the men and boys—a description of the trade in the East End was given in the chapter on " Women's Work " in Volume IV., and it only remains to treat of the trade in other parts of London, and the boys and men engaged therein.

The industry is mostly localized in Finsbury and the East End. In other districts the work more frequently forms a department of some business in which carton boxes are largely used, such as soap making. Workers come from all parts of London, but 4085 (or nearly half) are resident in the Eastern district.

The men who cut the paper and cardboard for the boxes make use of machines, worked some by steam and others by hand. As a rule, wages are paid by piece, but some firms pay by the day, and in such houses it is usual to fix a minimum task, giving a bonus when this is exceeded. Cardboard cutting is heavier work than paper cutting, and the men employed at it earn rather more money; cardboard cutters making 36s per week ; paper cutters 30s to 33s.

Boys tend the scoring machines, which make cuts in the cardboard along the lines on which the card has to be folded. If millboard, or other thick substance is used, a small groove is made, so that the card folds easily and evenly. Card-cutting machines, worked by steam power, are also fed by lads. They begin work at about fourteen years of age, and earn 6s a week. The majority of those employed are getting this sum, or a shilling more, a smaller number receiving 8s to 12s a week. Boys remaining in the trade develop into cutters. Usually a lad picks up a knowledge of the work as best he can, but in a few houses boys are apprenticed for five or six years, their wages rising to 21s a week at the end of the term.

Women and girls make the boxes from the materials prepared by the men and boys. Comparing the condition of these workers as represented in the returns now obtained with that found when the previous inquiry was made (1888), little difference is seen. The same methods of learning obtain, and the earnings of the girls do not differ materially. The ordinary worker's weekly earnings are still about 10s to 13s, but the proportion of young girls may have slightly increased, the number receiving less than 10s being rather greater in 1893-4. Home workers still play as important a part in the trade, small boxes of all kinds being almost entirely made outside the work-rooms. The material is cut and prepared, and then given out, usually to married women who have worked in one of the factories before marriage. A few minutes spent outside one of these establishments any afternoon towards the end of the week will give an observer an idea of the extent of this trade. Numbers of women and children may be seen returning the finished work to the warehouse, carried in carefully covered parcels or wheeled thither in perambulators.

Hours of Work vary. Some firms work from 8 A.M. to 8 P.M., allowing ten minutes interval for lunch, an hour for dinner, and half an hour for tea. Others do not commence until 9 o'clock, whilst some start at the earlier hour in the summer, and later on the dark winter mornings. To a certain extent this is a necessary concession, as it is very difficult to get the women and girls to start punctually, especially those who have household duties to perform before going to work.

Box-makers require plenty of bench-room for their work, and also to stack the boxes, so that there is generally ample air space. In the large factories the cutting and other heavy machines are placed on the ground floor or in the basement, and the men and boys work there, the upper floors being reserved for the women and girls. The smaller maker may have everything on one floor, his plant being of very limited extent—a cutting machine, scorers, glue-pots, and some boards to form a bench, is all that is necessary. Belonging to the poorer end of this class are a number of Jewish workers, cigarette boxes being one of their staple productions. In their workrooms the usual proportion of women to men does not obtain, the work being done by the family, or by personal relations, whether men, women, or boys. In these cases men and boys may be seen making the boxes. In one shop visited there were four men, two women, and a boy ; in another two men and two boys, one of the latter working on the floor.

The trade has grown rapidly of late years, as a result of an increasing demand from many industries, confectioners, chemists, soap-makers, boot-makers, and others being extensive users. At the same time the demand of the wholesale dealers in dress materials, formerly the most important part of the trade, has altered in character and importance. These houses now insist upon goods being supplied to them in boxes ready for delivery to the retailer. Much of the box making has consequently gone to the places where the goods are manufactured, and the orders of these wholesale houses are mainly for small quantities of many different kinds of boxes, to replace those damaged in handling. These orders are given just to supply the immediate need, no stock being kept, and they have to be executed at once.

Seasons.—Formerly the busy and slack seasons were sharply marked, and followed the fluctuations of the drapery trade, but the increased use of the cardboard box in so many and diverse trades has caused an equalization of the work, and except with firms whose business has developed mainly in one direction, the seasonal variations are much less. The influence of the dry goods trade is, however, still felt in the early months of the year, when spring and summer goods are being prepared for the market. Few, if any, of the workers are discharged at the slack time; the difference is mainly in the amount earned: instead of work awaiting them, when one order is finished the girls will have to wait their turn for the next. Thus in two firms making returns for busy and slack weeks, 307 females were employed in the busy week, of whom 197 earned 10s and over, and 110 under 10s; in the slack week 314 women were employed, but the proportion of earnings is reversed, only 134 earning 10s and over, and 180 under 10s.

Paper-bag Making.

Paper-bag making is largely concentrated in East and South London, the home workers and smaller workshops being found in Bow and near Victoria Park; the larger factories in Southwark or the neighbourhood. It is a women's industry; a few men are employed as cutters, but the proportion is less than one to twenty women.

Bags are made by hand and by machine, but the machines are only used in the large factories and for plain work required in great quantities, such as half-quartern flour or sugar bags.

The trade in the neighbourhood of Bow is largely a home industry. Some of the masters have workrooms, and employ girls on their own premises, but most of these also give out work to women working in their own homes; others simply cut the paper and employ none but outdoor hands, while a few give out the paper uncut to workers who can cut as well as make the bags.

As a consequence of the facility with which persons can commence on their own account, competition is very keen, and earnings and prices leave very bare margins for the support of the worker. The East End work consists mostly of plain bags made of thin yellow-tinted or brown paper, which are largely used by general shopkeepers, sweet and fruit sellers. The price paid for making the pint or half-quartern bag is 5*d* per 1000, with an additional 1*d* if the paper has to be cut. Some employers pay by the gross, and get their work done at slightly lower rates; one maker pays 1*s* for eighteen gross (2592), another 10*d* for twelve gross of the same size. Larger bags are paid 1*d* a gross. Women and girls, working eight hours a day, may, in some cases, make as much as 1*s* 6*d*. Twopence an hour may be regarded as the ordinary earnings; higher rates being only obtained by exceptional speed, or for peculiar work. The girls work at a bench or table, " fanning out " the sheets of paper, so that the edges of forty or fifty sheets may be pasted at the same time.

The men usually cut the paper, and endeavour to prevent the women learning this part of the work. Some have a small printing plant, and print customers' names and addresses on the bags. In addition to their own work, such men will do printing for other bag-makers. For this, 9*d* per 1000 is charged, or for larger quantities, 8*d* per 1000.

The usual selling price for these bags is 6½*d* per gross or 3*s* 6*d* per 1000, but they may be bought as low as 3*s* or 2*s* 10*d* in the slack time. The busiest time of the year for this part of the trade is from June to December, the fruit season increasing the demands of shopkeepers and street-sellers. When work is slack, women who can do the cutting will obtain paper and make bags on their own account, disposing of them to small shopkeepers.

The condition and earnings of the women in the large factories are better than those obtaining in the East End. The workrooms are larger and lighter, work is fairly constant, and the women must be regular and punctual in attendance. Beside the common sorts, bags with any peculiarity of shape or make are made in these establishments, such as the double bags in which some teas are sold. The light bags are cut as well as made by the girls, the piece price including both operations; the heavier work is cut by men (using machine knives), who earn 32s to 36s a week. Machine-made bags are cut, pasted and folded automatically, the women simply watching the machines and removing the bags. These women are chosen from the most experienced hand-workers. The working hours are from 8 A.M. to 8 P.M., with an hour for dinner and half an hour for tea, except on Saturday, when work ceases at 1 or 2 o'clock. Piece-work is the rule. Hand workers earn from 7s to 15s, but only the most adept bag-makers obtain the higher figures, the majority receiving from 8s to 12s a week. Machine workers are rather better off, and rise to about 18s. Learners and young girls, who pack and prepare the bags for delivery, receive from 4s to 7s or 8s a week.

The proportion of learners is usually large. With the small employers the desire to obtain cheap labour tends in this direction, and in the larger factories a considerable number are needed to replace those who marry, or from other causes leave the trade. In some places the learner is given a small wage, increasing at intervals; in others, she has to give three months,' during which time she is placed with another worker who teaches her, and as a recompense for the trouble is credited with any work the novice may do. At the end of the third month she will take her place as an ordinary piece worker. It is usual for the one with whom the girl is placed to give her a small bonus weekly to encourage her to work.

PAPER STAINING.

Paper staining, or the manufacture of paper-hangings, is one of a few sharply defined industries connected with the paper trade. The factories are distinct, and it is seldom associated with other businesses.

There are two branches—hand or block printing, and machine work. In hand-work the design is printed from wooden blocks, which the workman manipulates; in machine work steam-power is used, and the pattern is printed from rollers.

In London the trade is decreasing, the number of persons returned as paper-stainers falling from 1101 in 1881 to 1013 in 1891; these numbers include the dealers, and as there is no reason to suppose their numbers have declined, but rather the reverse, the proportionate reduction of the number of workmen is probably greater than shown above. The decrease seems to lie with the block printers, machine work and substitutes for paper-hangings not requiring so much labour in their production, taking the place of the block-printed papers.

Block Printing.—The paper is received from the mills in long rolls, and for block printing is cut into lengths of twelve yards. The paper first passes to the *colourer*, who applies a coat of colour to form the groundwork. For satin papers and some fine tints a second coat may be added when the first is dry. The colourer usually has two boys to assist him, one attends to the colour, keeping it "alive;" the other removes the paper as fast as it is tinted, and hangs it to dry in readiness for the block printer.

The designs are engraved on large blocks, faced with pearwood, varying in depth, usually from 10½ to 21 inches, and ordinarily a little over 21 inches wide, that being the usual width of the printed patterns. The other apparatus is very primitive, consisting of a wooden "table," with a clumsy-looking framework and levers, by which the requisite pressure may be brought upon the block. Close by the table stands the " slush-box "—a trough holding a large pad covered with felt or blanket. On this pad the printer's boy spreads the colour, and repeats the operation every time the block is used, the block going backwards and forwards from trough to table till the piece is finished ready for drying. For each colour in the design a separate block and printing is needed, save that with an open pattern a second colour may be introduced by patching— that is, by putting on the blanket pad a patch of the colour just where the pattern demands it.

Besides simply colouring the paper, other methods of ornamentation are adopted, such as flocking, bronzing, metalling, burnishing, and embossing. In _flocking_, the design is printed with colour having some oily or sticky ingredients, and then the paper is passed over a receptacle containing a quantity of finely cut wool or flock. The canvas bottom of this receptacle is struck sharply with a cane, and clouds of fluffy particles rise, which, in settling, adhere to the sticky design. The process may be repeated several times, according to the amount of relief desired. In _bronzing_ and _metalling_ the design is printed with varnish or gold size, but in bronzing metallic powder is applied with a brush, or is dusted on (as in flocking), while in metalling the gold or other leaf is laid on and rolled down, the portions not adhering being brushed away. The method of _burnishing_ varies with different papers, the object being to impart a polish or gloss to the surface. The surface of satin papers is brushed over with powdered talc, and afterwards burnished with a machine brush. Metallic work is rolled with polished metal rollers. _Embossing_ is the process by which a grained or ribbed surface is given to the paper by passing it under pressure between engraved steel rollers. In this way the appearance of silk, linen, grained leather, and other rough-textured materials is obtained. Various minor processes are also used in this manufacture, some being peculiar to particular firms, whilst a number of special preparations for wall and ceiling decoration have been introduced, and compete keenly with the hand-stained papers for the best work.

Machine Staining.—The great bulk of the paper hangings used for wall decoration are machine printed, and although London is the principal seat of "hand" work, the number of machine workers is fully equal to that of the block printers. Different kinds of machines are used; the ordinary kind being that in which the outlines of the pattern are formed ·by strips of metal fixed edgewise in wooden rollers, parts where the colour is to be solid being filled in with felt. Each roller prints one colour, and these rollers, with their ducts of colour, are mounted beside a large drum. The paper entering the machine, and travelling by lengths around the drum, is successively printed with each colour, and then passes from the machine to the drying-room, where it may be dried by heat, or is hung in long loops supported on rollers, which, travelling slowly on rods fixed near the ceiling, gradually fill the room with a series of loops, just sufficient space being left between to prevent the wet surfaces touching. The largest machine can print as many as sixteen colours, but smaller ones are employed for ordinary work. Various gums not affected by heat are used instead of size to fix the colours.

The trade is in the hands of comparatively few firms. Some of them do machine work only, and one or two old firms confine themselves to hand work. Most combine both systems. The tendency, however, is for machine to supersede hand labour.

Hours of Labour vary. In most houses the ordinary week is fifty-two to fifty-four hours, but the amount of work in hand, to a large extent, regulates the time. Block printers seldom exceed forty-eight or fifty hours, and, save when trade is active, a full week is exceptional. Machine men do not lose so much time as the block printers. When slack a factory may only run four or five days a week, but in busy times as many as seventy hours are sometimes worked. The legal restrictions on overtime for boys practically prevent the block printers working overtime, even when the opportunity occurs, as he cannot get on without his boy.

Wages.—Amongst the hand workers payment by piece is the more ordinary practice. Prices are reckoned per length of twelve yards, and vary according to the number of printings. When in full work the man's earnings vary from 40s to 48s a week, out of which he has to pay 5s to 7s to the boy, this being a fixed charge whatever his takings may be. When a man's money falls below a certain sum he is permitted to draw on account of the next week's work, and the amount is deducted from his earnings when a full week is made. A few men are day workers; they are employed to execute small orders for short lengths of paper, such as are required to match an existing paper, or the curtains or other appointments of a room. Machine workers are invariably on time. The men who are responsible for the machines earn 35s to 40s, a few rising as high as 50s. Beside these men there are a number of labourers who are paid from 25s to 30s a week.

Seasons.—Generally speaking, winter is the busiest and summer the slackest time. In summer, the new patterns are coloured and prepared for the market. In late autumn and winter they are shown to the wholesale trade, the factories being then busy printing the stocks which will be needed in the spring. With hand-stained papers the sequence is not so regular, as special orders, which are essentially capricious, form a large proportion of the work.

Method of Learning.—In the olden days the lads were regularly apprenticed, but apprenticeship is now the exception. With block printers, a lad will begin by colouring the blanket, probably helping his father, and may continue at this until he is about sixteen years old. If during this time he has shown general aptitude, an agreement may be made with the employer, and the lad will be taught the trade. With machine work there does not appear to be any regular system of teaching the trade. A lad is engaged, and given any work for which he appears suited, subsequent advancement depending upon his own efforts.

Men who have worked at the stainer's table are often employed as colour mixers, their experience in combining pigments being very useful.

Shifting.—There is very little shifting amongst the block printers. Many of the men have been with one firm all their life, and, perhaps, their fathers before them; they went as boys, and have remained ever since. Cases of men working twenty, and even thirty years, with one firm are not uncommon, and the man who has been in several shops is the exception. In one place visited by us, no man had been there less than ten years. In another instance, three generations were represented : grandfather, father, and son. Most of the lads who remain at the trade are the sons or other relatives of the men under whom they work.

Health.—Except in the case of the largest blocks, the work is not very laborious, and a man can continue at it until he is sixty years old, but it is difficult to get a new place after fifty, so that here, as elsewhere, there is a tendency for men to understate their age.

Nor are the surroundings such as to induce any special disease, and thus shorten the working life, now that the arsenical compounds, against which an outcry was made some years ago, are no longer used. To a certain extent, flocking and burnishing must be injurious, as it is impossible to avoid inhaling some of the dust with which the air is laden. The men, however, make no objection to this work.

Organization.—The block printers have a trade society, but the machine workers are not organized.

OTHER PAPER WORKERS.

Combined under the head of " Others," are a number of minor occupations, either using or distributing paper—such as alphabet-cutters, lamp shade and stove ornament makers paper collar and cuff makers, and many others. Only two are important so far as London is concerned—the bill-posters and board or sandwich men.

Billposters.—Bill-posting has largely developed in recent years, concurrently with—and probably influenced by—improvements in chromo-lithographic printing. Its demand gives employment to a considerable number of printers, as the extent and prominence of the advertisement hoardings testify, but the number of men directly employed as billposters is small, probably not more than six hundred. Of these, nearly three hundred work for the bill-posting firms, about one hundred for newspapers, and the remainder consists of men working on their own account and occasionally engaging other men to assist them: men of this class being found in all parts of Outer London.

Bill-posting is of two kinds—that on the protected stations, and fly-posting. The protected stations are hoardings rented by the billposter, who thus obtains an exclusive right. Most of the London posting stations are in the hands of fourteen or fifteen firms, who practically control this part of the trade. Fly-posting is mainly done by the small local men, each of whom would know every dead wall, fence, railway arch, or other suitable spot in his own district where he might affix his bills. This part of the trade is becoming restricted as the more eligible sites come to be rented by one or other of the large firms.

Apart from the sandwich-men, those employed form two classes—the hoarding builders and the billposters. Both belong to the same trade society, but the former are usually carpenters and are paid by the hour or occasionally by task work. Their number is small, and they are probably returned as carpenters in the census. The billposter himself is a semi-skilled worker: to make an effective display he must have some experience. He should know the different sizes of the bills, and must endeavour to completely cover the hoarding without any of the bill-overlapping, while the different rows should be ranged exactly in line. The most difficult part of his task is when he has to work at the top of a sliding ladder.

Working hours are usually fifty-two to fifty-six a week, commencing at 7 or 8, and working until 5.30 or 6, with an interval of one hour for dinner. Wages range from 24s to 40s a week, the higher limit being attained only by a few foremen; the majority of the men earn when at work about 28s a week, but excepting a fortunate minority, the average for the year would be lower, probably not exceeding 25s a week. The mode of reckoning the wages varies with different firms; one pays its men $5\frac{1}{2}d$ to $6\frac{1}{2}d$ per hour, others reckon the rate per day. The state of the weather affects the earnings, as in wet weather the men are put off. A wet morning often involves the loss of a day's work, and this, in such a season as 1894, makes a considerable difference. Only one firm is mentioned as finding the men work inside during rain.

A knowledge of the trade is picked up. Men are taken on and sent out with a billposter, and thus acquire a knowledge of the trade and of their employer's stations. The men object to this practice, regarding it simply as a device for obtaining cheap labour, the novices thus engaged exceeding the requirements of the trade, and some of them perhaps supplanting their instructors. Some men also come from the provinces.

For some years past the trade has been the object of periodic attacks from æsthetic folk, whose eye is offended by the glaring colours and incongruous surroundings of the poster; others have raised outcries against some offensive pictures, which, they contended, were subversive of public morality; while yet a third class see danger to pedestrians in the height to which some exposed hoardings are carried. Newspapers and magazines have been made the vehicles of these attacks, and two Bills were introduced into Parliament during 1894 to regulate or restrict the trade. The London Billposters' Protection Association has met these attacks in various ways. Offensive posters have been rendered almost impossible in London by the institution, in 1890, of a Committee of Censorship, whose duty it is to decide whether any bill brought before it by a billposter shall be exhibited. In the event of an adverse decision, it would be practically impossible to have the bill shown, as none of the members of the Association would post it. An arrangement has also been made by the London County Council which will limit the height of the hoardings to 12 feet, whilst the first objection is being removed by the great improvements made in printing these placards, and their arrangement on the walls.

Sandwich-men.—The ranks of the sandwich-men are recruited by the ne'er-do-wells of our complex civilization —men who in their earlier days have followed some calling, but either through misfortune or the indulgence of irregular and vicious habits have cut themselves away, not only from trade associations and the chances of work, but also from social and home influences. Most of these men are beyond middle life, and they have probably been married, although they invariably pass as single men. They drift from all classes, but not many labourers are found amongst them. As one of them put it, "they come from a more genteel sort of people"—such as clerks, valets, footmen, and even artisans, who have been ruined by drinking habits. The majority are Londoners; many of them are army pensioners, who adopt this means of livelihood until pension day, when they have a spell of enjoyment, only returning to their boards when the last shilling has been spent.

The number of men engaged in this work varies considerably. During the winter, which is the busy season, it is estimated that over two thousand are depending on it for their living.

The great bulk of them, however, are not returned in this section. Living, as most of them do, in registered lodging-houses, such men are probably returned by the deputy under the convenient though vague term "labourer."

In the summer (May and June) numbers of them go into the country, and, by pea, hop or fruit-picking, or in some other way, obtain a livelihood until September or October, when they return to their old haunts. Some belong to the militia, and with them the annual training provides occupation for a part of the summer.

Earnings vary from 1s to 1s 8d and 2s per day, the latter sum being paid by a few philanthropic societies. The lowest sum is paid by three employers; the minimum for ordinary boards being otherwise 1s 2d. A few firms give 1s 4d. For the overhead boards, or "high-flyers," the payment is rather more, ranging from 1s 2d to 1s 8d, but being usually nearer the higher figure, except for theatrical and publishers' work, which is the worst paid. On the other hand, the men like jobs for drapers or other large shops, as the remuneration, itself a little better, often involves some overtime, for which 2d per hour is given. Rainy days mean no work; in a few cases the men may be sent out for half a day, for which 8d is paid. The men gather at the contractors' yards at 8.30 A.M., and are despatched on their perambulations between 9 and 10, returning from 5 to 6 P.M., unless other hours are wished for by the advertisers.

If known, a man may reckon on regular employment throughout the season, and, for a certain number, there is always work.

Although the work is degrading and at first distasteful, and men rarely take to it unless compelled by stern necessity, after a while the feeling of shame wears off and they seldom give it up. The restraints are few. If they are engaged in the morning they are assured their supper, night's lodging and breakfast. They know shops where they can buy pieces of meat or bacon, sufficient for a good meal, for 2d or 3d. Their cooking is done over the lodging-house fire, and there they can enjoy warmth and light, as well as rough, yet not uncongenial company. On Sunday, if they cannot afford to indulge in an idle day, they perhaps sell matches or sweep a crossing: a broom can be purchased for $2\frac{1}{2}d$. When the man is not taken on, and if he has no money when night falls, he avails himself of a charitable shelter, or, in the last resort, goes to the casual ward.

Trades Unions.

The workpeople engaged in these industries are poorly organized. Out of 2459 who are of twenty years of age and upwards, only 220 are members of a trade society.

The London Paperstainers' Benevolent Society has 120 members, and gives out of work and death benefits, but only represents one section of this industry—the block printers. It is, however, strong as far as it goes, about 80 per cent. of the men being members. A strict watch is kept upon the lads working in the shops, and only those who are apprenticed are allowed to remain at the trade, while candidates for membership with the society must have worked four years at a printing or colouring table. A steward is appointed in each shop, and unemployed members have to report weekly to the steward at the shop nearest their home. The entrance fee varies from 1s to 5s, the subscription being uniformly 1s 4d a month. The Billposters' and Hoarding Builders' Society, with one hundred members, also offers out of work and death benefits. It is a general organization, but its influence is feeble, owing to the ease with which outsiders can be introduced into the business.

The employers in these trades have a medium of intercourse amongst themselves in the trade sections of the London Chamber of Commerce, and also to a certain extent in the Printing and Allied Trades' Association, to which many of the larger firms belong. The billposters have two employers' organizations : the United Billposters' Association, and the London Billposters' Protection Association. The former is a national society with about five hundred members, and publishes a monthly trade journal, and an official directory of billposters once a year; the latter includes the leading London firms, and deals exclusively with local questions, such as the regulation and renting of hoardings, and the employment of workpeople.

Wages Statistics.

In these industries 13,923 persons are employed, of whom 2459 are adult males. We have received wages returns from sixteen firms as under, employing 1239 persons, of whom 270 are adult men.

Wall-paper manufacturers......	6	= 16 firms employing
Paper-box makers	3	270 men
Paper-bag ,, ...	2	732 women
Envelope ,, ...	1	237 boys
Fancy card ,, ...	1	————
Paper ,, ...	1	1239 total.
Billposters ,, ...	2	

The wages of the men in an ordinary week are as follows :—

Under 20s	14, or	5	per cent.	
20s to 25s	37	,, 14	,,	Under 30s, 42 per cent.
25s ,, 30s	62	,, 23	,,	
30s ,, 35s	59	,, 21	,,	
35s ,, 40s	29	,, 11	,,	
40s ,, 45s	27	,, 10	,,	30s and over, 58 per cent.
45s and upwards	42	,, 16	,,	
	270	,, 100	,,	

The Board of Trade received twenty-two returns from firms employing 1372 persons engaged in these trades. Of these persons, 317 were adult men belonging to this section, and their earnings may be compared with our returns as under:—

	−20s.	20s—	25s—	30s—	35s—	40s—	45s.
Our returns	5 °/₀	14 °/₀	23 °/₀	21 °/₀	11 °/₀	10 °/₀	16 °/₀
		42 °/₀			58 °/₀		
Board of Trade returns	9 °/₀	21 °/₀	19½ °/₀	19 °/₀	13 °/₀	9½ °/₀	9 °/₀
		49½ °/₀			50½ °/₀		

The changes of seasons do not affect these occupations to the same extent as in other trades of the group. The Board of Trade returns show a difference of 14½ per cent. in the number of persons employed in busy and slack weeks, and those who retain their employment suffer a reduction of 14 per cent. in their earnings, the reduction of numbers and wages combined being 26½ per cent. from the high-water mark of the busy week to the ebb of slack work.

Our returns show a total reduction of only 16 per cent., but they are less complete, being limited to two industries. The greatest sufferers are the men, of whom 18 per cent. drop out. The same condition of things was noticed in bookbinding, and it admits here of the same explanation: the men being time workers, are discharged, the boys earning less wages, are retained, as are the women who work on piece.

The busy time varying in different occupations, this loss is spread over a longer period than where the seasons are sharply defined. As a whole, October to March are the busiest, and April to September the slackest months. Twenty-one returns gave the dates of busy and slack weeks; in fifteen cases the busy weeks occur from October to March, and in fourteen cases the slack weeks are from April to September.

In all these trades, except paper manufacture and paper-staining, the females greatly outnumber the males, and the proportion of women has risen from 67 per cent. of the total in 1881 to 72½ per cent. in 1891. There are 10,400 employed females enumerated in the 1891 census. We have received returns of the earnings of 836 of these women, and the Board of Trade returns give details concerning 752, as under:—

Earnings.	Our Returns, 1894.			Board of Trade Returns, 1886.		
	Net Nos.	Per cent.		Net Nos.	Per cent.	
5s and under ...	144	17	Under 12s, 67 per cent.	10	1	Under 12s, 65½ per cent.
6s „ 7s	142	17		32	4½	
8s „ 9s	142	17		278	37	
10s „ 11s	132	16		174	23	
12s „ 13s	113	13½	12s & over, 33 per cent.	176	23½	12s & over 34½ per cent.
14s „ 15s	79	9½		51	7	
16s „ under 20s ...	56	7		24	3	
20s „ over	28	3		7	1	
	836	100		752	100	

Except those earning 5s or less, who are probably learners, nearly all these women are piece workers. Comparing these returns, it will be seen that the effect of piece-work is to spread the earnings over a wider range than that of the standard wage, which for all branches of this trade is found between 8s and 13s.

The youths under twenty years of age number 1064, and of their earnings we have the following particulars:—

Earnings.	Our Returns, 1894.			Board of Trade Returns, 1886.		
	Net Nos.	Per cent.		Net Nos.	Per cent.	
5s and under ...	25	11	Under 12s, 73 per cent.	10	3½	Under 12s, 77½ per cent.
6s „ 7s	74	31		60	21½	
8s „ 9s	41	17½		96	34½	
10s „ 11s	34	14½		51	18	
12s „ 13s	21	9	12s & over, 27 per cent.	24	8½	12s & ove 22½ per cent.
14s „ 15s	17	7		26	9½	
16s „ under 20s ...	13	5½		12	4	
20s „ over	12	5		1	½	
	237	100		280	100	

Here, as in the case of the women, the number earning the lowest rates are greatest in our returns. It is possible that this may indicate an increase in the proportion of youthful labour.

Social Condition.

Of the 2459 adult men employed, about 1700 are classified as heads of families. Allowing for the large proportion of female heads of families—over one-fourth—and for the families and servants of the employers we can make the following comparison with earnings as given in the Board of Trade and our own returns.

Comparison of Earnings with Style of Life (Paper Trades).

Earnings as Returned.	Classification of Population.
Under 20s... 43, or 7 per cent.	3 or more in each room, 1000 or 13 per cent.
20s to 25s...103 „ 18 „	2 to 3 „ 1600 „ 21 „
25s „ 30s...124 „ 21 „	1 „ 2 „ 3000 „ 40 „
30s „ 35s...119 „ 20 „	Less than 1 „ ⎫
35s „ 40s... 70 „ 12 „	More than 4 rooms ⎪ 2000 „ 26 „
40s „ 45s... 57 „ 10 „	4 or more persons ⎬
45s and ⎱ 71 „ 12 „ upwards ⎰	to a servant ⎭
587 „ 100 „	7600 „ 100 „
	Families of employers and female heads, and servants ... 5000
	12,600

Thus we have 25 per cent. earning less than 25s a week compared with 34 per cent. living two or more persons to a room. Earning from 25s to 35s there are 41 per cent. corresponding with 40 per cent. living one and up to two to a room, and, lastly, there are 34 per cent. receiving

35*s* and upwards, as against 26 per cent. in the central classes.

The 10,400 employed women constitute the most important group in these trades. They are mostly young, about two-thirds (6900) being returned as under 25 years of age, and the number of heads of families amongst them is small; only about 860 are thus enumerated. Not less than three-fourths of these women and girls are box-makers, and of the remainder the majority make envelopes. Although all, or nearly all, belong to working-class families, social distinctions are clearly marked amongst them pointing to the character of the homes from which they come. Between factory and factory the difference may be great as shown both in dress and demeanour. Even under the same roof, in factories where all kinds of girls work together, the cleavage between the neatly dressed, quietly behaved artisan's daughter and the common type of factory girl with feathers and fringe, is distinct; and, if they are allowed to do so, the girls spontaneously sort themselves and form little coteries. The manager of a factory where this peculiarity was noticeable said the work went better so and he encouraged it.

Most of these women have their meals in the factories, at any rate in winter; few live near enough to go home regularly. Box-makers usually take their food in the work-rooms and boiling water can generally be had. In envelope factories where the workers sit closer together a separate room is usually provided with conveniences for cooking, and in these cases a woman is put in charge whose duty it is to prepare the meals. She is sometimes paid by the firm, but may perhaps add a little to her income by supplying food or will receive pennies from the girls for the services she renders. Dinner indoors in fine summer weather, when the streets are attractive, becomes a very short business, or may resolve itself into a pocketful of biscuits.

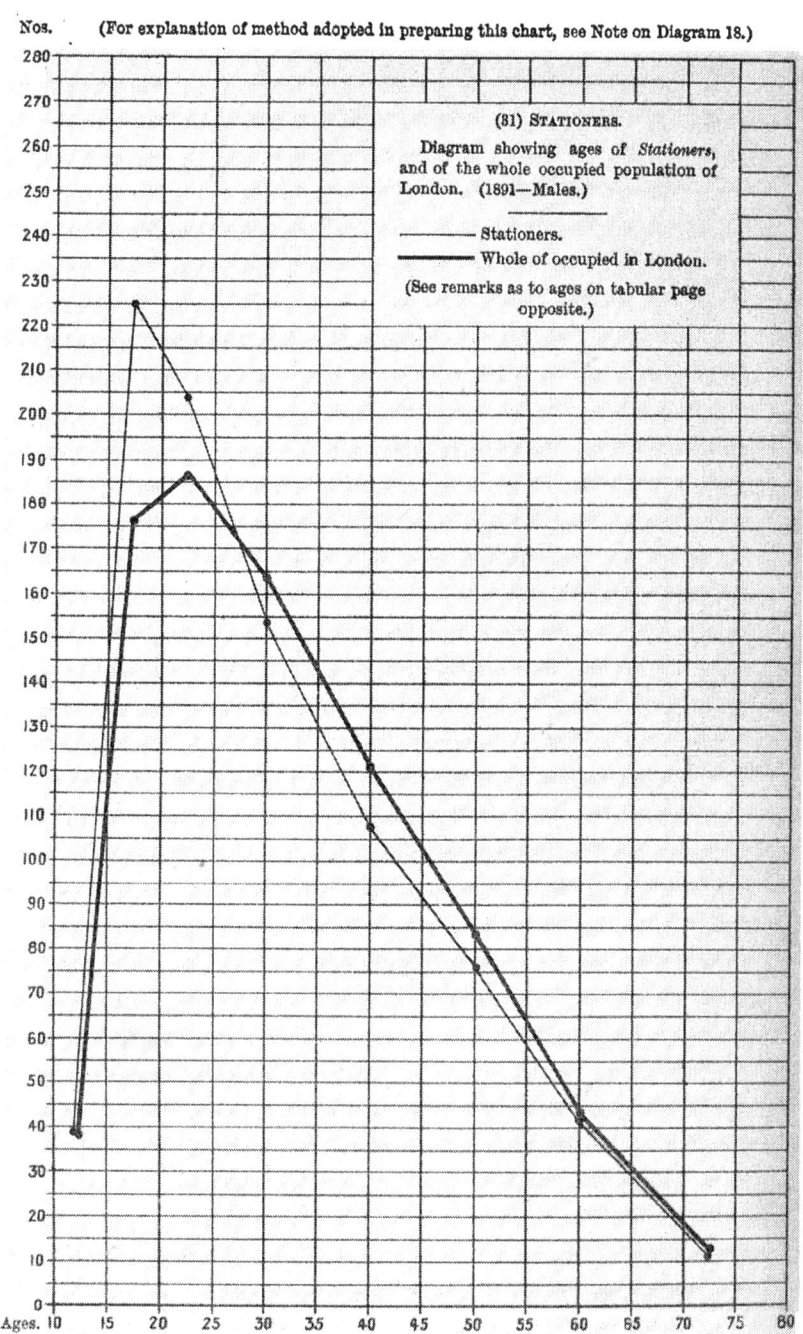

(81) STATIONERS.

Diagram showing ages of *Stationers*, and of the whole occupied population of London. (1891—Males.)

————— Stationers.
————— Whole of occupied in London.

(See remarks as to ages on tabular **page** opposite.)

CHAPTER IV.

STATIONERS. (*Section* 31.)

Persons Represented.

Census Enumeration.						Enumerated by Families.

Census Enumeration.

Census Division, 1891.	Fe-males	Males.				Total.
	All Ages.	—19	20—54	55—		
Stationers	3191	1196	3965	531		8883

In a minor degree these trades have the peculiarities of age distribution that have been remarked amongst printers and bookbinders. (*See* diagram.)

Enumerated by Families.

Sex	Males	3054	
	Females	369	
Birthplace	In London	70 %	2384
	Out of London..	30 %	1039
Industrial Status ..	Employers	25 %	864
	Employed......	64 %	2187
	Neither	11 %	372

Heads of Families, 3423.

DISTRIBUTION.

	N.	W. & C.	S.	Total.
	2700	1895	3025	8883

DETAILS OF OCCUPATIONS
FROM THE CENSUS DICTIONARY).

Stationer, law stationer, paper merchant, dealer, waste-paper dealer, monogram, heraldic and relief stamper, paper embosser, notepaper cutter, folder, sealer, stationer's sundries maker, dealer, stamp perforator.

TOTAL POPULATION CONCERNED.

	Heads of Families.	Others Occupied.	Unoccupied.	Servants.	Total.
Total.	3423	3556	7920	857	15,756
Average in family ..	1	1·03	2·30	·25	4·58

CLASSIFICATION.

Numbers living in Families.		%
3 or more to a room	985	6·2
2 & under 3 ,,	1746	11·1
1 & under 2 ,,	3163	20·1
Less than 1 ,,		
More than 4 rooms		
4 or more persons to a servant ..	7673	48·8
Less than 4 to 1 servant, & 4 or more to 2 servants ..	953	6·0
All others with 2 or more servants..	379	2·4
Servants	857	5·4
	15,756	100

	Inner.	Outer.	Together.
Crowded..	32 %	9 %	17 %
Not ,, ..	68 %	91 %	83 %

DISTRIBUTION.

East ..	Inner 1774	2031
	Outer 257	
North..	Inner 568	5034
	Outer 4466	
West ..	Inner 343	1683
	Outer 1340	
Central	Inner 1341	1341
South East..	Inner 437	2667
	Outer 2230	
South-West..	Inner 1156	3000
	Outer 1844	
		15,756

Inner 5,619, or 35½ %.
Outer 10,137, or 64½ %.

Status as to Employment (according to Census Enumeration).

Census Divisions (1891).	Employers.		Employed.			Neither Employer nor Employed.		Total.
			Males.		Females of all ages.			
	Males.	Females	Under 20.	Over 20.		Males.	Females	
Stationer, law stationer	850	211	1196	3301	2811	345	169	8883
TOTAL........	1061		7308			514		8883

Proportion of Employers to Employed, 1 to 7.

STATIONERS.

Stationers were originally the dealers in books and papers who occupied shops and stalls "stationed" in the neighbourhood of St. Paul's, or even in the very porches of the Cathedral, as distinguished from itinerant vendors. Their descendants are booksellers and publishers, and the organization known as "Stationers' Hall" remains to remind us of those days.

The stationer is now mainly a dealer in paper, but may call himself a manufacturer, inasmuch as, although he does not make paper, it is his business to prepare it for use. But many who would be properly described as manufacturing stationers appear in the census as paper manufacturers, and those returned in this section are probably, for the most part, shopkeepers, or assistants in stationers' shops. The wholesale houses form a connecting link with the actual manufacture of paper. They may have mills of their own, but they will also buy, cut, and handle paper made by others. Envelope making lies within their province. Retail stationers, with whom we are principally concerned, are simply dealers, but may be connected with printing or account-book binding, receiving orders for such work, and passing them on to others, unless able, perhaps, to execute them on their own machinery and by their own employees.

This group of trades affords examples of the growth of business by the inclusion, under one organization, of many branches of work, previously undertaken separately, department after department being added, and each involving a distinct trade; so that the establishment becomes a congeries of allied occupations whose relation to each other is mainly determined by the prominence of the particular trade which happened to form the nucleus of the business. This, it may be observed, is the

most modern form of trade development, and has very
little in common, economically or socially, with an increased
scale of operations.

Retail stationers employ countermen or salesmen, and to
these the wholesale or larger retail houses add warehousemen, cutters, embossers, stampers, folders and sealers. A
good counterman should be acquainted with every article
dealt in, and have sufficient technical knowledge to book
an order properly, so that it can be executed without
further reference or risk of blunder.

In the wholesale trade the counterman is usually promoted from the warehouse, where he will have become
acquainted with the stock; but not so many are employed
now as formerly, their services being superseded by those
of the "traveller." Time was when the buyer sought the
wares he needed, but this is changed, and now the seller
seeks his customers far and wide. Travellers and booking-
clerks take the place of countermen, and doubtless outnumber those whom they replace; advancement finds a
new road, and the men appear in the census under another
heading. The pay of wholesale countermen ranges from
28s to 35s a week, or in some cases a monthly salary will
be paid. In the retail trade the rate has a wider range,
and may be anything from 21s to 50s, or even more.

The wages of warehousemen and cutters vary from 30s
to 36s per week, and their assistants begin at 20s and may
rise to 30s. It is not possible to distinguish these men
from those returned under a similar name in the printing
section. Their pay is the same, and they belong to the
same union, if they belong to any union at all.

Notepaper folders and sealers are generally boys. They
either fold by hand or feed a machine. Neatness and
cleanness are essential. Some are paid by piece and others
by time. The earnings on piece would be about 10s, and on
time, 5s to 8s per week. Women and girls are also employed,
especially on fancy work. Girls begin at 3s or 4s a week,

but will mostly earn 5*s* to 8*s*. Women make 8*s* to 12*s*, or, in some cases, a little more.

Formerly lads were apprenticed, and the older men have generally served their time, but now lads come as errand or warehouse boys, and take their chance.

The busiest season is from October to Christmas, and the slackest from July to September. The beginning and end of each quarter bring special activity.

Foreign competition is almost entirely restricted to common lines of goods. Cheap printing papers are largely imported. Notepaper and envelopes of a common quality come from Germany and Austria, consigned to foreign houses, and push their way on the market. Provincial competition is unimportant, and in no way compares with that existing between London and country printing houses.

TRADE ORGANIZATION.

There are no trade unions belonging exclusively to this section. Some of the warehousemen and cutters are members of the Printer and Stationers' Warehousemen's Union or the Amalgamated Society of Printers' Warehousemen, but the unionist element is small. Two provident societies connected with the trade make provision for their members in sickness, distress, old age, and death. (1) The Stationers' Mutual Benefit Society, established 1845, which has 780 members and £12,000 of invested funds. It gives 22*s* a week in sickness, and deals with cases of distress out of a benevolent fund, and grants pensions of £15 per annum after sixty, as vacancies occur and funds permit. There were twenty-six pensioners in 1893. (2) The Stationers' and Paper Manufacturers' Provident Society, formed in 1840, of which the main object is the provision of annuities after sixty. Temporary help is also given in sickness and distress up to 20*s* a week. During 1893 the annuities, in sums not exceeding thirty guineas a year, amounted to £928, and other relief to £314. The invested funds are over £34,000.

Wages Statistics.

Seven returns have been received from stationers, employing 510 persons—263 men, 144 women, and 133 boys. These represent only the wholesale and manufacturing firms.

The number and percentage of those engaged at different rates are shown in the following table, and may be taken as representing the rates current generally in the trade, with the exception that men earning over 55s a week are only to be found in the larger houses, such as those making the returns :—

Adult Men.			Women and Girls.			Boys.		
Earning	No.	Per cent.	Earning	No.	Per cent.	Earning	No.	Per cent.
Under 15s	5	2	5s and under	17	15	5s	4	3
15s ,, 20s	17	6½	6s ,, 7s	21	18½	6s and 7s	37	28
20s ,, 25s	30	11½	8s ,, 9s	14	12	8s ,, 9s	25	19
25s ,, 30s	48	18	10s ,, 11s	11	10	10s ,, 11s	18	13½
30s ,, 35s	47	18	12s ,, 13s	7	6	12s ,, 13s	14	10½
35s ,, 40s	37	14	14s ,, 15s	13	11	14s ,, 15s	10	7½
40s ,, 45s	35	13	16s ,, 17s	9	8	16s ,, 17s	19	14
45s ,, 55s	18	7	18s ,, 19s	10	9	18s ,, over	6	4½
55s and over	26	10	20s ,, over	12	10½			
	263	100		114	100		133	100

The industrial element being comparatively small, no useful comparison can be made between these figures and those showing the general condition in which the population connected with this trade live. Even after allowance is made for the employers, the proportion living under crowded conditions is small. This is only what might be expected in an occupation where a large proportion are almost necessarily householders.

Classification of Population (Stationers).

3 or more in each room	...	...	980, or 9 per cent.
2 to 3 ,,	...	...	1740 ,, 16 ,,
1 ,, 2 ,,	...	...	3200 ,, 29 ,,
Less than 1 ,,	...	... ⎫	
More than 4 rooms	...	... ⎬	5000 ,, 46 ,,
4 or more persons to a servant		... ⎭	
			10,920
Employers' families and servants		...	4,830
			15,750

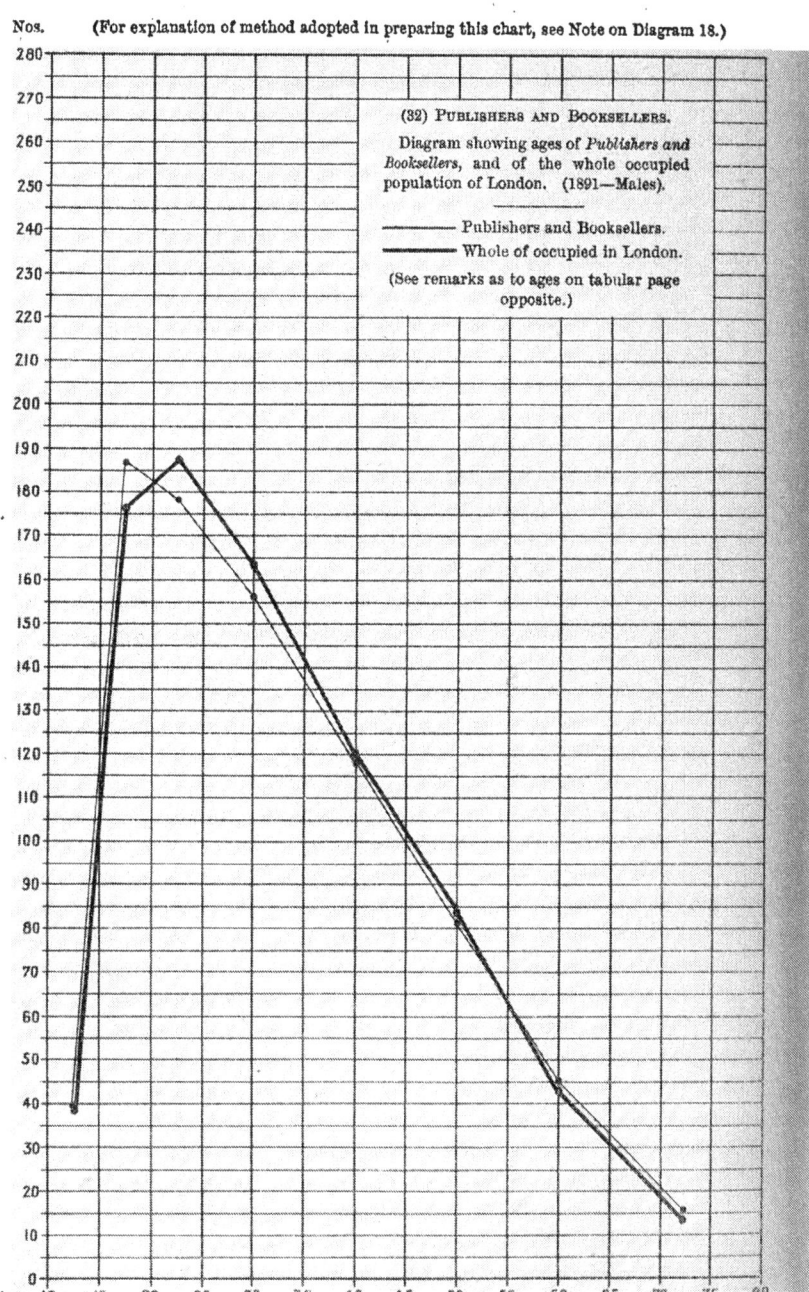

(32) PUBLISHERS AND BOOKSELLERS.

Diagram showing ages of *Publishers and Booksellers*, and of the whole occupied population of London. (1891—Males).

——————— Publishers and Booksellers.
——————— Whole of occupied in London.

(See remarks as to ages on tabular page opposite.)

CHAPTER V.

BOOKSELLERS, NEWSAGENTS. *(Section 32.)*

Persons Represented.

Census Enumeration.

Division, 1891.	Fe-males. All Ages.	Males. -19	20--54	55--	Total.
...lisher, ...kseller .. ...sagents	383	708	3067	434	4682
	565	429	1780	324	3098
1	948	1227	4847	758	7780

...proportion of males at various ages ...mates very nearly with that of the Occupied Males. (*See* diagram.) The figures evidently do not include the ...mber of lads of school age partially ...d by newsagents. Their inclusion ...give a line similar to those in other ... of the printing and paper trades, a ...erance of boy labour being a char-...ic feature of all.

DISTRIBUTION.

N.	W & C.	S.	Total.
2158	2082	2895	7780

DETAILS OF OCCUPATIONS (OM THE CENSUS DICTIONARY).

...lisher, bookseller, librarian; Book ...t, canvasser, colporteur, bookstall ...k, music seller, directory agent. ...svendor, news-room keeper; News-...r proprietor, publisher, despatcher. ...ertising agent, contractor, inspector, ...vasser.

Enumerated by Families.

Sex	Males .... Females	4064 322	
Birthplace	In London .... 58 % Out of London 42 %	2561 1825	Heads of Families, 4386.
Industrial Status ..	Employer .... 23 % Employed .... 54 % Neither ...... 23 %	1023 2386 977	

TOTAL POPULATION CONCERNED.

	Heads of Families.	Others Occupied.	Unoccupied.	Servants.	Total.
Total.	4386	4161	10,699	1436	20,082
Average in family ..	1	·95	2·30	·33	4·58

CLASSIFICATION.			DISTRIBUTION.		

Numbers living in Families.		%	East ...	Inner 1187 Outer 196	1383
3 or more to a room	915	4·6			
2 & under 3 ,,	2058	10·3			
1 & under 2 ,,	3838	19·1	North...	Inner 866 Outer 4841	5707
Less than 1 ,,					
More than 4 rooms	9805	48·8	West ...	Inner 527 Outer 2394	2921
4 or more persons to a servant ..					
Less than 4 to 1 ser-			Central	Inner 2244	2244
vant & 4 or more te 2 servants ..	1222	6·1	South-East .	Inner 299 Outer 2767	3066
All others with 2 or more servants..	808	4·0	South-West..	Inner 1575 Outer 3186	4761
Servants	1436	7·1			
	20,082	100			20,082

	Inner. Outer. Together.		Inner 6898, or 33 %
Crowded.. 29 % 8 % 15 %			Outer 13,384, or 67 %
Not ,, .. 71 % 92 % 85 %			

Status as to Employment (according to Census Enumeration).

Census Divisions (1891.)	Employers.		Employed.			Neither Employer nor Employed.		Total.
	Males.	Females	Males. Under 20.	Over 20.	Females of all ages.	Males.	Females	
...isher, bookseller, librarian	604	41	798	2581	290	316	52	4682
...spaper agent, news-room keeper	457	99	429	887	216	760	250	3098
TOTAL..........	1061	140	1227	3468	506	1076	302	7780
	1201		5201			1378		
	Proportion of Employers to Employed—1 to 4.							

DEALERS IN BOOKS AND NEWSPAPERS.

The occupations here grouped together differ widely in character, agreeing, however, in this :—that they all relate to the distribution or circulation of printed paper. The total numbers show a considerable increase since 1881, but are at the end of all less than would seem probable, leading to the belief that many who may be returned as warehouse-men, or collectors, or clerks, have escaped notice in the sections of the census with which we are now dealing.

BOOK PUBLISHING.

This trade is mainly in the hands of a few leading and well-known firms. It does not furnish employment directly to any large number of persons. The employees consist, for the most part, of clerks, receiving salaries ranging from £40 to £300 or £400 a year, and warehousemen or porters earning from 18s to 35s a week. The qualification needed for the warehousemen especially, but more, or less for everyone employed, is a knowledge of the works and editions published by the firm which employs them. Continued service alone can give this knowledge, and consequently we find great steadiness of employment. Changes are rare, and busy and slack times are encountered without any material increase or decrease of staff. Moreover, the work is much more continuous than it used to be. Formerly the publishing seasons were clearly marked, two busy periods being recognized : the winter season, beginning in October and lasting until about Christmas, and the summer season, lasting only for a shorter period before Easter. While if we go back to a still earlier date it seems that this second season did not exist, and that all or almost all books were published in winter. These old customs died hard, but gradually the periods of publication have been extended, and now every year they become less restricted, only July and August being avoided as holiday months. There are still special seasons for certain books: for instance, guide books, before the holidays begin; medical works in the autumn when the schools open; children's books, and gift books generally, at Christmas. Nearly every part of the year has its special feature.

A record of new books and editions from 1888 to 1894, compiled from the *Publishers' Circular*, affords an interesting view of the character and movement of the trade. The subjects are classified under fourteen general heads, as follows:—

	New books or new editions published.							Total.	New Books.	New editions.
	1888.	1889.	1890.	1891.	1892.	1893.	1894.			
Theology	912	764	708	627	673	533	556	4773	3916	857
Education	779	681	703	694	694	622	742	4915	4101	814
Medicine	199	182	193	175	177	151	156	1233	839	394
Law	172	106	79	109	65	50	149	730	471	259
Trade and Economics	135	126	109	136	175	85	162	928	776	152
Travel and Geography	297	260	257	271	336	319	350	2090	1597	493
Art and Science	253	146	73	116	209	123	128	1048	766	282
History	486	424	391	413	368	334	314	2730	2127	603
Belles Lettres	389	340	362	254	139	107	485	2076	1197	879
Poetry	231	187	188	201	227	234	181	1449	1098	351
Fiction	1314	1404	1204	1216	1537	1328	1652	9655	7143	2512
Children's books	470	511	538	447	345	695	298	3304	2786	518
Serials	327	346	319	316	373	371	330	2382	2352	30
Miscellaneous	627	590	611	731	936	1430	982	5907	4672	1235
Total	6591	6067	5735	5706	6254	6382	6485	43,220	33,841	9370
New books..............	4960	4694	4414	4429	4915	5129	5300	33,841		
New editions	1631	1373	1321	1277	1339	1253	1185	9379		
Total	6591	6067	5735	5706	6254	6382	6485	43,220		

Book Selling.

Cheap prices have resulted in a greatly increased demand for books. This, however, is only an incomplete measure of the extent to which habits of reading have increased, as newspapers and periodicals provide a still wider channel for the satisfaction of this need. But it may, perhaps, fully represent the increase in the reading of books; for there is a constant struggle between purchase and loan, and the more we buy because of cheapness the less likely are we to borrow books; the more readily we can read at home the less willing are we to sit at the table of a public library. This competition between borrowing and buying has various results—libraries either increase the comforts they offer or tend to become useful mainly as libraries of reference, where access may be had to books for which there is no general demand; and lending libraries pay a high price for the first editions which their readers desire to see at once, but could not afford to purchase. On this curious basis rests the continuation of the old-fashioned three volume form for fiction.

Another development connected with the effort to sell books as cheaply as possible, is the custom of the giving of discounts, first to wholesale dealers, then to retail sellers, and finally to the public at large; and as here, again, curious results have followed, it may be worth while to trace the devious course of "net prices."

Ordinarily books are supplied by the publisher at what is termed "sale" price, which may be 8d or 8½d in the shilling on the "published" or marked price. In addition to this, thirteen copies are charged as twelve, or sometimes it is twenty-five as twenty-four. These are the recognized established terms, involving no bargain. Beyond them, large buyers will sometimes obtain additional discount under one excuse or another. For export to the Colonies, or to find a market in America, or for an early order before publication to secure a certain sale, or when a large sum has to be spent in books on behalf of a public library; in such and other cases of the kind a special bargain is recognized as reasonable. Of a different character are the special prices accepted when superseded editions or neglected books must be cleared at great sacrifice—the alternative being their return to "pulp."

Wholesale bookselling, which was formerly in the hands of several firms, has been consolidated by amalgamation, and much of the work is now controlled by one firm. Booksellers can deal directly with the publishers; but even in London they often find it not worth while to do so, and almost all the country trade passes through the hands of the wholesale dealers. There is nothing disadvantageous in this. These dealers offer convenience to the trade for which both publisher and retailer are content to pay, and free to pay or not as they please.

Retail bookselling has been revolutionized—not to say demoralized—by the discount system, with the result that, except amongst second-hand booksellers, of intelligent appreciation of the books to be sold there is little left. A new book is a uniform article, exactly the same wherever it may be bought; and the most that can be asked for it, according to invariable custom, is the "published" price; consequently the retail seller must be remunerated by a discount. But the reasonable margin on a book which all the world desires to buy and read, of which half a dozen copies may be sold in a morning, would be quite inadequate to pay for the sale of some book which, however valuable, appeals to a limited circle of readers. And again, what is a necessary margin of profit on the sale of books in some remote country place, or exposed to the weather on a railway bookstall, is excessive under other and more favourable circumstances.

From these inequalities there crept in gradually the habit of giving part of the discount to the purchaser. It perhaps began with a return only to the buyers for "book societies," which, though now almost a thing of the past, were, thirty or forty years ago, to be found in every little provincial coterie. The return, which was first 5 or 10 per cent., rose gradually to twopence in the shilling; and when it became usual to give it to all "cash buyers," an increased allowance was sought and obtained by the bookseller from the publishers. For the moment a balance was maintained. Booksellers could still afford to keep a stock of all kinds of books, and were not expected to return the discount on works not in general demand nor to casual buyers, nor at all in out-of-the-way places. But later, when bookselling enterprise in London and large towns offered threepence in the shilling to all comers, keeping for sale only such books as sold readily, or for which "special terms" had been obtained, the position of the old-fashioned bookseller became almost untenable. He lost the cream of his trade, and was forced to become more and more a dealer in fancy stationery, ornaments, or games, and less and less an intelligent dealer in books.

From various sides attempts have been made to combat this evil. Ruskin published his books at high prices, and refused to allow any discount at all. Publishers combined to prevent under-selling, and proposed to refuse to supply any bookseller who allowed more than 10 per cent. for ordinary books or 15 per cent. for school books; but a legal decision was given by Lord Campbell against this proposal, and Lord Macaulay denounced it. More lately an attempt has been made to introduce net prices—that is, to publish books on which, as they are marked net, the buyer will expect no discount, or "only a very little one." Of course, the trade still has its discount, though a reduced percentage. The main advantage, perhaps, is that the public become used to varying terms of sale for different kinds of books. Only in this does there seem hope of a final settlement. Every book will still have its nominal price, and the amount of discount (if any) may vary with the circumstances of the case. In this way every buyer will be fairly treated whatever he may buy, and can have every variety of book laid before him. Whereas, those shops which give invariably the maximum discount must, perforce, restrict their stock to the books on which the maximum discount can be afforded.

The men employed by retail booksellers include assistants, clerks, collectors, and sometimes managers. They keep the ordinary hours of other retail shops, which close early on Saturdays.

Second-hand Bookselling is a distinct branch, about which there always hangs a certain flavour of romance. In how many stories of real life as well as fiction does not the hero hang over the books which lie exposed to tempt the passer by? What possibilities do the shelves of old bookshops offer for wonderful bargains to the collector, and of all the objects of interest collected by man which can compare to a rare edition of an old book? The dealers in second-hand books can hardly know too much of their contents, and must at least know something. They must be readers, and most probably also lovers of books. For them, business retains its individuality. They themselves personally buy what they themselves personally sell, and must put knowledge and judgment into every transaction, instead of being, as so many retail traders are, merely the channel through which wholesale production is distributed with the assistance of plate-glass windows and a smiling attendant.

They buy at book auctions, at which publishers' remainders and private libraries are offered; or they visit private houses to value books which are to be disposed of, and finally they are ready to pay its value on any book which may be brought into their shop. Holywell Street is the trade centre, and the name, unfortunately, is enough to remind us that this trade has its foul side.

NEWSAGENTS.

The distributors of newspapers and periodicals, wholesale and retail alike, are active servants of the public. Neither class have an easy existence. Long hours are general and early rising essential. Without methodical habits and promptitude success is impossible. This is true even of the ragged boys who sell papers in the streets.

Wholesale Newsagents.—There are a few " outside " agents, but the business is, for the most part, concentrated in the immediate neighbourhood of Fleet Street and the eastern portion of the Strand. The papers are collected from the publishing offices at the earliest moment and made up in parcels in accordance with lists received weekly from the retail agents. Most of the houses engaged in this business supply the country as well as London, but some deal with London only. One firm, as is well known, overshadows all the rest and has its own sorting vans on the leading railways.

The men employed are known as collectors and packers. The former must be familiar with the publishing offices of the various papers, the number of copies reckoned as a quire (which varies from twenty-four to twenty-seven), the regulations as to exchanging unsold copies, and even the trade prices. The packer makes up the parcels—working often against time—and dispatches them to catch the trains or for suburban distribution. There are two dispatches, one in the early morning, the other in the afternoon, this last consisting mostly of periodicals for country dealers, as the London newsagents usually come in the morning, and it may be a second time during the day, to fetch their own supplies, collecting special orders at the same time. At most newspaper offices unsold copies of the previous issue can be exchanged for the current number, but some restrict the quantity to a fixed proportion of those purchased. Collectors and packers are paid from 24s to 30s a week, with foremen at a higher rate.

The " outside " wholesale agents have their places of business in the suburbs, and supply the newsvendors in their own neighbourhood. Most of the City houses decline to distribute the Sunday morning papers, and this has given the suburban men their opportunity. The supply of Sunday editions to the retailers is almost entirely in their hands, and may be the means of introducing other trade.

Men engaged on the country trade must rise before the lark. Four days a week work begins at 4 A.M., and on Friday and Saturday an hour, and for some of the men two hours earlier, owing to the press of weekly journals. Soon after 6 A.M. the rush is over, and there is a break for four hours, work being resumed at 10 o'clock and continuing till 4 or 6 o'clock in the afternoon according to the pressure of work. For the London trade 5.30 A.M. is early enough from Monday to Thursday, with 5 o'clock on Friday and 3 A.M. on Saturday. Time is allowed for breakfast, dinner, and tea, and work finishes at about 7 P.M., or 4 P.M. on Saturdays.

A system of fines is usually adopted to secure punctuality, and if a man is very late he loses his day's work, and in his place another is selected from a number who usually stand ready for this chance. These hangers-on are men familiar with the work, but who have for some reason dropped into the ranks of the casually employed. Most of the men enter the trade as lads and work up. They usually retain their situations for long periods, and the seasons do not materially affect the numbers employed.

Retail Newsagents.—The day's work commences soon after 6 o'clock, when the parcel of papers is delivered at the door. After rapidly sorting, and in a few cases folding,* the papers, the newsvendor and his boys start on their early round, which will include such public-houses and coffee-shops as do an early morning trade. A second

* The improvements of folding machinery, and its adaptation to the printing press, has relieved the newsvendor of the task of folding the sheets, which pressed heavily at the moment when all his powers were taxed to deliver the journals. With one exception, the morning daily papers are now supplied ready folded and the majority of the weekly journals also. Indeed, newsagents are proposing a boycott of unfolded papers.

300 PRINTING AND PAPER TRADES.

journey is generally necessary to supply people who are not such early risers, but more often the newspaper is pushed beneath the front-door or flung into the area, or in some cases confidingly disposed under the knocker. In the course of the day it is probable that a visit has to be made to Fleet Street; and in the afternoon the carts of the evening papers deliver their successive editions, of which, however, the sale is not large till the "specials" and "extra specials" arrive, and the boys once more go over their districts. After 8 o'clock sales lessen, but it is not till 9 or 10 P.M. that the newsagent can close his shop. On Saturday it is still later, and Sunday is for him no day of rest.

If his business is sufficiently large, the retailer will deal with two wholesale houses, so that if one parcel should arrive late he may begin work on the other, and some advantage may be obtained in disposing of "returns," as the unsold copies are called.

The newsvendors' profits differ widely, depending on the extent of their trade; for, of course, the percentage made is the same to all. Few, however, depend only upon the sale of papers. Some light business is added—stationery or tobacco being the most favoured. Penny papers are sold to the retailers at 1s 4d to 1s 6d the quire, and, at twenty-four to twenty-seven copies to the quire, show about 33 per cent. profit. Smaller quantities are sold at ¾d to the 1d. If a retailer does a large enough business to make it worth while, he may himself send to the publishing offices, and in that case his profit on the sale of some journals may be 50 per cent. in place of 33 per cent. on their cost.

Competition is keen. Not only do the newsagents compete amongst themselves, but they have also to meet the opposition of the street sellers, and some of them complain that they are at a disadvantage in competing thus with those who pay neither rent nor rates—and have not even to take out a hawker's license—especially as they feel aggrieved when some street vendor by favour, or by custom, has acquired the right, or, at least, tacit permission, to display his bills and ply his calling at a particular spot, and even ask and receive rent for the use of his advertising boards.

In London there is a distinct falling off in the demand for papers during the summer months, as the result of the exodus to holiday resorts—this affects the retailers mainly— for wholesale work is probably transferred from town to country orders in the holiday season.

A large number of lads are engaged in the business, but few of these would be included in the census figures. Most of them are boys still at school, who do the work of carrying round papers before and after school hours. Such lads are paid 1s 6d or 2s a week, and may get breakfast or tea as well. When they leave school some will remain in the trade, but for most this work is only the introduction to some other calling, the recommendation of their employer giving them perhaps an advantage over other lads just leaving school.

Advertising Agents are also grouped under this head in the census, and some master billposters may be included under the heading of advertising contractors. As a rule the advertising agent deals only with advertisements inserted in newspapers, periodicals, &c. There are not many firms engaged and the number of persons employed is small, consisting principally of clerks and canvassers, the latter being paid by commission, or by salary and commission combined. Competition is very keen. The busiest times are in January and December, and, to some extent, at the end of each quarter.

TRADE ORGANIZATION.

Of the 5605 adult men included in this section, 3468 are described as employed, but they have no trade organization.

It is, however, possible, that a few may belong to societies connected with printing or other allied trades. There is one trades union, but it differs from the ordinary societies of this class in that it is an association of retail traders, combined to protect trade customs, and to increase profits.

This body, the Retail Newsagents' and Booksellers' Union, is a national society governed by a council. It has a number of country branches, and it is strongest in the northern counties. It is said to have four thousand members, of whom about six hundred are in London; nearly all being newsagents. Its principal object is the discussion and redress of trade grievances. The subscription is 5s per annum. Through its representations some newspaper publishers have taken to supplying their paper folded, and others have made concessions respecting the changing of unsold copies.

The booksellers are represented by the "Associated Booksellers of Great Britain and Ireland," a national society formed early this year (1895), which supersedes the old London Booksellers' Society. The annual subscription is 5s, and its objects are the maintenance of the net prices of books, and the limitation of the discount given on books issued upon the old terms of 25 per cent.

Booksellers and newsagents have each their own benevolent society. The Booksellers' Provident Institution was started in 1837 to provide temporary or permanent assistance to its members, their widows and children; all booksellers and their assistants being eligible. The minimum subscription is two guineas per annum. Temporary assistance is usually a weekly allowance, or a sum of money in case of death, while permanent help takes the form of a pension, which may reach but must not exceed fifty guineas a year. During 1894, the relief granted amounted to £1478, which was divided between seventy-five recipients, of whom thirty-two were pensioners. The

Institution has 435 members, and over £30,000 invested. Connected with this society is the Booksellers' Provident Retreat, at Abbots Langley, Herts, to which pensioners of the Institution, over sixty years of age, may be admitted. It was opened in 1846, and has an income of about £500 mainly derived from interest on its investment, which exceeds £12,000.

The other society, the Newsvendors' Benevolent and Provident Institution, grants pensions and other assistance to persons who have been engaged in the sale of newspapers. Benefit members subscribe 5s a year, and a donation of three guineas constitutes life membership. There are now 413 benefit members and twenty-eight annuitants. The latter received £485 in 1894, men receiving £20, and women £15 a year. The Institution had an income of £1462 in 1894. It has £14,000 invested, producing £500 per annum.

Wages Statistics.

Excepting the wholesale booksellers and newsagents, few employers in this section would have more than one or two men and a few boys in their service; while the business of the retail newsagent is very rarely large enough to enable him to employ more than one or two lads continuously, supplemented by a few boys working before and after school hours. There are also a large number who do all their own work, nearly one-fifth (1378) of the whole being returned as neither employers nor employed. Consequently, the following statistics must be regarded as referring only to the persons employed by the wholesale houses and not to the entire section.

Concerning the adult men employed, particulars have been received as to the average weekly earnings of 399, as follows:—

Under 20s............23, or 6 per cent. ⎫
20s to 25s............75 ,, 19   ,,   ⎬ Under 30s, 46 per cent.
25s ,, 30s............84 ,, 21   ,,   ⎭
30s ,, 35s............65 ,, 16   ,,   ⎫
35s ,, 40s............42 ,, 10½   ,,   ⎪
40s ,, 45s............34 ,, 8½   ,,   ⎬ 30s and over, 54 per cent.
45s and upwards ...76 ,, 19   ,,   ⎭
　　　　　　　　　　━━━
　　　　　　　399 ,, 100   ,,

These figures, which are mainly from one large firm, include managers and foremen who are not required in the smaller establishments, and bookstall clerks, who are paid commission on the sales, in addition to salary. Omitting the latter, the percentage is as under, and may more nearly represent the ordinary earnings :—

Under 20s............ 7½ per cent. ⎫
20s to 25s............25   ,,   ⎬ Under 30s, 56½ per cent.
25s ,, 30s............24   ,,   ⎭
30s ,, 35s............18   ,,   ⎫
35s ,, 40s............ 9   ,,   ⎪
40s ,, 45s............ 7½   ,,   ⎬ 30s and over, 43½ per cent.
45s and upwards... 9   ,,   ⎭
　　　　　　　　━━━
　　　　　　　100   ,,

Of the boys and youths under twenty, the census only shows 1227, but this would not include the boys working part time for newsvendors, who probably considerably outnumber the others. We have received information respecting 718, as under :—

2s & under ....105 or 14½ per cent. ⎫
2s to 3s ....142 ,, 20   ,,   ⎬ 4s and under, 40 per cent.
3s ,,   4s .... 40 ,, 5½   ,,   ⎭
4s ,,   5s .... 55 ,, 8   ,,   ⎫
5s ,,   6s ....109 ,, 15   ,,   ⎪
7s   .... 88 ,, 12   ,,   ⎬ Over 4s and under 10s, 45 per cent.
8s ,,   9s .... 71 ,, 10   ,,   ⎭
10s ,, 11s .... 40 ,, 5½   ,,   ⎫
12s ,, 13s .... 26 ,, 3½   ,,   ⎪
14s ,, 15s .... 24 ,, 3½   ,,   ⎬ 10s and over, 15 per cent.
16s & over .... 18 ,, 2½   ,,   ⎭
　　　　　　　━━━
　　　　　718 ,, 100   ,,

Most of those earning 4*s* or less are school-boys working part time, of whom but few may be expected to remain in the trade; whilst a considerable proportion of the others will stay either in the wholesale bookselling or newsagency or as bookstall clerks.

Social Condition.

Of the 5605 adult men enumerated, 4064 are classified as heads of families. The number of profit earners being so large, no useful comparison of earnings with style of life can be made. The proportion living under crowded conditions is very small, as might be expected in businesses involving in most cases the occupation of a shop. It is probable that the crowded families are chiefly those of men engaged in the wholesale newspaper trade who must live within walking distance of Fleet Street.

PART IV.—TEXTILES.

TEXTILES.

PRELIMINARY STATEMENT.

WHAT is left of Spitalfields silk weaving constitutes nearly the whole of Textile manufacture proper in London. The census, however, counts 2700 persons who give as their employment some form of cotton, woollen, or carpet manufacture; with them are placed in this chapter the dyers, who, however, are mostly cleaners, together with the manufacturers of rope and canvas, and of floor cloth and india-rubber goods. These are all small sections which do not together add up to 16,000 persons.

The total of those employed, divided by age and sex, is as follows :—

Persons represented: (A) *Census Enumeration.*

	ENUMERATED BY AGE AND SEX.						
	10—	15 —	20—	25—	55—	65 —	Total.
Males............	252	1259	1059	4641	881	571	8663
Females	289	2064	1345	2711	484	316	7209
Total.........	541	3323	2404	7352	1365	887	15,872

Females and males under twenty together comprise more than half of the total numbers employed, with the result that only 6546 count as heads of families. The total population included in these families is 28,815, made up as follows :—

Persons represented : (B) Enumerated by Families.

No.	Sections.	Heads.	Total numbers (excluding Servants).	Per family (excluding Servants).	Servants.
33	Silk Manufacture, &c.	1764	6703	3·80	331
34	Cottons, Woollens, Carpets	1076	4577	4·25	147
35	Dyers, Cleaners	896	4014	4·48	112
36	Hemp, Jute, and Fibre	1424	6294	4·43	97
37	India rubber and Floor Cloth	1386	6324	4·56	216
	Total	6546	27,912	4·26	903
	Servants.....................		903		
	Total population		28,815		

Of these heads of families, 1206 are women. These are mostly employed in silk weaving, and account for the small average number per family. In silk weaving 31½ per cent. of the heads are women, whereas in the other trades the proportion is only 13½ per cent.

The 903 servants attend 3100 persons, the remaining 24,812 being without any resident service. Of the servant keeping class, 1600 have only one servant to four or more persons served, 1000 have one servant to less than four in family, or two servants to four or more persons, and 400 live in other families keeping two or more servants.

Turning to the 24,800 who have no servant, we find that 7800 of them live in families which occupy more than four rooms, or have, on the average, more than one room to each person; 6700 live with one and under two persons per room; 6400 with two to three persons to a room; 2500 live three to four to a room; and 1400 individuals form households in which there are four or more persons to each room.

SOCIAL CONDITION OF FAMILIES OF TEXTILE WORKERS.

		Crowded: 35·8%
Lower Classes.	4 or more persons to a room ... 1400 or 4·9%	13·7%
	3 and under 4 " ... 2580 " 8·8%	
	2 and under 3 " ... 6380 "	22·1%
	1 and under 2 " ... 6681 "	23·2%

Not Crowded: 64·2%

Central Classes.	Less than 1 person to a room ... 913 " 3·2%	32·8%
	More than 4 rooms ... 6899 " 23·9%	
	4 or more persons to a servant... 1636 " 5·7%	
Upper Classes.	Less than 4 persons to a servant, or 4 or more to 2 servants ... 1059 "	3·7%
	All others with 2 or more servants 405 "	1·4%
Servants... ... ... 903 "		3·1%
28,815		100%

Social Condition (by Sections).

Section.	3, 4, or more persons to a room.	2 and under 3 persons to a room.	1 and under 2 persons to a room.	Less than 1 to a room. More than 4 rooms, or 4 or more persons to 1 servant.	Less than 4 persons to 1 servant.	Servants.	Total.
Silk, &c., Manuf..	643	1247	1699	2549	565	331	7034
Per cent......	9	18	24	36	8	5	100
Cottons, Woollen, &c.........	889	1234	1016	1195	243	147	4724
Per cent......	19	26	22	25	5	3	100
Dyeing and Cleaning.......	352	821	828	1865	148	112	4126
Per cent......	8½	20	20	45	3½	3	100
Hemp, Jute and Fibre	1201	1788	1567	1557	181	97	6391
Per cent......	19	28	24½	24	3	1½	100
Floor Cloth and India-rubber Manufacture.	854	1290	1571	2282	327	216	6540
Per cent......	13	20	24	35	5	3	100

CHANGES SINCE 1861 IN NUMBERS EMPLOYED.

	1861.	1871.	1881.	1891.
Silk, &c.....	12,400	8,900	6,100	4,800
Cottons, Woollens, &c.......	4,300	4,100	2,800	2,700
Dyeing and Cleaning..........	2,500	2,600	2,100	2,000
Hemp, Jute and Fibre	4,200	3,500	3,300	3,300
Floor Cloth and India Rubber	1,300	1,900	2,300	3,100
Total	24,700	21,000	16,600	15,900

Except in floor cloth and India rubber, the reduction in the numbers employed is very great and continuous decade by decade.

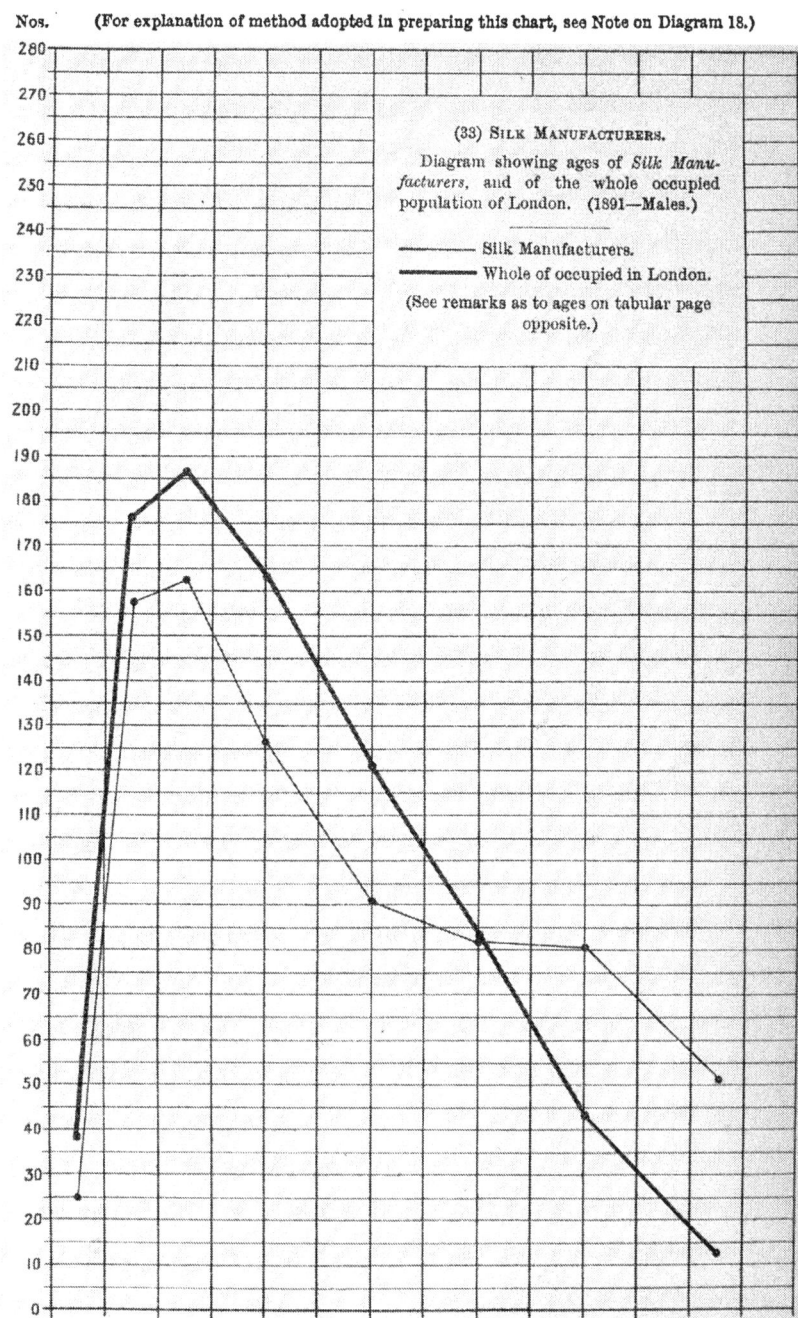

(33) SILK MANUFACTURERS.

Diagram showing ages of *Silk Manufacturers*, and of the whole occupied population of London. (1891—Males.)

———— Silk Manufacturers.

———— Whole of occupied in London.

(See remarks as to ages on tabular page opposite.)

CHAPTER I.
SILK AND WOOLLEN GOODS.
SILK AND FANCY TEXTILES. (Section 33.)

Persons Represented.

Census Enumeration.

Census Divisions, 1891.	Females All Ages.	Males -19	Males 20-54	Males 55-	Total.
1) Silk-weaving	1109	128	546	423	2206
2) Fancy Textiles	1744	155	636	70	2605
Total.........	2853	283	1182	493	4811

The diagram shows the natural age line of decaying industry with an abnormal proportion of old men. It is probable that the later development of this trade (such as it is) connected with female employment, as in the manufacture by machinery of silks especially intended for umbrellas, or the making of fancy textile goods.

Enumerated by Families.

Sex	Males	1206	
	Females..............	558	
Birthplace	In London 68%	1208	Heads of Families, 1764.
	Out of London.. 32%	556	
Industrial Status	Employer 15%	261	
	Employed 74%	1308	
	Neither 11%	195	

TOTAL POPULATION CONCERNED.

	Heads of Families.	Others occupied.	Unoccupied.	Servants.	Total.
Total.	1764	2132	2807	331	7034
Average in family ..	1	1·20	1·59	·19	3·98

DISTRIBUTION.

E.	N.	W. & C.	S.	Total.
1980	1059	664	1108	4811

DETAILS OF OCCUPATIONS (FROM THE CENSUS DICTIONARY).

1) Silk manufacturer, winder, warper, quill winder, twister, weaver, silk velvet weaver, silk braid.
2) Fancy dealer, dress warehouse-man, fancy goods importer, mounter, Berlin wool worker, repository keeper, knitter, hair-net maker, beader on net, babies' boot-maker, brace-maker, pinker, purse-maker, fancy-bag maker.

CLASSIFICATION.

Numbers living in Families.		%
3 or more to a room	643	9·2
2 & under 3 ,,	1247	17·7
1 & under 2 ,,	1699	24·1
Less than 1 ,,		
More than 4 rooms 4 or more persons to a servant ..	2549	36·3
Less than 4 to 1 servant, and 4 or more to 2 servants	405	5·8
All others with 2 or more servants ..	160	2·2
Servants...........	331	4·7
	7034	100

	Inner.	Outer.	Together.
Crowded ..	41%	10%	27%
Not ,, ..	59%	90%	73%

DISTRIBUTION.

	Inner	Outer	
East ..	2847	156	3003
North	187	1440	1627
West ..	45	289	334
Central	Inner 469		469
South-East	134	659	793
South-West	183	625	808
			7034

Inner 3865, or 55%
Outer 3169, or 45%

Status as to Employment (according to Census Enumeration).

Census Divisions (1891).	Employers. Males	Employers. Females	Employed. Males Under 20.	Employed. Males Over 20.	Employed. Females of all ages.	Neither Employer nor Employed. Males	Neither Employer nor Employed. Females	Total.
1) Silk, satin, velvet	77	6	128	852	1072	40	31	2206
2) Crêpe, gauze shawls	4	1	6	7	13	3	3	37
Fancy goods (textile)	171	96	149	452	1413	69	218	2568
TOTAL........	252	103	283	1311	2498	112	252	4811
	355		4092			364		

Proportion of Employers to Employed—1 to 12·

SILK AND FANCY TEXTILE GOODS.

Silk weaving is entirely an East London industry, and
as such is fully described in Vol. IV. (Vol. I. of original
edition). Since 1888, when the account was written, little
change has occurred in the condition either of the trade or
the operatives. The almost stationary character of the
industry, following a period of rapid decline, there noted, still
continues, the remnants of a once flourishing business being
held together partly by the superior character of the work,
and the special efforts of the manufacturers, and partly by
a semi-philanthropic endeavour to develop amongst the
wealthy a fashion for Spitalfields silk. This select demand
seems likely to go on for some time—quite possibly as long
as the supply lasts ; for the bulk of the operatives are getting
on in years, and there are very few learners to take their
place.

Under the name of "Fancy Textile Goods" are grouped
a number of small trades, but as they include fancy goods'
importers and merchants, Berlin-wool dealers, and repository
keepers, &c., it is quite likely that the majority of those
allotted to this heading are engaged in some branch of
dealing. Such manufacture as there is includes, amongst
males, silk-cord spinning and the tracing of various designs
on different textile fabrics, or of patterns for art needle-
work.

The silk-cord spinners are few in numbers, two or three
being employed by each of several trimming warehouses.
The silk threads are nearly always spun on a cotton body,
and the cord is used principally in the mounting of trimmings, or is twisted together to form girdles for dressing
gowns, or children's costumes and curtain loops. The men
work usually on piece, and skilled spinners may earn from
30s to £2 in a busy week, but, depending entirely on the

vagaries of fashion, work is precarious, and average earnings not much over 20*s*.

The tracing and marking of ornamental designs, crests, monograms, &c., on fancy or domestic articles such as antimacassars, handkerchiefs, night-dress cases and table linen, gives employment to a small number of men in two or three firms. If the design is an elaborate one, it is first drawn on tissue paper, and the lines of the drawing are then pierced with tiny holes by a perforating machine, an instrument with a fine steel point like a needle. Simple patterns can be drawn direct with this machine, which supplants the old method of pricking out the design by hand with a pin. One side of the design having been carefully rubbed or dabbed over with a preparation in the form of a dry coloured powder, it is laid, with the powdered side uppermost, on the article to be marked; a large cold flat-iron is passed smoothly over it, causing the colour to penetrate the perforated lines, and so leave on the fabric the impression of the drawing, which is then made fast by being pressed with a hot iron. In this way almost any number of articles may be marked from one design. The skilled man is, of course, the designer and draughtsman, who is well paid for his services; the other operations are comparatively simple, but, nevertheless, require knack and care to ensure a clear and even outline, and prevent the goods from getting dirty or having daubs of colour in the wrong places.

The men have good steady work throughout the year, with a considerable amount of overtime in the busy seasons, paid for in some instances at extra rates.

Wages vary from 25*s* to 35*s*, and hours from forty-eight to fifty-four per week.

Young women and girls, who form the bulk of those returned in this section, do beading on net, embroidery, basket lining, knitting, trimmings for furniture, and other fancy work.

These operations are carried on almost entirely by trimming manufacturers, and the position of those employed has been described in the chapter devoted to " Women's Work" (Vol. IV.). The work is generally done by the piece, and in the busy seasons wages rise to between 15s and 20s in the best houses, but more usual rates are 8s to 10s for competent workers, and 3s to 6s for learners. On common work, ordinary earnings are 5s to 7s. Outdoor hands (principally married women who have worked as indoor hands when single) are employed in periods of pressure, but in slack times they get little, such work as there is being shared by those engaged in the workshops.

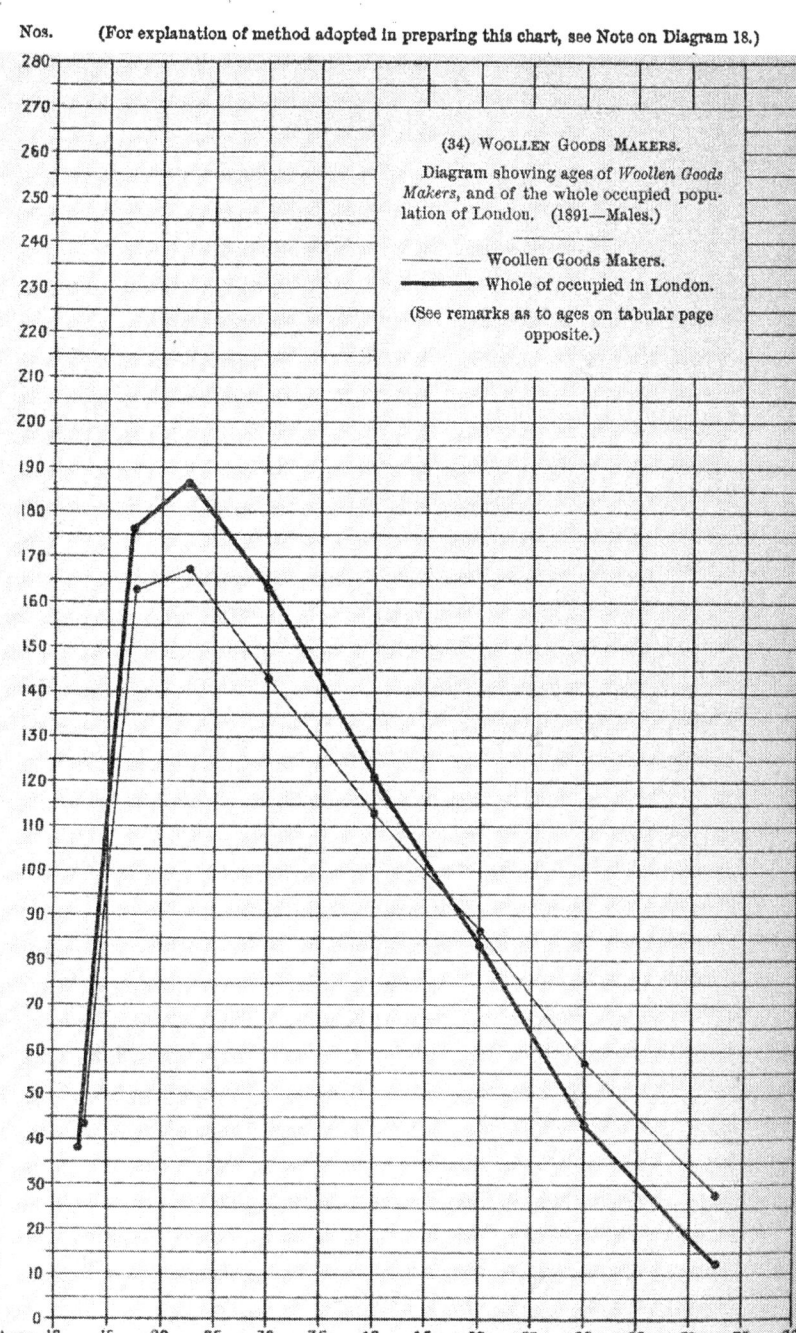

(34) WOOLLEN GOODS MAKERS.

Diagram showing ages of *Woollen Goods Makers*, and of the whole occupied population of London. (1891—Males.)

—————— Woollen Goods Makers.
———— Whole of occupied in London.

(See remarks as to ages on tabular page opposite.)

Persons Represented.

Census Enumeration.

sus Divisions, 1891.	Fe-males All Ages.	Males. −19	20−54	55−	Total.
llens, &c. ..	1201	246	1017	236	2700

with the preceding section (though not so ngly marked), we see evidence of a decay-.rade in the large proportion of the old small proportion of those in the active s of life.

DISTRIBUTION.

	N.	W. & C.	S.	Total.
s	509	489	844	2700

DETAILS OF OCCUPATIONS (FROM THE CENSUS DICTIONARY).

on-goods manufacturer, woollen-cloth manufacturer, worker, clothier, weaver, factory hand, carpet manufacturer, weaver, hearthrug - maker, curtain maker.

Enumerated by Families.

Sex	Males	913	
	Females	163	
Birthplace	In London .... 68 %	727	Heads of Families
	Out of London.. 32 %	349	1076.
Industrial Status ..	Employer ...... 10 %	104	
	Employed .... 85 %	918	
	Neither .... 5 %	54	

TOTAL POPULATION CONCERNED.

	Heads of Families.	Others occupied.	Unoccupied.	Servants.	Total.
Total.	1076	1143	2358	147	4724
Average in family ..	1	1·06	2·19	·14	4·39

CLASSIFICATION.

Numbers living in Families.		%
3 or more to a room	889	18·8
2 & under 3 ,,	1234	26·2
1 & under 2 ,,	1016	21·5
Less than 1 ,, More than 4 rooms 4 or more persons to a servant ..	1195	25·3
Less than 4 to 1 servant, and 4 or more to 2 servants	163	3·5
All others with 2 or more servants ..	80	1·6
Servants	147	3·1
	4724	100

	Inner.	Outer.	Together.
Crowded ..	55 %	30 %	45 %
Not ,, ..	45 %	70 %	55 %

DISTRIBUTION.

East...	Inner 1217 Outer 130	1347
North	Inner 282 Outer 668	950
West...	Inner 104 Outer 260	364
Central	Inner 520	520
South-East	Inner 261 Outer 437	698
South-West	Inner 388 Outer 457	845
		4724

Inner 2772, or 59 %
Outer 1952, or 41 %

Status as to Employment (according to Census Enumeration).

Census Divisions (1891).	Employers.		Employed.			Neither Employer nor Employed.		Total.
	Males.	Females	Males. Under 20.	Over 20	Females of all ages.	Males.	Females	
ton, cotton goods	37	3	29	84	114	5	4	276
rsted and stuff	10	1	5	13	48	—	1	78
ollen cloth	47	3	77	467	221	11	7	863
x and linen................	8	5	5	19	25	1	4	67
avers (undefined)................	—	—	16	154	183	—	—	353
tory hand (textile), undefined	—	—	74	31	425	—	—	530
pets and rugs................	33	—	23	204	81	11	4	356
ers................	11	3	17	75	61	2	8	177
	146	15	246	1077	1158	30	28	2700
TOTAL..........	161		2481			58		2700

Proportion of Employers to Employed–1 to 15.

The Woollen Trades.

The ancient saw, "first catch your hare," might appropriately be accepted as the motto of the inquirer into the condition in London of the various manufacturing trades scheduled in this section. At one time or another several of them have had a place in the multitudinous category of metropolitan productive industries, but so steady and effectual has been their decline that not even men who have spent half a lifetime in the commercial side of the London trade could say for certain whether the business with which they were connected still existed here in the shape of manufacture.

Clothworking.

The principal item included in our section is, according to the census, the making of woollen cloth—a generic term embracing astracan, baize, listing, shoddy, mungo, nap, millpuff, &c.—but, so far as we have been able to ascertain, not a yard of these goods is now woven in London. On the other hand, every provincial manufacturer of repute has either an establishment or agency in or near the City, and about one half of the 860 persons returned under this heading may be considered to be working at the City warehouses, offices, or show-rooms.

The other half, or some 450 persons, are employed in *clothworking*, which consists in shrinking and finishing the cloth after it leaves the loom. The business is carried on in London by about ten firms, two of which employ one hundred or more hands, the others being much smaller. In addition, there are two or three wholesale cloth merchants who do their own work. The industry is mainly a metropolitan one, and with the growing use of Scotch and similar fabrics, which require a good deal of working, has increased somewhat of late years. London has a special reputation for the perfection of finish imparted to the cloth, so much so, that goods are sent from distant parts of the kingdom, as well as from abroad, to be manipulated here. The words "London shrunk" on the label attached to a piece of cloth are deemed to be a guarantee of good work.

Process.—The cloth, having been received from the woollen draper, goes first to the damping room. A long and narrow piece of cloth or canvas, termed a "damping sheet," is soaked in a large tank of water and then roughly spread out for the water to drain off. The men, working in pairs, station themselves one at either end of an oblong board or stand, raised a few inches from the ground, having on one side of them the pile of cloth to be shrunk, and on the other the wet sheet. Then, taking first a fold of the damp sheet of the width of their board, and then a fold of the cloth, they proceed to arrange alternate layers or loops of each until the pile is completed. The period during which the cloth remains in the damp varies greatly, from one hour or less to twelve or more, generally according to the nature and quality of the fabric, but sometimes also according to the speed with which it is required.*

Scotch cloths, vicunas, &c., for men's coats, take a great deal of shrinking, whilst other and inferior goods only just get "shown" the damping sheet. Material for guinea suits and 4s 6d trousers will not pay for much shrinking. Stuff for ladies' garments, too, it is confidentially stated, need to be shrunk very little; the wearers look rather to a glossy and bright appearance; but it follows that an unexpected shower of rain causes vexation and disappointment.

In the case of particular lines of goods the foreman of the room may give instructions as to the shrinking: otherwise

---

* The recognized time required for shrinking and finishing a piece of cloth is at least three clear days, but sometimes an order may come for the work to be completed in one day.

the responsibility rests with the man at the head of each board, who must therefore exercise considerable care and judgment. There are two opposing classes of clients to please, and a clear course must be steered between them. If the material is insufficiently shrunk there may come, *viâ* the tailor and wholesale dealer, angry remonstrances, and perhaps the garments as well, from the wearers of coats which have shortened at the sleeves and tightened at the waists; whilst, on the other hand, if the wetting has been done "not wisely but too well," the colour may run, or the cloth shrink to less than the regulation width, and so lose much of its value. An experienced hand is therefore placed at the head or "bout end," as it is called, of each damping pile; the man or youth at the lower or "fag end" is an assistant, and has no responsibility, being usually a learner. The goods, on being drawn out of the pile, are carried from the shrinking department, and hung in long loops or "cuddles" across laths in a hot room, and, when sufficiently dry, are taken down and spread out in another department ready for examination. These two processes, which in the larger houses are each performed by a distinct set of men, are simple and require little skill. The examiner, on the other hand, must be a fully competent man. The cloth hangs before him on a "perch," or horizontal bar, with a strong light shining through, and he must be able to detect a flaw of any kind. If the defect be in the shrinking the piece is returned to the damping room; if in the manufacture, particulars of it are noted in a book, to be afterwards sent with the cloth to the merchant. This scrutiny completed, the cloth is folded in widths between alternate sheets of millboard by the press hands— work requiring skill and care. Hot plates are placed at the top and bottom of the pile, and one is pushed into the centre, in a space which has been reserved for it by means of extra boards. The pile is then placed in a large press under the direction of a pressman, who must be able to

judge of the amount of pressure and heat which are needed
to impart the proper finish and lustre to any given material.
Subsequently the goods are taken out and folded or rolled
ready for return to the customer.

In one or two small firms machinery is used both for
shrinking and folding. In the shrinking-machine the cloth
is hung over iron pipes, through which hot steam passes;
it does not then require any special process of drying.
This method, however, appears to be less thorough than
hand work.

Machinery has also been introduced recently to prevent
"rain-spotting." Cloths which have too stiff a surface
(usually foreign-finished goods) are softened by being
passed rapidly through steam vapour.

Hours and Wages.—The standard week is one of fifty-
four hours' work, continuing usually from 8 A.M. to 7.30 P.M.
on five days of the week, with twenty minutes for lunch,
one hour for dinner, and half an hour for tea. On Saturday
the hours are from 8 A.M. till 2 P.M., with the luncheon
interval only.

The men are all paid a weekly wage, piece-work being
unknown in the trade. In the damping-room the "bout"
hands get from 20s to 30s, and "fag" hands from 12s to
22s. Wages in other departments are about as follows:—
drying hands (usually labourers), 20s; head examiners,
32s; assistant examiners, 28s; folders and press-hands, 32s;
pressmen, 36s. The press-hands often take it in turns,
week and week about, to take charge of the press, and so
each share in the 4s extra given for this work.

Overtime is paid for at ordinary day rates, save that
time and a half is allowed after 2 o'clock on Saturdays, and
double time for the few occasions on which Sunday work is
necessary.

Seasons.—There are two busy periods in the year, one in
preparation for the summer trade, lasting from the beginning
of November to the latter part of February; the other, for

winter goods, beginning in April and ending in July.
Practically there are seven busy and five slack months. In
the periods of pressure a good deal of extra time is worked.
The present winter season (1894-5) has been an exceptionally
good one; in some firms the men have worked till
10 o'clock every night for two months, and men whose
ordinary wages are 32s have been taking from £2. 2s to
£2. 5s per week. In the slack time, about a fourth of the
men are discharged; there is nothing else in particular that
they can turn to, and their livelihood is generally a very
precarious one until the busy season comes round again,
when they return to the clothworking, "looking very
seedy," we are told. The other three-fourths are kept on
full time, even though there may not be much work for
them, so that they are in pretty comfortable circumstances,
and seldom change their employers.

Training.—There is no system of apprenticeship; lads
are taken on as van boys, to assist in fetching and delivering
the goods, and after a period as general helpers are promoted
to the fag end of the damping pile, whence they may rise
to the work of the other departments.

Health.—The men are not as a class robust, nor is the
work of any section of them conducive to good health.
The moist atmosphere of the damping-room induces rheumatism;
the heat of the drying-room (over 100 degrees
Fahrenheit) makes the men very susceptible to colds; the
eyes of the examiners are severely tried, and are said, after
a spell on scarlet or other brightly-coloured fabrics, to
become quite yellow; the press-hands complain of the
sulphurous fumes emitted from the coke fires with which
the plates are sometimes heated; and, affecting all departments,
fluff rises into the air, and may be a possible cause
of lung affections. Well-ventilated workshops are essential
in such a business, but are not always found.

Rug Weaving.

Of the other textile trades enumerated in this section, rug weaving is the only one that needs any description here. For neither in the manufacture of cotton, worsted, flax, linen, nor carpets is anything done in London, whilst the 350 undefined weavers are probably nearly all working in silk, and the five hundred textile factory hands may be spread over a dozen different industries.

Rug weaving by hand has long since seen its best days, and is a dying trade. In London only about a couple of firms carry it on, and there are not fifty people employed all told. The men are mostly past middle life, and the boys who are taken on to wind the bobbins and fill the quills for the men, do not usually stay at the work, so that hardly anyone is learning. The rugs, which are made of wool or yarn, are of the very best and most expensive description; no machine work can approach them for richness and depth of pile. They are executed generally to the special orders of furnishing-houses, and designed to match the carpets with which they are sold. The busy season, as with furniture-work generally, is in the spring : from March to June, when, by working overtime, fairly large earnings *might* be made, but seldom are. The weavers, who are all on piece and share whatever work is to be had, have got into somewhat leisurely habits, both as to hours worked and speed attained, and, being elderly men, are perhaps not equal to doing much better, so that even in busy times 30*s* represents a good week's pay, whilst taking the year through 20*s* to 22*s* is about the average. The shearers, who, after the weaving is finished, cut the woollen threads to form the pile of the rug and shear off the ends to produce an even surface, are on time wages, 24*s* a week, with 6*d* per hour overtime. Boys are paid 6*s* or 7*s* a week. It is a healthy trade, and the operatives are long-lived.

Trade Organization.

The trades included in this chapter are without any representative organization. The London Broad Silk Weavers' Society, after lingering for some time as a funeral club, has now broken up, and a similar fate has just befallen the Clothworkers' Union, although a few years back this society included four-fifths of those employed, and has been the means of obtaining some undoubted advantages for the workpeople.

Wages Statistics.

In these trades, 2388 adult men are employed, but we have wages returns for 90 only, employed by six firms, as under :—

Under 20s............ 2, or 2 per cent.		Under 30s, 56 per cent.
20s to 25s............32 ,, 36 ,,		
25s ,, 30s............16 ,, 18 ,,		
30s ,, 35s............29 ,, 32 ,,		
35s ,, 40s............ 8 ,, 9 ,,		Over 30s, 44 per cent.
40s ,, 45s............ 1 ,, 1 ,,		
45s and upwards... 2 ,, 2 ,,		
90 ,, 100 ,,		

The women and girls earned from 3s to 20s a week, and the lads from 7s to 16s, but the evidence is insufficient for any safe generalization.

Social Condition.

In the census, 6593 persons are returned as employed in these industries; 2388 are adult men, and of these about 1800 come under classification as heads of families. Making the usual allowances for servants and for the families of employers and female heads, the following approximate statement is obtained as to the manner in which these men live :—

Classification of Population According to Style of Life (Silks, Woollens, &c.).

3 persons or more to a room	1000 or 12 per cent.	
2 and under 3 ,,	1500 ,, 18	,,
1 and under 2 ,,	2700 ,, 33	,,
Less than 1 ,,		
More than 4 rooms	} 3000 ,, 37	,,
4 or more persons to a servant		
	8200 ,, 100	,,
Employers' families, servants, and families with female heads	} 3500	
	11,700	

CHAPTER II.

DYERS, &c. (Section 35.)

Persons Represented.

Census Enumeration.					
Census Divisions, 1891.	Fe-males.	Males.			Total.
	All Ages.	—19	20—54	55—	
Dyers & Cleaners	752	171	826	197	1946

The diagram tells the story of a trade that has left London, or at least has found its growth elsewhere—the old in it are out of proportion numerous.

Enumerated by Families.

Sex	{ Males	773	
	{ Females	123	
Birthplace	{ In London 62%	554	Heads of Famili. 896.
	{ Out of London.. 38%	342	
Industrial Status ..	{ Employer 20%	182	
	{ Employed 68%	608	
	{ Neither 12%	166	

TOTAL POPULATION CONCERNED.

	Heads of Families.	Others occupied.	Unoccupied.	Servants.	T
Total.	896	1023	2095	112	4
Average in family ..	1	1·13	2·34	·13	4

DISTRIBUTION.

E.	N.	W. & C.	S.	Total.
236	529	519	662	1946

DETAILS OF OCCUPATIONS

(FROM THE CENSUS DICTIONARY).

Dyer, scourer, bleacher, calenderer, clothes cleaner, French cleaner, dyer's ironer, cloth printer, wool dyer, silk dyer and printer.

CLASSIFICATION.

		%
Numbers living in Families.		
3 or more to a room	352	8·6
2 & under 3 ,,	821	19·9
1 & under 2 ,,	828	20·1
Less than 1 ,,		
More than 4 rooms	1865	45·2
4 or more persons to a servant ..		
Less than 4 to 1 servant, and 4 or more to 2 servts.	128	3·1
All others with 2 or more servants ..	20	·4
Servants	112	2·7
	4126	100

	Inner.	Outer.	Together.
Crowded ..	42%	22%	28%
Not ,, ..	58%	78%	72%

DISTRIBUTION.

East ..	{ Inner	447 }
	{ Outer	60 }
North	{ Inner	165 }
	{ Outer	688 }
West ..	{ Inner	75 }
	{ Outer	916 }
Central	Inner	152
South- East	{ Inner	227 }
	{ Outer	557 }
South- West	{ Inner	215 }
	{ Outer	624 }

Inner 1281, or 31%
Outer 2845, or 69%

Status as to Employment (according to Census Enumeration).

Census Divisions (1891).	Employers.		Employed.			Neither Employer nor Employed.		Tot
			Males.		Females of all Ages.			
	Males.	Females	Under 20.	Over 20.		Males.	Females	
Cotton, calico printers, dyers, &c.	3	——	——	19	1	——	1	
Wool, woollen goods dyer, printer........	——	——	——	11	1	——	——	
Silk dyer, printer	3	——	7	52	3	2	——	
Dyer, scourer, bleacher, calenderer	166	36	164	668	646	99	64	18.
	172	36	171	750	651	101	65	19.
TOTAL..........	208		1572			166		
	Proportion of Employers to Employed–1 to 7½.							

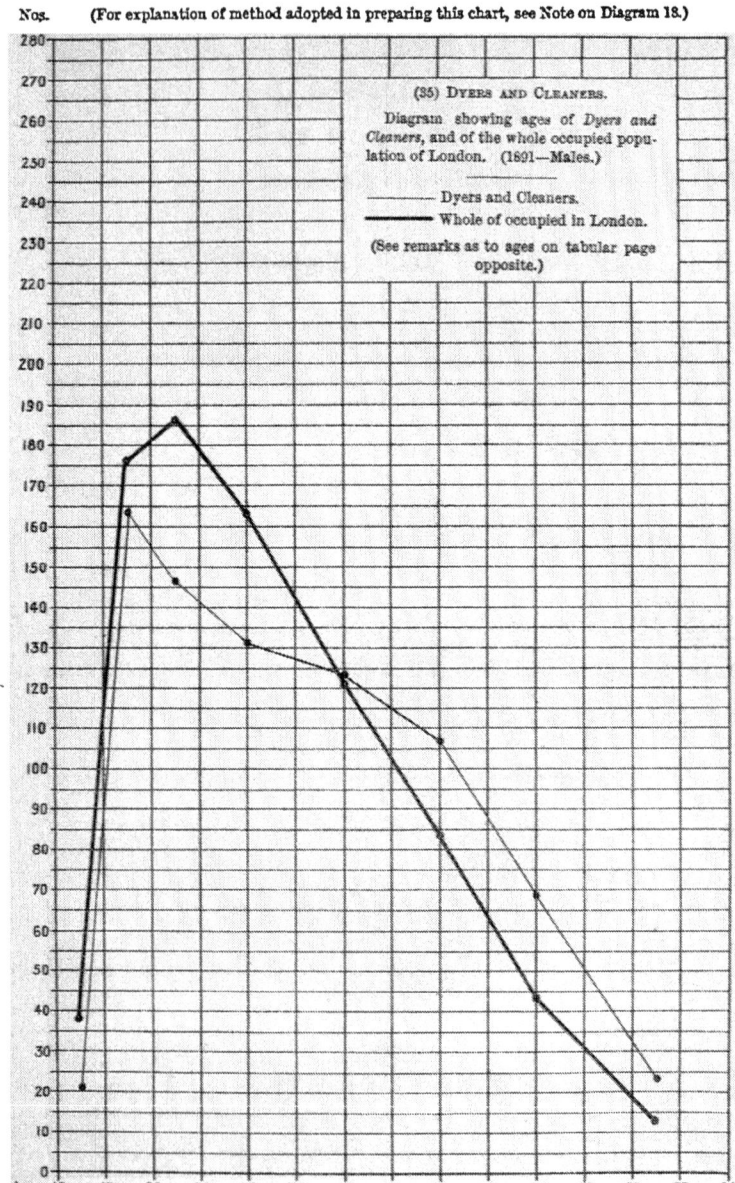

(35) DYERS AND CLEANERS.

Diagram showing ages of *Dyers and Cleaners*, and of the whole occupied population of London. (1891—Males.)

——————— Dyers and Cleaners.

——————— Whole of occupied in London.

(See remarks as to ages on tabular page opposite.)

DYEING AND CLEANING.

London has scarcely any original dye works for fabrics. Most of the persons coming under this section are engaged in re-dyeing or in cleaning. There are, however, some special kinds of dyeing, such as that of ostrich feathers— of which London is the principal seat—skin rugs and furs; also the dyeing of leather, a process connected with leather finishing. The dyeing of silk skeins, which once held a prominent place in London, decayed with the Spitalfields silk weaving, upon which it was dependent, and is now of little account.

The trades of re-dyeing and cleaning have seen great changes in London during the last twenty-five years. Before 1870 the work was done rather inefficiently by a large number of small firms. These were beaten by the establishment of collecting agencies by dye works in Scotland, proving that the expense of collection and carriage could be more than saved by improved systems, the economies possible in work done on a large scale, and the advantage of lower rent and rates of wages, as well as of purer air and better supply of water in Perth, as compared to London.

Now, however, things are changing again. The incompetent masters have been driven out, and new firms have arisen. Thus the London trade is being concentrated in the hands of a comparatively few enterprising firms, who are in touch with all the latest improvements, and, provided with the newest machinery, are ready to adopt for their leading hands workmen from Scotland, France or Germany, as need may be. It is now the turn of the Scotch firms to feel the pinch of competition, and the proportion of work leaving London diminishes every year; but meanwhile the whole trade of re-dyeing and cleaning has greatly increased, owing partly to the facilities offered, and the success with which old stuffs can be made to look like new; but, above all, to the invention of systems of cleaning which can be applied without undoing and re-doing the stitches in made-up materials.*

Processes of Work.—The trade of the "jobbing dyer" includes the cleaning or re-dyeing of every article of dress or furniture, except underclothing and bed linen. The workshop is divided into four main departments—

1. Wet cleaning,
2. French or dry cleaning (a process introduced in 1880),
3. Dyeing,
4. Finishing,

and in each there are a variety of sub-divisions of employment. There is also a department for sorting and packing, which serves all the others.

When the articles reach the works, they are first sorted and arranged according to their requirements—whether dry cleaning, wet cleaning, hand cleaning or dyeing. This requires considerable skill, and a certain familiarity with every branch. The goods are numbered and labelled, and sent to their respective departments. After cleaning or dyeing, they go to the finishing department, to be ironed, pressed, glazed, stretched, calendered or what not, either by hand or by numerous machines. Every article is examined after each process, and is finally sent from the finishing to the packing-room, checked off on the ledger, and returned to the owner. This "circular tour" of a piece of stuff through the works generally occupies from four to fourteen days.

Wet cleaning is simply a careful and scientific mode of washing. Dry or French cleaning, by which a great amount of labour has been saved, is effected by soaking the articles in naphtha or benzoline spirits, and then placing

---

* This improvement in cleaning displaced the labour of many upholsteresses or seamstresses, who previously prepared the goods for cleaning or dyeing, and made them up again afterwards.

them, just as they are—it makes no matter what they are, whether flounced gowns or silk handkerchiefs—into a rotary machine containing the same liquid, and afterwards into a cylinder with perforated sides, which, revolving at very great speed—as much as eight hundred revolutions a minute—throws off the spirit by centrifugal force, and leaves the fabrics clean and dry. The spirit is re-collected, and after refinement can again be used, though some of it is lost each time. The cleaned articles, though dry, still smell strongly of the spirit used, and have to be hung up for forty-eight hours in a hot chamber, after which the process is complete.

Busy and Slack Seasons are clearly defined. Spring is the busiest season, autumn stands next, and mid-winter is the slackest time. In spring, curtains and furniture covers and light dresses are cleaned for summer use. In autumn, preparations are made for the winter season, including work for the theatres.. It is the spring rush that causes irregularity of employment. It rather takes the shape of full work and some overtime, balanced by short time in the slack season, than in the taking on of extra hands and their discharge. There may be in the year eight months of full work and overtime to four months of half or three-quarter time. Those who are discharged will usually be women, and some of them may be able to find employment in the india-rubber works in winter, or at laundries in summer.

Hours of Work.—The hours vary, being in some houses only fifty-two or fifty-three, while in most fifty-six or fifty-eight are worked. Men begin at 6 or 7 A.M. and work to 6 or 7 P.M., with one hour and a half for meals. Women usually begin an hour later. The overtime in spring, necessary to avoid introducing more hands than could possibly find employment at other times, is worked according to the regulations for female labour under the Factory Acts. It is complained that laundries sometimes undertake "cleaning," and possess an unfair advantage, not being included in the Act. It is also said that the ninety-six hours overtime allowed would be more service-able if it might be taken on ninety-six days, an hour each time, instead of two hours on each forty-eight occasions.

Wages for Men.—We find dyers earning, on an average, about 30s a week—the foremen having from 35s to 50s, dry cleaners 25s to 30s, and fancy cleaners (wet), dealing with the more delicate fabrics, about the same. Leading hands are paid a little more. Rough wet cleaning, such as is used for blankets and counterpanes, is the least skilled work, and wages do not average over 24s or 25s.

Women's Wages show more than ordinary variation, due to gradations in skill, and connected also with age. Fifteen shillings to 18s are not unusual rates, and forewomen receive from 20s to 30s. On the other hand, many, probably young women or girls, receive only 10s. Beginners start at 4s or 5s a week.

Both dyeing and cleaning are skilled trades. A dyer, to have a thorough knowledge of his trade, must give five years to learning it; and a good cleaner ought to know something of dyeing as well as of the work of his own department. The work, however, when once learned, is not in itself difficult or very laborious.

Training.—The sub-division of the various branches has brought with it, as in other industries, the decay of the apprenticeship system, and tends to the extinction of the all-round skilled workman. Hence, perhaps, the necessity of the importation of foremen managers from Scotland and elsewhere. In the cleaning department, however, Londoners still hold their own, and nearly all those employed are said to have been born in the metropolis. Moreover, London has a high reputation for excellence in this branch; especially since the introduction of "French" cleaning.

Health and Age capacity.—As the work is light, it may be maintained to a good age—sixty or sixty-five being not uncommon, if the worker has robust health to start with, and the shops worked in are well ventilated and arranged. But the dye-houses and cleaning-rooms, with their sloppy floors and steaming atmosphere, are not suitable places for men with weak constitutions, and the finishing-rooms are extremely hot in summer. In the process of dry-cleaning, good ventilation is essential; large quantities of gases being given off, which are not only injurious, or, at least, intoxicating, to breathe (with an effect something like laughing-gas), but are also dangerous as liable to "spontaneous combustion" under conditions not yet fully understood, and therefore not entirely to be guarded against. Every known precaution is, however, taken, and the work is under the supervision of the inspectors of the London County Council, whose orders must be carried out, on pain of withdrawal of the license held under the Petroleum Acts.

Character.—Dyers and cleaners have a particularly good reputation in regard to character, whether for sobriety and general steadiness or for honesty. It is essential for the conduct of the business that the employees should be above suspicion on this latter point, for many articles of value and small size pass daily through the hands of a number of persons, and it would be difficult to say who was the culprit if finally a piece were missing. It is for this reason especially that employers object to taking on strange hands in the busy season, or to part with those they know when work is slack, preferring to make use of overtime and short time.

Trade Organization.—There are no unions in the dyeing trade. The men have always worked in perfect amity with their employers.

Wages Statistics.

There are 1946 persons employed in these trades, of whom 1023 are adult males. As to these, we have wages returns for 114 men working for four firms, who also employ twenty-nine boys and 280 women and girls, and nine men belonging to other sections, as porters and vanmen.

The earnings of the 114 men in an average week are as follows:—

```
Under 20s............11, or  9½ per cent. ⎞'
20s to 25s............30  ,, 26½    ,,     ⎬ Under 30s, 59½ per cent.
25s ,, 30s............27  ,, 23½    ,,     ⎠
30s ,, 35s............18  ,, 16     ,,
35s ,, 40s............10 ,,  8½     ,,     ⎞
40s ,, 45s............ 7  ,,  6     ,,     ⎬ 30s and over, 40½ per cent.
45s and upwards...11  ,, 10         ,,     ⎠
                    ─────  ───
                    114 ,, 100      ,,
```

Returns to the Board of Trade in 1886 from seven firms employing sixty-six adult men show very similar results.

	20s.	20s—	25s—	30s—	35s—	40s—	45s—
Our returns ...	9½ %	26½ %	23½ %	16 %	8½ %	6 %	10 %
		59½ %			40½ %		
Board of Trade returns... ...	10½ %	33½ %	17 %	20 %	9 %	—	10 %
		61 %			39 %		

The fluctuations in numbers and average earnings between busy and slack seasons are as follows:—

	Busy.	Slack.	Percentage Reduction.		
			In numbers.	In earnings per head.	Combined.
Our returns (1893)	172	151	12	6	17½ %
Board of Trade returns (1886)	171	140	17½	12	28 %

The busiest month appears to be May, and the busy time lasts till August. January and February are the quiet months, but there is a further period of slackness, according to these returns, in September and October.

Concerning the earnings of the women and girls, we have the following particulars:—

AVERAGE EARNINGS OF WOMEN AND GIRLS.

Our returns, 1893.			Board of Trade returns, 1886.		
Earnings.	Net Nos.	Per cent.	Earnings.	Net Nos.	Per cent.
6s and under ...	21	7½ ⎫	6s and under ...	10	14 ⎫
7s	21	7½ ⎪	7s	2	3 ⎪
8s	36	12½ ⎬ 52	8s	8	11 ⎬ 44
9s	30	10¾ ⎪	9s	—	— ⎪
10s	39	14 ⎭	10s	11	16 ⎭
11s and 12s ...	64	23 ⎫	11s and 12s ...	16	23 ⎫
13s, 14s, and 15s	38	13 ⎬ 48	13s, 14s, and 15s	10	14½ ⎬ 56
16s and under 20s	19	7½ ⎪	16s and under 20s	8	11½ ⎪
20s and over ...	12	4½ ⎭	20s and over ...	5	7 ⎭
	280	100		70	100

As in other trades employing females, if we compare the two returns we see signs of the tendency to increase the number of women at the lower rates of pay, but to what extent this affects the men's employment it is difficult to say. The ordinary earnings of the women are evidently from 8s to 12s a week.

The number of lads and boys is small, compared with the men and women: the census only enumerates 171 under twenty years of age. Their earnings vary from 5s to 15s a week, but not more than a fourth of them, according to our returns, earn more than 8s, the greater number receiving 6s to 8s a week.

Social Condition.

Of the 750 adult males employed, about 525 are counted as heads of families, and so come under classification socially. Taking the wages returns as a test, we have 36 per cent. earning less than 25s a week to compare with 37 per cent. living under crowded conditions; 40 per cent. earning from

25*s* to 35*s*, as compared with 26 per cent. living in small tenements, but not crowded; and 24 per cent. earning 35*s* or more, compared to 37 per cent. of the central classes.

Comparison of Earnings with Style of Life (Dyers and Cleaners).

Earnings as returned.		Classification of Population.		
Under 20*s*...11, or	9½ per cent.	3 or more in each room,	352, or 11 per cent.	
20*s* to 25*s*...30 ,,	26½ ,,	2 to 3 ,,	821 ,, 26 ,,	
25*s* ,, 30*s*...27 ,,	23½ ,,	1 ,, 2 ,,	828 ,, 26 ,,	
30*s* ,, 35*s*...18 ,,	16 ,,	Less than 1 ,,		
35*s* ,, 40*s*...10 ,,	8½ ,,	More than 4 rooms	1175 ,, 37 ,,	
40*s* ,, 45*s*... 7 ,,	6 ,,	4 or more persons		
45*s* and upwards } 11 ,,	10 ,,	to a servant		
114 ,, 100 ,,			3176 ,, 100 ,,	
		Employers' families and servants	950	
			4126	

Nos.   (For explanation of method adopted in preparing this chart, see Note on Diagram 18.)

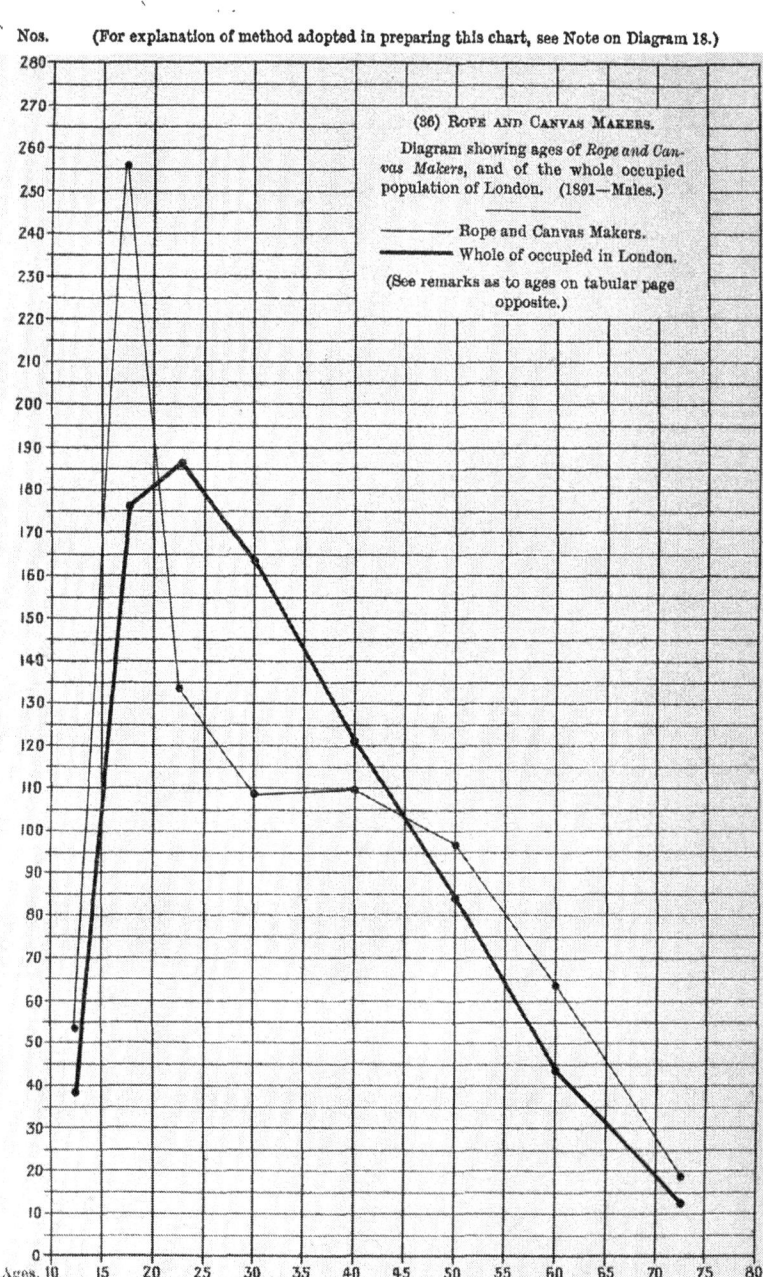

(86) ROPE AND CANVAS MAKERS.

Diagram showing ages of *Rope and Can-vas Makers*, and of the whole occupied population of London. (1891—Males.)

————— Rope and Canvas Makers.

━━━━━ Whole of occupied in London.

(See remarks as to ages on tabular page opposite.)

CHAPTER III.
HEMP, JUTE AND FIBRE. (Section 36.,

Persons Represented.

Census Enumeration.					
nsus Divisions, 1891.	Fe-males All Ages.	Males.			Total.
		—19	20—54	55—	
Rope, &c.	412	435	858	219	1924
Canvas, &c. ..	831	81	418	87	1417
TOTAL....	1243	516	1276	306	3341

The diagram shows the age peculiarities of trade in which machinery (in rope making) superseding hand labour—many boys, few ung men, and an excessive proportion of e old. Coupled with this and acting in the me general direction, there has been a moval of canvas work to the provinces.

DISTRIBUTION.

E.	N.	W. & C.	S.	Total.
1787	311	192	1051	3341

DETAILS OF OCCUPATIONS
(FROM THE CENSUS DICTIONARY).

) Coir manufacturer, rope and cord-maker, cord spinner, hemp dresser, twine spinner, ropewalk labourer, mat-maker, bassock-maker, bass dresser.

) Net-maker, canvas-bag weaver, sack mender, hammock-maker, Russian mat and bag-maker, tent and marquee-maker, mop-maker.

Enumerated by Families.

Sex ...... { Males .... 1181 } Females.............. 243 }		
Birthplace { In London .... 67 % 950 } Out of London.. 33 % 474 }	Heads of Families, 1424.	
Industrial Status .. { Employer .... 9 % 134 } Employed...... 83 % 1172 } Neither .... 8 % 118 }		

TOTAL POPULATION CONCERNED.

	Heads of Families.	Others Occupied.	Unoccupied	Servants.	Total.
Total.	1424	1635	3235	97	6391
Average in family ..	1	1·15	2·26	·07	4·48

CLASSIFICATION.

Numbers living in Families.		%
3 or more to a room	1201	18·8
2 & under 3 ,,	1788	28·0
1 & under 2 ,,	1567	24·5
Less than 1 ,,		
More than 4 rooms	1557	24·4
4 or more persons to a servant ..		
Less than 4 to 1 servant,& 4 or more to 2 servants ..	135	2·1
All others with 2 or more servants..	46	·7
Servants	97	1·5
	6391	100

	Inner.	Outer.	Together.
Crowded..	55 %	34 %	47 %
Not ,, ..	45 %	66 %	53 %

DISTRIBUTION.

East ..	{ Inner 2303 } { Outer 732 }	3035
North..	{ Inner 70 } { Outer 668 }	738
West ...	{ Inner 21 } { Outer 273 }	294
Central	Inner 149	149
South-East..	{ Inner 729 } { Outer 565 }	1294
South-West..	{ Inner 684 } { Outer 197 }	881
		6391

Inner 3956, or 62 %
Outer 2435, or 38 %

Status as to Employment (according to Census Enumeration).

Census Divisions (1891).	Employers.		Employed.			Neither Employer nor Employed.		Total.
			Males.		Females of all ages.			
	Males.	Females	Under 20.	Over 20.		Males.	Females	
Rope, twine, cord-maker	60	5	373	575	283	33	4	1333
Mat-maker	35	—	62	329	88	36	8	558
Net-maker	—	—	—	6	23	3	1	33
Hemp, jute, cocoa fibre manufacturer	7	2	18	108	64	3	1	203
Canvas,sail-cloth,sacking,bag manuf.	31	4	49	153	588	26	10	861
Others working in hemp, &c.	11	—	9	89	146	13	2	270
Dealers in hemp, jute, &c.	22	1	5	25	12	17	1	83
	166	12	516	1285	1204	131	27	3341
TOTAL........	178		3005			158		
	Proportion of Employers to Employed–1 to 17.							

HEMP AND FIBRE WORK.

There are included in this group, according to the census, no less than seven separate sections, although the total number employed, male and female, young and old, is only 3341. The three more important are :—

	Males.	Females.
Rope, twine, and cord ....employing	1041	292
Mat making ....:................. ,,	462	96
Canvas, sacking and bags .... ,,	259	602
	1762	990
The other four sections .... ,,	336	253
TOTAL..................	2098	1243

As to the men, these figures may be taken as correct, but as to the women it is not so; in these trades it is certain that there are many women, the wives and daughters of dock or other casual labourers, who do not return themselves as connected with any trade.

ROPE MAKING.

Ropes are manufactured chiefly in the eastern and south-eastern districts of London, and high-class work is confined to a few firms. The tendency of the day is to use machinery for nearly every process of rope making. Hand made ropes are better and stronger, but too dear. It is only for mountaineering or such special purposes, where life " hangs by a thread," and money is no object, that hand work is insisted on. It owes its superiority to the fact that it is difficult with a machine to avoid putting too much strain at times on the strands as they are twisted up, and a weak spot or a flaw may thus be established which a test strain may only further develop, if the rope does not actually give way under the test. Of the two fibres principally used—Manilla hemp and Russian hemp—the last-named, up to six or seven years ago, was largely spun by hand, because of the nature of its staple; but the more modern machinery has conquered the difficulty. In the "line" trade—a very small business in London—half is still spun by hand and half by machinery, to be afterwards made up by hand. This applies to fishing lines, for which the utmost strength is required with the smallest possible thickness.

The prevalence of improved mechanical contrivance has had the result of diminishing the number of those employed, and of dispensing with special skill in the workman. The rope-maker has become more and more a machine minder, and one more typical artisan is lost—the man, who may still be remembered, with a coil of spun hemp round his body, walking slowly backwards, while the turning of a wheel, it might be by power or it might be by hand, gave the necessary twist to the threads it was his business to combine. The machine tender requires but little skill; the technical knowledge needed is supplied by the foreman, who issues all the directions as to number of yarns, &c., and then the machines work as they are set.

Manilla hemp makes the strongest rope, and other kinds come from India. Some called "sisal" is grown in South America, and used principally for small light ropes. In this trade, as in most others, shoddy articles are not uncommon, and ropes are known to have been fabricated from sacking, gunny bags, and any sort of fibrous rubbish that can be tortured and twisted into a yarn, but woe betide the man, if any there be, who places his trust in such a rope.

A "rope" is understood by the trade to imply an article of a certain size—not less than 1 inch in circumference, and may be either "cable" *laid,* when three or four thin ropes are twisted together, or "shroud" *laid,* when made from three or four strands of untwisted yarn. Shroud-laid ropes are the stronger of the two.

Process and Wages.—When the bales of hemp arrive at the factory they are cut open by women, who, on piece-work, earn about 12s a week. We have heard of a case when a woman earned nearly double this sum, but anything of the kind would be quite exceptional. The hemp is spread out with the aid of machinery, and "hackled" with coarse strong teeth. A man tends this machine, the materials being handed to him by girls, who get 7s 6d to 9s a week for this laborious, but unskilled work. The man is paid from 20s to 26s. The stuff goes on to another similar machine with finer teeth. At this only girls work, and they are paid 9s.

The fluffy stuff is now passed through at least three "drawing frames"—for very fine work through as many as six—taking the shape of a rounded stream of fluff, and gradually contracting in size. In this state the product is called "sliver," and conveyed to the spinning-room, where it is twisted gradually into yarn, passing from bobbin to bobbin, through holes smaller and smaller till the required size is reached. Boys, as well as men, work at the "forming machines"—wages from 16s to 25s, according to the size of the plate upon which they work.

In the last and most important process, the strands are "laid" into ropes by mechanical means. Those who do this are all men, and are called "rope-makers." In the best firms only skilled workers are employed in this department, and the wages are 30s to 35s, but other houses are content to rely chiefly on the foreman of this branch, who may receive 40s, while the two or three unskilled hands who work under him earn about 20s.

The product is either "white" or "tar" work. If it is to be tarred, this is done by taking the white stuff from the spinning-room and passing it through a kettle of best archangel tar, and coiling it on a capstan before being wound on the bobbins to begin its course of being twisted and spun out, and gradually reduced in thickness, as with the untarred yarn.

Other Particulars.—The work does not seem to be un-healthy. In spite of the fluff and dust raised by hackling the material, the lungs of the workers do not appear to suffer. Perhaps the smell of the tar is a counter agent. As regards regularity, Christmas is usually a time of slack work, but the fluctuations in this trade are less than in most. The usual factory hours are worked, and there is very little overtime.

There is now no system of apprenticeship, but formerly there used to be a sort of guild, known as the Rope-makers' Association, to which all rope-makers belonged, and in which learners had to serve a regular term before they were considered qualified. During the last twenty years, however, all this has been changed by the revolution in methods of manufacture, due to the introduction of machinery.

There is one union in this trade of recent origin, called the East London Rope-makers' Union, a body which origin-ally comprised both men and women. Its existence dates from the time of the great dock strike in 1889. After a time differences arose and the men seceded, without, how-ever, forming a union of their own. The women, on the other hand, have adhered with tenacity to their organiza-tion. The number of women in the union is now about two hundred and never exceeded five hundred. There was at the outset some difficulty between the union and a prominent employer, but the greatest harmony now pre-vails. Many of the women are enthusiastic trades unionists, and in this present a strong contrast to the apathy of the men. They are mostly the wives and daughters of carmen or dock labourers, and are generally of strong build, and capable of heavy work, such as lifting large coils of yarn and rope. Considerable powers of endurance also are needed to keep pace with the machines, whether at hackling or spinning. The major part of the women are married, and their wages serve to eke out the irregular earnings of the men, on whom they nominally depend, but who in reality too often depend on them.

The arrangements of some of the rope and jute factories in London, from a hygienic point of view, are stated to be very inadequate, and this is confirmed by the general evidence on the subject recently published by the Labour Commission. One large firm, it is said, has a workshop with no lavatory accommodation whatever, and in other cases necessary provision is most meagre. Complaint is also made that the machinery is insufficiently guarded, and that in several cases serious injuries have been suffered, in more than one instance with fatal results. With the increase recently made in the staff of factory inspectors of both sexes, there is no doubt that the fencing of machinery will receive more attention.

MAT MAKING.

The art of working in cocoa-nut fibre was introduced into this country about sixty years ago, and the first English mat factory was established in London shortly afterwards, so that mat making can be legitimately claimed as a metropolitan industry. Indeed, for a long period, London was the centre of the trade, and supplied the world, but gradually other countries acquired the art, and this, combined with the setting up of provincial factories, has led of late years to a considerable decrease in the numbers engaged in the work here.

The business is now carried on by four fairly large firms, and a few small ones, employing altogether about three hundred men and women, besides which a certain number of persons of either sex make small mats at home, and carry them round to sell.

Process of Manufacture.—The work is divided into two branches, viz. matting weaving and mat making.

The material of which both are manufactured, is imported principally from Ceylon, Malabar, and Cochin, the latter country sending the lightest and finest description. It comes over packed tightly in bales, in the form of loose cocoa-nut fibre, and skeins of coir yarn (or twisted fibre).

The yarn is first dealt with by women, who sort the skeins according to hue, unwind them, so as to form long, loose coils, and prepare the yarn for the warp, or wind it on large shuttles for the weft. It then goes to the weavers, who are usually men. They spread the work on the rollers of their loom, and otherwise affix it so as to form the basis of their work; and, by throwing in the weft, or "shute," from side to side, weave it into plain matting, or work in any required pattern, which, as it runs in lines only, can be done in the same loom.

In the manufacture of mats, yarn is, as a rule, only used for the warp, fibre being employed to form the "pile," and jute for the weft. The fibre first goes through a machine called a "devil," which cleans and tears it into a fine, loose, silky substance, easily manipulated with the fingers. Seated at his loom, with a large hammock-shaped sackful of the fibre at his side, the weaver, with a motion of his foot on the treadle, raises the top layer or "shade" of threads which comprise the warp, and catching up a handful or "take" of the fibre, twists it deftly around each thread, so that the ends stand upright like an unkempt head of hair, thus forming the pile of the mat; he then secures it with two or three throws of the shuttle, packs it tightly by striking it with the heavy batten frame of the loom, and with a huge pair of shears trims it off evenly, and starts a fresh row, so continuing until the mat is of the proper size. When patterns have to be made, the operative has a copy of the design before him, and introduces at the right point in each row, the coloured fibre or wool of which the pattern is formed. Where mats have a woollen border, the wool is plaited in loops, which are afterwards cut in the centre so as to make the pile. The cutting is usually done

by a woman, who also turns in the ends and binds the
mats. Mats which have no borders have their rough ends
secured with a binding of plaited yarn, which is sewn
round them.

Subsequently the mats pass through a shearing machine,
and the finishing touches are given by hand, the result
being to give a perfectly even surface to the smooth dense
pile. "Skeleton," or chain mats, are of a different character.
They are made of coir yarn, worked into a curious but
perfectly regular design. The artificer stands at a bench,
and twists the stout threads in and out with a bent steel
instrument known as a yarn needle.

Mats are of many sizes, patterns, and qualities, ranging
from the splendid "Imperial," with elaborately worked
designs, crest, monogram, initials, or motto, which may be
seen in the hall of some great public building or stately
mansion, to the most common "diamond" or little oblong
bordered apology, which does duty at the door of the
docker's best parlour. But all alike are distinguished above
all textile goods for one quality, and that is durability. So
much is this the case, that some of the operatives consider it
to be one of the causes of the limited extent of their trade.
"The worst of our work," they say, "is that it never wears
out."

Conditions of Employment. — Hours of work vary in
different factories, but are usually about forty-eight per
week. Work, however, is extremely intermittent, and
probably the average hours worked do not exceed thirty
a week.

It being all piece-work, earnings differ greatly; for apart
from the ordinary divergencies of skill, speed, and steadiness, a good deal depends on the nature of the material
used. Prices, being based on the number of "ends" or
threads used in any given piece of work, have no reference
o the quality of the fibre, and it is possible to earn with
some kinds of material twice the amount that can be gained

with other sorts. On the whole, 30s for men represents a fairly good week's work, and £1 is about the average amount per week, taking the year through. For women, the usual wage is from 5s to 10s; in a few cases, from 12s to 15s is earned.

The trade is not much affected by seasons, but is, on the whole, busiest in spring and autumn. When things are very slack a few men are discharged, but the more general practice is to share the work.

Boys are apprenticed for three years, the trade rate being one lad to ten men. They are put on piece-work, and the employer deducts usually a penny in the shilling off their earnings.

The work is dusty, but not unhealthy, and men keep at it to an advanced age. They rarely change employers.

Prison Labour.—The trade is one which has been largely affected by prison labour. Until recent years, mats were made in many English gaols, and were disposed of under conditions which pressed hardly upon men who had to obtain a living by making them. The method usually adopted was for a manufacturer to supply the prison with the material, and a man to instruct the prisoners, and then to pay a certain price for the work produced, perhaps one-third of what he would have had to pay for the same work if done outside. Ridiculous prices are stated to have been sometimes paid to the prison authorities by the contractors, in some cases amounting to little more than a penny a week per man. The mats were made in frames (looms not being used), and were generally of inferior kind, but long-term prisoners sometimes got very skilled, and turned out good work. As a result of continued agitation, principally on the part of the men's trade union, mat making has now been abolished in English gaols, excepting to supply the requirements of the establishments themselves, but it is complained that the work is still done in Scotch and Irish prisons. Mats are also made in the gaols of Belgium, but public opinion being (so it is said) strong enough to prevent their being sold in that country, they are sent over here to be disposed of.

Efforts are now being made to abolish the sale in this country of prison-made goods, whether home or foreign.*

One curious result of prison labour, is that " mat-makers " have figured in the charge-sheets of Police Courts out of all proportion to their numbers in the population. The explanation of this is that many old gaol-birds, having learnt the trade during a previous period of enforced confinement, have described themselves as mat-makers when arraigned for fresh offences.

Social Habits.—Most of the men in this trade live near their work, and so can go home to meals.

There is no special dress, but some have a piece of leather fastened on the chest to prevent the chafing caused by the breast beam of the loom.

Some of the shops have a sick and loan club, into which the members pay 6d per week ; men may borrow sums of £1, repayable at 2s a week, with 1d in the 1s interest, and fines in default of regular repayment. Sick pay of 10s 6d or 12s a week is given for eight weeks, and half those amounts for a second eight weeks; and £4 is paid for a member, and £2 for a member's wife at death. Any surplus is shared out at Christmas, excepting 1s per member. Friendly meetings are also usual for distressed fellow-workmen, and, with trade union subscription, bring the outgoings for purposes of this kind to about 1s per week.

Some of the men's wives do warping, winding, &c., many of the women in these branches being married.

Trade Organization.—The Mat and Matting Weavers' Trade Society, founded 1868, now numbers about one

---

* It is asserted, on the other side, that it was only by means of these prison-made mats that England kept its hold on the poorer part of the trade. The common work has now gone to the lower-paid foreigners.

hundred financial members, but has had a much larger membership. It exercises a considerable influence on the trade, its price list being readily acceded to by the employers, and most of the shops being entirely unionist. The main effort of the society has been directed against prison work, and it has spent a large proportion of its funds in carrying on the agitation. The entrance fee is 10s, and subscription 3d a week, in return for which benefits are offered of 10s a week out of work pay for twelve weeks in the year, £2 on emigration, and, in case of death, £6 for a member, and £4 for a member's wife. Strike pay, if needed, is met by a levy. Slackness of trade lately has, by largely increasing the amount paid to unemployed members, reduced the society's funds rather seriously, and proposals are now being considered for replenishing the diminished exchequer.

Bass Dressing.

This is a small distinct industry in London, employing about 150 men, some of whom work for firms of brush-makers, and others for a Co-operative Society of Bass Dressers, which was established as the outcome of a strike a few years ago.

The best fibre comes from Peru, and is known as "Piassava." It is made up in bundles, tied at the ends like the tail of a cart-horse at a fair. An inferior article is imported from Africa and other tropical countries.

To "dress" the fibre, it has to be first freed, and then steamed in a tank so as to straighten it out; it is next sorted, the short fibre being divided from the long, and once more steamed. Then it goes through a process of combing, similar to that to which bristles are subjected, in order to separate the thick and strong fibres from the thinner and weaker, after which it is cut to certain fixed lengths as required. Lastly, the long ends are trimmed off with a pair of shears, and the short pieces eliminated by a deft process of shuffling. The bass is then ready for use, and has only to be weighed and tied up into bundles.

Bass Dressers all work on piece, and earn on an average 7*d* to 9*d* per hour, or about 28*s* per week. The trade price usually is 6*s* per cwt., not including cutting. In some shops 8*s* is paid per cwt., including cutting. The hours of work are about fifty-two per week, but the men seldom make full time.

The work is said to be particularly healthy, in spite of the dust which flies from the bundles of bass as they are shaken out and sorted. In a good, well-ventilated workshop there is nothing to fear. Men go on for thirty or thirty-five years without losing their capacity for earning good wages at the trade.

Boys are employed, and start by making themselves generally useful, learning by degrees how to handle the bass. In some places apprentices are still taken, but this is unusual.

A trades union was established in 1888. It is known as the "Bass Dressers' Trade Union Society," and has about ninety members. The subscription is 6*d* per week, entitling to out of work pay for twelve weeks in the year (5*s* for six weeks, and 2*s* 6*d* for a further six weeks), £5 at death, and £3 at death of wife. Members called out of any shop by the executive in consequence of a reduction in the price of work, receive 12*s* per week whilst unemployed.

Sack and Tarpaulin Manufacture.

There is no canvas made in London, but a large quantity of it is sent from the North, and is used by several firms, principally in the manufacture of sacks, but also for tarpaulins, tents, marquees, ships' sails, rickcloths, &c. The preparation of the canvas was at one time in the hands of the sail-makers, but, excepting for the actual making of sails, has now become a separate industry. The best canvas is made of flax, and inferior kinds of jute, or a mixture of flax and jute. It is woven in long narrow strips, and when received by the London house is first cut in lengths suitable to the article required, and is then given out to be made up. The sewing is at present chiefly hand-work, being performed by women in their own homes; but machinery is steadily superseding hand labour, the natural tendency in this direction being assisted by the fact that as houses make way for business premises in South and East London the women are forced to live further from the centre of their work; and also because the landlords of blocks of buildings and newer houses will not allow nails to be driven into the doorposts, as is the practice in doing this work. Consequently, an increasing proportion of the work is done in factories by power, the lighter machines being attended to by girls and women, and the heavier ones by men.

Sacks and bags are made in infinite variety to hold coals, corn, seed, onions, flour, money, &c. In hand-work the woman stands with the material hung up before her; one side of the bag is held in the left hand, and the worker, sewing over and over the edges, bends the body forward at each stitch. She uses, in lieu of a thimble, an indented metal disc, termed a palm; which is fastened round the centre of the hand and kept in position by the thumb. The twine used is found by the employer; the needle and " palm " are the property of the worker.

The work, whether in home or factory, and whatever the article made, is nearly all done by the piece; and the variety of the amounts earned, as well as the unwillingness of most of the employers to afford information, makes it very difficult to give any standard weekly wage. Amongst female workers, quick hands will earn 2*s* a day, and medium hands 1*s* 6*d*—8*s* to 12*s* being, it is said, common amounts paid for a full week's work in the factory. But

trade is very irregular, and in addition there is, as regards
home work, the irregularity of the women themselves,
most of whom are the wives or widows of labourers, and
have household duties to perform, so that to outdoor
hands 4s to 5s a week are the most usual sums paid.   The
women take out their work direct from the firm, no middle-
man distributors being employed in the trade.   The
earnings of men are stated to range from about 18s to 30s
a week, the tent and marquee-makers being the more
skilled and better paid section.   The cutter-out is the most
responsible man, and commands regular work at a good
wage.

Hours of work in factories are from about fifty-eight to
sixty per week, and seasons vary with the article required,
the demand for sacks being greatest in the early autumn,
when the crops are gathered; for seed bags, the winter;
and for tarpaulins and rickcloths, the summer.

Tarpaulins.—When these have to be made, the canvas
sheet, which, as in the other branches, is usually prepared
by women, has to be waterproofed, and this is done by men
called dressers.   The sheet is stretched on a frame or
"jigger," and the dressing (the chief ingredient of which
is generally linseed oil) is applied with a wide long-handled
broom, which is dipped into the pail containing the composition, and then worked backwards and forwards over
the sheet, which is spread out at the feet of the operator.

After the first coating, it is taken off the frame, folded
up and left for some hours, in order that the composition
may evenly permeate the material.   Subsequently it
receives two or three further coats, being hung up to dry
between each process, and finally cords are inserted by
boys into the metal rings, which have been sewn in to
receive them.

In addition to private firms, one large railway company
makes tarpaulins in London, but entirely for its own use,
employing about half a dozen men, thirty women and forty

youths and boys. The women who do the sewing at home for the railway company, are nearly all widows of former employees, and for this reason no machinery is introduced. They are on piece, and earn from 5*s* to 10*s* a week, the smaller amount being taken by those who only devote part of their time to the work. The men who do the dressing make from 30*s* to 35*s* (also piece-work), and boys from 7*s* to 15*s*, and both men and boys are provided with uniform. Hours here are about fifty-four per week, and work is practically constant throughout the year.

Second-hand Trade.—There is a growing second-hand trade in sacks, owing to the increasing import of flour from America. The sacks are collected from bakers by costers and others; and are then cleaned and darned. They are used for many purposes—for potatoes and other produce, as well as for repacking flour. Attempts have been made to adopt machinery to darn these sacks, but hitherto without success.

Wages Statistics.

Of the 3341 persons returned in this section, 1285 are employed males over twenty years of age. Detailed returns have been received from five firms employing 353 persons, of whom 134 are adult men. The earnings of these men are as under:—

Under 20*s*	21, or 15½ per cent.	}	Under 30*s*, 71½ per cent.
20*s* to 25*s*	42 ,, 31 ,,		
25*s* ,, 30*s*	33 ,, 25 ,,		
30*s* ,, 35*s*	23 ,, 17½ ,,	}	30*s* and over, 28½ per cent.
35*s* ,, 40*s*	3 ,, 2 ,,		
40*s* ,, 45*s*	3 ,, 2 ,,		
45*s* and upwards	9 ,, 7 ,,		
	134 ,, 100 ,,		

It is noticeable that more than half the men (56 per cent.) earn from 20*s* to 30*s* a week.

Of the women employed more than 70 per cent. are

returned as earning 9s or 10s a week, nearly 20 per cent. earning more than the latter amount. Only one return from a sack-maker is included in these figures, which, therefore, apply more especially to cocoa-fibre matting and rope-makers. The sack-makers are largely home workers, and their earnings are less than those of the rest. Boys receive from 6s to 16s, and their earnings are evenly distributed down the scale, 60 per cent. receiving 10s or less per week, and 40 per cent. over 10s.

Social Condition.

Of the 1285 employed men, about 970 come under social classification as heads of families. The wages returns received do not provide a sufficiently wide basis for comparison. The figures are, however, stated side by side as follows, as in other sections:—

Comparison of Earnings with Style of Life.

Earnings as returned.	Classification of Population.
Under 20s...21, or 15½ per cent.	3 or more in each room, 1100, or 20 per cent.
20s to 25s...42 ,, 31 ,,	2 to 3 ,, 1600 ,, 31 ,,
25s ,, 30s...33 ,, 25 ,,	1 ,, 2 ,, 1550 ,, 28 ,,
30s ,, 35s...23 ,, 17½ ,,	Less than 1 ,, ⎫
35s ,, 40s... 3 ,, 2 ,,	More than 4 rooms ⎬ 1150 ,, 21 ,,
40s ,, 45s... 3 ,, 2 ,,	4 or more persons ⎭
45s and ⎫ 9 ,, 7 ,,	to a servant
upwards ⎭	
134 ,, 100 ,,	5400 ., 100 ,,
	Employers' families ⎫
	and servants, and ⎬ 1000
	families with fe- ⎪
	male heads ⎭
	6400

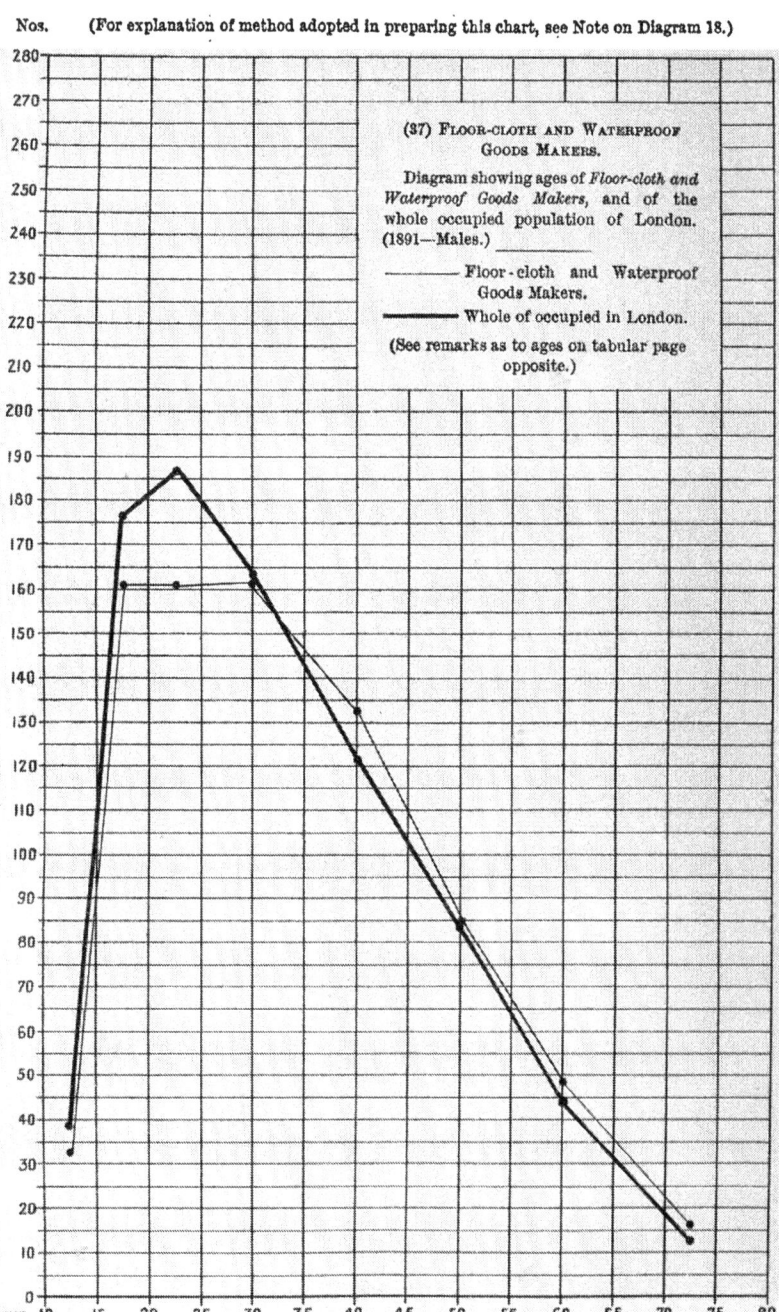

(37) FLOOR-CLOTH AND WATERPROOF
GOODS MAKERS.

Diagram showing ages of *Floor-cloth and Waterproof Goods Makers*, and of the whole occupied population of London. (1891—Males.)

———————— Floor-cloth and Waterproof
Goods Makers.

━━━━━━ Whole of occupied in London.

(See remarks as to ages on tabular page
opposite.)

CHAPTER IV.

INDIA-RUBBER GOODS, FLOOR-CLOTH, &c. (Section 37.)

Persons Represented.

Census Enumeration.						Enumerated by Families.					

Census Enumeration.

Census Division, 1891.	Females All Ages.	Males.			Total.
		—19	20—54	55—	
1) India-rubber..	1034	182	756	98	2070
2) Floor-cloth,&c.	126	113	643	122	1004
Total.......	1160	295	1399	220	3074

These are not trades which employ many boys or young men, and consequently the entire proportion of men over 30 is above average. They are new industries and employ a large number of women and girls.

DISTRIBUTION.

E.	N.	W. & C.	S.	Total.
1214	665	272	923	3074

DETAILS OF OCCUPATIONS
(FROM THE CENSUS DICTIONARY).

1) India-rubber and water-proof goods worker, elastic band and webbing manufacturer, gutta-percha manufacturer, india-rubber mill-band maker, rubber stamp maker, xylonite manufacturer.

Balloon maker, tarpaulin, rick cloth, van cover and tilt maker, oil-sheet maker, japan, lacquer and varnish maker, sealing-wax maker, shellac bleacher.

2) Floor-cloth manufacturer, cork miller, linoleum printer, oil boiler, American cloth maker, oil-skin maker, japanned goods manufacturer, furniture japanner, black polisher.

Enumerated by Families.

| Sex | Males .... 1267 |
| | Females............. 119 |

| Birthplace | In London .... 63% 875 |
| | Out of London.. 37% 511 |

Heads of Families 1386.

Industrial Status..	Employer 14% 187
	Employed 80% 1111
	Neither 6% 88

TOTAL POPULATION CONCERNED.

	Heads of Families.	Others Occupied.	Unoccupied	Servants.	Total.
Total.	1386	1331	3607	216	6540
Average in family ..	1	·96	2·69	·16	4·72

CLASSIFICATION.

Numbers living in Families.		%
3 or more to a room	854	13·1
2 & under 3 ,,	1290	19·8
1 & under 2 ,,	1571	24·0
Less than 1 ,,		
More than 4 rooms	2282	34·9
4 or more persons to a servant ..		
Less than 4 to 1 servant, & 4 or more to 2 servants ..	228	3·5
All others with 2 or more servants..	99	1·5
Servants	216	3·2
	6540	100

	Inner.	Outer.	Together.
Crowded ..	45%	23%	33%
Not ,,	55%	77%	67%

DISTRIBUTION.

East ..	Inner 1396	1862
	Outer 466	
North..	Inner 143	1511
	Outer 1368	
West ..	Inner 74	348
	Outer 274	
Central	Inner 376	376
South-	Inner 384	1187
East ..	Outer 803	
South-	Inner 658	1256
West..	Outer 598	
		6540

Inner 3001, or 46%.
Outer 3539, or 54%.

Status as to Employment (according to Census Enumeration).

Census Divisions (1891).	Employers.		Employed.			Neither Employer nor Employed.		Total.
			Males.		Females of all ages.			
	Males	Females	Under 20.	Over 20.		Males	Femal	
1) India-rubber, water-proof goods worker	103	7	182	708	1027	43	...	2070
2) Floor-cloth, oil-cloth manufacturer..	14	—	21	136	12	10	2	195
Japanner	16	3	40	284	75	15	2	435
Others........................	76	2	52	189	25	25	5	374
Total..........	209	12	295	1317	1139	93	9	3074

221   2751
Proportion of Employers to Employed—1 to 12.   102

India-rubber Goods.

The india-rubber and floor-cloth industries are extremely secret trades, and, for this reason, but little information has been received in regard to them.

As to india rubber, there is no general method of treatment, each firm having its own system of mixing the different raw rubbers with alloys, and a variety of machinery for working out the various products.

If we exclude the chemists and those who hold the secrets of the mixings, there are but few really skilled workers in a rubber factory; and, as far as skill is concerned, the preparation of rubber may be compared with the manufacture of chemicals, in which the men simply carry out the instructions of their superiors, and know but little of the why and wherefore. They learn a certain routine of work with which some acquaintance is necessary before it can be discharged with ease and efficiency, but their skill is often of no use outside their own factory, and they thus rank—that is, the great majority of them—as unskilled labourers.

There are something over fifty different kinds of rubber, each with its own particular properties and its own particular uses; and in the selection and classification of these as they enter the shop lies one of the skilled branches of rubber manufacture.

Rubber comes to England in various forms, from Brazil and from Africa, and elsewhere. It is formed from the glutinous sap of a tree, congealed in thin layers on some object made of wood or clay. This object is dipped again and again in the liquid sap, and exposed after each bath to the action of smoke. The best Brazilian rubber, prepared in this way on a wooden disc or paddle end, assumes the shape of a hollow cake, when the paddle is withdrawn. It used originally to be brought over in the form of bottles and shoes, and the hollow cakes are sometimes still called "bottles." _ Other kinds are wrapped, sausage-like in shape, round pieces of twig or bamboo. The rubber is at first nearly white in colour, and only gradually goes black with age and exposure. The commoner descriptions are often much mixed with earth and clay.

Method of Preparation.—The first thing to be done with raw rubber is to free it from all impurities. It is softened by immersion in hot water—a process producing a most disagreeable but not unhealthy smell; then it is sliced open, and the slices crushed between grooved rollers, over which water passes. All solid impurities are ground out in this way and carried off by the water, and the pure rubber emerges in porous, irregular-shaped sheets. These have to be hung in heated rooms for some days to dry. The next object is to get rid of the air-bubbles—of which the sheets are full—and for this purpose it is passed through a machine called the masticator, which reduces it to an almost solid pulp. Incorporation with sulphur—which is necessary for vulcanization—may be effected either before or after this process. Having passed through the masticator, the rubber is sometimes compressed in moulds into a solid cylinder, from which sheets can be cut off, or else it may be passed through "mixing rollers," under the action of which sulphur for subsequent vulcanization, as well as colouring matter, are generally incorporated with it. Evidently, few of the workmen employed on the above processes can be called skilled, since their duties, as a rule, consist simply in feeding a given machine with a given material. The manipulation, however, of the next machine, the calender —so called from a resemblance to the machine of that name used in paper manufacture—calls for considerable skill, and calender men are the most highly paid in the works. The machine consists of three rollers, one over the other, between which the rubber paste passes to be formed into a sheet. The proper production of the sheet depends upon the temperature both of the rubber and of

the calenders. Considerable experience and constant attention are requisite on the part of the men who work the
machine, to prevent failure.

After calendering, rubber sheets are ready for vulcanization, which is produced by exposure of the sulphur-laden
rubber to heat for some hours, and it is then fit for cutting
into other shapes required for tubes, tyres, rings, or whatever the ultimate product required.

This completes what may be called the process of preparation, which, in a large factory, continues from year's
end to year's end in what is termed the central shop without
slackening, except through some unusual cause.

The rubber having left its original barbarous form of
"bottle" or "sausage," and having become a sheet,
plays a useful part in life, whether as a water-proof, a
football bladder, the core of a packing, an engine valve,
a pneumatic tyre, the stopper of a mineral water-bottle,
a surgical instrument, a lawn tennis ball, an invalid's water-
bed, a submarine cable, or any of the thousand and one
purposes to which it may be put.   The industry is still in
its infancy, in spite of the extraordinary development of
late years, and there appears to be no limit to the usefulness
of rubber.

Gutta-percha which, though also the gum of a tree, is a
totally different substance, is mainly used for telegraphic
work.   It also is an excellent non-conductor, but differs
from rubber in being plastic in place of elastic.

Busy and Slack Seasons.—In large rubber factories, of
which the number in London may almost be counted on
the fingers of one hand, the variety of products is
generally so great that the various departments, being
busy and slack at different times, are able to transfer their
workmen from one to the other, while the central shop is
always kept busy. Few persons are, therefore, discharged
through slackness. The only considerable industry connected with rubber, in which this is not the case, is that of

telegraph appliances and submarine cables, which depends entirely on large contracts. The result of this is the existence of a floating body of workers who move from factory to factory, as required by the firms that obtain the contracts.

Wages.—Deducting such skilled men as calenderers, ebonite fitters and turners, some water-proof cutters, &c., the rank and file of rubber workers receive, on the average, about 5d an hour, ranging—for youths of nineteen and twenty years of age—from 4d to 5d, and for older men, from 5d to 6d or 6½d.

Perhaps one-third of those employed will be in receipt of wages amounting to over 25s a week, but quite two-thirds will not exceed that sum, and may thus be reckoned as on a par with ordinary unskilled labour. Men do not care to stay longer "at the rubber" than they can help, and seize the first opportunity of other employment that offers a better prospect.

Piece-work men, who are not a numerous class, can usually earn better money, but they also frequently work longer hours.

Women, of whom a large number are employed in nearly all departments except the "central shop," seem to earn good wages, as women's wages go. Girls begin at a nominal rate of 2s 6d, but the average is from 12s to 15s, while some are able to earn 20s, and forewomen even up to 30s, an unusually high figure.

Hours.—The usual hours for time workers are about fifty-four—from 6.30 to 6, less one hour and a half for meals. Sometimes rather shorter hours are worked in winter. Male piece workers are, however, not tied and bound by any hard and fast rule, and work sometimes in excess and sometimes short of the regular factory hours.

Method of Training.—No special method of training workers is attempted. Deftness, attention, and obedience are the principal qualities needed, and having these it does not take a lad or girl long to learn what is required of them.

Health.—In regard to the general health of those employed, one only of the processes in a rubber factory can be termed injurious. This is that known as "cold vulcanization," used on woollen and silk materials after the rubber paste for water-proofing has been applied.

Besides the *bonâ fide* London rubber factories, the Directory contains the names of a great number of rubber manufacturers who have their works scattered about in the provinces, and sometimes in France and Germany, with only a depôt here; and there are also an innumerable quantity of persons "manufacturing" some speciality requiring the use of rubber, but obtaining their material almost finished from the large factories, and working it up to suit some particular fancy of their own. These are probably not returned in the census as rubber workers.

WATERPROOF GOODS.

It is said that certain firms in the east employ a large number of girls on waterproof clothing, sending their material in to the rubber factories to be waterproofed, or buying it in prepared sheets at wholesale rates, and paying at the rate of 3*d* per garment for having it made up, while the price at a good firm ranges from 1*s* to 1*s* 6*d*.

Process of Waterproofing.—As waterproofing is a large industry, it may not be amiss to give a slight sketch of the process. There are two methods, the first and least common being to insert a very thin layer of rubber between two sheets of the other material.

The second consists in dissolving rubber with naphtha or benzol, and so producing a sort of paste of the consistency of butter on a warm day. The sulphur for vulcanization is incorporated into the paste in the case of cotton or linen, but not wool or silk. The material is then spread out over a long flat slab and slowly drawn along by a roller at the further end. A kind of knife, fixed just above it, butters the sheet, as it passes underneath, with the rubber paste as thinly as the most meagre "bread and scrape." As the sheet is drawn along, the naphtha evaporates and leaves a dry coating of rubber. This process may be repeated two or three times.

In the case of wool or silk, to which the ordinary method is not adapted, " cold vulcanization " has to be resorted to. This is done by bringing the fabric in contact with a mixture of chloride of sulphur and carbon disulphide, when vulcanization takes place without the action of heat.

These are the two chemical substances which are injurious to health. Few men can withstand their effects for any length of time, and it is very necessary to remove the workers from the department in which it is carried on as soon as they appear to be suffering.

FLOOR-CLOTH, &c.

Floor-cloth and *linoleum* manufacturers, as well as makers of gum, lacquer, varnish, household cement, &c., also fall within this section.

In regard to the former, although there are a few large factories within and around London, little or no information has been received, and no wages' returns have been obtained, doubtless on account of the secrecy already alluded to. Each firm conducts business on its own line, and has its own methods of manufacture. So far as we can learn, men are paid much on the same scale as in rubber factories. When first taken on they receive 18s a week, and after six months' employment, when they are classed as ordinary labourers, rise to 20s. By diligence and steadiness they may attain to the position of semi-skilled labourers earning from 22s to 26s a week. Men of these two classes form something like 70 per cent. of those employed, the other 30 per cent. being really skilled men, earning between 30*s* and 40*s* a week. Employment is regular throughout the year. Hours range from fifty-four to fifty-six and a half.

Makers of gum, varnish, household cement, &c., are generally to be found in small workshops. They prepare their own mixtures—almost each one claiming some particularly valuable receipt—with perhaps a couple of men to help them, and a number of boys or girls to fill, stop, and label the bottles. Boys stay at this kind of work usually from the ages of fourteen to sixteen, receiving from 5*s* to 7*s* a week, and leave as soon as they can find some more permanent employ. There is no lack of applicants, since the work is light, easily learned, and suitable for boys to do.

Trade Unions.—No special trade union has as yet been established for this industry, nor is it likely that one will be formed at present. There is scarcely sufficient solidarity among the employees to enable them to establish a society of their own, and, as with the chemical workers, the bulk of the men are more likely to join the General Labourers' Union.

Wages Statistics.

In these trades 1317 adult males are employed. As to these, we have received particulars of wages for 518, employed by twelve firms, as under :—

India-rubber and gutta-percha works 5	= 12 firms employing usually
India-rubber type and stamp makers 4	1443 persons, of whom 899 are
Asbestos and india-rubber manuf. 1	adult males, but of these 381
Tarpaulin maker...................... 1	belong to other sections, being
Waterproof clothing maker 1	employed in various ways.*

* This abnormal proportion belonging to other sections, is due to one large firm who combine an entirely different business with rubber works.

The wages of these men in an ordinary week are as follows :—

```
Under 20s ......... 75, or 14 per cent. ⎫
20s to 25s ......... 103  „  20    „     ⎬ Below 30s, 58½ per cent.
25s „  30s ......... 126  „  24½   „     ⎭
30s „  35s ......... 85   „  16½   „     ⎫
35s „  40s ......... 62   „  12    „     ⎬ 30s and over, 41½ per cent.
40s „  45s ......... 39   „  7½    „     ⎬
45s and upwards  23  „  5¼    „          ⎭
                   ———    ———
                   518  „  100   „
```

A comparison may be made between our figures and those obtained in 1886 by the Board of Trade, from five firms employing 1393 persons, of whom 710 were adult men belonging to this section :—

	—20s.	20s—	25s—	30s—	35s—	40s—	45s.
Our returns ...	14 %	20 %	24½ %	16½ %	12 %	7½ %	5¼ %
		58½ %			41½ %		
Board of Trade returns	1 %	26 %	40 %	12 %	4 %	11 %	6 %
		67 %			33 %		

The discrepancy between these returns is mainly accounted for by the difference in method adopted, already so often referred to. The increase in the number of those earning over 30s probably points to a real rise in wages. The large proportion who appear in our returns as earning less than 20s are, no doubt, to be explained by short time. In both returns the bulk of the men earn from 20s to 30s.

As to regularity of work, we have particulars from three firms to combine with the Board of Trade figures, as follows :—

	Busy.	Slack.	Percentage Reduction.		
			In numbers.	In earnings per head.	Combined.
Our returns	1017	586	42½	16	51½ °/o
Board of Trade returns ...	1550	1224	21	16½	34½ °/o

The busy weeks fall mostly in May, June, and July; and the slack ones are mostly in the winter; but some factories were slack in August and September, and others were busy in October and November. It, therefore, seems that the seasonal variations, though marked, are not uniform, and, as much of the work does not need special skill, some of the workpeople shift from one part of the trade to another as work offers. The actual reduction in numbers employed is consequently not so great as that shown above.

The following tables show the difference between busy and slack weeks in more detail. They are compiled from returns supplied by one of the largest employers in the trade:—

Men.		Busy Week.					Slack Week.				
		Men.	Wages.		Hours.	Rate.	Men.	Wages.		Hours.	Rate.
			s.	d.		d.		s.	d.		d.
Time-work	Under 5*d* per hour	114	21	8¼	63¼	4	60	19	7¼	59½	4
	5*d* and 6*d*...........	170	30	4	68	5¼	141	26	2	59	5¼
	Over 6*d* to 8*d*	43	38	11	68	6¾	35	34	10½	59¼	7
	Over 8*d*..............	7	49	5	69¼	8½	3	44	0	60¼	8¾
		334					239				
Piece-work	Under 15*s* a week	4	10	6	56	2¼	6	11	6	48¾	2¾
	,, 20*s*.........	9	16	6½	53½	3¾	10	16	6	51½	3¾
	20*s* ,, 25*s*.........	20	21	9	60¾	4¾	8	22	9	54	5
	25*s* ,, 30*s*.........	6	27	6	54½	6	9	27	4	48	6¼
	30*s* ,, 40*s*.........	50	34	1	63¼	7¼	29	34	2½	57¼	7
	40*s* and upwards...	36	49	11¾	69	7¾	7	46	3	52½	9¼
		125					69				

According to the census, these trades furnish employment for 1160 women and girls, and we have particulars of wages earned by 343, as under:—

5*s* and under......	39, or 11½ per cent.		Below 12*s*, 38½ per cent.
6*s* „ 7*s*	16 „ 4½ „		
8*s* „ 9*s*	27 „ 8 „		
10*s* „ 11*s*	49 „ 14½ „		
12*s* „ 13*s*	56 „ 16½ „		12*s* and over, 61½ per cent.
14*s* „ 15*s*	45 „ 13 „		
16*s* „ under 20*s*	67 „ 19 „		
20*s* „ over	44 „ 13 „		
	343 „ 100 „		

As to boys and lads under 20, there are 295 employed, and we have particulars concerning 159, as follows:—

5*s* and under......	2, or 1 per cent.		Below 12*s*, 55½ per cent.
6*s* „ 7*s*	11 „ 7 „		
8*s* „ 9*s*	37 „ 23½ „		
10*s* „ 11*s*	38 „ 24 „		
12*s* „ 13*s*	20 „ 13 „		12*s* and over, 44½ per cent.
14*s* „ 15*s*	16 „ 10 „		
16*s* „ under 20*s*	14 „ 8½ „		
20*s* „ over	21 „ 13 „		
	159 „ 100 „		

The following details are interesting, as showing the prevalence of piece-work amongst the women, the great irregularity of the work, and the high earnings that can sometimes be made:—

Women.		Busy Week.				Slack Week.			
		Women.	Wages.	Hours.	Rate.	Women.	Wages.	Hours.	Rate.
			s. *d.*		*d.*		*s.* *d.*		*d.*
Time-work	Under 5*d* per hour	55	9 7	51¾	2¼	25	11 1	53½	2½
Piece-work	Under 5*s* a week	2	2 6	42	¾	49	2 9	24½	1½
	„ 10*s*.........	20	7 5	54¼	1¼	32	7 1	36¼	2½
	„ 15*s*.........	54	12 5	55¾	2¾	34	12 0	48	3
	„ 20*s*.........	113	17 3	57	3¾	31	15 9	54	3½
	„ 25*s*.........	53	21 3	57¼	4¼	1	8 0	22	4½
	„ 30*s*.........	13	26 6	58	5¼	—	—	—	—
	30*s* and over......	5	33 3	55	7¼	—	—	—	—
		260				147			

The boys are mostly on time, but the older lads are on piece, and some of them earn men's wages, as is shown below :—

Boys.		Busy Week.					Slack Week.				
		Boys.	Wages.		Hours.	Rate.	Boys.	Wages.		Hours.	Rate.
			s.	d.		d.		s.	d.		d.
Time-work	Under 5*d* per hour	126	11	5	61	2¼	74	10	0	56¼	2¼
Piece-work	Under 10*s* a week...	7	7	9	59	1½	2	8	0	39½	2½
	,, 15*s*...........	14	11	5	60	2¼	4	11	9	58¼	2¼
	,, 20*s*...........	3	17	0	75	2¾	3	16	4	58	3½
	,, 25*s*...........	11	22	0	71¾	3¾	2	21	0	57	4½
	,, 30*s*...........	5	26	3	72¼	4½	—	—	—	—	—
	30*s* and over........	7	32	10	74	5½	—	—	—	—	—
		47					11				

Social Condition.

Of the 1317 adult men employed, about 1015 come under social classification as heads of families. Tested by our wages returns, 34 per cent. earn less than 25*s* in an average week, and may be compared to the 40 per cent. who live under crowded conditions. Next, we have 41 per cent. earning from 25*s* to 35*s*, as compared to 28 per cent. who live one and up to two persons in a room in small tenements; and, finally, we have 25 per cent. earning over 35*s* to compare with 32 per cent. of the central classes; as is shown in the following table :—

Comparison of Earnings with Style of Life (India Rubber, &c.).

Earnings as returned.	Classification of Population.
Under 20s... 75, or 14 per cent.	3 or more in each room, 850, or 15½ per cent.
20s to 25s...103 ,, 20 ,,	2 to 3 ,, 1300 ,, 24 ,,
25s ,, 30s...126 ,, 24½ ,,	1 ,, 2 ,, 1550 ,, 28½ ,,
30s ,, 35s... 85 ,, 16½ ,,	Less than 1 ,,
35s ,, 40s... 62 ,, 12 ,,	More than 4 rooms
40s ,, 45s... 39 ,, 7½ ,,	4 or more persons 1740 ,, 32 ,,
45s and } 28 ,, 5½ ,, upwards }	to a servant
518 ,, 100 ,,	5440 ,, 100 ,,
	Employers' families
	and servants 1100
	6540

APPENDIX.

PART I.—PRECIOUS METALS, &c.

TABLE A.—*Distribution of whole Population.*

Registration Districts.	(18.) Goldsmiths, Lapidaries.		(19.) Watch and Clockmakers.		(20.) Surgical &Electrical Instrument makers.		(21.) Musical Instruments, Games, &c., makers.		Total Precious Metals.	
	No.	%	No.	%	No.	%	No.	%	No.	%
Poplar	184	·8	136	1·1	347	1·9	358	1·4	1025	1·5
Mile End Old Town and Stepney	375	1·7	249	2·0	381	2·1	420	1·7	1425	1·8
St. George's-in-the-East Whitechapel	329	1·5	164	1·5	107	·6	155	·6	755	1·0
Bethnal Green	258	1·2	203	1·6	285	1·5	931	3·7	1677	2·2
Shoreditch	802	3·7	505	4·2	416	2·2	707	2·8	2430	3·1
Total of East London	1948	8·9	1257	10·4	1536	8·3	2571	10·2	7312	9·4
Hackney	1476	6·8	923	7·5	1164	6·3	1708	6·8	5271	6·8
Islington	4890	22·5	2598	21·4	2901	15·7	4373	17·4	14,762	19·0
St. Pancras	1864	8·6	602	5·0	1354	7·3	6403	25·5	10,223	13·2
Marylebone and Hampstead	1365	6·2	445	3·6	651	3·5	1158	4·6	3619	4·6
Total of North London	9595	44·1	4568	37·5	6070	32·8	13,642	54·3	33,875	43·6
Paddington	421	1·9	233	1·9	345	1·8	363	1·4	1362	1·8
St.George's, HanoverSquare	458	2·1	238	1·9	425	2·3	448	1·8	1569	2·0
Kensington	433	2·0	319	2·6	350	1·9	356	1·4	1458	1·9
Chelsea	233	1·1	138	1·2	252	1·3	227	·9	850	1·1
Fulham	744	3·4	369	3·0	846	4·6	1107	4·4	3066	3·9
Total of West London	2289	10·5	1297	10·6	2218	11·9	2501	9·9	8305	10·7
City	192	·9	51	·4	77	·4	47	·2	367	·5
Holborn	2493	11·5	1874	15·4	1338	7·2	1001	4·0	6706	8·7
Strand, Westminster, and St. Giles	1057	4·9	312	2·6	423	2·3	349	1·4	2141	2·8
Total of Central London	3742	17·3	2237	18·4	1838	9·9	1397	5·6	9214	12·0
Woolwich	70	·3	161	1·4	1449	7·9	334	1·3	2014	2·6
Greenwich	268	1·2	268	2·2	885	4·8	252	1·0	1673	2·2
St. Olave, Southwark	101	·5	134	1·1	212	1·1	223	·9	670	·9
Camberwell	941	4·4	537	4·4	892	4·8	871	3·5	3241	4·1
Lewisham	265	1·2	186	1·5	210	1·1	166	·6	827	1·1
Total of S.-East London	1645	7·6	1286	10·6	3648	19·7	1846	7·3	8425	10·9
St. Saviour's, Southwark	481	2·2	349	2·9	774	4·2	791	3·1	2395	3·1
Lambeth	1131	5·2	506	4·2	1441	7·8	1251	5·0	4329	5·6
Wandsworth	892	4·2	655	5·4	990	5·4	1156	4·6	3693	4·7
Total of S.-West London	2504	11·6	1510	12·5	3205	17·4	3198	12·7	10,417	13·4
GRAND TOTAL OF LONDON	21,723	100	12,155	100	18,515	100	25,155	100	77,548	100

TABLE B.—*Classification of whole Population.*

Classification. See Vol. V. page 404.	(18.) Goldsmiths, Lapidaries.		(19.) Watch and Clockmakers.		(20.) Surgical & Electrical Instrument Makers.		(21.) Musical Instruments, Games, &c., makers.		Total.	
	No.	%	No.	%	No.	%	No.	%	No.	%
Without Servants										
Families averaging— 1. 4 or more persons to a room	628	2·9	283	2·3	610	3·3	1074	4·2	2595	3·4
2. 3 & under 4 persons to a room	1095	5·0	538	4·4	1057	5·7	2005	7·9	4695	6·0
3. 2 & under 3 persons to a room	3160	14·5	1743	14·3	3171	17·1	5093	20·3	13,167	17·0
	4883	22·4	2564	21·0	4838	26·1	8172	32·4	20,457	26·4
4. 1 & under 2 persons to a room	4874	22·5	2518	20·7	5090	27·5	6529	26·0	19,011	24·5
5. Less than 1 person to a room	766	3·5	499	4·2	774	4·2	863	3·5	2902	3·8
6. All families occupying more than 4 rooms (mainly house-holders)	6511	30·0	4741	39·0	5382	29·0	7340	29·1	23,974	30·9
Families averaging— A 4 or more persons to 1 servant	1743	8·0	915	7·5	1030	5·6	1110	4·4	4798	6·2
	9020	41·5	6155	50·7	7186	38·8	9313	37·0	31,674	40·9
With Servants										
B 1 to 3 persons to 1 servant, &c.	1303	6·0	422	3·5	538	2·9	512	2·0	2775	3·6
C 1 to 3 persons to 2 servants, &c. ...	336	1·7	97	·8	147	·7	103	·5	683	·9
D 3 or 4 persons to 3 servants, &c. ...	116	·5	14	·1	74	·4	41	·1	245	·3
	452	2·2	111	·9	221	1·3	144	·6	928	·2
E 1 or 2 persons to 3 servants, &c. ...	61	·2	4	—	39	·2	10	—	114	1·2
F 1 or 2 persons to 4 servants, &c. ...	25	·1	—	—	10	—	—	—	35	—
G 1 or 2 persons to 5 servants, &c. ...	4	—	—	—	—	—	6	—	10	—
H 1 or 2 persons to 6 servants, &c. ...	—	—	—	—	—	—	—	—	—	—
	90	·3	4	—	49	·2	16	·1	159	·2
Servants	1101	5·1	381	3·2	598	3·2	469	1·9	2544	3·2
GRAND TOTAL...	21,723	100	12,155	100	18,515	100	25,155	100	77,548	100

Without servants... 66,344, or 15,269 families = 4·34 ⎫
With servants ...... 8,660, or 1,757 „ = 4·87 ⎭ persons per family.

PART II.—SUNDRY MANUFACTURES.

TABLE A.—*Distribution of whole Population.*

Registration Districts.	(22.) Earthenware and Glass.		(23.) Chemicals.		(24.) Tallow, Soap, and Glue.		(25.) Leather Dressing, Tanning, &c.	
	No.	%	No.	%	No.	%	No.	%
Poplar	227	1·9	1549	14·2	409	8·3	594	1·5
Mile End Old Town and Stepney	311	2·7	394	3·6	219	4·4	1248	3·3
St. George's-in-the-East and Whitechapel	58	·5	86	·8	180	3·6	1828	4·7
Bethnal Green	457	3·9	206	1·9	224	4·5	979	2·5
Shoreditch	579	5·0	293	2·7	152	3·1	1716	4·5
Total of East London	1632	14·0	2528	23·2	1184	23·9	6365	16·5
Hackney	823	7·1	1084	10·0	281	5·7	2055	5·4
Islington	779	6·7	975	9·0	285	5·8	2957	7·7
St. Pancras	821	7·1	679	6·1	89	1·8	737	1·9
Marylebone and Hampstead	289	2·5	279	2·6	50	1·0	657	1·7
Total of North London	2712	23·4	3017	27·7	705	14·3	6406	16·7
Paddington	121	1·0	105	1·0	41	·8	283	·7
St. George's, Hanover Square	88	·7	93	·8	26	·5	371	1·0
Kensington	69	·6	79	·7	54	1·1	227	·6
Chelsea	80	·7	43	·4	16	·3	148	·4
Fulham	352	3·0	146	1·3	65	1·3	333	·8
Total of West London	710	6·0	466	4·2	202	4·0	1362	3·5
City	96	·8	29	·3	12	·2	214	·5
Holborn	880	7·6	347	3·2	129	2·6	1690	4·5
Strand, Westminster, and St. Giles	108	·9	197	1·8	101	2·1	657	1·7
Total of Central London	1084	9·3	573	5·3	242	4·9	2561	6·7
Woolwich	47	·4	701	6·4	24	·5	166	·4
Greenwich	201	1·7	642	5·9	537	10·8	1241	3·2
St. Olave, Southwark	166	1·4	322	3·0	219	4·4	11,186	29·2
Camberwell	596	5·1	531	4·9	216	4·4	3385	8·8
Lewisham	88	·7	261	2·4	56	1·1	437	1·2
Total of South-East London	1098	9·3	2457	22·6	1052	21·2	16,415	42·8
St. Saviour, Southwark	837	7·2	468	4·3	210	4·3	3060	8·0
Lambeth	2727	23·4	479	4·4	546	11·1	1133	3·1
Wandsworth	865	7·4	904	8·3	805	16·3	1054	2·7
Total of South-West London	4429	38·0	1851	17·0	1561	31·7	5247	13·8
GRAND TOTAL OF LONDON	11,665	100	10,892	100	4946	100	38,356	100

PART II.—SUNDRY MANUFACTURES (continued).

TABLE A.—Distribution of whole Population (continued).

(26.) Saddle and Harness Making.		(27.) Brush and Comb Making.		Total Sundry Manufactures.		Registration Districts.
No.	%	No.	%	No.	%	
162	1·5	574	5·1	3515	4·0	Poplar.
287	2·7	498	4·5	2957	3·4	Mile End Old Town and Stepney.
123	1·2	148	1·3	2423	2·8	St. George's-in-the-East and Whitechapel.
300	2·8	1312	11·8	3478	4·0	Bethnal Green.
818	7·7	864	7·7	4422	5·0	Shoreditch.
1690	15·9	3396	30·4	16,795	19·2	Total of East London.
436	4·2	1426	12·7	6105	6·9	Hackney.
671	6·3	1070	9·5	6737	7·6	Islington.
619	5·9	281	2·5	3226	3·7	St. Pancras.
659	6·3	184	1·6	2118	2·4	Marylebone and Hampstead.
2385	22·7	2961	26·3	18,186	20·6	Total of North London.
382	3·6	66	·6	998	1·1	Paddington.
376	3·5	61	·5	1015	1·2	St. George's, Hanover Square.
338	3·2	41	·4	808	·9	Kensington.
411	3·9	74	·7	772	·9	Chelsea.
460	4·4	85	·7	1441	1·7	Fulham.
1967	18·6	327	2·9	5034	5·8	Total of West London.
85	·8	19	·1	455	·5	City.
495	4·8	588	5·2	4129	4·7	Holborn.
398	3·8	141	1·3	1602	1·9	Strand, Westminster, and St. Giles.
978	9·4	748	6·6	6186	7·1	Total of Central London.
508	4·8	—	—	1446	1·7	Woolwich.
174	1·6	113	1·0	2908	3·3	Greenwich.
290	2·7	567	5·0	12,750	14·5	St. Olave, Southwark.
715	6·7	678	6·1	6121	7·0	Camberwell.
119	1·1	89	·8	1050	1·2	Lewisham.
1806	16·9	1447	12·9	24,275	27·7	Total of South-East London.
514	4·8	1759	15·7	6848	7·8	St. Saviour, Southwark.
611	5·7	338	3·0	5834	6·7	Lambeth.
627	6·0	239	2·2	4494	5·1	Wandsworth.
1752	16·5	2336	20·9	17,176	19·6	Total of South-West London.
10,578	100	11,215	100	87,652	100	GRAND TOTAL OF LONDON.

Table B.—*Classification of whole Population.*

	Classification.	(22.) Earthenware and Glass.		(23.) Chemicals.		(24.) Tallow, Soap, and Glue.		(25.) Leather Dressing, Tanning, &c.	
		No.	%	No.	%	No.	%	No.	%
Without Servants.	Families averaging—								
	1. 4 or more persons to a room	643	5·5	370	3·4	159	3·2	1647	4·3
	2. 3 & under 4 persons to a room	1168	10·0	746	6·8	276	5·6	3262	8·5
	3. 2 & under 3 persons to a room	3225	27·6	2074	19·1	980	19·9	9184	23·9
		5036	43·1	3190	29·3	1415	28·7	14,093	36·7
	4. 1 & under 2 persons to a room	2964	25·5	2589	23·8	1179	23·9	9697	25·3
	5. Less than 1 person to a room	339	2·9	344	3·2	196	4·0	1046	2·7
	6. All families occupying more than 4 rooms (mainly householders)	2529	21·7	2651	24·3	1405	28·3	9657	25·2
With Servants.	Families averaging—								
	A 4 or more persons to a servant	368	3·2	677	6·2	232	4·7	1716	4·5
		3236	27·8	3672	33·7	1833	37·0	12,419	32·4
	B 1 to 3 persons to a servant, &c.	176	1·5	450	4·1	183	3·7	948	2·5
	C 1 to 3 persons to 2 servants, &c.	43	·4	267	2·5	55	1·1	241	·6
	D 3 or 4 persons to 3 servants, &c.	12	·1	88	·8	24	·5	66	·2
		55	·5	355	3·3	79	1·6	307	·8
	E 1 or 2 persons to 3 servants, &c.	2	—	33	·3	18	·4	13	—
	F 1 or 2 persons to 4 servants, &c.	14	·1	18	·2	28	·5	17	·1
	G 1 or 2 persons to 5 servants, &c.	3	—	7	—	4	·1	—	—
	H 1 or 2 persons to 6 servants, &c.	—	—	8	·1	—	—	—	—
		19	·1	66	·6	50	1·0	30	·1
	Servants	179	1·5	570	5·2	207	4·1	862	2·2
	Grand Total...	11,665	100	10,892	100	4946	100	38,356	100

TABLE B.—*Classification of whole Population (continued).*

(26.) Saddle and Harness Making.		(27.) Brush and Comb Making.		Total Sundry Manufactures.		Classification.
No.	%	No.	%	No.	%	
421	4·0	685	6·1	3925	4·5	
761	7·2	962	8·6	7175	8·2	
2432	23·0	2868	25·6	20,763	23·7	
3614	34·2	4515	40·3	31,863	36·4	Without servants, 78,824 persons, or 17,496 families = 4·5 persons per family.
2802	26·5	2837	25·4	22,068	25·2	
416	3·9	339	3·0	2680	3·1	
3130	29·6	2841	25·3	22,213	25·2	
309	2·9	356	3·2	3658	4·2	
3855	36·4	3536	31·5	28,551	32.5	
150	1·5	161	1·4	2068	2·4	
23	·2	36	·3	665	·8	With servants, 6752 persons, or 1352 families = 5·0 persons per family.
3	—	—	—	193	·2	
26	·2	36	·3	858	1·0	
3	—	—	—	69	·1	
—	—	—	—	77	·1	
—	—	—	—	14	—	
—	—	—	—	8	—	
3	—	—	—	168	·2	
128	1·2	130	1·1	2076	2·3	
10,578	100	11,215	100	87,652	100	

PART III.—PRINTING, &c.

TABLE A.—*Distribution of whole Population.*

Registration Districts.	(28.) Printers.		(29.) Bookbinders.		(30.) Paper Manufacturers.		(31.) Stationers.		(32.) Publishers and Booksellers.		Total.	
	No.	%	No.	%	No.	%	No.	%	No.	%	No.	%
Poplar	1533	1·9	331	1·8	451	3·6	257	1·6	196	1·0	2768	1·9
Mile End, Stepney	2096	2·5	563	3·1	322	2·6	478	3·0	368	1·8	3827	2·6
St. George's E. & Whitech'p'l	822	1·0	181	1·0	267	2·1	120	·8	147	·7	1537	1·2
Bethnal Green	2438	3·0	811	4·4	1165	9·3	589	3·7	228	1·1	5231	3·4
Shoreditch	3913	4·8	1436	7·9	1963	15·6	587	3·7	444	2·2	8343	5·6
Total E.London	10,802	13·2	3322	18·2	4168	33·2	2031	12·8	1383	6·8	21,706	14·7
Hackney	5464	6·7	1452	8·0	826	6·6	1832	11·6	1248	6·2	10,822	7·2
Islington	9613	11·7	2235	12·3	1302	10·5	1794	11·4	2101	10·5	17,045	11·5
St. Pancras	4886	5·9	772	4·2	458	3·7	746	4·7	1165	5·8	8027	5·3
Marylebone and Hampstead	1326	1·6	217	1·2	200	1·6	662	4·2	1193	5·9	3598	2·5
Total N.London	21,289	25·9	4676	25·7	2786	22·4	5034	31·9	5707	28·4	39,492	26·5
Paddington	648	·8	60	·3	89	·7	420	2·7	525	2·6	1742	1·2
St.George, H. Sq.	1066	1·3	190	1·1	68	·5	343	2·2	527	2·6	2194	1·4
Kensington	398	·5	68	·3	76	·6	317	2·0	698	3·5	1557	1·1
Chelsea	600	·7	154	·8	181	1·4	173	1·1	326	1·6	1434	·9
Fulham	1212	1·5	107	·6	221	1·8	430	2·7	845	4·2	2815	1·9
Total W.London	3924	4·8	579	3·1	635	5·0	1683	10·7	2921	14·5	9742	6·5
City	679	·8	365	2·0	103	·8	125	·8	287	1·4	1559	1·0
Holborn	7606	9·2	2687	14·7	1450	11·6	826	5·2	967	4·8	13,536	9·1
Strand, West'r and St. Giles	2482	3·0	498	2·8	260	2·0	390	2·5	990	4·9	4620	3·1
Total C.London	10,767	13·0	3550	19·5	1813	14·4	1341	8·5	2244	11·1	19,715	13·2
Woolwich	279	·3	37	·2	32	·2	41	·2	155	·8	544	·3
Greenwich	2057	2·5	220	1·2	79	·6	399	2·5	562	2·8	3317	2·2
St. Olave, Sthwk.	2598	3·2	529	2·9	380	3·0	437	2·8	299	1·5	4243	2·8
Camberwell	8681	10·5	1702	9·3	496	4·0	1404	9·0	1561	7·8	13,844	9·3
Lewisham	700	·8	46	·2	90	·7	386	2·5	489	2·4	1711	1·3
Total S.-E. Lon.	14,315	17·3	2534	13·8	1077	8·5	2667	17·0	3066	15·3	23,659	15·9
St.Saviour,Sthwk.	9889	12·1	2192	12·0	1072	8·5	986	6·2	1090	5·5	15,229	10·2
Lambeth	7073	8·6	958	5·3	384	3·1	938	6·0	1884	9·5	11,237	7·6
Wandsworth	4160	5·1	430	2·4	623	4·9	1076	6·9	1787	8·9	8076	5·4
Total S.-W.Lon.	21,122	25·8	3580	19·7	2079	16·5	3000	19·1	4761	23·9	34,542	23·2
GRAND TOTAL	82,219	100	18,241	100	12,558	100	15,756	100	20,082	100	148,856	100

TABLE B.—*Classification of whole Population.*

Classification.	(28.) Printers.		(29.) Bookbinders.		(30.) Paper Manufacturers.		(31.) Stationers.		(32.) Publishers and Booksellers.		Total.	
	No.	%	No.	%	No.	%	No.	%	No.	%	No.	%
Without Servants: Families averaging—												
1. 4 or more persons to a room	4035	*4·8*	1016	*5·6*	1107	*8·8*	399	*2·5*	321	*1·6*	6878	*4·6*
2. 3 & under 4 to a room	6926	*8·4*	1931	*10·6*	1670	*13·3*	586	*3·7*	594	*3·0*	11,707	*7·9*
3. 2 & under 3 to a room	17,338	*21·1*	4580	*25·1*	3372	*26·9*	1746	*11·1*	2058	*10·3*	29,094	*19·5*
	28,299	34·3	7527	41·3	6149	49·0	2731	17·3	2973	14·9	47,679	32·0
4. 1 & under 2 to a room	23,155	28·0	5431	29·8	3023	24·1	3163	20·1	3838	19·1	38,610	25·9
5. Less than 1 to a room	23,084	*3·7*	564	*3·1*	309	*2·5*	644	*4·1*	844	*4·2*	5445	*3·7*
6. All families with over 4 rooms (mainly householders)	23,404	*28·4*	4062	*22·3*	2142	*17·1*	5357	*34·1*	6764	*33·7*	41,729	*28·0*
With Servants : Families averaging—												
A 4 or more persons to a servant	2349	*2·8*	388	*2·1*	307	*2·4*	1672	*10·6*	2197	*10·9*	6913	*4·6*
	28,837	34·9	5014	27·5	2758	22·0	7673	48·8	9805	48·8	54,087	36·3
B 1 to 3 to a servant, &c. ...	853	1·3	101	·6	221	1·7	953	6·0	1222	6·1	3350	2·3
C 1 to 3 to 2 servants, &c. ...	160	·2	34	·2	103	·8	309	2·0	459	2·3	1065	·7
D 3 or 4 to 3 servants, &c. ...	40	—	10	—	12	·1	35	·2	107	·5	204	·2
	200	·2	44	·3	115	·9	344	2·2	566	2·8	1269	·9
E 1 or 2 to 3 servants, &c. ...	14	—	—	—	18	·2	30	·2	115	·6	177	·1
F 1 or 2 to 4 servants, &c. ...	1	—	—	—	15	·1	3	—	84	·4	103	·1
G 1 or 2 to 5 servants, &c. ...	3	—	—	—	4	—	2	—	24	·1	33	—
H 1 or 2 to 6 servants, &c. ...	3	—	—	—	4	—	—	—	19	·1	26	—
	21	—	—	—	41	·3	35	·2	242	1·2	339	·2
Servants.........	854	1·3	124	·5	251	2·0	857	5·4	1436	7·1	3522	2·4
GRAND TOTAL	82,219	100	18,241	100	12,558	100	15,756	100	20,082	100	148,856	100

Without servants ... 133,463 persons, or 30,972 families = 4·3 } persons per family.
With servants ...... 11,871 ,, or 2,410 ,, = 4·0 }

PART IV.—TEXTILES.

TABLE A.—*Distribution of whole Population.*

Registration Districts.	(33.) Silk & Fancy Textile Workers.		(34.) Woollen and Carpet Manufacturers.		(35.) Dyers.		(36.) Hemp, Jute, and Fibre Work.		(37.) Floor Cloth and Waterproof Goods Makers.		Total.	
	No	%	No.	%	No.	%	No.	%	No.	%	No.	%
Poplar	156	2·1	130	2·7	60	1·5	732	11·4	496	7·6	1574	5·5
Mile End, Stepney	173	2·5	132	2·8	73	1·8	1177	18·5	368	5·6	1923	6·8
St. George's E. & Whitech'p'l	214	3·0	136	2·9	113	2·7	361	5·6	175	2·7	999	3·4
Bethnal Green	2154	30·6	575	12·2	181	4·4	535	8·4	475	7·3	3920	13·6
Shoreditch	306	4·5	374	7·9	80	1·9	230	3·6	348	5·3	1338	4·6
Total E.London	3003	42·7	1347	28·5	507	12·3	3035	47·5	1862	28·5	9754	33·9
Hackney	795	11·3	207	4·4	313	7·6	428	6·7	537	8·2	2280	7·9
Islington	459	6·5	296	6·3	232	5·6	171	2·7	633	9·6	1791	6·2
St. Pancras	169	2·4	275	5·8	133	3·2	65	1·0	191	2·9	833	2·9
Marylebone and Hampstead	204	2·9	172	3·6	175	4·2	74	1·1	150	2·3	775	2·7
Total N.London	1627	23·1	950	20·1	853	20·6	738	11·5	1511	23·0	5679	19·7
Paddington	73	1·0	49	1·0	90	2·2	56	·9	92	1·4	360	1·2
St.George, H. Sq.	45	·6	104	2·2	75	1·8	21	·3	74	1·1	319	1·2
Kensington	91	1·3	71	1·5	325	7·9	23	·3	65	1·0	575	2·0
Chelsea	53	·7	48	1·0	168	4·1	1	—	40	·6	310	1·1
Fulham	72	1·0	92	1·9	333	8·1	193	3·1	77	1·2	767	2·6
TotalW.London	334	4·6	364	7·6	991	24·1	294	4·6	348	5·3	2331	8·1
City	96	1·4	11	·2	4	·1	36	·6	30	·5	177	·6
Holborn	275	3·9	302	6·6	56	1·4	95	1·5	302	4·6	1030	3·6
Strand, West'r. and St. Giles	98	1·4	207	4·4	92	2·2	18	·3	44	·7	459	1·6
Total C. London	469	6·7	520	11·2	152	3·7	149	2·4	376	5·8	1666	5·8
Woolwich	13	·2	25	·5	14	·3	84	1·3	131	2·1	267	·9
Greenwich	108	1·5	104	2·2	112	2·7	194	3·0	162	2·5	680	2·4
St. Olave, Sthwk.	134	1·9	261	5·5	227	5·5	729	11·4	384	5·9	1735	6·0
Camberwell	419	6·0	275	5·8	387	9·4	226	3·5	459	7·0	1766	6·1
Lewisham	119	1·7	33	·7	44	1·1	61	1·0	51	·8	308	1·1
Total S.-E. Lon.	793	11·3	698	14·7	784	19·0	1294	20·2	1187	18·3	4756	16·5
St.Saviour,Sthwk.	171	2·5	292	6·2	165	4·0	622	9·7	505	7·7	1755	6·1
Lambeth	287	4·1	241	5·1	224	5·4	166	2·6	356	5·4	1274	4·4
Wandsworth	350	5·0	312	6·6	450	10·9	93	1·5	395	6·0	1600	5·5
Total S.-W.Lon.	808	11·6	845	17·9	839	20·3	881	13·8	1256	19·1	4629	16·0
GRAND TOTAL	7034	100	4724	100	4126	100	6391	100	6540	100	28,815	100

TABLE B.—*Classification of whole Population.*

Classification.	(33.) Silk and Fancy Textile Goods Manufacturers.		(34.) Woollen and Carpet Manufacturers.		(35.) Dyers.		(36.) Hemp, Jute, and Fibre Work.		(37.) Floor Cloth and Waterproof Goods Makers.		Total.	
	No.	%	No.	%	No.	%	No.	%	No.	%	No.	%
Without Servants : Families averaging—												
1. 4 or more persons to a room	202	2·9	351	7·4	108	2·6	449	7·0	299	4·6	1409	4·9
2. 3 & under 4 to a room	441	6·3	538	11·4	244	6·0	752	11·8	555	8·5	2530	8·8
3. 2 & under 3 to a room	1247	17·7	1234	26·2	821	19·9	1788	28·0	1290	19·8	6380	22·1
	1890	26·9	2123	45·0	1173	28·5	2989	46·8	2144	32·9	10,319	35·8
4. 1 & under 2 to a room	1699	24·1	1016	21·5	828	20·1	1567	24·5	1571	24·0	6681	23·2
5. Less than 1 to a room	272	3·9	150	3·2	105	2·5	183	2·9	203	3·1	913	3·2
6. All families with over 4 rooms (mainly householders)	1751	24·9	852	18·0	1418	34·4	1204	18·9	1674	25·6	6899	23·9
With servants : Families averaging—												
A 4 or more persons to a servant	526	7·5	193	4·1	342	8·3	170	2·6	405	6·2	1636	5·7
	2549	36·3	1195	25·3	1865	45·2	1557	24·4	2282	34·9	9448	32·8
B 1 to 3 to a servant, &c. ...	405	5·8	163	3·5	128	3·1	135	2·1	228	3·5	1059	3·7
C 1 to 3 to 2 servants, &c. ...	114	1·6	55	1·1	17	·4	42	·7	54	·8	282	1·0
D 3 or 4 to 3 servants, &c. ...	30	·4	18	·4	3	—	4	—	31	·5	86	·3
	144	2·0	73	1·5	20	·4	46	·7	85	1·3	368	1·3
E 1 or 2 to 3 servants, &c. ...	16	·2	4	—	—	—	—	—	12	·2	32	·1
F 1 or 2 to 4 servants, &c. ...	—	—	—	—	—	—	—	—	2	—	2	—
G 1 or 2 to 5 servants, &c. ...	—	—	3	—	—	—	—	—	—	—	3	—
H 1 or 2 to 6 servants, &c. ...	—	—	—	—	—	—	—	—	—	—	—	—
	16	·2	7	·1	—	—	—	—	14	·2	37	·1
Servants.........	331	4·7	147	3·1	112	2·7	97	1·5	216	3·2	903	3·1
GRAND TOTAL	7034	100	4724	100	4126	100	6391	100	6540	100	28,815	100

Without servants ... 24,812 persons, or 5,938 families = 4·2 } persons per family.
With servants ...... 3,100 ,, or 617 ,, = 5·0 }

INDEX.

INDEX TO VOL. VI.

THE next volume (VII.), which should be ready within six months, will contain an account of the population included in Sections 38 to 89, beginning with the Makers of and Dealers in Dress, and ending with Domestic Servants. In volume VIII., which will conclude the Industrial Series, an attempt will be made to compare the trade groups with each other, and to draw into one focus a general view of the Industrial Condition of London.

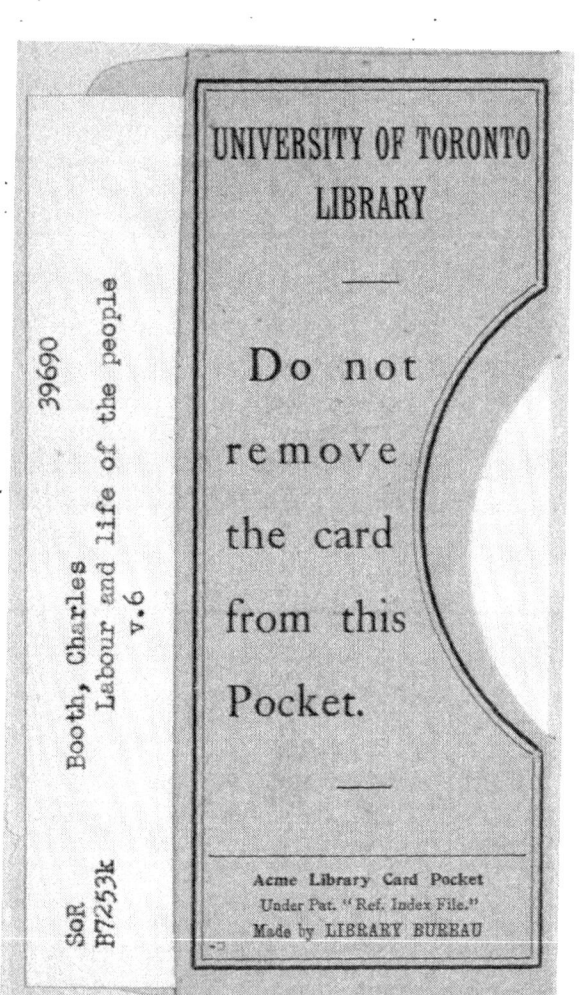

Ingram Content Group UK Ltd.
Milton Keynes UK
UKHW021258290623
424274UK00015B/347